Mike Grant

ALWAYS READY

The Drill Halls of Britain's Volunteer Forces

by
Mike Osborne

Published by Partizan Press

Copyright Dr. Mike Osborne 2006

Mike Osborne has asserted his right under the Copyright Designs and Patent Act 1988 to be identified as the author of this work

Design & Production by Jay Forster (www.generate.me.uk)

Partizan Press
816 - 818 London Road, Leigh-on-Sea,
Essex, SS9 3NH
Ph/Fx: +44 (0) 1702 473986
Email: ask@caliverbooks.com

www.caliverbooks.com

ISBN: 1-85818-509-2

Printed in the UK by JH Haynes, Somerset

Front Page:
Ardwick Green, Brunswick, Manchester
© Pam Osborne

Back Page:
Broadgate, Lincoln
© Mike Osborne

Other Partizan Press publications:

Partizan Historical series:

1   The Origins and Development of Military Tartans
James D Scarlett

2   The Last Scots Army 1661-1714
Stuart Reid

3   The Armies and Uniforms of Marlborough's Wars Pt1
CS Grant

4   The Armies and Uniforms of Marlborough's Wars Pt2
CS Grant

5   Cossack Hurrah! - Russian Irregular Cavalry Organisation and Uniforms During the Napoleonic Wars
Dr S Summerfield

6   The King's Ships - Henry VIII's Royal Navy
Jonathan Davies

Partizan Special Edition series:

1   Sieges and Fortifications of the Civil Wars in Britain
Mike Osborne

2   Partizan Press Guide to Solo Wargaming
Stuart Asquith

Partizan Army Guides series:

1   The Organization of the Texan Army
Stuart Reid

Partizan Battledress series:

1   The Heart and the Rose - The Battle of Linlithgow Bridge 1526
Jonathan Cooper

Contents

Foreword

Mike Osborne's pioneering study of drill halls, based on inspection of every known example in England, Wales and Scotland, is an invaluable addition to the study of the barracks and other buildings of the British army and its volunteer forces.

Militia armouries and drill halls were briefly examined by English Heritage in its thematic study of barracks in the mid-1990s [James Douet, "British Barracks: their architecture and role in society"; London, 1998, HMSO], one of a number of studies prompted by the Ministry of Defence's reassessment of its estate, and the historic buildings in its ownership and care. In their planning and architecture they reflect the importance attached to the volunteer as well as regular forces by successive governments after the 1852 Militia Act. Some of these such as the combined drill halls and militia armouries at Cirencester, Lincoln and Grantham, are architecturally pretentious, even iconic in the way they were designed to foster pride as well as a military air through their use of castellations, turrets and other devices. These, and several examples of the highly distinctive 'keeps' built following the Military Localisation Act of 1872, are now listed buildings. The examples that followed the establishment of the Territorial Force in 1908, under the imperative of the then Secretary of State for War, Lord Haldane, are generally more utilitarian in style although they could range from lavish Wrenaissance to streamlined Moderne in their treatment. Dr Osborne's study will help inform decisions about the protection of the best surviving examples. It will also underline the important role that these buildings have played in the life of their surrounding communities.

Jeremy Lake
Inspector of Historic Buildings
English Heritage
January 2006

Introduction

Few Victorians would not have been inside the local drill hall. A high proportion of the male population served in the Volunteer Force, and their parades and drills often provided entertainment for the rest of the family. Shooting was only the most obvious of a wide range of sports and pastimes provided for volunteers, and opportunities for self-improvement through education, or commercial advantage through networking, also proved significant. Fund-raising activities, for what was essentially a self-financing venture, provided all the fun of the fair- a mix of spectacle, jumble-sale and social event. Into the twentieth century, the drill hall impinged on people's lives no less. The drill hall was where young men and women enlisted for the forces in two world wars; where those involved in home defence against bombing or invasion were enrolled, equipped and trained; and where the ends of those wars were celebrated with parties. Often, the drill hall remained the social centre of its community long after its warlike rationale had been forgotten. For over a hundred years, the drill hall was as essential a part of the built environment as the church, the school or the market. Since the 1960s the size of the Nation's volunteer forces has steadily decreased. At the same time, the training requirements of the volunteers have seen a corresponding growth in order to match both the professionalism and the technological sophistication of the regular forces, within the context of a lessening of any perceived external threat at a global level, but an increase in local threats. Many drill halls have, over the years, been adapted for a whole range of social, commercial and recreational activities. Many another has been demolished either because the structure had come to the end of its natural life, or, more recently, because it occupied valuable building land, needed for homes, offices, roads or shops. Large numbers, however, do still survive, and often enrich our townscapes.

This study came about, at first, out of curiosity. I had been involved as a volunteer co-ordinator in the Defence of Britain Project, recording twentieth century military structures. The local surveys in several areas included those drill halls which had fulfilled specific military functions, as bases for the Home Guard in World War ll, for instance. I then began to look into surviving drill halls, and the history of their provision generally, at first in East Anglia and the East Midlands, and then across the whole of Britain. In five years, I have visited over 2500 sites, extant or formerly used by the volunteer forces. Despite the old army maxim: 'never volunteer for anything', this country has a long tradition, in widely differing fields, for volunteering. For many reasons, there has always been a place, often an urgent necessity, for the voluntary warrior. The drill hall is one of the few tangible reminders of this phenomenon.

The terminology of the volunteers' home-base is relatively straightforward. The first requirement of a volunteer unit was secure storage for its weaponry and ammunition. This was the 'Armoury'. Next, was the need for somewhere to drill, preferably under cover. This was the 'Drill Shed', often part of a larger building containing an office or 'Orderly Room' and an indoor shooting facility, or 'Range'. Together, these three elements formed the 'Drill Hall'. In Wales, drill hall is translated as 'Neuadd Ymarfer'. Many units were spread over a wide geographical area, making it impractical to gather the whole unit together more than once or twice a year at special parades, inspections or annual camps. Small detachments of the unit might then meet for their weekly drills at an out-lying 'Drill Station'. A number of factors determined whether this should be in dedicated premises, a village hall or a school, a public house, or a grander residence. The majority of the volunteer coast defence units were based in the actual forts and batteries whose garrisons they had been raised to form, and this arrangement continued in some cases right up until 1956, when Coast Artillery was stood down. Only some of these are included in the gazetteers. Similarly, in the early days of the Territorial Force, a number of stately homes were initially used as bases for newly-raised units. Warwick Castle, for instance, provided a base for the Warwickshire Royal Horse Artillery in 1908 until their move to more appropriate premises in Leamington three years later.

It had occurred to me that association of the drill hall with youth organisations in the local folk memory might be down to its subsequent use. When asked about the existence of a local drill hall, people are often inclined to mention the Boys' Brigade, or the Boy Scouts and Girl Guides. However, it must be remembered that from 1908, Boys' Brigade and Church Lads' Brigade units were affiliated to the Territorial Force, and often, quite firmly attached to particular TF formations. There was also, at least one instance of a drill hall being built and designated purely for the use of youth organisations, notably the 1909 Miners' Welfare Hall at Forest Town, Mansfield Woodhouse. This was specifically built to accommodate youth organisations, initially the Boys' Brigade, apparently never hosted military units, despite having a WWl machine-gun mounted on its porch for some considerable time, and is still, to this day, referred to locally as the 'Drill Hall'.

After the reconstitution of the Territorial Army in 1947, drill halls tended to be called 'TA Centres'. New TACs often received names, deriving from a regimental hero, such as Harry Weale VC Hall TAC at Queensferry, or Hollis VC Armoury at Coulby Newham, Middlesbrough. Other sources of names are the roll of inspirational generals from past campaigns, such as Napier House in south-east London or Montgomery House in Birmingham or Dudley. Regimental battle honours also provide names as at Kohima House TAC at Redditch, or Somme Barracks in Blackburn.

This book seeks to record both the context within which drill halls were originally built, and how they developed as buildings within both the military and civilian communities. By means of the Gazetteers, it also records as many of the individual sites and buildings as it has been possible to identify throughout Britain. As will be re-iterated at several points in the text, there is no way in which it can be totally definitive, for both new discoveries and demolitions frequently occur. Readers should regard it as a snap-shot of the situation at a given moment in time. I continue to welcome information in order that the database might be continuously up-dated.

As far as I am aware, this book is a first. Apart from a few articles in specialist building-trade journals, there is no literature at all. There is hardly any literature on barracks. Douet's excellent book for English Heritage [1998] brings the story only as far as 1914, and May's Shire Book on barracks [2002] gives two pages to the twentieth century. Both these books refer, in passing, to drill halls. My own "Defending Britain" [Tempus, 2004] included a chapter on buildings for the army and the navy, which only briefly referred to barracks and drill halls in the twentieth century. Pevsner's 1976 History of Building Types, covering a wide range of buildings, which includes prisons, hospitals, railway stations, government buildings, theatres, hotels, shops and museums, in its introduction, cites barracks as one of those types, along with schools and observatories, "which would have been rewarding but would have swelled the book to unmanageable proportions". This would appear to be one reward Pevsner denied himself throughout his prolific output. Apart from this semi-comprehensive approach, a number of building types have enjoyed dedicated volumes. These include markets, lighthouses, follies, almshouses, railway buildings, and public houses. But not drill halls. It is my hope and intention that this book remedies this deficiency.

Mike Osborne,
January 2006

[Illustrations are referenced throughout by page numbers in brackets. All illustrations are by the author unless otherwise indicated.]

Acknowledgments

Julie Adams [NW England & Isle of Man RFCA, Liverpool]
Ian Angus [Lympstone]
Adrian Armishaw [Daventry & Rugby]
David Atkinson [Morley]
Mike Bardell [East Anglia RFCA]
Arthur Bevan [Briton Ferry]
Bristol City Archaeology Service
Neil Busby [Thrapston]
Graham Cadman [Northants SMR]
Robert Carter [Kirkburton]
Peter Cobb [Portsmouth]
Wayne Cocroft [Kent etc]
Barbara Deacon [Totton]
Jeanne Dingle [Looe]
Colin Dobinson [sources]
Rosemary Edwards [Oswestry]
Dr David Evans
John Goodwin [Worthing etc]
Guildford Museum
Janet Gyford [Witham]
John Harding [Ripon etc]
Alwyn Harvey [Cornwall]
Mike Heaton [Falmouth]
Richard Hillier [Peterborough]
Nick Howell [Oldham]
Chris Jakes [Cambridgeshire Collection]
Alan Johnson [English Heritage]
Richard Johnston [Yateley]
Kingston-upon-Thames Arch. Soc.
Kirkwall Library [Kirkwall & Stromness]
Bernard Lowry [Shropshire]
Col. Tim May [Oxfordshire]
Colonel Macfarland [Co Durham]
Dr Michael McGregor [Bourne]
Pauline Marples [Mansfield Woodhouse]
Hywel Matthews [Pontypridd]
Henry Meir [Derbyshire & Nottinghamshire]
Merton History Society [Mitcham]

The McIntosh family [Ventnor]
Nancy Morland [Wilton]
Brian Nolan [Kings Rochester CCF]
David Osborne [Thetford]
Martin Pakes [Crewkerne]
Trevor Pearce [Portsmouth]
Bill Pitchford [Wetherby]
Plymouth City Museum
Tony Podmore [Yorkshire]
John Powell [Ironbridge etc]
Tony Priestley [Buckinghamshire]
Simon Purcell [Norwich]
Alan Rankin [Strichen]
Alan Robinson [Wallsend]
Sarah Rodger [Arundel]
Angela Rush [Kington]
Geoffrey Salvetti [Portsmouth]
Eric Sharpe [Lincolnshire]
George Shaw [Ashbourne]
Bob Sheldon [Banbury]
David & Margaret Sibley [Nottinghamshire]
Norman Skinner [Caterham]
Martin Smith [Hunts Cyclists]
Spen Valley Local History Society [Cleckheaton]
Staffordshire Record Office
Neil Storey [North Norfolk]
Surrey History Centre
Mike Suttill [East Midlands RFCA]
Keith Ward [London]
Ray Westlake [Gwent and London]
West Sussex Record Office
West Yorkshire Archaeological Service
The Watt family of Oldmeldrum
Mick Wilks [Worcestershire]
Paul Williams [Dolgarrog]
Tony Wiseman [Horwich]
Dave Wood [Ipswich]

Thanks are also due to officers, teachers and archivists at the 30 schools listed in Appendix 6, who so kindly provided information about CCF premises. Much of the identification of drill hall locations was accomplished with the help of officers and staff of the Reserve Forces & Cadets' Associations [RFCAs] which continue, on a regional basis, the work of the original County Territorial Associations and thanks are due to them all. All over Britain, library staff, especially local studies librarians, have unearthed maps, local directories, and other sources of local knowledge, often live ones. We are most grateful for all their help.

Pam & Mike Osborne, January 2006

Abbreviations

A

AA	Anti-aircraft
ACF	Army Cadet Force
AFV	armoured fighting vehicle
A&SH	Argyll & Sutherland Highlanders
aka	also known as
APU	Anglia Polytechnic University
AT	Anti-tank
ATC	Air Training Corps
ASC	Army Service Corps

B

Bde	Brigade
Beds	Bedfordshire
Berks	Berkshire
Bn	Battalion
BT	British Telecom
Bty.	Battery
Bucks	Buckinghamshire
BW	Black Watch

C

CA	Coast Artillery
CAB	Citizens' Advice Bureau
CCF	Combined Cadet Force
CCS	Casualty Clearing Station
CD	Civil Defence
CH	Queen's Own Cameron Highlanders
Col.	Colonel
Col	Column
Coy	Company
CPS	Crown Prosecution Service
CRA	Commander Royal Artillery
CRE	Commander Royal Engineers

D

DCLI	Duke of Cornwall's Light Infantry
DCO	Duke of Cambridge's Own [Middlesex] **OR** Duke of Connaught's Own [Hampshire Regiment]
DG	Director General
Div/Div'n'l	Division/Divisional
DLI	Durham Light Infantry
DoB	Defence of Britain Project
DoW	Duke of Wellington's [Own West Riding Regiment]

E

E	east
EH	English Heritage
EM	East Midlands

F

FANY	First Aid Nursing Yeomanry
FE	Further Education [College]
F'sters	Foresters [Sherwood] the Nottingham & Derby Regt.

G

GH	Gordon Highlanders
Glos	Gloucestershire
GOC	General Officer Commanding

H

HAA	Heavy Anti-aircraft
HAC	Honourable Artillery Company
Hants.	Hampshire
HDC	Horsham District Council
H'ders	Highlanders
HG	Home Guard
HLI	Highland Light Infantry
HQ	Headquarters

I

Imp Yeo	Imperial Yeomanry

J

JTC	Junior Training Corps

K

KOSB	King's Own Scottish Borderers
KOYLI	King's Own Yorkshire Light Infantry
KSLI	King's Shropshire Light Infantry

L

LAA	Light Anti-aircraft
LAD	Light Aid Detachment
Lancs	Lancashire
Leics	Leicestershire
Lincs	Lincolnshire
LDV	Local Defence Volunteers, later Home Guard

N

N	north
NACRO	National Association for the Care & Resettlement of Offenders
NF	Northumberland Fusiliers

Northants	Northamptonshire		SLI	Somerset Light Infantry
Notts	Nottinghamshire		SP	self-propelled [artillery]
O			Sqdn	Squadron
OS	Ordnance Survey		Stn	Station [as in drill station]
OTC	Officers' Training Corps		SWB	South Wales Borderers
P			**T**	
PH	public house		TA	Territorial Army
PSI	Permanent Staff Instructor		TAA	Territorial Army Association
Q			TAC	Territorial Army Centre [after 1947]
QOOH	Queen's Own Oxfordshire Hussars [Yeomanry]		TA&VRA	Territorial, Auxiliary & Volunteer Reserve Association
R			T&AVR	Territorial & Army Volunteer Reserve
RA	Royal Artillery		TAER	Territorial Army Emergency Reserve
RAC	Royal Armoured Corps		TAFA	Territorial & Auxiliary Forces Association
RAMC	Royal Army Medical Corps		TF	Territorial Force
RAOC	Royal Army Ordnance Corps		TIC	Tourist Information Centre
RASC	Royal Army Service Corps		**U**	
R Aux AF	Royal Auxiliary Air Force		u/g	underground
RBL	Royal British Legion		UKWMO	United Kingdom Warning & Monitoring Organisation
RC	Roman Catholic		**V**	
RCT	Royal Corps of Transport		VF	Volunteer Force
RE	Royal Engineers		VTC	Volunteer Training Corps- WWl Home Guard
Regt	Regiment		**W**	
REME	Royal Electrical & Mechanical Engineers		W	west
RFA	Royal Field Artillery		Warwicks	Warwickshire
RFCA	Reserve Forces & Cadets Association		WD	War Department
RGA	Royal Garrison Artillery		WMC	Working Men's Club
RGJ	Royal Green Jackets		WO	War Office
RHA	Royal Horse Artillery		WR	Welch Regiment
RHF	Royal Highland Fusiliers		WR	West Riding [of Yorkshire]
RHQ	Regimental Headquarters		WWl	First World War
RHR	Robin Hood Rifles		WWll	Second World War
RLC	Royal Logistic Corps		WYREs	West Yorkshire Royal Engineers
RMR	Royal Marines Reserve		**Y**	
RN[V]R	Royal Naval [Volunteer] Reserve		Yeo	Yeomanry
ROC	Royal Observer Corps			
RS	Royal Scots			
RSF	Royal Scots Fusiliers			
RTR	Royal Tank Regiment			
RWF	Royal Welch Fusiliers			
S				
S	south			
SA	Salvation Army			
SH	Seaforth Highlanders			
SL	searchlight			

CHAPTER 1
Britain's Volunteer Forces

Britons' attitudes towards the armed forces have always been characterised by ambivalence, notions of freedom and repression underpinning how we feel about, in particular, the army. In times of peace, a standing army has often been seen as expensive, unnecessary, and an ever-present threat to democracy and individual freedom. In times of international tension, however, it has become the citizen's responsibility to take up arms in defence of homeland, kith and kin, and collective freedom. Once the danger had past, then weapons were returned to the armoury, and normal, civilian life was resumed. At times, there have been internal tensions, when economic or political influences have exacerbated friction between different sections of society, and one man's perception of freedom, did not necessarily always coincide with that of his neighbour. Striking the balance between a citizen's rights and responsibilities has never been easy, and we must remember that Britons are anyway subjects, not citizens. Over the centuries, the State has called on people to serve under arms in a variety of ways, usually by managing both to represent such service as voluntary, and to maintain the acquiescence of those called to serve, and the wider Society from which they are drawn. It is interesting to note that the British pre-occupation with the professional/amateur dichotomy, always very relevant in the military arena, is still alive, even in these days of a wholly professional army. The think-tank Demos, in December 2004, has, once again, revived the notion that organised networks of amateur enthusiasts, working in areas that are also the preserve of the professional, are contributing to the good of society, expanding corporate knowledge, developing new techniques and skills, and generating social capital, by breaking down the barriers between work and leisure. Examples cited by Demos, and dubbed Pro-Ams, include amateur archaeologists, wildlife experts, activists in the Arts, and, where else could this be leading, but to the amateur soldiers of the Territorial Army, some of whom, at the time of writing are on active service in

Iraq. Whether or not proof exists for these assertions in the case of the TA is unclear, but the claim has been made. Let us now see how the system of voluntary militarism developed, taking each element in turn.

The Militia

Few Militiamen would have regarded themselves as volunteers, but the Militia provides an essential backdrop, against which can be seen all the other elements of the military scene. In the absence of a standing army, sovereigns from Canute to Charles ll, were criticised for maintaining corps of mercenary troops for their personal protection. Militias, on the other hand, had a long history of popular approval, based on romantic notions of the Sovereign's dependence on her subjects' loyalty, patriotism and self-sacrifice. Subsequent portrayals of Elisabeth l rallying her militia at Tilbury in 1588 to counter the threat of the Armada, have become a familiar expression of this feeling. Paradoxically, it was negative feelings toward the regular troops of the eighteenth- and early-nineteenth centuries which were to rub off onto the Militia. Society's view of licentious soldiery, neatly summed up by Kipling at a later date, tarnished the Militia too, who began to be seen as inept. As early as the 1740s, with regular troops committed to the War of Austrian Succession on the Continent, the double danger of Jacobite invasion from Scotland, and French incursions across the Channel, coupled with a lack of confidence in the effectiveness of the Militia, prompted the establishment of Defence Associations raising volunteer forces, funded by subscription, locally armed and led, and with little Government influence or control. Once the dangers had passed it was time to reform the Militia, establishing county quotas, introducing training regimes, and imposing the same Articles of War and Mutiny Act, which regulated the regular forces. A succession of conflicts through the second half of the eighteenth-century ensured that the Militia became established as a semi-professional force, many of its members being long-term substitutes for those balloted men, often engaged in well-established trade or business, who, not unnaturally, preferred their lives un-interrupted by military service. It also became more common for the Line Regiments to recruit from this pool of trained men. Militia units could also be deployed outside their home counties. All these factors contributed to the Militia's movement toward becoming a reserve for the Regular Army. The Napoleonic Wars provided plenty of opportunity for the Militia's embodiment, and for the parallel recruitment of volunteer corps for solely local defence. A stream of legislation throughout the 1790s created a bewildering array of defence forces, further complicated by the measures which exempted volunteers from service in the Militia if balloted. Unsurprisingly, volunteer recruitment became healthier with, in 1800, 24000 men enrolled in the Yeomanry Cavalry, and 87000 in the Volunteer infantry and artillery. Rowlandson pictured the members of nearly 100 volunteer corps in London alone, in their handsome uniforms. Meanwhile, the Militia remained at least 10% short of its required strength of 40000 men, and attempts to raise a Supplementary Militia fell short of its target. In 1805, the year of Trafalgar, there were 87000 regular troops, 80000 more in the Militia, but, by one estimate, some 343000 volunteers, and 400000 by another. Legislation now sought to provide a system for expanding recruitment to the Regular Army. As the threat of invasion receded, the Government took steps to absorb many of the Volunteer Corps into a new Local Militia, while simultaneously withdrawing support for the Volunteers. By 1813, most Volunteer infantry and artillery units had either transferred to the Local Militia, or disbanded. For the Yeomanry Cavalry, it was a different story, as we shall see in due course.

After the end of the French Wars, the Militia was allowed to stagnate. Numbers fell, positions were unfilled, and budgets more-closely regulated. By 1852 and the likely return to hostilities, a new Act was passed providing a Militia of 80000 by county quota, initially to be met by voluntary recruitment with bounties payable, and then, by ballot, with substitution permissible. Two years later, the Regular Army was so desperate for ready-trained recruits to fight the Crimean War, that it was allowed to take up to 25% of the Militia. In 1855, legislation was introduced to remove the upper limit of 56 days annual

service by Militia-men. About 40% of the force agreed to serve for longer periods if so required. So acute became the problem of losing numbers of trained personnel to the regulars, that recruitment to the Regular Army from the Militia became limited to 17% of strength, and individuals would be guilty of desertion if they attempted to transfer outside these limits. Other changes were made, however, which effectively reinforced the position of the Militia as a reserve for the regulars. It became normal for superannuated regular soldiers to put in further service in the Militia. Officers were encouraged to undertake specialised training at establishments such as the School of Musketry at Hythe. By 1875, the initial training of recruits to the Militia was increased to a possible six months, and during this time, they were expected to be accommodated in barracks, local to their homes. Annual training obligations were increased to a normal 28 days, the likely possibility of up to 56 days, and, for artillery, 84 days. At the same time, a most fundamental change to the Militia as a Constitutional or Emergency Force, was instituted. The Cardwell reforms through the 1870s, had formalised the local ties of Line Regiments into rigid geographical relationships. Each regiment of the Regular Army, was now to have a local depot, usually in the county town; it would recruit from that catchment; it would foster local loyalty and support, thus attempting to build an organisation, analogous to the family. One battalion would serve abroad, and one at home, in rotation. Recruits would be trained at the local depot, and drafts despatched to the absent unit. In 1882, the local militia units were taken into this system becoming, depending on the size of regiment, the third and fourth battalions of the regiment. Thus, for instance, the 8th North Lincoln Regiment of Militia, based in Lincoln, became the 3rd Bn. Lincolnshire Regiment, and the 29th South Lincoln Regiment of Militia, with HQ in New Sleaford in 1850, but ensconced in their barracks in Grantham ten years later, became the 4th Bn. [p66] Similarly, the 23rd [Royal South Gloucester Light Infantry] Regiment of Militia with barracks where Gloucester Prison now stands, and the 69th Royal North Gloucestershire Regiment of Militia whose barracks still stand in Cirencester, became, respectively, the 3rd and 4th Bns. Gloucestershire Regiment. [p66] In a larger regiment like the Royal Fusiliers [City of London] Regiment, the Militia became the 5th, 6th, and 7th Battalions. As there was, at that time, no

OAKHAM, the Riding-school of the Rutland Fencibles

Cambridgeshire Regiment, the 68th Cambridge Regiment of Militia, whose barracks may still be seen in Ely, became the 4th Bn. Suffolk Regt. The Militia from then on served as a Reserve for the regulars, even serving overseas, especially during the South African Wars, when many campaign medals were awarded to units, casualties were sustained through disease as well as enemy action, and individuals received Mentions and the odd gallantry medal. A total of 60 battalions of Militia had served in South Africa, with another ten on overseas garrison duty, plus 14000 reservists serving with their Line battalions. All this was highly efficient, but, even though a Militia Reserve, recruiting straight into the regulars, had been disbanded in 1901, the system continued to ship trained men into the regulars. Evidence, from the most exalted in the land, to the Norfolk Commission in 1904, emphasised the inferior training, and undefined role of the Militia. It must have come as no surprise, therefore, that the machinery which set up the Territorial Force, in 1908, also put an end to the Militia. What survived through the next 20 years was a Special Reserve, and, in well-recruited regiments, an Extra Reserve, neither having any affinity with a traditional Militia. Only in mid-1939, in the lead-up to WWll, was it temporarily re-formed to provide conscripts with six months of recruit training.

The Yeomanry Cavalry
Some of the volunteers raised by the Defence Associations of the 1740s were organised into troops of cavalry, such as the Yorkshire Light Horse, whose initial task was to shadow the Jacobite invasion, reporting as scouts to the regular troops. They were completely autonomous, and their subsequent name, 'The Royal Regiment of Hunters', as sanctioned by George ll, gives some clue as to their composition and predelictions. The French Wars saw a proliferation of volunteer troops of yeomanry cavalry, so much so, that an attempt by the Government to raise a mounted equivalent of the Militia: the Provisional Cavalry, found itself completely undermined by them. In 1800, there were 24000 men serving as volunteer cavalry. It has been suggested that exemption from the horse tax, and immunity from Militia ballot, were powerful incentives to volunteer for the Yeomanry. Officers tended to be country gentry, even nobility, and other ranks were their servants or tenants. There was certainly a presumption that the Yeomanry were a cut above

their urban counter-parts socially. [p12] After the end of the French Wars in 1815, when most of the infantry were either disbanded or absorbed into the Militia, many of the Yeomanry units were kept in being, their major usefulness being seen as their availability to aid the Civil Power in times of industrial unrest. The notorious instance of the use of the Cheshire, and Manchester & Salford Yeomanries in the Peterloo Massacre of 1819, is one of very many occasions upon which Yeomanry regiments were used, in the absence of a police-force, to put down Luddite demonstrations across the country. It must be pointed out that the Government was often irked by the willingness of local Justices to call out the Yeomanry, as they then had to be paid, whilst use of the better-disciplined regular troops came free. Throughout the second quarter of the nineteenth century Yeomanry units were either active in support of the Civil Power, or were disbanded. From the 200 or so units existing in 1805, the Royal Militia and Yeomanry Cavalry Army List for April 1850, shows 66 regiments in existence, some of them like the Royal Kettering Troop, or the Whittlesey & Cambridgeshire Troop having strengths of only around 60 effectives, whereas Prince Albert's Own Leicestershire Regiment of Yeomanry Cavalry had over 600. In 1871, the Yeomanry was taken under the direct control of the Crown. Some units disappeared and, a list of 1885, shows a strength of 39 Yeomanry regiments, each of four squadrons. An expansion of the Yeomanry occurred at the time of the South African War, when the tactics of the Boer Commandos suggested a role for an equivalent cavalry force on the British side. Because the Yeomanry were prevented by law from being deployed overseas, special legislation was drafted to enable volunteers to be formed into companies of Imperial Yeomanry. Much of the cost was raised by public subscription, whilst troopers contributed their own horses and equipment, and even, sometimes, paid their own passage. In all, some 35000 men served in these companies. By 1908, there were 53 regiments of Yeomanry cavalry, two of which, the Scottish Horse, and Lovat's Scouts each had eight squadrons. The Welsh Horse was raised in Glamorgan in 1914, but recruited in Montgomery, and appears never to have operated in a cavalry role. In WWl, Yeomanry regiments served as horsed cavalry in the Middle East, as infantry on the Western Front and elsewhere, and formed the nucleus of a new regiment, the Machine-Gun Corps.

In 1920, many regiments were converted to field artillery, and some, in 1938, again to AA artillery. Others became armoured or reconnaissance units with tanks or armoured cars. Some even began WWll with horses, the Yorkshire Dragoons fighting against Vichy French troops in Syria in 1942 were the last troops to operate as horsed cavalry. Since the end of WWll there have been innumerable amalgamations, disbandments and conversions. Some regiments have completely disappeared; some are mere squadrons in composite regiments; others are commemorated by no more than a unit's title in parenthesis, some as batteries of artillery, signals squadrons, or, even, infantry companies. A particularly good example of the cumulative effect of amalgamations is the resident unit of Dudley TAC: A [Staffordshire, Warwickshire, and Worcestershire Yeomanry] Squadron, The Royal Mercian & Lancastrian Yeomanry. Here, twelve squadrons in three former regiments have been whittled down into one squadron, whilst the new parent regiment represents the descendants of at least seven former complete regiments. Based at Stratford-upon-Avon and Stourbridge TACs, are units of the 67th [Queens Own Warwickshire & Worcestershire Yeomanry] Signal Squadron, 37th Signal Regt. [Volunteers]. At Shrewsbury TAC is 95th [Shropshire Yeomanry] Signal Squadron, 35th [South Midlands] Signal Regiment [Volunteers]. All these represent laudable, if cumbersome, attempts to keep alive memories of former regimental pride.

The Rifle Volunteers 1859-1908
There were many amongst, especially, the middle classes who, throughout the middle years of the nineteenth century, had watched the activities of the Yeomanry with something approaching envy. Quite simply, they wanted to do their bit for the country, and saw no reason why their occupations as grocers, clerks, or house-builders should prevent them. Some, even felt that the freehold of a suburban villa conferred no less a status as an officer and gentleman, than did a farm or a small country estate. International events were such that, once again, the country saw itself as likely to be invaded by France, which was developing superior sorts of warship. One response, that of Government, was to convene a Royal Commission, commencing work in August 1859, and ultimately to advocate throwing large sums of money at the construction of monolithic

fortifications to defend the naval bases. These, we have since come to refer to as Palmerston's Follies. An alternative, more populist, response was for individuals to learn to fire rifles effectively. A [civilian] National Rifle Association was formed in November 1859, and Queen Victoria naturally pulled the [pre-aimed] inaugural trigger on Wimbledon Common. Throughout the 1840s and 1850s successive Governments had been politely declining offers from well-intentioned gentlemen of military bent, to raise Volunteer Corps to defend the country from foreign aggression. Finally, in May 1859, the Secretary of State for War, issued a circular to Lords Lieutenant, authorising the formation of volunteer rifle corps. In an exercise, to be repeated in the formation of the Local Defence Volunteers in 1940, volunteers rushed forward to serve in the Rifle Corps. By the end of 1860, over 120000 men had enrolled in Rifle Volunteer Corps, predominantly in cities. Although the emphasis had initially been on the independence of each unit to make its own rules, design its own uniforms, please itself as to training and conduct, and appoint its own officers, these freedoms were to last only a short while. Almost immediately, Administrative Battalions were formed, into which neighbouring corps were directed, and this inevitably led to a reduction of individuality, as consistency assumed greater importance. In 1863, the Volunteer Act was passed by Parliament, both establishing the principle of annual inspection, and setting the standard for drills. Whilst the regulation of the corps was increased, successive governments continued to rely on the enthusiasm of the volunteers, seeking to get away with funding as little as possible. This presented problems for any volunteer officers who were without private means as they found themselves unable to fund the shortfall between government grant, and the not inconsiderable cost of running private armies. Whilst the early spirit of adventure, patriotism and enthusiasm had caught people up in the novelty of the movement, once much of what was perceived as the fun element had been taken away with government, not unjustifiably, demanding accountability for the spending of public funds, then many, both officers and other ranks found themselves losing interest.

We have already seen how the Militia were absorbed into the regimental system of the regular army through Cardwell's reforms. In 1881 the 215 battalions of the Rifle Volunteers were allocated to Line Regiments. Thus, for instance, the 1st, 2nd and 3rd Hampshire, and the 1st Isle of Wight Rifle Volunteer Corps were re-organised into five Volunteer Battalions of the Hampshire Regiment. Similarly rifle volunteer corps in Renfrew, Stirlingshire, Clackmannan & Kinross, Dunbartonshire and Argyll found themselves re-designated as the seven Volunteer Battalions of the Argyll & Sutherland Highlanders. The volunteers of Sutherland were joined with those of Ross and Moray to provide three volunteer battalions for the Seaforth Highlanders. Prior to this rationalisation, the Rifle Volunteers had fallen a little behind in the public confidence department, and this strengthening of the connection between regular and volunteer was good for morale on one hand, and, to some extent, restored public faith in a force of volunteers who nevertheless were now perceived as nearer to the professionals. When the test came with the South African Wars, for which many volunteered for overseas service, there came the opportunity for public acclaim for a generally creditable performance, even if there were reservations in the High Command, mainly relating to deficiencies in physical fitness and training. Attempts to demand higher levels of, particularly, training, after the war, were obstructed by some of the many Volunteer officers who sat in Parliament. However, the Liberal Secretary-of-State for War, RB Haldane, managed to bring about reform when, on 1 April 1908, the new Territorial Force [TF] came into being.

We shall presently look at the horsed elements of the Rifle Volunteers, but we must not forget that there were, however, other, better-established specialist units within the Volunteer Force, the many artillery and engineer units, in particular, but also such innovative units as the Volunteer Medical Staff Corps, formed in Maidstone in 1886, the fore-runner of an entire volunteer medical organisation.

Artillery and Engineer Volunteers 1859-1908
In 1859, a significant number of volunteer units elected to become gunners. These were mainly in coastal areas, particularly ports, where they expected to man coast artillery in times of threatened invasion. Many of these units were quite small, but the specialist nature of their work demanded that

they put in, on average, twice as much drill-time as the infantry. In 1885, there were 62 Artillery Volunteer Corps in existence, the most senior being the Honourable Artillery Company, already, then, approaching its bi-centenary. Many of these units were effectively combined but deployed to operate in quite widespread locations. They were not all confined to coastal areas since Worcestershire, Shropshire and Staffordshire all boasted artillery units.

In January, 1860, the staff of the South Kensington Museum formed the 1st Middlesex Engineer Volunteer Corps. They were followed by two dozen or so others, the last-formed being Bedford Grammar School in 1888, attached to the Tower Hamlets Corps, along with the 1st Northamptonshire Corps, who had built their own HQ building & workshops in Peterborough in 1867. Some units specialised in railway construction and operation, others were Fortress Engineers, mainly concerned with coast defence works. In 1886 a number of additional volunteer engineer units were raised as Submarine Miners/Electrical Engineers, responsible for controlling defensive minefields in the major ports, although these duties at Hull and Falmouth were shortly afterwards transferred to the Militia. In 1908, many of these specialisms, along with the new science of signals, would be carried forward into engineer units in the Territorial Force.

Light Horse & Mounted Rifle Volunteers 1860-1901
As we have earlier seen, many of the volunteer cavalry units had disbanded by the middle of the century, and the resurgence of the volunteers in 1859, encouraged the formation of new ones. Some of these units, generally designated Light Horse Volunteers were raised and led by aristocrats, examples including the Earl of Rosslyn's Fife Mounted Rifles, but shortly changed to Light Horse, Viscount Macduff's Elgin Mounted Rifles, the Earl of Yarborough's Lincolnshire Light Horse at Brocklesby Park, and the Duke of Manchester's Huntingdonshire Light Horse, based at Kimbolton Castle. This latter body led the march-past at the Volunteers' Review at Windsor in 1868, when Queen Victoria took the salute, and were already veterans of such royal reviews. A number of factors limited the lives of these units. The threat of invasion from France receded as some of the initial enthusiasm of their

membership waned. At the same time, the cost of maintaining horses and their accoutrements, and of providing the splendid uniforms, became a burden on their members, particularly those officers who did not enjoy great wealth. Many units had dissolved by the end of the1860s, Huntingdonshire hanging on until 1882, and Lincolnshire to 1887. Despite absorptions and amalgamations, or the transformation of Mounted Rifles into the more prestigious Light Horse, the concept was not a successful one. It must be remembered that few of the longer-established, and better-supported Yeomanry regiments had survived even into the second half of the nineteenth century. Only the Fife & Forfar Light Horse Volunteers made it into the new century, becoming Imperial Yeomanry in 1901, and serving as infantry in WWl. They then fought in WWll in armoured cars as a reconnaissance unit, and, within the 79th Armoured Division, with flame-thrower tanks in north-west Europe. They survive as an armoured unit in the Scottish Yeomanry.

The Territorial Force 1908-20
The TF was designed as one thing, but, for the usual political considerations which accompany radical change, was presented as another. Haldane's wish was that of some amongst the earlier architects of volunteer armies, particularly Earl de Grey and Lord Ranelagh, who wanted the Volunteer Force to be a fully self-sufficient force of all arms which would mirror the Regular Army, acting as a reserve in time of war. The Duke of Cambridge in 1860, and pillars of the military establishment in 1908, were extremely worried by this, as it seemed to them, to pose a threat to the Regular Army by under-cutting it cost-wise, and by diluting professional values by appearing to promote those of amateurism. The TF was, therefore, presented solely as a home-defence force, and only the stated possibility of its members' option to volunteer for overseas service offered a possible contra-indication of this purpose. Within a short time 20000 officers and men had declared a willingness to serve abroad if asked. The actual organisation, recruitment and day-to-day administration of the TF was in the hands of locally-appointed County Territorial Associations. It had been with Edward Vll's backing that Haldane had been able to set up the TF at all, and it was with influential support from both Houses of Parliament that the TF Associations could operate effectively. In 1909, for instance, 115 Peers served as Association members.

MONMOUTH, the 1673 house,
home to the senior TA unit

A couple of years later, and nearly 100 MPs were serving as TF officers. With such support, Haldane was able to organise the new TF to fulfil its shadow role: in 14 regional divisions, each with three infantry brigades; a mounted brigade of three Yeomanry regiments with horse artillery; field and heavy brigades of artillery; engineers and signallers; service corps transport & supply columns; field hospitals and field ambulances. There were further garrison artillery and engineers to defend the ports. [p16] Thus the capacity to understudy the regulars was there, but not fully appreciated. It has been suggested that Kitchener's refusal to turn to the TF in the immediate aftermath of the Old Contemptibles' demise in 1914 after the retreat from Mons, was rooted in stories he had heard of the failure of volunteer units in the American Civil War. His preference for raw recruits may, however, lie in his under-estimating the capabilities of the TF, and a more basic ignorance of their intended role as a Reserve Army. Nevertheless, the TF played its part in WWI, many entire units volunteering for overseas service on the Western Front, the Dardanelles, the Middle East or the Home Front, guarding the East Coast against invasion, or shooting down Zeppelins. Territorial units garrisoned India and Africa, releasing regulars to fight more effectively elsewhere. Despite Kitchener's refusal to use the TF and its administrative networks in the creation of his New Armies, such was the demand for trained troops that virtually all TF units were ordered to duplicate themselves, sometimes more than once. In 1915, the Volunteer Training Corps was formed to train as a last line of defence. Their GR brassards provided them with a nickname: Grandpa's Regiment, thus setting the precedent for Dad's Army one short generation later.

The Territorial Army 1920-46
After the end of the war to end all wars, many territorial units were disbanded. Only against a back-drop of War Office opposition, was the Territorial Army [TA] re-constituted in 1920, and then with the old problem of ill-defined and misunderstood aims. In 1923 the TA was given responsibility for AA defence, and, in 1926, for coast defence, but little was done to further these fresh tasks in terms of planning, the development of tactics, provision of weapons or training. Recruitment was down, partly due to the unclear function of the TA in the eventuality of civil strife, strikes and strike-breaking. However,

by the late-1930s, the force was up to its establishment of 200000, finding no less than 77000 new recruits in 1938 alone. Many TA units had undergone radical change. By this time most of the Yeomanry regiments had, unsurprisingly, become either field artillery or armoured units. In addition, many infantry units had been converted into AA regiments. Added to this disruption was the demand that TA units should clone themselves, thus producing duplicate units. This gave some earlier-amalgamated units the opportunity to become re-inventions of their former selves. For others it must have been a strain to provide two COs, two adjutants, two quartermasters etc. all whilst preparing for full mobilisation. Whilst the First-Aid Nursing Yeomanry [FANY] had been around since 1908, there had hitherto been no opportunities for women in the TA, until the ATS was founded in 1936. By 1944, women would be serving in mixed AA batteries. In 1939, the TA was organised into 13 infantry divisions with bases across Britain, six AA divisions, and two cavalry brigades. This force was to be immediately doubled as war approached, and TA units served with distinction in every theatre of war. Significantly, in 1940, the job of organising the Home Guard was given to the Territorial Associations.

The Territorial Army from 1947

It was a very different TA which was re-constituted on 1 January 1947. There were nine infantry and two armoured divisions, with the remaining 25 Yeomanry regiments organised into armoured brigades. Within this framework were specialist units meeting the technical, medical, and logistical needs. By 1950, national servicemen were serving in the TA, and by 1953, they made up two-thirds of its strength. A number of factors, not least the need for national economies, were from now on to force a succession of scaling down of the armed forces in general. The recognition, by the mid-1950s that airplanes travelled too fast to be shot down by conventional AA fire, however brilliant the radar technology, meant that AA Command was disbanded in 1955. Coast Artillery went the very next year. Changes in defence thinking, the ending of National Service in 1960, and the ever-present problem of escalating costs, all contributed to conversions, amalgamations and contraction. The argument was that a leaner, more professional, better-trained TA could, amongst other duties,

contribute more to NATO operations, and be much closer in terms of training, equipment and commitment, to the regulars. In those post-war years we have seen the TAER [Ever-Readies]; the T&AVR; units earmarked for service in Germany; and others as home defence forces. Since the thawing of the Cold War and the Options for Change White Paper, further reductions have been made in the numerical strength of the TA, with the accent on forming cadres of specialists with specific roles to play in emergencies. There have also been fundamental changes in the legislation governing the TA. The 1996 Reserve Forces Act allows the mobilisation and deployment of TA personnel alongside the regulars. At the time of writing, the implementation of this policy may be seen in Iraq and elsewhere. On the administrative side, the County TA Associations have been brought together into the thirteen regional Reserve Forces and Cadets Associations [RFCAs], with some specialist units centrally administered by their parent formations.

Social Class and the Volunteer Force 1859-1908

We have already seen how the Rifle Volunteer Corps was intended by its founders as a middle-class institution. This was motivated by a desire prevalent amongst the middle-classes to be seen as committed to the well-being of the country in the same way as was the aristocracy. The cynical might argue that it was also a product of a reluctance to put weapons in the hands of the poor and the politically-disaffected, especially in times of social and political change. In the event the rifle volunteers came very much from the artisan class. Many of those tradesmen and professionals, expected to join up, were either too busy, too lacking in interest or military enthusiasm, or unwilling to subsidise what many of them must have seen as essentially a function of government. So the majority of the volunteers were from the artisan and labouring classes. A large number of corps were sponsored by individual firms who might provide uniforms and equipment, as well as structuring working practices to accommodate training activities. Other corps came from particular occupational groups. Even interest groups such as temperance movement members, got in on the act. Examples of all these types of membership could be found in Glasgow: 22nd Corps from Messrs Cogan's spinning factory, 28th Corps from the Edinburgh & Glasgow Railway, 81st Corps from Law

& Co's Port Dundas Ironworks; 31st & 75th Corps, both recruited from workers in the leather trade, 38th Corps of mechanics, 63rd Corps of bakers, 83rd Corps of joiners; 54th, 82nd & 91st Corps, all of total abstainers. These types of group far exceeded those from the professional classes such as the 9th Corps of bankers, or 17th Corps of stockbrokers & accountants. It is interesting that the 25th Middlesex Corps, with HQ at Somerset House, and recruited in the Bank of England, drew its membership from the porters, not the clerks. The thorniest questions universally were, however, about the qualifications needed to be an officer and a gentleman. It was suggested that those in trade or working as artisans could not possibly aspire to command, and this was generally resolved by the appointment of members of the professional classes as officers in companies made up of working-class volunteers. Those companies based on commercial concerns had a ready-made solution: managers, often family members of the firm's owner, could be officers; foremen became NCOs; and the workers found their place as rank-and-file. There are even instances of the work-place becoming an extension of the corps, with workers in uniform overalls, those of foremen being decorated with rank badges. Other types of volunteer unit found similar solutions, and the early practice of electing officers seems to have died fairly quickly, solicitors and doctors providing the officers for many small town corps, almost ex officio. We must not, however, forget the nuances of Victorian social stratification. When it was suggested by regular army officers that the volunteers were depriving the Militia of recruits, it was forcefully pointed out by Rifle Volunteer Corps officers that their men's attitude to the Militia could best be summed up by statements using words such as 'not touching' and 'barge-pole'. The pecking-order was alive and well. Although it took a while, society gradually accepted the notion of Volunteer Force officers being drawn from an enlarged social constituency, one wider than had hitherto been traditional. No similar problem appeared to affect the Yeomanry. A comment of 1879, quoted by J Mordaunt Crook, recognises, with some hint of resignation, wealth as the governing force of the prevailing social system, and that wearing the 'gorgeous uniform of the Yeomanry' constituted one of several ways in which the arriviste might buy his way into the landed gentry. The Yeomanry regiments and the Honourable Artillery Company in London all stressed that members, who had to be proposed by existing members, should be of independent means or in permanent and secure employment. It should also be noted here that many of the public schools supported Cadet Companies, some of whose members would eventually have gone on to become officers in the Volunteer Force. These companies were absorbed into the TF, in 1908, as Junior Officer Training Corps [OTC], and many still exist as the Combined Cadet Force [CCF]. Cadet Battalions, attached to Rifle Volunteer units had been formed from 1863, and, in 1883, the Boys Brigade was founded along the same lines. When the Territorial Cadet Force was sanctioned by the War Office in 1910, these cadet units were absorbed. They would ultimately become the Army Cadet Force [ACF] still flourishing today, with attitude.

The Social Dimension of the Volunteers & Territorials

Although the first Rifle Volunteer Corps were formed in London, the highest level of recruitment in the first two years, in terms of proportion of the male population, was in Scotland, and particularly the more sparsely-populated parts of the Highlands. The only English county which came anywhere near these Scottish levels was rural Westmorland. In 1881, between 5% and 7.5% of Scottish males aged from 15-49 were enrolled in the corps, with the higher turn-out in the counties with lower population density. Lorna Jackson has suggested that it was the activities, incidental to the major thrust of volunteering, which attracted young men to the colours in such numbers. It was the rifle-shooting at competitions offering good prize-money; it was the opportunity to meet contemporaries for competitive sport; it was the provision of other, sometimes educational, more often recreational facilities in the drill halls which were built in small towns, and in the Highlands in small villages, which went a long way to explaining the popularity of the Rifle Volunteers. It would appear that drill halls were providing a venue, equivalent to the Mechanics' Institute more often found in urban areas. It was used for a wide range of social events such as dances, concerts, plays and festivals. These would, no doubt, have involved the wider community, but it was predominantly the young men in their late-teens and early twenties who could make best use of these facilities on a regular basis. In remote, rural areas, it seems likely that membership of the volunteers

provided, were designed in such a way, that easy conversion to workers' housing remained an option. The possession of a secure, easily accessible Armoury, provided at its own expense, was key to the very existence of a volunteer corps. No issue of arms by Government could proceed until a successful inspection of armoury facilities had taken place, which deemed them appropriate. The Volunteer Regulations of 1881 listed the relevant criteria. The Armoury had to be dry, well-aired, free from worm-eaten timber, white-washed and clean. Once an Armoury had been inspected and approved, it could only be moved with the written permission of the GOC District. It was also expected that arms would always be stored in the Armoury, volunteers only being allowed to take weapons home in extraordinary circumstances, and only then, with the express written permission of their CO. The ever-present anxieties about weapons falling into the wrong hands were aired constantly, and the 1881 Regulations repeat the licence given to volunteers to defend their armouries and storehouses against attack by rioting mobs, using force of arms as necessary.

TONBRIDGE, the Corn Exchange which served as the drill hall

Chapels were often ideal buildings to use, especially when amalgamations of non-conformist congregations caused redundancies, making numbers of them available to alternative users. This process seems to have provided solutions most often in Scotland and Cornwall. [p65,p25] Chapels in Auchterarder, Dunblane, Halkirk, Jedburgh, Leslie, Lossiemouth, Nairn, New Scone, in Scotland, and in Bude, Falmouth, Helston and Launceston, in Cornwall, exemplify this re-cycling of buildings. There are other examples across Britain which include Meeting-Houses at Axminster, Kirkintilloch and Witney, and chapels at Burnham-on-Crouch, Llangollen and March. Some of these, as at Falmouth, had quite substantial, secure outbuildings added along the sides to store specialist equipment and weapons.

JEDBURGH, the C18 chapel, once the drill hall, now a RBL club

Schools also often provided suitable premises for the volunteers. The British School at Horncastle, the National School at Chapel-en-le-Frith, St Marks School at Sidcup, and others at Aberlour, Kirkintilloch, North Walsham, Wilton, and elsewhere, were all used. At Faversham, the owner of the Gunpowder Mills had built a school for the children of his employees, and used these premises for a drill-room in 1859 for the newly-raised artillery volunteers whose captain he was. When he moved his school into larger premises he fitted them out with an armoury at the same time. Local tradition has it that the former drill hall in Beauly, was a school-room, brought from Lairg and re-erected. The Yeomanry in Winchester occupied a building in Hyde Close, designed, in 1795, by Sir John Soane, as a school.

A wide range of industrial and commercial buildings were utilised as well. In Bacup, a corn-mill; in Worksop, a disused malt-kiln; at Mountsorrel, quarry offices; King's seed ware-house in Coggeshall; at Galashiels, the offices of textile mills; the malt-house and kilns at Petersfield, and at Melrose, a water-mill. Three artillery drill halls in Cornwall, at Charlestown, Marazion and St Just, were adapted from featureless granite buildings which probably had commercial origins, possibly as stores. At the other extreme, a very imposing 1840 bank at Alnwick [p67] housed the Percy Rifle Volunteers, and, somewhat bizarrely, at Torquay, a circus school was taken over. Many units went straight for hostelries: the Station Hotel at Kimberley, the Crown at Diss, the Cattle-Market Hotel at Worksop, the Queens Hotel at Blaina, the Royal Station Hotel at Carnforth, and Clacton's Osborne Hotel, for instance. Sometimes, only the Officers' Mess was accommodated in licensed premises as at the Lovat Arms in Beauly, and at Chester's Eastgate Hotel. At Bradford-on-Avon, the Rifle Volunteers shared with G & T Spencers Ale & Porter Store, a fine, stone, castellated building on Silver Street from 1881, certainly until 1911. [p67] Institutes were also used at Egham, Lanark, Fauldhouse, Llanfair Caereinion, Melton Constable, and Rothbury. At both Poole and Knaresborough, premises were shared with the Oddfellows, and at Williton, with the Girls' Friendly Society. At Dursley the Masons' premises, now a Tandoori restaurant, were shared. Theatres were used at Lyme Regis, Downham Market, and Morecambe. Even ancient monuments provided venues: the Cathedral Tithe Barn at Wells; the Newarke Gate at Leicester; Barr Castle at Galston; the old court-house at Cuckfield; and local landmarks like the Round-house at Melksham, possibly the Dean's Library at St Asaph, the Parish Rooms at Midhurst, and the Museum Hall at Bridge of Allan.

Houses, both humble as at Nuneaton or Usk, and grand as at Dumbarton, Fulham, Hertford, Kilmarnock, Leamington Spa, Monmouth [very], Norwich, Reading, and Torrington were often used as the front-block of a drill hall complex. Some, as we have seen, stood alone, as office, armoury and orderly-room.

The Yeomanry, being dependent on the supply of recruits with their own horses, were forced to be more flexible in their provision of accommodation. Very often, Saddle Rooms were provided, where the military-issue harness could be stored, only being issued on drill nights, as the men arrived on their own mounts with their own saddles. These Saddle Rooms were often in those public houses, most convenient for the greatest number of troop members. Centres of gravity could switch, as when a squadron of the QOOH moved its base from Witney to Chipping Norton for a year or so, in recognition of the fact that the recruitment catchment had shifted, albeit only temporarily. A general point to be made here relates to attempts to cut down unnecessary travelling on drill nights. Drill stations were quite far-flung, especially in rural areas, and units were staffed with PSIs to reflect this. It was even possible for a CO to request that inspections be carried out at drill stations rather than always at HQ, providing he could guarantee a two-thirds turn-out on the day.

So much for those buildings which were adapted. Now we must look at the earliest examples of purpose-built drill halls. Much depended on a whole range of factors which would determine the scope of the venture. These included the general size and affluence of the community, the existence of patronage or leadership, the enthusiasm of the volunteers, the level of civic pride, the availability of sites and materials, and the density of population. So, for instance, the Drill House of the Kent Rifle Volunteers [25th Kent Rifles] proudly displayed in the Illustrated London News of 15 February 1862, is a large hall, 100 feet [30m] long, and 53 feet [16m] wide, with a high, pedimented classical facade, with two tiers of arched windows, and the Kentish horse and *Invicta* motto over a grand entrance arch. Part of this hall may still be contained within the Holly Hedge House complex on Blackheath, in use by the 2nd Volunteer Battalion of the Royal West Kent Regiment in 1903, by the 20th [County of London] Battalion The London Regiment in 1914, and ever since, by the TA and ACF. It would appear that the good burghers of south-east London had both the resources to provide such a splendid structure, and the presence of other units in close enough proximity to motivate them to compete for recruits. Other imposing drill halls were built at Newport [1860] for Princess Beatrice's Isle of Wight Rifles, St Helens [1861],

Hull's Londesborough Barracks [1864],[*p27*] Norwich's Chapelfields drill hall [1866], now demolished, Selkirk [*p68*] and Great Yarmouth's York Road [1867], Wakefield's George Street [c1867], Boston, Brighton, Runcorn [*p27*] and Sandwich [all 1869], Inverurie [1870], Chirnside [1871] for the Berwickshire Rifle Volunteers, Forrest Hill in Edinburgh, Colliergate in York [1872], and Thurso's Olrig Street [1873] [*p69*]. In almost total contrast are Settle [1865], and Roy Bridge [1869]. Settle is a rough stone barn-like building, which may not be a purpose-built drill hall at all, as, although in the centre of the village, it has the look of an agricultural building about it. Roy Bridge [*p28*] was built by Alexander Aeneas, 27th Chief of Clan Mackintosh for the 10th Inverness-shire Rifle Volunteers. A plain stone oblong formed the drill hall with an apartment for the drill instructor. Another pressing need in the village was for a post office, and this occupied a wing which projected forward from the drill hall. Later, in 1903 it was taken over by Lovat's Scouts, who added an ammunition store at one end, and adapted the interior to the needs of cavalry by installing storage for saddlery etc. Although fulfilling similar functions perfectly efficiently, the drill halls at Blackheath and at Roy Bridge could not be further apart in size and appearance. That at Roy Bridge, moreover, housed the families of both the drill instructor and the postmaster, in 1881, a total of four adults and eleven children.

The use of adapted premises involving varying degrees of improvisation, and the first attempts at the purpose-built, began the process of defining the drill hall as a building type, with specific component elements and relationships of internal spaces setting it apart from other building types. These elements divide neatly into four headings. The first concerns the running of the unit, and includes the office, or Orderly Room; perhaps a separate office for the CO; a secure Armoury for storing the unit's weapons; and a Stores, for all the un-issued items of uniform and equipment. Next, are those areas concerned with training: the Hall itself, preferably an unencumbered space in which a Company of around 100 men can drill; and an Indoor Range for target-shooting practice. The third element is accommodation for the drill instructor and his family. This might consist of a two-storey house, a flat, or even a space shared with the offices. Finally, comes the social space. This would be the optional element and could consist of luxurious facilities to rival

LONDESBOROUGH Barracks, Hull, built in 1864

RUNCORN, the drill hall with Rifle Volunteer badge & datestone

ROY BRIDGE, drill hall & post office

ILKLEY, the artillery drill hall, now in commercial use

any gentlemen's club, a fully-equpped gymnasium, or a simple reading-room. There might be an Officers' Mess, even a Sergeants' Mess, and perhaps a canteen for the other ranks. There appear to have been several basic layouts by which these elements were combined into a coherent building. More often than not, the offices, armoury and stores were accommodated in a one-, or two-storey block fronting the site. The hall lay behind this, usually with the indoor range along one side. A cross-wing, behind the hall, might then contain the staff accommodation. If circumstances demanded it, because of a restricted site, for instance, or a particularly generous provision of facilities, then the front-block might, as at Chenies Street, rise to three storeys. Variations included side-by-side hall and office-wing or house; the hall might lie laterally behind the front-block, or might lie alongside the front-block but laterally to the street. [See Figure 1]. Examples of the side-by-side lay-out include Eastbourne, Lutterworth, Felixstowe, Inverurie and Cowie. Lateral halls, behind the front-block, may be seen at Tarbert, Lochcarron, Elland and Barnsley. At Ilkley, [p28] a hall with two cross-wings has been rotated through 90 degrees, to lie sideways to the street, and at a number of other sites, including Basingstoke, Camberley, Haverhill, Lampeter and Pwllheli, the two main elements of hall and offices form a single block along the street-frontage.

It is significant that a large proportion of both the earliest purpose-built drill halls, and the early adaptations were for volunteer artillery units. Clearly the needs of the artillery for gun-sheds, ammunition stores, indoor practice areas and so on were more acute than those of the riflemen. There was also new construction at the sharp end. The Duke of Northumberland Battery, built in 1861 for the defence of Alnmouth was manned by the Percy Volunteer Artillery, who also manned a battery at Lindisfarne Castle on Holy Island throughout the later 1860s. They had a drill hall from 1860 in a converted chapel in Percy Street, Amble, and one of their drill instructors lived round the corner in Lamb Street. In North Wales the Napoleonic period forts of Belan opposite Anglesey, and Williamsburg, now in the Glynliffon Country Park, were built by Lord Newborough, commander of both the Loyal Newborough Volunteers and the Militia. They served as militia stores, but also as practice batteries for the Carnarfonshire Artillery Volunteers. The War

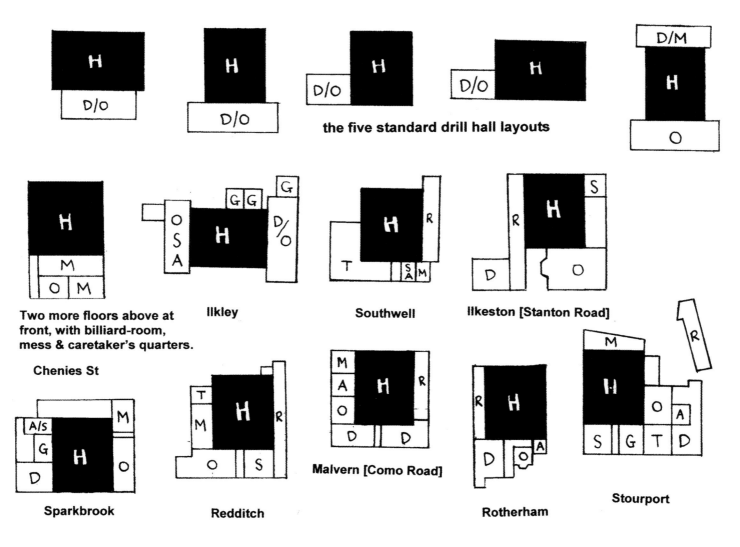

the five standard drill hall layouts

Two more floors above at
front, with billiard-room,
mess & caretaker's quarters.

Chenies St

Ilkley

Southwell

Ilkeston [Stanton Road]

Sparkbrook

Redditch

Malvern [Como Road]

Rotherham

Stourport

Key: H hall   O orderly-room/offices   R indoor-range   M mess

A armoury   S stores   G garage/gun-shed   D staff-house

Figure 1 Sketch block-plans of Drill Halls up to 1914   [not to scale]

Office, unsurprisingly, kept a close eye on proposals which involved the raising of new volunteer artillery units. A specialist artillery officer was appointed as inspector, and he had to approve the site of the new battery, the site and capacity of its magazine building, the relative distances of the unit's HQ from battery and magazine, and the security both of any armoury storing carbines, and the magazine storing powder, shot and shell. Particular attention was paid to the volunteer gunners' observance of safety practices in the magazine, with specific reference to lighting and the wearing of stud-less footware. The volunteers were also required, at their own expense, to install a lightning-conductor on the roof of the magazine. Where guns were to be emplaced permanently, the construction and maintenance of any necessary earthworks were the responsibility of the volunteers. Where there was no permanent battery, then the War Office provided two practice guns, to be kept in the gunshed at the drill hall. All these stipulations are laid down in volumes issued by the War Office. The 1881 edition runs to 1042 articles, to which are added over 50 pages of appendices which provide technical explanation, cross-references to Statute Law, and samples of forms and returns.

Some specialist units were thrown onto their own resources entirely. The 1st Northamptonshire Engineer Corps, formed in Peterborough in 1867, with responsibilities in the field of railway engineering in the military context, finding the Wentworth Room and the Corn Exchange unsuitable for their practical activities, built their own premises with their own hands, in St Leonards Street. These contained the usual orderly room, but, additionally, a modelling studio and store-shed for their construction materials. No doubt nowadays, we might describe it as a bonding experience, or an exercise in team-building. The pragmatic Victorian engineers may have seen it simply as making a virtue of necessity.

Although the Volunteer Act of 1863 granted Volunteer units the legal right to acquire land or buildings for purposes approved by the Secretary of State, such as the construction of drill sheds, ranges or storehouses, nevertheless, the funding of drill halls could be a problem. Bolton provides a good example. The Bolton Artillery Volunteers were founded in 1860 and constructed rudimentary gun-platforms in order to practise on their 32 pounder guns. By 1867, a drill shed had been erected on waste ground on Orlando Street, but they really needed a more permanent home somewhere. Eventually, a company was formed to purchase Silverwell House and its adjoining land. A public appeal raised £980 from 85 subscribers, the largest donation being £100 each from Musgrave and Sons, and a Mr Thomasson, then £50 each from Colonel Ainsworth, the Marquess of Rothwell, and J Garnett, through donations of 20, 10 and five guineas or pounds, down to the lowest of £1. The company acquired the property for £2500 and spent the same again in adapting the house into offices, stores, messes, canteen, armoury etc. and adding a large drill hall, underground rifle range, stables and covered riding school. In 1900 Colonel Musgrave took on the mortgage and bought the whole property, which he then sold to the Lancashire Territorial Association in 1908. It was clearly only through the combination of wealthy officers putting in their own money, and the local community chipping in generously, that such enterprises could stay afloat. In Hull, a Bazaar lasting three days raised £1200, which enabled Londesborough Barracks to be built in 1864 for the 1st Corps, East Yorkshire Rifle Volunteers, to plans drawn up by one of their officers. In 1867, the 11th Corps of Worcestershire Rifle Volunteers in Malvern, formed a Drill Shed Company with capital of 1000 shares of £1. It was expected that rent would be paid out of the Government Capitation Grant, and that the hall would be let out for events thus creating a regular income. Many such companies, however, were to come unstuck, and they were fortunate if they found a wealthy patron to bail them out. All sorts of fund-raising took place, like the Bazaar at Selby held 21-25 May 1864 when tickets were 2/- [10p] on the first day, and bargains could be purchased from stalls run by ladies including the Countess de Grey and Ripon, and Lady Londesborough, whose husband was Lt Col of the 38th West York Rifle Corps. Their unofficial title, the Selby Rifles, is still emblazoned over the doorway of the Drill Shed and Armoury, built from the proceeds of, amongst other initiatives, this bazaar. The presentation of a Silver Bugle and Colours to the 4th Bucks Rifle Volunteers on 13 August 1860 at Velvet Lawn with the band of the Life Guards playing, was presented as a public spectacle, and admission was charged accordingly, tickets bought in advance attracting a saving. Corps members were already paying an annual subscription of one guinea [£1.05] after an initial levy of two guineas. Such funds went towards running costs, camps and permanent accommodation. As late as 1901, the 2nd Volunteer Battalion of the Gordon Highlanders found the solution to their accommodation problem by combining their funds with the proceeds of a public subscription to build the Victoria Hall at Ellon. For their money they got exclusive use of an Armoury, 24 feet x 16 feet [7.3m x 4.9m] and shared use, at no charge, of a large building with hall, offices, and outbuildings. For them, this was, apparently an ideal arrangement. At Wordsley, the money was raised by public subscription to build a handsome drill hall for D Company, 1st Volunteer Battalion South Staffordshire Regiment, which was opened with a concert on 17 October 1884. By 1907 it was being presented to the village by a William Richardson of Glasgow, presumably being surplus to the requirements of the TF, in memory of his late sister. Now known as the Richardson Hall, it was still referred to as the Drill Hall on a hand-bill for a meeting on 3 July 1916, to recruit civilians for military training in the cause of Home Defence. At Sidmouth, the drill hall on the sea-front, in use by 1897, had been gifted in perpetuity to the volunteers by a serving officer. The drill hall at Jardine Street, North Kelvinside in Glasgow reputedly still belongs to whichever unit is currently in occupation, for some reason not having been taken over by the local TF Association in 1908. It would most likely take more than the engineer unit who set it up in 1894 to find a way through all the implications of such a [legal] minefield. [p31]

By the early-1870s drill halls were becoming much more sophisticated in terms of both provision and demarcation of specialist spaces. Rotherham [1873] and Grove, on the Isle of Portland [1874] [p69] both display this in their layout and components. The first indication of this elaboration was, somewhat paradoxically, the anachronistic use of architectural motifs from mediaeval castles. Many of the Militia Barracks and Storehouses of the 1850s and 1860s had employed these features, so it is probably unsurprising that they should be repeated. In fact, this style seems to have been that favoured across Europe for fortifications generally, from Fort Picklecombe defending Plymouth, to the gates of Ulm, defending Bavaria. The classicism of Blackheath or Selkirk apparently merely represented blips in the process of creating a martial ambience. Whether home-grown Scots Baronial north of the border, or other forms of faux mediaeval a la Violet-le-Duc, these romantic echoes of the middle

GLASGOW's Jardine Street drill hall now used by a TA Signals unit

WOKINGHAM, the entrance lodges looking through to the site of the hall

ages were to be exploited until beyond the end of the nineteenth century, by which time there seems to have been a drift more toward the Tudor palace, finally recognising the military features as no more than token. A few drill hall architects appear to have opted either for the ecclesiastical version of mediaeval rather than the popularly more appropriate military one, or, more commonly, a domestic Tudor style, perhaps more often seen in almshouses, village schools or cottage hospitals, but both, nevertheless, presenting an institutional image, if on a small scale. It must, however, be noted that these architecturally stylish features appeared only where an attempt was consciously made to lift a building above the hum-drum. Many drill halls were quite undistinguished, utilitarian structures.

Early examples of drill hall as mediaeval castle can be seen at Bury [1868 & 1907], Chester [1865], Grove [1874] and Macclesfield [1872]. [p70,p72] Rotherham [1873], now demolished, was another good example. Grove, built for the Portland Artillery Volunteers, is, like Bury, the product of several builds, but in its original form it comprised a hall with a two-storey addition to the front containing an armoury and stores. It is of local stone, with narrow windows, and castellated. Later additions, notably in 1901, simply further developed the style of the existing structure, adding a tower/gateway, another two-storey projection on the front, and a two-storey, three-bedroomed cottage with crow-stepped gables, for the staff instructor/ caretaker, alongside the hall. For some, and not before time, the lavatory block on the rear corner, may well have proved as welcome an addition as the new billiard-room, as for the previous thirty years, the building had been a stranger to plumbing. At Rotherham, in Wharncliffe Street, the drill hall had a tall, off-centre, three-storey gate-tower with a higher, circular stair-turret with a pointed roof. To each side, gabled two-storey wings contained, on one side the armoury and orderly room, and, on the other, living accommodation for the staff instructor. Behind these was the hall, measuring 99 feet [30m] x 60 feet [18m]. Along one side ran a shed, probably containing the indoor range, and, at the back, was a stage with a room to each side. It was important that such halls earned their keep from outside lettings for dances and parties, as well as from the occupants' own fund-raising events. Macclesfield, built for the 8th Corps Cheshire Rifle Volunteers, although its hall has

been replaced by apartments, retains its front-block and tall, four-storey, pinnacled tower. A plaque on the tower records the volunteers' gratitude to the town for building them such a splendid drill hall. At Wokingham [1881], the style was more an informal Tudor, with, instead of a front-block, a pair of lodges, each containing two cottages, flanking an archway into a courtyard, across which faced the hall. The hall has gone but the lodges remain with the re-set datestone. [p31] The hall was built by Captain Arthur Walter, meeting the cost, which the architects estimated at £2350, from his own funds. The hall was of seven bays and measured 70 feet [21m] x 33 feet [10m], with a separately-accessed armoury and stores behind. This left the lodges as orderly room and accommodation for permanent staff. Photographs taken prior to its demolition in c1975, show aisles, one of which probably contained an indoor range. The hall was built in red brick with bands of grey and yellow bricks to relieve the blandness, and patches of diaper-work on the outside. A dado and cornice of pitch pine were installed, and a double floor, the upper, again, of pitch pine. Rendall's Patent Glazing in a wood and iron roof ensured good natural lighting and ventilation, and artificial light came from three Sugg's 100-candle burners. A moveable platform allowed the hall to be used for plays and lectures, and 500 people could be seated. The contemporary account of the dinner at which the hall was handed over to L Coy. 1st Volunteer Bn. Princess Charlotte of Wales Royal Berkshire Regiment, described it as the best room in Wokingham, and, no doubt it would have been in great demand for the town's main social events. The glazing in the roof, whether Rendall's or others, tends to be one of the defining features of drill halls from this period.

Sometimes, what seems a perfectly adequate building, was either replaced, or significantly enlarged within a relatively short period of opening. At East Street, Bromley, a drill hall was built in 1872 with £2000 capital raised by a Limited Liability Company. Provision included a galleried hall, 98 feet [30m] by 43 feet [13m], fitted out with gymnastic equipment etc. and with accommodation for the drill instructor. By 1875, as there was no other hall in the town, demand for the use of this space continued to increase, so, with another £1000 of capital, retiring rooms were added to the back of the hall, with a new, small hall, suitable for entertainments, band-practice etc. over these rooms.

This annexe, equipped with catering facilities, had a separate entrance. Fifteen years later, a further drill shed, 48 feet [15m] by 36 feet [11m], with a new armoury and orderly room were added, and the original buildings were renovated and given new gas lighting. The building is now a public house. [p33] At Horncastle, where the British School of 1814, had been adopted as the drill hall in 1867, this, despite it being a fairly generous space with gallery above, was deemed, by the end of the century, inadequate, and a new, much larger drill hall with adjoining house on one side, and indoor range along the other, was built in 1901.

The basic requirements of the drill hall were relatively simple in terms of space. The one universal demand for the provision of specific training facilities was for a range which enabled volunteers to practise their marksmanship. In rural areas, it was often possible to find the large expanses of land needed to create safe shooting outdoors where rifles with their effective ranges of up to two miles could be used. A good example is the range in the Trent's water-meadows below Long Eaton, used by the Robin Hood Rifles in the latter part of the nineteenth-century. A detached villa acted as lodge for the supervisor, [p33] and substantial earth banks supported the butts; all-in-all, an expensive and complex set-up. Urban units were usually denied such provision. London units were lucky, in the early days to get some firing on Wimbledon Common, and, later on, far into the country-side at Bisley. For drill nights, they had to make do with 25 yard indoor ranges in their own drill halls. They could not, of course, fire their rifles in these circumstances, without modification to them, and so the Morris Tube was invented. This consisted of an insertion into the barrel of the normal issue rifle, enabling smaller ammunition to be fired at a shorter range. Nor were Morris Tube ranges always confined to dedicated drill halls, for the volunteers had use of one in the Bull Hotel on Bell Street in Henley-on-Thames. It is clear that the provision of good facilities for shooting practice was seen as a priority. Around 1900, the 3rd Volunteer Bn. of the Kings Own Scottish Borderers had just the two proper drill halls at Dumfries and at Annan, but its eight companies had the use of no less than twelve ranges. As well as the general practice of shooting, there were specialist units which had their own particular training needs. The gunners of the 2nd East Yorkshire artillery volunteers, for example, were

BROMLEY, the East Street drill hall, now a public house

NOTTINGHAM, Trent Rifle House, built by 1895 for the Range warden

praised in a report by Major General Dalton, in 1906, for the 'ingenious and costly contrivances' that they had assembled, 'at their own cost' in their Colonial Street, Hull, 'model drill hall', for training in the specialist techniques of coast defence.

Whilst the basic components of a drill hall were the same regardless of most other factors, there was some variation in terms of social provision. We have seen how some of the big city drill halls were basically clubs for middle-class gentlemen, with billiards room, bar and reading-room. Others, catering for urban working-class members, often sought to provide more facilities of the physical and gymnastic type. The drill hall in the market town, with its members drawn from a more socially-mixed population, seems to have concentrated more on providing a venue for mass social events and entertainments. It may not be too much of a generalisation to suggest that the sedentary office-worker needed to take up fencing after a hard day's clerking, while the agricultural worker may have been content with less physically-taxing activities, after a different sort of working day. There is another point to be noted here regarding the general usefulness of the drill hall within the community. We have seen how, in many towns, the drill hall was the prime social venue for dances, concerts, meetings of societies, and national celebrations. In times of emergency it could also provide facilities of a different sort. Lincoln's Broadgate drill hall, for instance became an overflow for the city's hospital during the typhoid epidemic of 1905.

Around 1880 the connection between the volunteers and the regulars was strengthened when the previous Administrative Battalions became the Volunteer Battalions of Line Regiments. So, for instance, the six battalions of rifle volunteers from Fifeshire, Forfarshire and Perthshire, became the 1st-6th Volunteer Battalions of the Black Watch, whilst continuing to have their companies spread around their same catchment areas. It may have been this re-organisation, or it may have been other economic and social factors which appear to have triggered a spate of new drill hall building. Many of these new drill halls, especially in the densely-populated industrial towns of the north-west, were designed to accommodate whole battalions of infantry. Manchester [Ardwick Green 1886, and Burlington Street 1885], [p35] Bury [1868 & 1907], Salford, now demolished as are Liverpool's Shaw Street and Fraser Street,

Oldham [1897] [p35], Accrington, Warrington, Blackburn, Southport, and Ashton-under-Lyne [p35] all fall into this category. Some of them are quite cavernous, and a former adjutant of the Lancashire Fusiliers [TA] was to wax lyrical, recounting his memories of drilling the entire battalion of some 600 men inside the drill hall at Bury in the 1950s. He also maintained that Bury is the largest drill hall of them all. Other appreciably capacious drill halls of this time include Halifax, and, slightly later, Bournemouth [1895] [p35], Huddersfield [1899] [p70], Portsmouth [1902] Gosport [1902] and Southampton [1890] [p36]. The infantry had no monopoly on size. The artillery drill hall in Edmund Road, Sheffield [1880] measured 180 feet [55m] x 90 feet [27.5m], and also had a gun-shed, riding-school and first-floor stables accessed via a ramp.

It has sometimes been suggested that the activities of the volunteers provided the Victorians with one of their most popular spectator sports. In the early days, crowds would turn out to watch field days and parades. This may be one of the reasons why a number of the larger drill halls [Southampton [St Mary's] [p36] and Smethwick are good examples] had galleries for spectators across at least one end of the hall. No doubt it prevented the less nimble visiting brass-hat from sustaining injury whilst inspecting bayonet-drill, but it would appear likely that the facility was on occasion available for the local supporters to see, albeit from a safe distance, how their brave lads were doing.

Most of these large drill halls featured elements of mediaeval or Tudor architecture. A group of Scottish drill halls from this same period were built in Scots Baronial style. These included Stirling [1892] [p36], Huntly [p36], Elgin [p71], Castletown [p37], Ellon [1901] and Blair Atholl [1907] [p37], all with lots of bartizans, pepper-pots, crow-stepped gables and towers, both round and square. Another flurry of building, early in the new century, produced a number of Tudor examples which included Somme Barracks, Sheffield [1907] [p72], Kings Road, Manchester [1902] [p38], and Chorley [pre-1900] [p168].

If the external appearance of these drill halls harked back to days of yore, then, very often, the construction was cutting-edge. One of the most important features in terms of the functional workings of a drill hall was the extent of clear space in which troops could be drilled or guns manoeuvred for practice firing

MANCHESTER's Burlington Street drill hall, built for a whole battalion

ASHTON-under-LYNE, the front block containing offices & messes

OLDHAM's Rifle Street drill hall's cavernous interior

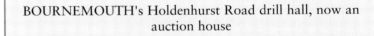

BOURNEMOUTH's Holdenhurst Road drill hall, now an auction house

SOUTHAMPTON's St Mary's drill hall opened by War Minister Stanhope

STIRLING, built 1892 for a volunteer Bn. of the Argyll & Sutherland Highlanders

SOUTHAMPTON's St Mary's drill hall showing the balcony for spectators

HUNTLY, a compact drill hall with front block, hall, and indoor range

drills. This meant that a wide roof-span needed to be supported without columns. It is significant that when the TA took over Leslie Church to be adapted as a drill hall, the first thing they did structually, was to remove the columns and substitute a system of cantilevered roof beams. A number of different solutions were tried. At Edmund Road, Sheffield [1880] [p39], the solution for spanning the 90 foot [27.5m] width was that adopted by Barlow at St Pancras Station, some twenty years earlier, its arch ribs springing from the floor, bearing on brick buttresses, with shallow pointed arches between each buttress. This would appear to be a common method with other examples, among many, at Dumfries [1890] [p39] and Lincoln [1891]. If the inspiration for Edmund Road came from St Pancras Station, then it was Kings Cross from which the next model was to originate. The senior Engineer Volunteer Corps was formed by the staff of the South Kensington Museum in January 1860. Six years later they moved their HQ from the Museum to College Street, Fulham. Their new drill hall was designed by Fowke, who had adapted an old method of making roof trusses from laminated timber, similar to those used in railway stations, but using his own techniques. This method was, apparently, used in other drill halls. Some drill halls, however, were just as revolutionary on the outside. The building acquired by the 2nd Volunteer Bn. Royal West Surrey Regiment for their Guildford drill hall came from the Edinburgh International Exhibition of 1886, and had stood in Edinburgh's Meadows. It was designed by a Glasgow engineer, in the tradition of Paxton's Crystal Palace, of glass and iron construction, measuring 122 feet [37m] x 60 feet [18m]. What it would have been like to drill in on a hot day, in thick serge uniforms, can only be imagined. By the 1890s, ferro-concrete, with all its advantages, was coming into use, and a number of systems were available. The Chatham drill hall of the 2nd Volunteer Bn. Queens Own Royal West Kent Regiment was built using the Hennebique method. Formerly standing on the corner of Boundary Road and Albany Terrace, it has been demolished for housing.

We have seen how buildings evolved throughout this period of the volunteers' own development as a viable force. Some places had adequate accommodation from the start. In others, the improvisation and extemporising of the early days, often gave way to more functional solutions. [p39] Some places never got proper buildings at all. At Kyle of Lochalsh, for instance, the

CASTLETOWN, this orderly-room block & the hall alongside are now flats

BLAIR ATHOLL, built in 1907 for A Squadron, the 1st Scottish Horse

shed [there is no other word for it] used by E Squadron, 2nd Lovat's Scouts, raised for service in the South African War, still stands in use as a furniture store. When the present owner was asked, perfectly diplomatically, how a proud regiment could be associated with such a sorry construction of plaster-board and corrugated-iron, his reply was to the effect that they probably intended to do something about it but never quite got around to it. This seems odd when contrasted with the magnificent Skeabost, [p39] across the water on Skye, which provided a home for C Squadron, 1st Lovat's Scouts. Maybe it was the luck of the draw, along with all the other factors to which reference have already been made, which determined the quality of a unit's accommodation. There are quite significant discrepancies between the provision enjoyed by different units. We have seen how in 1900, 3rd Bn. KOSB with only two drill halls, had to wait until about 1914 before having one for each company, whereas the Orkney RGA, with HQ in its Kirkwall drill hall, had use of seven further drill halls or armouries, each with a four-room cottage for the PSI, much earlier than that.

There are a few very obvious instances of how the Volunteers' accommodation needs have been met over successive decades A good example can be seen at Horncastle, where the first drill hall, a converted British School, stands some 100 yards from the 'new' drill hall which replaced it in 1901. This clarity is, however, not the usual picture. To explore both the range of provision and the sheer complexity of tracking units' occupation of premises, this chapter concludes with a number of examples, some of which take the story on a little, beyond the period so far under examination here.

ALLOA [Clackmannanshire] provides a good example of complications in both the occupation of different premises by the volunteers, and in the history of individual buildings. In 1860 the drill hall and armoury are reported in Bank Street. There are references to a drill hall in use in Union Street in 1864 and 1866, and to the Corn Exchange, also in Union Street, being used, with the house next door to it occupied by the drill instructor. Another reference gives the Armoury as being in the Old Court House, and by 1871, it has moved to The Whins. Ochil House, in Marshill, was built in 1806 as The Tontine Inn, and later served as a jail, prior to being acquired in 1882 as the drill hall. Its new occupants added a hall behind the main house, as well as an

SHEFFIELD's Edmund Road artillery drill hall, with first-floor stabling

HERNE BAY, the drill hall which may have started life as a tin church

DUMFRIES, showing the roof construction derived from railway architecture

SKEABOST, the grand mansion on the Isle of Skye which served as a drill hall

ALLOA, Ochil House & the archway through to the former drill hall

armoury, forming a complex of buildings around a yard entered through an arch with the inscription: *1st C & K R V DRILL HALL 1882.*

There was a 900 yard rifle range at Hillend. The 1st Clackmannan & Kinross Rifle Volunteers had been consolidated in 1880 out of corps which had at times belonged to Stirlingshire. From 1880 they had HQ and A & C Coys. in Alloa, B Coy. in Sauchie, D Coy. in Dollar, E Coy. in Tillycoultry, F Coy. in Alva, and G Coy. in Kinross. A new H Coy. was formed in Kincardine in 1883. In 1887, the battalion became the 7th Volunteer Battalion Argyll & Sutherland Highlanders. Ochil House survives, along with the arch, but the rest has been re-developed for housing. [*p40*]

AMBLE [Northumberland] is another town with opaque provision. In 1860, the drill hall was in Percy Street, but was taken over as a chapel by the Primitive Methodists in c1885. There is still a methodist chapel in Percy Street, but it looks to be grander than the early drill hall would have been. In 1887, the Percy Volunteer Artillery took over the Old Assembly Rooms in Church Street, adding a gymnasium, a reading-room, and a billiards room. This building later became Ballantynes Workshop and had been demolished for housing by 1985.

BOURNEMOUTH [Dorset] is a good example of a large town with a high level of volunteer activity and a consequent proliferation of drill hall locations. The rifle volunteers were formed in 1860, but had to wait a long time for adequate accommodation. Their first HQ was at 2 Granville Villas, on Lansdowne Road, the home of their drill instructor. This was followed by Lornend Villa, on Dispensary [now Stafford] Road, again, their instructor's home. Next, the same situation at Kilmore House on Stafford Road, and again in shop premises on Wolverton Terrace at the junction of Stafford Road and Old Christchurch Road. In 1885 they had a drill shed on Oxford Road, near the junction with St Pauls Road, which, at some stage was enlarged. Although many of their camps and drills were held in the New Forest, or on the coast, Bournemouth was, at this time, the base for two whole companies of the 4th Volunteer Battalion of the Hampshire Regiment. In 1891 a speculative housing development in Boscombe included a chapel-like hall in Portman Road, earmarked in the plans for community use. [*p41*]

This quickly became the drill hall of G Company of the 4th Bn. Hampshire Regiment, and is still used by cadets. At last, in 1895, the long-awaited new drill hall was built at 177 Holdenhurst Road [p35], and was officially opened as the HQ of 4th Bn. on 23 May 1896 by Viscount Wolseley. It comprises a very large hall, behind a front block containing orderly room, armoury, reading and billiards rooms, canteen, officers' mess, and staff flat. Behind, are stables and other utbuildings. The facade is double-fronted with two-storied bow widows, and an oriel over the entrance archway, all very smart, in brick with stone dressings. It is now Riddett's auction house. In 1903, there were four companies based here including one of transport, and one of cyclists, as well as a fifth company at Boscombe. In addition to the rifle volunteers, Bournemouth raised an artillery volunteer unit in 1867. Though their officers were sworn in at the Belle Vue Assembly Rooms, and a temporary drill shed was found behind some shops, more suitable provision had to be made for storing and maintaining their heavy 60 pounder guns as, no doubt, their instructor's wife would have objected to keeping them in her front room. Premises were found in the stables of a house on Old Christchurch Road, demolished for the Grand Hotel. The coach-house provided offices and accommodation for the sergeant-major instructor and the stables were stripped out as an armoury. When these premises were re-developed as Regents Terrace, the gunners were forced to move, by 1875, to more stables in Tregonwell Road on West Cliff. This was their home until 1896 when they took over a hall, now remembered as the Old Fire Station on Wimborne Road, Winton. It had been built as a Congregationalist mission hall and British School in 1869. It stayed in military use until 1906, when a purpose-built artillery drill hall was built in Winton on the corner of Bingham and Wycliffe Roads. Subsequently used by the Boys Brigade, this hall with adjoining gun-shed still stands. In the meantime, a fund had been started in 1897 to build a suitable HQ and drill hall for the artillery. Hence, in 1900, the Victoria Artillery Drill Hall came into service, and was officially opened by Lord Roberts on 22 October 1902. It has since been demolished for road-widening. The third element in the equation was the Yeomanry. Bournemouth, itself, had no local troop but hosted Yeomanry Brigade exercises from time-to-time. In 1896, the Hampshire Carabiniers had their orderly room in Verulam Place, off Yelverton Road, and their HQ and mess was in the Royal Exeter

BOSCOMBE, the community hall quickly adopted as the drill hall

DONCASTER, Nether Hall used as the drill hall until sold to the local council

DORNOCH, the Jail with the drill hall entrance on the right

LLANGOLLEN, built as a chapel, it was converted into the drill hall

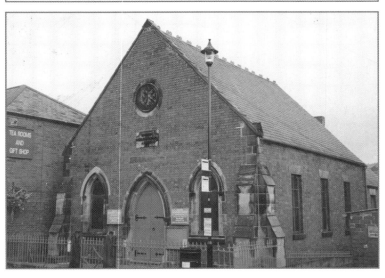

Hotel. The Dorset Yeomanry had their HQ and mess in the Hotel Mont Dore. In 1908, the TF re-organised the Yeomanry, and the town became home to D Squadron, Hampshire Carabiniers, probably based in Holdenhurst Road. It is also worth noting the Victoria Hall, on Victoria Park Road, Winton, looking for all the world, the very embodiment of a drill hall, but, apparently never used for that purpose. With three Victoria Halls in town, one hopes that invitations to social events were precise in stating their venues.

DONCASTER [South Yorkshire] is another town where the volunteers waited a long time for proper accommodation. The first rifle volunteers, formed in the Plant Works of the Great Northern Railway, used the Wagon Shop for drill, and appear to have been supported for some time by the GNR. The Yeomanry generally used the Mansion House [built 1744] as their base. Parades were held outside, and during the annual camps on the Race-course every year, the Mansion House served as officers' mess and social centre up to 1889. By the time that the 20th Corps West Yorkshire Rifle Volunteer had been re-organised into the 2nd Volunteer Bn. York & Lancaster Regiment, their HQ was, from 1893-1908, at 19 French Gate, as was that of the Yorkshire Dragoons. In 1908, the Doncaster units were hived off to become the 5th Bn. Kings Own Yorkshire Light Infantry. Following the departure of elements of the local yeomanry to fight in South Africa, the 66th Company of Imperial Yeomanry was raised in Doncaster with its HQ at Dolphin Chambers, Market Place. From 1908, the Yorkshire Dragoons had Nether Hall, a large mansion with a columned porch, as their HQ, but in 1920, this was sold to Doncaster Rural District Council for their offices, and is still in use. [p41] This left the yeomanry embarrassed, and they set up a temporary HQ in a shop on the corner of Nether Hall Road, then moved into old army huts on the corner of Bennetthorpe and Racecourse Roads. Meanwhile, the 5th Bn. KOYLI, returned from World War 1 to the new Scarbrough [sic] Barracks in Sandford Road, now modernised and still in use as a TAC. The Yorkshire Dragoons finally got their purpose-built drill hall in Danum Road in 1938. This is a two-storey front block with large hall behind, set in a yard with garaging etc. In 1938, they were still horsed, so stabling and a riding-school would have been provided. They kept their horses until 1942, serving as cavalry in Palestine. In 1947 they became an armoured regiment, still based at Danum Road, until 1967, when they handed it over to the Parachute Regiment.

DORNOCH [Sutherland] is a good example of development taking place on one site. In 1842-5 a jail was built in the square, functioning as such for forty years, until in 1882 it was purchased, for £220, by the Sutherland Highland Rifle Volunteer Corps as their headquarters. Over the years a number of improvements and additions were made. A grand staircase leading to the first floor, which was probably the officers' mess, was inserted. In 1896-7, a new entrance was built to one side of the building, and possibly this was when the free-standing drill hall was built in the yard behind. Later, came an indoor rifle range, garages, and, most recently, a cadet hut. The former jail is now a craft-centre, gallery and museum. [p42]

LLANGOLLEN [Clwyd] has two multi-purpose buildings. The Town Hall was built in 1835 and has, over the years, functioned as Armoury and Eistedffod office; the label over the door says Police Station, and it is currently the office for the Canal Trust and the Armoury Video store. In Market Street is the Memorial Hall, built in 1862 as a chapel, but used as the drill hall, having an adjoining house and store behind [p42].

PETERSFIELD [Hampshire] The 12th Corps Hampshire Rifle Volunteers must have spent a great deal of time in removals operations. Their first home in 1860, was the Town Hall [replaced in the 1930s]; then, in 1867, the Corn Exchange, built in the previous year. From there, in 1894, they moved to the Clarendon Room, where they had use of a hall, plus a secure magazine and armoury. The final move came in 1899 to Dragon Street, where a new drill hall was fashioned out of a malthouse and kilns, with a two-storey front block and hall behind. [p43] This was also the home, from 1901-1935 of the Petersfield Music Festival. After military use ceased, BT took over, and, more recently, the building has been converted to apartments.

THURSO [Caithness] shows the way in which building use changes over a long period of time. An imposing drill hall was built on Olrig Street [p69] in 1873, very ornate with bartizans and turrets. A second drill hall was built at 21 Sinclair Street, less impressive visually, but more functional with a lateral first-floor hall with range alongside, an adjoining house, and a yard behind.

PETERSFIELD, the malthouse converted into the drill hall, and then into flats

THURSO, Sinclair Street built to supplement the Olrig Street drill hall

WITNEY, the meeting-house which served as a drill hall until 1927

[p43] Both these drill halls were in use in 1904. The original drill hall became a masonic hall, perhaps in 1908, when it might have proved surplus to the requirements of the TF. Sinclair Street continued in use, but at some time, possibly quite recently, the chapel in Princes Street, which backs onto it, built in 1875 for the United Original Secessionist movement, became a drill hall, and is currently a Cadet Centre.

WITNEY [Oxfordshire] has three buildings used by the volunteers. The earliest is a Friends' Meeting House in Marlborough Lane, built in 1712, but used from about 1860 by the 5th Oxfordshire Rifle Volunteer Corps. [p44] It is also likely that the Corn Exchange, built in the High Street in 1863, was used. It certainly gave the Home Guard a base in World War ll. In 1914, the town was the base for a company of the Oxfordshire & Buckinghamshire Light Infantry, and a drill station for B Squadron of the Oxfordshire Hussars Yeomanry, but it was not until 1927 that a purpose-built drill hall was provided. This building is now the Langdale Hall, a community centre.

This first fifty years or so of the volunteers' existence had been characterised by a certain amount of flair and initiative: personal, corporate and municipal; a great deal of make do and mend; much flexibility and patience. The next period in our story sees consolidation and moves made toward uniformity, as the TF comes into being, is mobilised for war, and tested, in some instances, to destruction.

CHAPTER 3
The Development of Drill Halls 1908-2005

The creation of the Territorial Force in 1908 had a number of immediate effects on drill hall construction and design. First of all, the rationalisation of the volunteer forces meant that numbers of new units had to be accommodated. The Yeomanry, who had been revived in the South African Wars, were now integrated into the new force, and needed drill halls, riding schools and stables, with less reliance on the stately homes of their original sponsors. Across each of the regional divisions of the TF, a balance between infantry, cavalry, artillery etc was required, which resulted in a certain amount of movement of units, and the concomitant juggling of training spaces. The Militia was subsumed into a new Reserve Force, and responsibilities previously shared with the volunteers had to be re-allocated. Where volunteer units were well-established in adequate premises, it was relatively straight-forward to accommodate extra troops, but some places became venues for the first time. The establishment of the new Territorial Force Associations brought a move toward standardisation, in that some of the inequalities of provision would no longer be tolerated. It was not the case now, that units should be dependent on patronage, local enthusiasm or charity for the quality of their accommodation. The War Office was now funding the TF, and those funds were to be distributed equitably, and as a response to needs and priorities. A number of the TF offices themselves may still be seen, in Kirkcaldy [Fife] [p325] and Mold [Flintshire] [p162], for instance. The London office is in Hunter Street, part of the Handel Street complex of drill halls. In many instances, these TF Associations were able to purchase existing drill halls from their owners, sometimes private companies, sometimes joint stock companies owned by the volunteers themselves, and sometimes wealthy local benefactors, sponsors or patrons. From 1907, where new accommodation needs had been identified, a widespread building programme was embarked on, and this work was to continue through into1914, and the very outbreak of war.

In terms of an architectural style one could be forgiven for seeking homogeneity. To a large extent, however, the previous approach of laissez-faire was maintained, with a mixture of adaptations, improvements and enlargements of existing drill halls, new adaptations of existing buildings, and entirely new builds. Adaptations on widely differing scales took place. Dr Tobin of Ilkeston, who had leased land for a new drill shed to the TF in 1909, was surprised to find the surrounding shrubs removed three years later for the erection of an indoor range. Whilst he was loth to interfere with the activities of the Sherwood Foresters, his solicitors did feel that they should point out that the terms of the lease demanded some consultation prior to building works, however modest, being carried out. At the other end of the scale were places like Endcliffe Hall in Sheffield [p71,p46]. This Italianate mansion, the grandest of the city's steel magnates' houses, had been built in 1863 for Sir John Brown, its interior full of sumptuous decoration. It was taken over by the TF in 1913 when a large drill hall was added beside the stable block, and the lodge became a guard-room. It is still the HQ of the successor units of theYork & Lancaster Regiment. Other such conversions, albeit on a less impressive scale, include the Workhouse at Cullompton [Devon], 44 Bethel Street, Norwich, and Arden Street, Halifax, built as a roller-skating rink, and then a cinema, prior to conversion as a drill hall. The technical school on East Road, Cambridge, was converted in 1914, into a drill hall, since demolished, and London Brick Company's Coffee Palace in Peterborough, also demolished, built in 1898, had been acquired by the TF by 1914. There are five quite large complexes, all named 'Barracks' which would appear to be earlier foundations, enlarged and modernised c1908 [and again subsequently]. They are Croydon Barracks, Greater London; Picton Barracks, Carmarthen; Chyandor Barracks, Penzance [Cornwall]; Seaforth Barracks, Dingwall [Ross & Cromarty]; and Crelake Barracks, Tavistock [Devon]. Each of the five appears to consist of an open quadrangle of buildings around a parade-square. None of them

SHEFFIELD's Endcliffe Hall, the drill hall added in 1913

GRANTHAM, the drill hall added to the Militia Barracks in 1913

SHEFFIELD's Endcliffe Hall, interior of the drill hall, still in TA use

NEWPORT, Isle of Wight, the 1910 artillery drill hall

was ever a depot for regular troops, although maybe two of them had Militia connections, and may have come to the TF by the same route as did the Militia barracks at Lincoln and Grantham, which both had drill halls added in 1913 [p46].

It is clear that finding any sort of uniformity in the design of adapted buildings would be most unlikely, but it is no more possible to find any universal building style in new builds of the period either. In 1909, the War Office had despatched a civil servant, one AWA Pollock, to the United States to inspect Armouries there, with a brief to explore the feasibility of adopting US designs. Pollock found many grand buildings, looking like mediaeval castles, with vast halls and social spaces. They were too big, and, more to the point, too costly. Britain would continue with the traditional local initiative in all its individuality. This diversity is well illustrated by the drill halls of this period on the Isle of Wight. Here, one might reasonably expect some attempt at uniformity, but there is none. The new artillery drill hall of 1910 on Drill Hall Road, Newport [p46], opposite the much earlier one built for the Isle of Wight Rifles, is entirely different to that built in Ryde, for use by the same, freshly-deployed, units, and in the same year. Different again is that at Denmark Road, Cowes [p47], built in 1912. This latter example comes close to the only style that one might argue is at all universal across Britain, but best exemplified by small clusters of drill halls in a locality, possibly sharing a common architect. The style could be described loosely as Edwardian-Baroque. In many cases, their scale gives these buildings a domestic feel, usually missing in military structures. The prevailing motif is the pediment, sometimes broken, sometimes open, over the central entrance in a, normally symmetrical, facade. The effect is often heightened by the use of stone dressings and door-cases, on these predominantly brick buildings. Sometimes the quoins are rusticated, and in odd cases, vermiculated as well. In Spalding and Boston, the local architects Scorer and Gamble designed the new drill halls in 1913. One is the mirror image of the other. That at Scunthorpe is remarkably similar, and may also be by them. It is likely that the group of similar drill halls at Melton Mowbray [p47], Oakham, and Shepshed were designed by the same person. Another group which includes Holywell, Ruthin, and Acrefair, may be the work of a common architect, as may a fourth group of Rugeley and

COWES, the Denmark Road drill hall opened in 1912

MELTON MOWBRAY, one of a group of similar drill halls opened in 1914

UPHALL, a more domestic style favoured in this part of central Scotland

STEWARTON, a very plain & utilitarian design for the front block

Kings Heath, and yet another, Devon, group which includes Thorverton, Tiverton and Totnes. Other individual examples across England and Wales, from Southend to Guisborough to Barry may share similarities, but no two examples are identical. This style appears to be completely missing in Scotland where the front blocks of this period tend to be much more informally domestic, as characterised by a group which includes Fauldhouse, Bathgate, Uphall [p48] and West Calder; or with just a hint of decoration such as the simple gablet over the entrance as at Musselburgh, or Alva; or almost completely unadorned as at Castle Douglas, Dalry, Sanquar or Stewarton [p48]. As echoes of the mediaeval style of previous drill halls, many still featured just a hint of castellation, as at Blantyre and Larkhall outside Glasgow, or Milnsbridge and Mossley, between Manchester and Huddersfield, with their slender battlemented towers. Three further groups from this period deserve mention. There is almost a house-style evident in several of the Staffordshire TFA's buildings. Booth Street, Stoke-on-Trent [1913], Park Road East, Wolverhampton, Sedgley Road West, Tipton [1910], Corporation Street, Tamworth [1911] [p49], and Whittimere Street, Walsall [1910] lean toward a Tudor look. Of entirely different appearance, a group of stone-built, single-storey Cornish drill halls, could be mistaken for village schools, with porch, lateral hall, and small, gabled projections to the rear. It includes Hayle [p161], Redruth and St Just, all dated 1911 or 1912. Similar buildings can be seen at Bonar Bridge, and in brick at Northwich [1911]. These quasi-school buildings must not, of course be confused with instances such as Batley, Hailsham or Hawkhurst, where former schools have been taken over as drill halls, one of them in quite recent times. The final defineable group from this period is in Somerset. A simple two-storey front block, often with a gable over the entrance, has a hall behind it. Examples can be found at Chard, Frome, and Yeovil, and, with slight variations, at Castle Cary [p49], Clevedon, Shepton Mallet, and Glastonbury. Again, similar buildings in this simple style can be seen across Britain from Fakenham to Merthyr Tydfil [p50], and from Abertillery to Wooler.

Having attempted some categorisation, however loose, we must look at some of the more individual examples from this time. Some drill halls were still extremely modest, in the tradition of the earlier armouries. In East Grinstead, the

Armoury of 1911 on De La Warr Road subsequently became a chapel for the Countess of Huntingdon Connection, is now the office for a Civil Engineering consultancy, and is really quite tiny, although well-built in brick [p50]. Not much bigger, but a more-or-less featureless stone box, is the drill hall of the RGA at Bishops Waltham, opened in 1914. Many drill halls were small and little more than sheds like those at Lerryn, in timber [recently restored], and Southend [Argyll] [p50], Kemnay, Gairloch, Gourock and Horton Kirby, all in corrugated-iron. Herne Bay, also in green-painted corrugated-iron, with its gothic windows, looks like a tin church. There were also the very splendid. Two, in west London, are particularly outstanding. Hownslow, now 'Treaty Lodge' on Hanworth Road [p50], has a very fine porch with an elaborate coat-of-arms of the 8th Bn. Middlesex Regiment which includes the battle honour 'South Africa 1900-02', over the door. High up on the corners of the building are plaques with 'TFA 1911' inscriptions. The building itself is otherwise fairly plain but elegant and symmetrical. Willesden, in Pound Lane, on the other hand has no time for restraint [p51]. The front block is the same width as at Hownslow, but has a gabled mansard roof with dormers, and a single-storey pedimented pavilion at each end. The central bay has a pediment over the porch and another at roof level. Some of the windows have open segmental pediments, there are stone dressings right up to the top of the central bay, and a stone cornice below the roof-line. Over the porch are coats-of-arms, and the TFA plaque is contained in a trophy of standards and drums, all carved in what may be Coade Stone. Hampton [1914] may have been to a similar standard and its recent remodelling has retained its impressive facade with a coat-of-arms in a panel over the door. As grand in detail, but on a wholly larger scale as well, is the drill hall on Derby Road, Nottingham, built around 1910 [p51]. It is four storeys in height with rusticated stone ground floor and brick above. Copious stone dressings include pediments, foliage, window surrounds and cornices. Along the top is a balustrade. The E-shaped building formerly enclosed a double-height hall, but this space is now car-parking since the building's welcome conversion to offices. Its exterior has been restored to a magnificent standard. Of similar standard in terms of preservation, but simpler in style are Sherwood House in Newark [1914] [p52], and Woodbridge Road, Ipswich [1909-10] [p52].

TAMWORTH, one of a group of drill halls built c1911 by the Staffordshire TFA

CASTLE CARY, typical of several Somerset drill halls from this date

MERTHYR TYDFIL, showing many of the features of drill halls of the date

SOUTHEND, Kintyre, the most basic of design & materials, now Dunaverty Hall

EAST GRINSTEAD, the Armoury, subsequently a chapel, then offices

HOWNSLOW, Treaty House, awash with splendid detail

The organisation of the TF into discrete formations at Brigade or Division level, created a new need for HQs. Very often these were accommodated in drill halls along with their local constituent units, but, in other cases, the preference was for stand-alone premises, usually taking the form of private houses. Just as, in the early days, the drill sergeant's house, or the CO's residence, initially became the focus for unit activities, or housed the Armoury, so, once again, a domestic dimension can be seen. In Norwich, Oxford, and Lichfield, for example, quite unpretentious houses, often semi-detached, housed the HQ staff. In Oxford's Lonsdale Road [p53], the Brigadier, Brigade Major, Quartermaster, and secretarial staff of the South Midland Mounted Bde, consisting of the Berkshire, Buckinghamshire, and Oxfordshire Yeomanries and the Berkshire Royal Horse Artillery, inhabited number 14. One is prompted to wonder whether the milkman found himself with an unexpectedly large order on Field Days.

Whatever the architectural style, however pretentious or humble the building might be, it still had to be functional. We have seen how the East Yorkshire RGA had developed ingenious training devices in order to simulate their operational duties as coast defence gunners. A permanent problem faced field gunners, in making their drills realistic. A simple solution lay in the sand-tray. Here, different terrains could be modelled in sand, and at a scale which simulated distance. Field gunners could therefore, in the comfort of their drill halls, and all the year round, usefully train in circumstances which began to approach the reality of the battle-field. As Colonel Helyar pointed out, this was greatly preferable to aiming at "a chimney, the door of an out-house, or a white spot on the wall". All sorts of ways of making training meaningful, stimulating and enjoyable had to be found for troops, who, on reporting to the drill hall, had already put in a full day's work, and these techniques had to fit into the local drill hall. The annual two-week training camp was generally devoted to integrating dispersed units and exercising in larger formations, and the basic skills were expected to be learned, and then practised, over and over, ad nauseam, throughout the year, in local drill halls.

The outbreak of war in August 1914 put a stop to building operations, and drill halls assumed a greater importance in

WILLESDEN, an exuberant exercise in regimental pride

NOTTINGHAM's Derby Road drill hall, now minus its hall but used as offices

NEWARK, built in 1914 & enlarged in the '30s and the '50s

HORSHAM, built 1922 for the Royal Sussex Regiment

IPSWICH, the only survivor of several local drill halls, now in community use

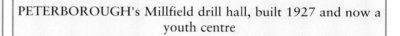

PETERBOROUGH's Millfield drill hall, built 1927 and now a youth centre

doing the things for which they were designed. At the start of hostilities they were where the territorials gathered on mobilisation in order to be kitted out for wherever they were sent: to garrison duties at home; to relieve regulars serving abroad in places like Malta or India, away from the battlefields; or to active fighting service on the Western Front or in the Middle East. Despite Kitchener's distrust of the TF, virtually the whole force ended up on active service, but not necessarily in the self-contained divisions that had been envisaged as their embodiments. Older territorials often found themselves on training duties, freeing younger men for active service, and helping to inculcate regimental values into well-intentioned but innocent recruits. Later, there were the Voluntary Training Corps [VTC] to train. Drill halls also served as Recruiting Offices for the million men demanded by Kitchener for the New Armies. Public buildings were also used for this purpose, but sometimes fresh premises were requisitioned. In West Street, Bourne, there is a lock-up shop whose sign reads: '[2ND] **BATT. LINCS. V R[EGT]**', from which Sgt. Murray operated. In the basement of the Institute opposite was the miniature range where the VTC practised. In Hemel Hempstead, the VTC were allowed to use the drill hall in Bury Road, and to use the miniature range at Lockers Park School, under the supervision of Sgt Maj Cumner of the 5th London Bde. RFA. There appears to have been very little building during the war itself. In 1915, a drill shed was moved in numbered sections from Winchelsea Beach to be re-erected on Winchelsea Road, Rye, where it still stands as a boat-building shed, but this would appear to be an isolated instance of such activity. Limited building work resumed after the end of hostilities, the extension to Fareham's Connaught Drill Hall in West Street being dated 1918, but, generally there was little enthusiasm, even after the TA re-formed in 1920. It must also be remembered that following demobilisation, many volunteer units were never reconstituted and there must have been many towns which lost their connection to the TA completely, finding new uses for their drill halls, or, depending on their condition, demolishing them altogether.

Once necessary building did get under way again, from the point of view of style at least, it seems to have been a case of carrying on from where they left off. Of the small number of new buildings appearing in the 1920s, most employed the now-

OXFORD, 14 Lonsdale Road served as HQ of a TF Mounted Brigade

53

NEWBURN-on-TYNE, a very ornate drill hall for the
Northumberland Fusiliers

traditional Edwardian-Baroque style. These included Horsham [1922] [*p52*], Hinckley [1923], Rushden [1928] and very probably the quite similar Wellingborough, Peterborough [1927] [*p52*], Dalton-in-Furness [1927], and Barrow-in-Furness [1928]. There were several notable exceptions however. Newburn [1924] [*p54*] has a three-storey front block in brick and stone with lots of decorative detail including an oriel over the entrance, and a three-storey projection next to it. Langdale Hall at Witney [1927] [*p55*] also has a three-storey front block but of Dutch gable profile with dormers in a tile-hung top storey. The projecting porch is gabled, and a loggia runs along the side of the hall behind. Tynemouth [1928] [*p56*] is probably the most eclectic of all. It has two long plain blocks to the street with a cornice, and a pediment over the gateway framing a carved relief of art deco character [*p56*]. On one end is a cross-wing with a balcony and Tuscan outlook tower. At the other, is a house with a hipped roof, for the PSI. As well as new building, the custom of adapting existing buildings had not disappeared. In 1920 the Derbyshire TAA took over a property in Phoenix Street, Derby, which had been built in 1880 as a house, smithy and stables. It has been considerably altered but is still a cadet centre. Dover's immediate needs for extra accommodation were met by the purchase, in 1922, of a redundant sea-plane shed on the sea-front, still in use 50 years later. In 1927, new premises were needed in Guildford, and so Webbers 'Churchacre' Ironworks, which had been bankrupted during the current depression, was acquired by the TA. The two-storey administration block provided a suitable orderly-room, armoury and mess, while the ironworks itself, two large sheds with three projecting annexes, served as the hall. The building is now the Bellerby Theatre.

The inter-War years were difficult ones for the new TA. Having had to rebuild from scratch, a combination of war-weariness, lack of job security, and government parsimony all conspired to make recruitment slow. Whilst it was easy to fill motor-related units to the point of over-subscription, the real problem was attracting infantry-men. In Oldham, for instance, it took several years to reach establishment, and then men moved away to the Midlands to find work. One way of getting recruits was to improve the social facilities. The Oldham drill hall in Rifle Street was open most evenings for officers and other ranks alike to use the billiard tables, piano, and bar. Money was

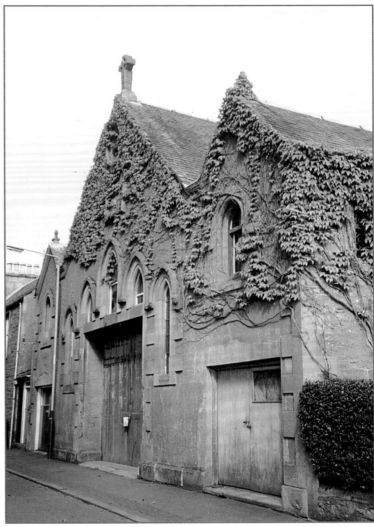

STOCKPORT, the Armoury of the Cheshire Militia; still a TAC

AUCHTERARDER, the chapel, converted into the drill hall

GRANTHAM, the South Lincolnshire Militia Armoury

CIRENCESTER, the Militia Armoury, now offices

| ALNWICK, the Northumberland Artillery Volunteers HQ in a former bank | BRADFORD-on-AVON, the liquor store which doubled as drill hall |

PAIGNTON, the public hall used as the town's drill hall

SELKIRK, the Volunteer Hall of 1867, in unusual classical style

THURSO, the Olrig Street drill hall now a Masonic centre

GROVE on the Isle of Portland in mediaeval castle style

BURY, reputedly the largest drill hall of them all

HUDDERSFIELD, opened by Lord Roberts in 1899

ELGIN, the drill hall with fine Scots Baronial detail, now a library-store

SHEFFIELD's Endcliffe Hall built for a steel magnate & bought for the TF

MACCLESFIELD, the tower & front block survive as apartments

SHEFFIELD's Somme Barracks, home to West Riding volunteer engineers

inflammables should be stored separately in self-contained, brick-built stores. Pairs of such structures may still be seen behind many drill halls. Surviving examples include Luton, Oundle, Loddon, Guiseley and Peterborough. By early 1941, cities and most large towns had formulated an anti-invasion plan which laid down the forces and weaponry available, the main vulnerable points, defensive perimeters, and, as control point and last ditch stronghold, the Keep, as it was designated. In many places, the Keep was a block centred on the drill hall, and this was the case in Aylesbury, Derby and Northampton for instance. One has to wonder for how long Northampton's toy fort Militia Armoury would have withstood a pounding from Stukas and 88mm guns. A small number of drill halls did actually succumb to enemy action. The drill hall in Landguard Road, Shanklin was among several destroyed or severely damaged by enemy bombing, along with others in Bristol, Campbeltown, and Teignmouth. One of the London drill halls, referred to by General Pile, the AA supremo as "the Signals Drill Hall" in Brompton Road [p73], occupied a station, surplus to the London Underground's requirements, and became the Operations Room for London's AA defences. Slough also served as an AA plotting-room. At the end of the war, drill halls assumed fresh functions, hosting parties to celebrate VE or VJ Day, as at Beverley, and then providing facilities for the demobilisation of returning troops.

By the time the TA was re-formed in 1947, the whole country was already facing an accommodation crisis. It was usually expedient to put troops into the dozens of hutted camps which littered the country, such as was the case at Colchester and Edmonton. It was to be several years before as low a priority as the TA could expect new premises to be built, however urgent the perceived priority. Inevitably, buildings were acquired and converted, such as the bus-garage in Prestatyn [p74] in 1953. There had been some new building in the meantime. The plans for Harlow New Town were completed in 1949, but the TA Centre in Old Road had been built by 1947. There were also plans interrupted by the war in the queue. At Braintree, land had been earmarked on Coggeshall Road for a new drill hall in 1939. A hutted transit camp had been put up there during the war, and it was for this that the local territorials, 313 Sqdn. of 134 [Essex] Construction Regiment RE [TA], had to settle in 1950, and other

WYMONDHAM, in use from the 1930s but completely refurbished in the 1990s

KENSINGTON, Old Brompton Road drill hall in redundant Tube station

PRESTATYN, the bus garage converted for TA use in 1953

NOTTINGHAM's Triumph Road drill hall, showing the anti-bomb blast-wall

units right up to 1993, as the promised centre was never built. At Portsmouth's Peronne Road, a new drill hall had been scheduled for 1940, but a postponement in construction was forced. It was eventually built 1947-9, but with modifications. The lessons of a large building's vulnerability to attack by incendiary bombs meant that changes were introduced into the design of the eaves and tiling, window size was reduced, and a walk-way at roof level was included, in order that fire-watchers with stout footwear might take immediate action. It must have been comforting to the occupants, as they entered the nuclear age, to know that there were men in wellies with buckets up on the roof.

Another area of concern at the end of WWII must have been security. Many buildings which had been used to store arms and ammunition were now subject to lower levels of oversight. At Lewes, in March, 1946, youths broke into the old Mountfield Road drill hall, presumably needing little more than a tin-opener, stealing three rifles and 4000 rounds of ammunition. The local citizenry must have been relieved when their ballistic ambitions were confined to shooting up only road-signs. More sinister was the series of raids by the IRA on school armouries, and, here action resulted both to limit the weapons in circulation, and to make them harder to steal. This failed to prevent at least one CCF CO from secreting surplus weapons around the school during War Office inspections.

Just as building had continued after the first war with little discernible change in design, so did it after the second. Two new TA Centres in Nottingham: Triumph Road [1953] [p74] and Wigman Road, Bilborough [1957], Retford [1956], and further extensions to Newark-on-Trent [1956] and to Sutton-in-Ashfield [1953] are barely distinguishable from pre-war building. Triumph Road had an anti-terrorist bomb blast-wall added in 1990, but can still be taken for a much earlier model. Farnham [1953] shows direct continuity. Its layout as base for an AA unit is quite familiar. It is quadrangular with the hall in the middle, with generous vehicular access to the hall. A large, full-height training space is actually labelled as *Dome Trainer*. The front block is of two-and-a-half storeys, as at Bilborough, and the miniature range runs along the back on the first-floor. Harcourt House in Oxford's Marston Road, was opened by Earl

Alexander of Tunis in May 1957 for units of the Oxfordshire Hussars, then field artillery, the 4th Bn. Oxford & Bucks Light Infantry, and a LAA battery. It is a long brick block with projecting, gabled wings, and a pediment over the main door. Old stone crests of its occupants are reset in the wall. To one side, are garages, the whole presenting a very traditional image, and apparently high production values. A similar building may be seen at Penicuick [1957] [p75]. There was also a requirement for smaller-scale TACs to house infantry units with fewer storage and equipment needs. Minehead [1953] [p75], built for a company of the Somerset Light Infantry, has a single-storey front block, with a lateral hall behind. It is, in fact, very similar in both scale and lay-out to Wigton [1938], Golborne, Warminster and Westbury. Minehead is built to resemble an adjacent school, and is very reminiscent of local authority buildings of the time: clinics, libraries and primary schools. Marsh Road, Luton [1955], on the other hand, may well be as solid and well-designed a building as Harcourt House, and many of those other buildings we have looked at, but, despite its smart royal coat-of-arms over the main door, it otherwise presents itself as a featureless factory building. Still looking like factory buildings but with a little more detailing are Cinderford [1957] [p76], Eastern Avenue, Gloucester [1950], Cheltenham, Cardiff's Norbury Road, Crawley, Leominster [1962] and Windsor [1963]. There are also locations where up-dating has taken place by the addition of new buildings to established sites, as has occurred at Pontypridd, for instance.

TA Centres in the last quarter of the twentieth century appear to fall into three main categories. First, are the multi-purpose industrial buildings, often erected on business or industrial estates, and comprising large, hangar-like structures which offer versatility in the use of space, and are set in plenty of space to allow vehicles to manoeuvre. In out-of-town locations, they can be reached easily by their car-owner occupants, who enjoy the added advantage of being the only ones on site at weekends, when drills take place. Thus there are fewer neighbours to disturb, and less of an audience to observe what might be happening. Security is seen as an issue, but, as has lately been pointed out, finding out what goes on in the TA is as easy as signing up. Such industrial or business park TACs can be seen at Dunoon, Newcastle's Kingston Park, Washington, Dundee's

PENICUICK, the front block of this extensive complex south of Edinburgh

MINEHEAD, a small post-WWll TAC for a company of Somerset Light Infantry

CINDERFORD, the main door of this 1957 TAC, still with pre-WWll features

Mid-Craigie and Dalkeith Road, and Cwmbran. An urban exception to this rule is Glasgow's Houldsworth Street. Another advantage of these buildings, is that once they become surplus to requirement, they can be easily returned to civilian commercial use. This has in fact already happened at Long Benton, outside Newcastle, and at Whiteinch on the Clyde.

A second category is of buildings which could be taken for office-blocks or hospitals. Here, substantial two- or three-storey blocks, often with pyramid roofs are set in large yards filled with garages and workshops. Again, for reasons of access, they tend to be placed near arterial roads. Examples include Coulby Newham and Brambles Farm [p77], both in Middlesbrough, Queensferry, Runcorn, Coventry's Canley and Radford Road, Longton, Irvine, Livingston, Glasgow's Carmunock Road, East Kilbride, Paisley, Salford's Haldane Barracks [p77] and Cumbernauld. It will be apparent that many of these new TACs are located in areas of re-generation, or designated new towns, where young, skilled men and women will be found, where green-field sites are available, and where the transport infrastructure is sound. At least one TAC in this particular style, however, at Rutherglen, has already succumbed to redundancy.

The third category is arguably arbitrary and subjective, consisting of structures which may lay claim to some architectural merit. This is clearly a move into dangerous territory for the present writer. The two previous categories are clear statements of form following function, and there is absolutely nothing wrong with them, since, almost without exception these are inoffensive buildings, perfectly in tune with their contexts. In many cases enormous effort has gone into producing something which is functional yet sympathetic. Nowhere is this seen better than at Fulham where the monolithic hall, added, in the very same yellow brick, to the solid nineteenth-century house, actually enhances the whole. There do seem, however to be a small group of buildings where the design brief may have encouraged something above the merely functional. As to whether they work as well as those of more mundane outlook, must be left to their occupants to comment. Meanwhile, to this observer at least, this handful of buildings does seem to be rather special. The first is Polmadie Road, Rutherglen [p77], where there has been a clever attempt to

MIDDLESBROUGH's Brambles Farm TAC, typical of recent styling

GLASGOW's Polmadie Road, Rutherglen, TAC echoing an earlier feature

SALFORD, Haldane Barracks named for the architect of the TF

SOUTHALL, a thoroughly modern replacement on an old drill hall site

LIVERPOOL's, Chavasse House TAC in Childwall, more hospital than barracks

BIRMINGHAM's Tennal Grange, built 1904, now OTC & RFCA HQ

incorporate that iconic emblem of the drill hall, the long glass skylight. This very conscious feature lifts this otherwise un-remarkable building above the common-place. At Hayes Bridge, Southall [p77], in west London, the great glass canopy sweeping over the hall, suggests that something at the very cutting-edge of technology is going on inside. This is a building which would be very much at home on a science park. Alnwick's Lisburn Terrace [1983] is entirely different, its scale suggesting the traditional drill hall, but in modern materials. It somehow manages to hint at the mock-Tudor of Hexham's drill hall but without compromising its modernity or looking twee. Another interesting building in Northumberland is the University OTC Centre, St Cuthbert's Keep at Fenham Barracks. Here colour is used to produce something a bit different. Colour also features strongly at Chavasse House, Childwall, Liverpool [p78] where a red-tiled roof, oriels with green glazing-bars, and pink brickwork, sparingly banded with a darker red, together produce a sunny, un-military effect, quite appropriate for a medical unit. Perhaps the most striking of all, though, is Ty Llewellyn TAC in Morgan Street, Cardiff [p163], provided by the Welsh Rugby Football Union in exchange for the Park Street drill hall demolished to make room for the Millennium Stadium. A building of slanting planes, asymmetric faces, a tall, prow-like corner turret, and glass everywhere. Over two widows are sculptures, in stainless steel of the dragon of Wales, and of Mercury, symbol of the signallers who are stationed within.

We have seen the University OTC building at Newcastle-upon-Tyne already, and it is worth noting that such buildings themselves present a microcosm of volunteer provision generally, ranging from Southampton's Regency Carlton Place drill hall cum riding-school, to Glasgow's 1900 granite; Birmingham's original base in the 1904 Tennal Grange [p78]; London's Handel Street hall of around 1908; right through to Dundee's post-WWll centre on Park Wynd; Edinburgh's 1970s Duke of Edinburgh House; Manchester's University Barracks and Aberdeen's Don Street centre of the 1980s; and, up to the moment, Liverpool's Crawford House, with its pyramid roof, next to the 1930s drill hall on Mather Avenue, or Oxford's Oxpens Road, resembling a corporate, rather than a military, HQ. Montgomery House in Stoney Lane now gives Birmingham OTC a modern home but on an established site with buildings going back to 1914.

Whilst many cadet units still inhabit Victorian drill halls, and many more occupy the ubiquitous cadet hut, there are some newer buildings around. The Yorkshire and Humberside Association have re-invented the smaller purpose-built gable-ended drill hall with examples at Ripon [1989], Frodingham [1991], Brigg [1993], Leeds, and Howden [1997] [p79]. Another universal design is the square hall with pyramid roof, a smaller version of Crawford Hall. Examples can be seen at Harrow, Aberdeen's Fonthill Barracks, and Campbeltown.

One other factor must be noted here, and that is the re-cycling of military buildings. A good example is the TAC which occupies the station HQ of the former RAF Old Sarum. Similarly, the TA's main transport training base occupies the Expansion Period buildings of the old RAF Spitalgate outside Grantham. Other examples include the presence of territorials sharing barracks with the regulars at Aberdeen, Cardiff and Shrewsbury, and inheriting from them at Lincoln, Newcastle-upon-Tyne and Perth.

The continuous reduction in numbers in the TA caused by perceived lack of need and by a, possibly temporary, reluctance to enrol, and rash of resignations during the Iraq and Afghanistan campaigns, would suggest that few drill halls will be built in future. The plans to replace the demolished Stonecot Hill TAC at Sutton, with new premises for the TA would apparently represent what may become an increasingly rare occurrence.

HOWDEN, ACF hut built 1997, from a new generation of such permanent builds

CHAPTER 4
Case Studies

The wide diversity which characterises almost every aspect of the drill hall is best illustrated by a range of in-depth examples. These are approached in two ways. The first approach is a geographical one, working through a heirarchy of centres from medium-sized towns: Brighton, Dover, Ripon and Scarborough; through county towns: Ayr, Lancaster and Lincoln; through medium-sized cities: Aberdeen, Cardiff and Portsmouth; to larger cities: Glasgow and Liverpool; then to the predominantly rural counties of Borders [Berwick, Roxburgh and Selkirk], Clwyd [Denbigh and Flint], Cornwall, and Norfolk. This attempts a spread of geography, size, and character, to enable the identification of both similarities and differences. The second approach is through the territorial units themselves, and is designed to highlight distribution. Here will be examined the provision made for the Highland Division and its attached units in 1914; for the 26 battalions of the London Regiment, in 1914, with a detailed look at the drill hall of one of those battalions, the 24th, based at Braganza Street, Lambeth; and, finally for the units administered by the Nottinghamshire Territorial Association in 1950. It is intended, in this way, to show how the demands of different units in contrasting areas necessitated a range of provision to meet their individual needs. Throughout this section, the use of bold type will denote that the building still stood during the survey period, 2001-present .

Drill Halls in BRIGHTON & HOVE, East Sussex
The 1st Corps of the Sussex Rifle Volunteers was formed at Brighton on 23rd November 1859, and by 1863, with six companies, was made a battalion in its own right, becoming in 1887, the 1st Volunteer Bn. Royal Sussex Regt. There was also a Corps of the Sussex Artillery Volunteers from 1860, but the Yeomanry of the Napoleonic era had all been disbanded by 1848, but for a Brighton troop, still serving with the Middlesex Hussars in 1880. A new Sussex cavalry regiment was raised in 1901 as 69 Coy. Imperial Yeomanry, for service in the Boer War.

In 1914, the HQ and eight companies of the 6th [Cyclist] Bn. Royal Sussex Regt. were based in Brighton, as were HQ, A Sqdn. and part of B Sqdn. of the Sussex Yeomanry; the RE Signalling and the Army Service Corps Transport and Supply Companies of the Home Counties Division; 3rd [Sussex] Bty. of the Home Counties Bde. of the RFA; the HQ and No 1 Coy. of the Sussex Royal Garrison Artillery [Defended Ports], and 2nd Eastern General Hospital. After WWl when they had become an infantry unit, the Yeomanry were amalgamated with the Surrey Yeomanry, and converted to field artillery. In 1939, they formed a duplicate Field Artillery Regiment, the 144th. This unit's engineer successors are still based in Brighton. The scale of military activity is reflected in the range of premises used over the years. In 1910, no less than 24 different locations were in use by TF units. An artillery drill hall had been built at **117 Gloucester Road** in 1869 [*p81*]. It consists of a two-storey, battlemented administrative block, with a hall alongside, entered through a large arched opening with fancy, brick mock machicolations above. It is now apartments, with the hall as car-parking. As well as the artillery, it housed the Army Service Corps and RAMC units in 1914. In **Church Street** stands the large drill hall which housed the Yeomanry in 1914. A three-storey front-block of eleven bays, with ornate Baroque doorcase, is backed by a large hall. At one end is the Sussex Martlets crest of the Yeomanry. The riding school in the **Old Market** was used by the military [*p81*], as was the skating-rink which formerly formed the southern edge of the County Cricket Ground. The RFA were based in the **Marmion Street** drill hall. The Cyclists' HQ was at **18 Montpelier Place**, a four-storey early-Victorian terraced house, but they drilled in Church Street, premises they had occupied since it had been built in 1890. In 1914, the base for the Royal Engineers Signalling Company of the Home Counties Division, was 23 Gloucester Place, but by 1939, they appear to have moved to the **Queens Square** drill hall, now a sports centre and sometime ice-rink. Apart from these earlier drill halls there is, on **Dyke Road**, a grand neo-Georgian building of the 1930s, three storeys, of 20 bays, with projections, an elaborate stone porch and balcony over, and a Royal Artillery crest [*p82*]. This must have been opened for the Yeomanry gunners. It stands in large yards with out-buildings and an Edwardian villa, and remains in TA use. The old regular Preston [Cavalry] Barracks on **Lewes Road**, accommodates TA units in 1980s buildings which occupy parts of the square where once the illustrious 11th Hussars [Prince Albert's Own] paraded.

Drill Halls in DOVER, Kent

Although no Rifle Volunteer Corps were formed here, various re-organisations resulted in the HQ of the 1st Volunteer Bn. East Kent Regt. [the Buffs] being moved, in 1901, from Canterbury to Dover, where one company had been based since, at least, 1880. Dover was also home to C Sqdn. East Kent Mounted Rifles, raised in 1863. In 1908, HQ and H Coy. 4th Bn. the Buffs, C Sqdn. of the Yeomanry; H Coy. of the Kent Cyclists; HQ and the Kent Battery 3rd Home Counties Bde. RFA; 6 Coy. Kent RGA; and HQ Cinque Ports [Fortress] REs were all based in Dover. In 1914, No 1 Electric Lights Coy. Cinque Ports [Fortress] REs had been added to Dover's volunteer garrison. The Yeomanry, after horsed service in Palestine and Egypt, completed the WWl as infantry on the Western Front. In 1920, both Kent Yeomanry regiments were amalgamated and, ultimately, converted into 97 and 143 Field Artillery Regts. At the start of WWll, other re-organisations had produced Kent & Sussex Heavy Regt. RA [TA] by 1932, and the converted infantry of the Buffs who formed 75 HAA Regt. RA [TA] in 1938, both in recognition of the vulnerable point Dover occupied in another country's invasion plans, and the need for the trained gunners who might help to frustrate those plans. Dover has had a number of drill halls over the years. Up until 1876, there was a drill hall in Snargate Street, now vanished, which was replaced by one in Northampton Street, now itself also re-developed, and this was the base for the Buffs and the RGA in 1908, although much of the RGA's drill took place in **Archcliffe Fort**. There was a RGA Reserve and **Mobilisation store** in **Dover Castle**, built in 1901, and the regular RGA had new **barracks** there in 1913, so, no doubt regulars and territorials must have worked together. The HQ of the Yeomanry was at 18 de Burgh Hill, but they must have used

BRIGHTON's, Gloucester Road artillery drill hall of 1869, now flats & garaging

HOVE's Old Market; it once functioned as a riding school used by the Yeomanry

BRIGHTON's Dyke Road Yeomanry drill hall built for the conversion to artillery

RIPON's Somerset Row drill hall, built 1912, now a community centre

the riding-school in Liverpool Street, part of a drill-hall complex used by the RFA as well. Castle House in Dolphin Lane, was used from 1866, and other premises in Castle Street were also in use by the Fortress REs in 1908. Little had changed by 1914, but the REs had moved to 16 Bench Street. In 1932, the Kent & Sussex heavy gunners were ensconced in Liverpool Street, where a large hall fronted the, larger, riding-school. Also in Liverpool Street through the 1930s were the Buffs, whose sergeant drill-instructors lived at numbers 65-67. The Buffs moved out, sometime after 1936. In 1938, when their conversion to HAA gunners meant they needed larger premises both to train, and to store all their new kit when it eventually arrived, 233 Field Battery, moved into an old WWl seaplane-hangar, [once also, apparently, an ice-rink], displacing the Buffs again. This seems to have been a temporary measure, until a new drill hall for the AA gunners was finished. The Liverpool Street hall continued in use by 7 Coy. ATS. It was demolished after the War and the site re-developed. The old **administrative building** of the seaplane base on **Marine Parade**, still stands, below Motes Bulwark, and is marked on a 1960s street-map as a TA Centre. A combination of WWll bomb damage, and the development of the Port facilities, means that very little of this military heritage can be traced on the ground. Only the **London Road** TA Centre, dating from around the 1970s can now be seen.

Drill Halls in RIPON, North Yorkshire
The 27th Corps of the Yorkshire [West Riding] Rifle Volunteers was formed at Ripon on 13 April 1860. By 1880, the town provided a base for H and J Coys. of the 1st Volunteer Bn. The Prince of Wales Own West Yorkshire Regt, and in 1914, for H Coy. of the 5th Bn. with a drill station at Pateley Bridge. It would appear that after the end of WWl, there was no territorial unit based in Ripon. There was a drill hall in **Park Street**, by 1896, probably much earlier since it had been converted from an eighteenth century theatre, comparable to that at Richmond. This building was in use until 1912, when the new drill hall in Somerset Row was opened. It was a garage in 1914, then became the garrison cinema for the town's massive military training camps; more recently it was used to store buses, and has lately been re-furbished for continuing commercial use. The new purpose-built drill hall, now **Hugh**

Ripley Hall, in Somerset Row, consists of a two-storey front block with attached staff-house, and hall behind. It now serves as a community centre [*p82*]. In 1989, the Yorkshire & Humberside Association provided a new, brick-built cadet centre for the ACF next to Claro Barracks at the top of **Clotherholme Road**. This T-shaped building is similar to those built around the same time at **Howden, Frodingham, Leeds** and **Brigg**.

Drill Halls in SCARBOROUGH, North Yorkshire
The 6th Corps of the Yorkshire [North Riding] Rifle Volunteers was formed on 28th February 1860. By 1881, the HQ and D & E Coys. of the 2nd Volunteer Bn. of the Princess of Wales's Own Yorkshire Regt. were based in the town. In 1914, the HQ plus E & F Coys. had been joined by units with drill stations in the town: D Sqdn. of the Yorkshire Hussars, and the Army Service Corps Transport and Supply Column of the Yorkshire Mounted Brigade. The North Riding Battery of the Royal Field Artillery's 2nd Northumbrian Bde. was also based in the town. After WWI the 5th Bn. was reconstituted in 1920 with HQ in Scarborough, forming a duplicate 7th Bn. in 1939. In March 1947 the unit was converted into 631 [Green Howards] Anti-Tank Regt. TA, continuing as a Light Regt. until its amalgamation with the 4th Bn. in 1961 to become 4/5th Bn. The Green Howards. Through a number of contractions and re-structurings, this unit has survived to the present with a company based in the town, and HQ at **Coulby Newham** [Middlesbrough]. From at least 1880, there was a drill hall in North Street, and the nearby Temperance Hall served as the HQ of the 2nd Volunteer Bn. Both these sites have been re-developed. The North Street drill hall was in use until 1934, when a new drill hall was built in **St John's Road**. This building, with hall, indoor range, and garaging still exists as a factory [*p83*]. In 1958, a new drill hall was opened in **Coldyhill Lane**, and this continues in service. It consists of a two-storey, symmetrical front block of eleven bays, with a stone door-case, a hall behind and garages. In 1861, **Burniston Barracks** had been built for the regular artillery, and it is possible that the TF RFA unit was based there. Many of the brick huts remain, next to new housing named for the Green Howards. There was an even earlier barracks in the castle, built into the mediaeval Mosdale Hall, which was destroyed by enemy coastal bombardment just before Christmas 1914.

SCARBOROUGH's St Johns Rd drill hall's offices, hall & range, now a factory

AYR, this house in Citadel Place appears to be the front block of the drill hall

AYR, these houses were accommodation for PSIs at the Chalmers Street drill hall

LANCASTER, the Phoenix Street drill hall, now a church, dates from c1880

Drill Halls in AYR

This county town on the south-west coast of Scotland had buildings belonging to both the regular and the volunteer forces. From 1836, the 115th or Prince Regent's Royal Ayrshire Militia were based in Ayr, possibly in the barracks built near the harbour, the Cromwellian Citadel and the old bridge during the Napoleonic Wars. A corps of Rifle Volunteers was formed at Ayr in 1860, becoming A Company of the 1st Volunteer Bn. Royal Scots Fusiliers in 1887, and 4th Bn. in 1908. The barracks, now demolished and replaced by apartment-blocks, incorporated a drill hall, shown on the 1909 OS map, which may have been shared by the regulars and the volunteers. In 1914, Ayr was home to the HQ and A Sqdn. of the Ayrshire Yeomanry, and the Lowland Mounted Brigade's attached Royal Horse Artillery unit. Their drill hall was at **24 Wellington Square**, a substantial Victorian terraced house with large hall and other outbuildings behind. It is now a fitness centre. At the other end of the terrace, on the corner site, **40 Wellington Square**, is the Riding School, a similar house, but extending the full depth of the plot, and now a cafe. In **Citadel Place**, is an imposing double-fronted stone house with, in the yard behind, a building, now offices, but marked on the 1934 OS map as a drill hall [*p83*]. This was likely to have been the HQ of the Fusiliers. The Ayrshire Yeomanry are still in Ayr, at their **Chalmers Street** HQ, a mix of 1950s and earlier buildings: deco-style hall, arts & crafts staff houses [*p84*], early stables, and brick and glass entrance tower with Yeomanry crest. In **Seaforth Road**, is the 1970s block, built for, and still occupied by the Lowland Regiment [TA].

Drill Halls in LANCASTER

This is another county town with almost a full set of military establishments. In 1850 there were three regiments of Militia in Lancashire. The 113th was based in Liverpool, the 125th in Preston, but the senior regiment, the 45th Royal Lancashire Militia, was based in the barracks in **South Road**, built in 1854 in Scots Baronial style with corner towers and tourelles. A gatehouse, dated 1899, has bartizans with pepper-pot turrets. The building is now Storeys Mill social centre and offices. The 10th Corps of Rifle Volunteers was formed in Lancaster in late 1859, re-organised in 1883, as the 2nd Volunteer Bn. the Kings Own Royal Lancaster Regt, becoming the 5th Bn. in 1908. In

1914, HQ and four companies were based in Lancaster. An elaborately-decorated stone drill hall with lots of baroque detail had been built in **Phoenix Street**, probably sometime around 1880 [*p84*]. Also built around then was the depot of the Kings Regt. in **Bowerham Road**, now forming the core of St Martins College. It has the characteristic keep, bastioned and loop-holed perimeter-wall, and elegant messes and barrack-blocks of its type. Also in Lancaster in 1914, was the 10th Lancashire Bty. of the 2nd West Lancashire Bde. RFA, based in the Dallas Road drill hall [*p85*], of apparently unique design, demolished for housing in the 1970s. In 1983, **Alexandra Barracks, Kingsway**, a new TAC was built to house the OTC and a medical unit. It is a two-storey, L-shaped block with a roof-tiled turret in the angle, set in a yard with garages. Strangely, whilst Lancashire supported two regiments of yeomanry cavalry, there was no presence ever in Lancaster.

Drill Halls in LINCOLN

On 26 October 1859, the 1st Lincolnshire corps of Rifle Volunteers was formed in Lincoln, and by May 1860, had joined with nine other corps in the north of the county, to form the Administrative Battalion, which in 1883 became the 1st Volunteer Bn. Lincolnshire Regt. A grand drill hall, partly paid for by Joseph Ruston, the engineer whose firm would go on to pioneer the production of tanks in WWl, was opened in **Broadgate** in 1891 [*p162*]. Built in red brick, it has turrets, castellations, an oriel over the main door, stone dressings, arrow-loops and coats-of-arms. It has recently been restored as a concert venue and social centre. Lincoln was the base for the 8th or Royal North Lincolnshire Militia, whose barracks in **Long Leys** was built in 1857 as a red-brick mediaeval fort with gatehouse, corner towers and arrow-loops. Adjacent, are the Adjutant's house, and a terrace of cottages for permanent staff. A drill hall was added in one corner of the quadrangle around 1913. The complex is now the Museum of Lincolnshire Life. Incidentally, the South Lincolnshire Militia had an identical building, but in stone, built in Grantham. There too, a drill hall was added at about the same time as that in Lincoln. About 1876, the Lincolnshire Regiment acquired their new Sobraon Barracks in **Burton Road**, typically furnished with keep, gatehouse and bastioned, loop-holed perimeter-wall, and, soon after, the Militia became their 3rd Bn. After the Militia's final

LANCASTER, the artillery drill hall, stood in Dallas Road [photo: NW RFCA]

LINCOLN's Newport drill hall, built in 1938, was for an AA searchlight unit

departure, the Old Barracks was occupied, in 1901, by the re-formed Lincolnshire Yeomanry, who took a 21-year lease. However, having served as horsed cavalry in Palestine early in the War before acting as the nucleus of the newly-created Machine Gun Corps, formed at Belton House in 1915, they were disbanded in 1920. Towards the end of the 1930s, the 5th Bn. Lincolnshire Regiment also underwent a traumatic conversion to become AA Searchlight units of the RE. The new drill hall in **Newport**, opened in 1938 carries the traditional Sphinx badge of The Tenth Foot, but also an inscription announcing the arrival of 385 Coy. 46th [Lincolnshire] AA Battalion [*p85*]. The new building provided all the usual messes, offices, orderly room, and armoury etc, but, additionally, garages for the searchlights and their tractors, and specialist training spaces for learning new and unfamiliar skills and techniques. The infantry of the 4/6th Lincolns stayed on at the conventional **Broadgate** drill hall, in fact until into the 1960s. In 1961, the Old Barracks was still in use by REME Workshops and a detachment of RAOC. In 1963, Princess Alice opened a new TAC next to the much shrunken Sobraon Barracks, and this is still active. A number of other locations must be mentioned here. In 1914, the HQ of the 4th Northern General Hospital [RAMC TF] was at **6b Guildhall Street**, now a shop with flats over. **Stonefield House**, Church Lane served as HQ of the Lincolnshire Territorial Association up until 1968. A Victorian school, attached to a house, became the **Westgate** drill hall of the cadets for some time in the 1960s, and there is another cadet centre in Church Drive, off Boultham Park Road.

Drill Halls in the city of ABERDEEN

In contrast to several rather smaller towns we have so far explored, there is much less to be seen in Aberdeen, but it is included here to show the volume of military activity in a small city, rather than to show how quickly so many traces may be removed. Aberdeen is Clan Gordon country, and the Colonel, the Lt. Col. and at least two other officers of the 89th or Aberdeenshire Regiment of Militia in 1850 were Gordons, based at **Gordon Barracks** by the Bridge of Don, which would, in the 1870s, become the depot of the Gordon Highlanders, whose 3rd Bn. the Militia would constitute in 1881. The City's response to the formation of the Rifle Volunteers in early 1860 was to raise a complete battalion of nine corps at once, and it

was essentially this unit which became the 4th Bn. of the Gordons in 1908, with its HQ in the city's elegant Custom House at **28 Guild Street**. By 1914, Aberdeen had four large drill halls. That next to the Royal Infirmary in Woolmanhill, housed its HQ and the entire 4th Bn. Gordon Highlanders. At North Silver Street, in the angle of Ruby Place and Ruby Lane, were the whole of 1st Highland Bde. RFA, three batteries and the ammunition column. Here also may have been based HQ and G Sqdn. of the 2nd Scottish Horse yeomanry cavalry. At 80 Hardgate were based the RE units: HQ and a field company of the Highland Divisional engineers, the divisional signals company, and the City's fortress engineers who defended the port with minefields and coast defence searchlights. The barracks in Fonthill Road, accommodated the Highland Division's ASC column, the RGA unit that manned the coast defence guns, and the Highland Division's two complete field ambulances. The Gordons' stretcher-bearer companies had been based at Albert Hall, 14 Union Wynd, in 1908. All those sites have now been re-developed but for the Custom House, and a small cadet enclave at Fonthill Road. The Gordons have only in recent times occupied their HQ at **St Luke's**, Viewfield Road, a beautiful arts-and-crafts house. Near the University, the OTC have a modern TAC at **125 Don Street**. Given the recent development of Aberdeen as a centre of the Oil Industry, it is probably unsurprising that so much has been swept away in the change.

Drill Halls in the city of CARDIFF

Here is another city with a strong military tradition, and whose recent history has involved wholesale re-development. A number of volunteer units were composed of dock-workers who petitioned to have the Bute name included in their unit titles, hence 16th [Bute] Corps Glamorganshire Rifle Volunteers raised in 1869. In all, some 22 corps were formed around the Cardiff area, resulting in the 2nd Volunteer Bn. Welch Regiment having 24 companies in 1900, reduced to 14 in 1905. Cardiff Castle was the location of the **Armoury** of the 44th Royal Glamorgan Light Infantry Regiment of Militia, in a building restyled by William Burges about 1860. The depot of the Welch Regiment at **Maindy Barracks** was built in 1881, with a keep, built to the same design as those still standing at Bedford and Worcester. Barrack blocks and a gymnasium, amongst later additions to this active depot, remain from the earliest buildings. Currently, TA units of the Royal Welsh Regiment and the RAMC are based there alongside the regulars. The Glamorganshire Yeomanry was raised in 1796, and stayed in existence into the 1830s being involved in suppressing industrial unrest in Merthyr. It was re-formed in 1901 for service in South Africa. Its HQ and C Sqdn. were based in Yeomanry Hall, 76 St Mary's Street, a property listed in a 1914 Directory as the Philharmonic Restaurant and Hall as well. In 1920 they were converted to artillery so probably moved to Dumfries Place. This was known as the Volunteer Drill Hall in 1901 so was probably home to the Rifle Volunteers, but by 1914, it is referred to in Kelly's Directory as the Artillery Drill Hall, and housed 3rd & 4th Glamorgan Batteries 2nd Welsh Bde. RFA. The drill hall at 11-15 Newport Road on the corner of West Grove was the base for HQ and A & B Coys.7th [Cyclist] Bn. Welch Regiment [at no.11] and 2nd Welsh Field Ambulance [at nos.13 & 15], along with HQ 3rd Western General Hospital. The city's RE units were based in Park Street at the drill hall marked on a 1920 OS map as RE Headquarters [Territorial]. These included, in 1914, the Divisional works and signals companies, and the fortress REs. The RE HQ was at **59 Charles Street**, part of a Regency terrace. Park Street has disappeared under the Millennium Stadium re-development. The Newport Road premises next to University College are now part of the hospital. Dumfries Place has been re-developed, as was St Mary's Street in the 1930s, and the Submarine Miners' base in Burt Road. A new drill hall was built at **Gabalfa Road** in the 1930s, and this is still active. It has a wide front-block with white stone dressings and door-case, and a balcony. The two-storey block wraps around a large transverse hall, all set in a large yard with garaging. There is a post-War TAC in **Norbury Road**, now in commercial use [p87]. It has a two-storey front-block with large garage-doors at each end giving access to the hall behind. In **Morgan Street** is the 1990s Ty Llewellyn TAC, with quite sculptural forms, and steel Dragon and Mercury emblems set across two windows. It was paid for by the Welsh Rugby Union as part of the deal to re-develop Park Street. It currently houses a signals squadron and elements of artillery and medical units. A Victorian stone-built three-storey villa at **14 St Andrew's Crescent** currently houses the OTC, who also use facilities at Maindy Barracks.

CARDIFF, a post-WWll TAC to an old layout, in Norbury Road

PORTSMOUTH, the St Pauls Road artillery drill hall, used by the University

PORTSMOUTH's RE drill hall on Hampshire Terrace has labels over the doors

PORTSMOUTH, the c1935 drill hall in Tudor Crescent occupies the site of a fort

Drill Halls in the city of PORTSMOUTH

For long, Britain's premier naval base, Portsmouth has always had fortifications manned by both regular and volunteer troops. Accommodation for these, added to which the introduction of barracks rather than hulks for sailors between ships, has given the city very much the look of a garrison town. One element of this is a large collection of drill halls for the numerous volunteer units based here. In 1879, the HQ of the 3rd Corps of Hampshire Rifle Volunteers, five of whose 11 companies were based in Portsmouth, was at **4 Grand Parade**, a Regency house on the north side of the parade-ground. This corps became, a year later, the 3rd Volunteer Bn. Hampshire Regiment. The South Hampshire Militia was in Southampton, but a unit of Submarine Miners RE [Militia] was in Portsmouth from 1878, possibly having their HQ in High Street. The Rifle Volunteers would have been based at the original Connaught Drill Hall in **Alfred Road**, opposite the RC Cathedral. This red-brick castellated building with towers was used until 1902, when it was handed over to the Navy to form the nucleus of HMS Nelson. In 1902, the new Connaught Drill Hall [p163] was opened in **Stanhope Street**, and in 1914, the HQ and A B C & D Coys. 6th Bn. Hampshire Regt. and D Coy. of the 9th [Cyclist] Bn. were based there. The 6th Bn. was still there in 1937, but a year later they had converted into AT artillery, first equipped with 2 pdr. guns, and later with SP 17 pdr Archers. By the 1960s they were 383 Field Regt. RA [TA]. Since then it has been, amongst other things, a Casino, and currently awaits sympathetic development. It is a cavernous structure with all the mediaeval motifs of a late-Victorian drill hall. The Hampshire Carabiniers stayed in existence through the 19th Century, sending a company of the Imperial Yeomanry to South Africa. In 1914, HQ and A Sqdn. were based on Governor's Green sometimes known as the Pembroke drill hall. In 1920, they were converted to artillery, and in 1938, to 72nd [Hampshire] HAA Regt. The Hampshire Volunteer Artillery had their HQ at **22 Marmion Road**, from 1879-1886. Now a public house occupies what may be the original building. In 1898, they were at 33 Marmion Road, but by 1914, had moved into the drill hall on Governor's Green, as No.4 Coy. Hampshire RGA, along with the Wessex divisional field ambulances. In 1937, Governor's Green was occupied by 155th & 156th Batteries, Hampshire Heavy Bde. RA [TA]. It would appear that, until recently, a hut survived on the Green, near the guardhouse of King William Gate, now a cottage, whose occupants relate how, in dry weather, outlines of the old TA buildings may be seen in the grass. The drill hall itself probably stood on the SE corner of Penny Street and Pembroke Road. Other artillery units were based in the **St Pauls Road** drill hall, a tall, thin block with ornate gables and stone dressings, fronting a large hall [*p87*]. Here, in 1914, were HQ and the two batteries of 1st Wessex Bde. RFA. By 1937, these had become 57th Wessex AA Bde. The engineers were based close by at **Hampshire Terrace** which still carries the inscription 1st H R E V over two of the archways to its road frontage. Again, a large hall lies behind [*p88*]. Both these buildings are now used by the University. In 1914, 1st, 2nd, & 4th Coys. Electric Lights Fortress REs were at Hampshire Terrace with their HQ in Commercial Road, possibly at number 19, in use by 1937 as an Army Recruiting Office. In 1937, the Hampshire Fortress REs were still there but other RE units, such as 206th [Hampshire] Field Coy. had moved out to **Burnaby Road** drill hall, possibly the old gymnasium of Milldam Barracks, used by the regular engineers, and now used by HMS Temeraire. This site was still used by RE and REME into the 1950s. All these buildings dated back to the late 1800s, and it was time for improvements. The drill hall in **Tudor Crescent** with its stylish deco touches probably dates from the late 1930s [*p88*], and that in **Peronne Road** would also have done had it not been delayed by the outbreak of WWll. When, finally it was built in 1947-9, it incorporated modifications forced by the experience of incendiary bombing. This long two-storey block, had its window sizes reduced, and roof-top walk-ways constructed. This TAC with its much more recent neighbour in **Peronne Close** are both still in use.

Such is the density of military buildings in Portsmouth that it is often difficult to disentangle the regulars and the volunteers. The present Armed Forces Careers Office, for instance, on Burnaby Road, began life in 1908 as a Military Reception Station for recruits, in the charge of a Major in the RAMC. Next door was overspill from the Milldam Barracks complex which includes a building most usually identified as a riding school or a gymnasium similar to those at St Georges Barracks, Gosport, or at Hilsea Barracks. Milldam was used by the

GLASGOW's drill hall in West Princes Street is now home to the Scottish Ballet

GLASGOW, the RNR drill hall in Whitefield Street, Govan, is now a TAC

BLANTYRE, one of several similar drill halls of the Cameronians

regular army RE in 1915 and in 1937, but already accommodated TA units whose needs could not be met elsewhere. Thus dual-use may have been more common than it appears, where buildings are jostling for space, and boundaries become blurred.

Drill Halls in the city of GLASGOW

This densely-populated city has always had large numbers enrolled in volunteer units, and this is reflected in the number of drill halls. By the end of the 1860s, there were ten Corps of Rifle Volunteers in the Glasgow area, each of battalion strength. The period 1884-1905 saw the construction of at least eight drill halls, designed for whole battalions:

Yorkhill Parade/Gilbert Street	1900	6th Bn. HLI [*p164*]
81 Greendyke Street, Glasgow Green		9th Bn. HLI
261 West Princes Street	1895	5th Bn. Cameronians [*p89*]
149 Cathedral Street		8th Bn. Cameronians
24 Hill Street, Garnethill	1895	5th Bn. HLI
James Street, Bridgetown	rebuilt 1938	7th Bn. HLI
130 Whitefield Road, Govan	1905	RNReserve [*p90*]
Victoria Rd, now 35 Coplaw St.	1884	7th Bn. Cameronians
21 Jardine Street	1894	Lanark Vols./ Cameronians

Several of the smaller drill halls, provided for the outlying companies of the 6th Bn. Cameronians, such as **Blantyre** [*p90*], **Larkhall** and **Uddingston**, or for the 8th Bn. HLI, such as Carluke [1905], or **Law** were built at around the same time in similar style. The 6th Bn. Argyll & Sutherland Highlanders was based in Renfrew, with HQ in **Paisley**, some of whose companies spread into Glasgow, as at **Pollockshaws** built c1900 [*p164*]. The Queen's Own Glasgow Yeomanry were based at **Yorkhill Parade**, with one squadron of the Lanarkshire Yeomanry at Coatbridge. The University OTC was given an impressive drill hall in **University Avenue**, in 1900. Artillery units enjoyed equally grand accommodation:

Earls Park Ave, Cathcart	3[Highland] Howitzer Bde.
Berkeley St / Newton Terr.	3[Lowland] Bde. RFA
Butterbiggins Road, Govanhill	4[Lowland] Howitzer Bde.
21 Jardine Street in 1914	3[Lowland] Bde. RFA

90

and whose site is now occupied by a RC church. Harry Weale VC TAC at **Station Road, Queensferry,** and **Groes Road, Colwyn Bay** have both been opened as active TACs in relatively recent times.

Drill Halls in CORNWALL

Although the County retains only three active TACs, there is a high survival rate amongst former drill halls exhibiting a wide range of styles over a long time span. By 1865, two administrative battalions of Rifle Volunteers had been formed with 12 corps based on Penzance, and another ten on Bodmin. As well as these, there were three Militia units, the 38th or Duke of Cornwall's Rifles, which moved from Torpoint to its new, French chateau-style **Bodmin Armoury** in 1857; the 118th or Royal Cornwall & Devon Miners' Light Infantry, which converted to artillery and moved into Pendennis Castle in 1853; and the Falmouth Division of the Submarine Miners RE formed in 1892 from a previous unit of volunteers, and responsible for operating the minefield which protected Falmouth's deep-water anchorage. The Armoury became the centre-piece of the Duke of Cornwall's Light Infantry's new depot in around 1880. The Miners' Militia had added their HQ building to the Henrician keep at Pendennis, from which, it was removed by the Office of Works in 1921, in an ill-conceived and senseless sanitisation exercise. Falmouth's buildings have been demolished for re-development.

The beginnings of the Rifle Volunteer movement in Cornwall saw a number of instances of adapting existing buildings as drill halls. In **Launceston, Helston, Bude, Falmouth**, and, possibly, **Truro**, non-conformist chapels were taken over. **Penryn Town Hall**, and Liskeard Market Hall provided shared use. Pre-1860 artillery drill halls at **Charlestown** and **Marazion**, simple rectangular granite halls may have been existing industrial buildings. The re-organisation of 1880 may have produced the drill halls at **Newquay, St Columb Major** and **Camborne**, whilst those at **Delabole** and **Saltash** [*p95*] may be slightly later in date. In 1908, the newly-formed Cornwall Territorial Association commissioned a group of new drill halls, apparently built to the same design, but with small individual differences, at **Hayle, Redruth** and **St Just**, all dated 1911 or 1912. At the same time were built the extensive **St Austell** [East

SALTASH, the Cornish badge is visible over the door

95

LISKEARD, this post-WWl drill hall has modern features

KINGS LYNN, this Wellesley Street drill hall is now a church

Hill], **Penzance's Chyandor** artillery barracks, **Camelford's** fine hall, and **Lerryn's** tiny, timber hut, recently restored to its original state. It is likely that **Lostwithiel's** corrugated-iron-clad hall also dates from this surge of building activity. A number of Corwall's TA units converted to AA gunnery in the 1930s and this change prompted the next phase of drill hall construction. A revolutionary design was used in new drill halls at **St Ives**, [**Alexandra Road**], **St Just**, and Falmouth. It has been suggested that **Redruth [Foundry Row]**, now the Brewery Museum, and the former drill hall at Station Road, St Blazey, were further examples. Technically, they were geodetic barrels, designed on the same principles as Junckers hangars, and Wellington bombers. That at Falmouth has only recently been demolished. More conventional buildings but in the *international moderne* style were built in **Moresk Road, Truro**, and **Barras Cross, Liskeard** [*p96*]. The huts at **Torpoint**, and at **South Street, St Austell** may date from WWll. The later drill hall at **North Roskear Road, Camborne**, may be of the 1930s, but that at **Castle Canyke Road, Bodmin**, is dated 1958. Recent additions are the modern Cadet Centres at **St Blazey**, and **Wadebridge**.

Drill Halls in NORFOLK

In the 19th Century, Norfolk was a comparatively densely-populated county. At one time, Norwich had been England's second city, and Kings Lynn and Great Yarmouth had been important ports. This is reflected in the number of units sustained in what was an essentially rural area. In the 1860s there were some twenty, company-sized, Rifle Volunteer corps, and a unit of Light Horse. In 1908, the TF had three battalions of the Norfolk Regiment, the Norfolk Yeomanry, re-formed in 1901, a brigade of the RFA, a field ambulance, and an ASC transport & supply column. The Yeomanry's squadrons were based in Norwich, North Walsham, Fakenham and Kings Lynn. The infantry were spread across 15 main centres plus a further fifty odd drill stations. Norwich itself had four main drill halls in the early part of the 20th Century. Chapelfields, also referred to as Theatre Street or St Giles, was built into the city walls, in 1866 with a mock mediaeval facade of castellated towers and arrow-loops. This was the HQ of 4th Bn. Norfolk Regiment and a base for A & B Coys. It was demolished soon after 1966 for road-widening. **Ivory House**, or **52 All Saints Green**, is a grand, four-storey Georgian house of 1772. It became the

Militia Barracks in 1860, but by 1900 had become Surrey Street Barracks, base for the artillery volunteers. In 1914, the 1st East Anglian Bde. RFA was based there. In 1931, the gunners had moved out and 161st East Anglian Field Ambulance had taken their place. Until recently there was a Victorian drill shed behind the house, along with other outbuildings. The drill hall at **23 Cattlemarket Road**, also started life as a three-storey Georgian house of about 1800. In 1914, it was HQ and base for A Sqdn. Norfolk Yeomanry; and HQ and base for A Coy. 6th [Cyclist] Bn. Norfolk Regt. After WWl it was the base for the East Anglian divisional RE and ASC units. In 1931, the Yeomanry were still based there, but as field artillery, having combined with the Suffolk Yeomanry in 1923. Only in 1942, did they, once again, form an independent unit, still as artillery, but now as an AT regiment. The premises at **44 Bethel Street**, had been built in the 1870s, and requisitioned by the TF in 1908, as a base for the 2nd East Anglian Divisional Field Ambulance [*p165*]. A Regency house at **22 Tombland, Erpingham House**, was the Norfolk Territorial Association's office from 1912-31, and also provided HQ facilities for the Yeomanry, the Eastern Mounted Bde, and later, in 1931, 163 East Anglian Infantry Bde. which included the two battalions of the Norfolk Regiment, and the Cambridgeshire Regiment. Other quite humble houses were used as unit HQs at different times: **18a Prince of Wales Road, 41 Silver Road, 21 Northcote Road**, and **137 Rosary Road**. Sometime in the mid-1930s, a new drill hall was built, probably to house the artillery unit which the Yeomanry now formed. This is **325 Aylsham Road**, with neo-Georgian front-block with RA crest and stone dressings on stylish semi-circular projections, and extensive garages, gun-sheds etc in the surrounding yard. This TAC is still active. We must not, of course, forget that both **Britannia Barracks**, the depot of the Norfolk Regiment, dating from around 1875, now fronting Norwich gaol, and the much earlier Nelson Cavalry Barracks of 1791, now represented only by a few bits of boundary wall, made Norwich an important garrison town.

Elsewhere in the county, were other concentrations of troops. At Great Yarmouth, the **Nelson Road** drill hall in brick and flint with stepped gables, built in 1867, was the base for G & H Companies 5th Bn. Norfolk Regiment and a battery of field artillery. At **Southtown Road** is a depot of the regulars, but opposite at the Victorian **Hampstead House** [No 80], and its neighbour, a 1930s drill hall, now a printworks, can be seen the town's later provision for the volunteers. In 1914, the HQ 5th Bn. Norfolk Regiment was **First House, Quebec Street**, East Dereham, now an estate-agent's office. There is an active Cadet Centre, built in 1952, at **44 Norwich Road**. In Kings Lynn, there are three sites remaining. A faded painted inscription on the side of a building, once a **warehouse** near the Custom House, announces its function as the HQ Army Service Corps Norfolk & Suffolk Bde. The Broad Street drill hall has disappeared under the bus-station, but its 1936 replacement in **Wellesley Street** is now a church [*p96*]. In **Providence Street** is another former TAC in the standard neo-Georgian of so many government buildings. An earlier Volunteer Stores, further along the street, was demolished in the re-development of the 1960s. One of the earliest drill halls in the county is the adapted theatre in **Playhouse Yard, Downham Market,** in use in the late 19th Century, and there is a reset 1876 date-stone at Watton. Several towns apparently never had dedicated drill halls. In Diss, the **Crown Hotel** [1878] was succeeded by a Victorian house, **Sunnyside**; and in Thetford, the **Guildhall** [1902] gave way to Burrells Works in Minstergate, used by 2/50 Field Coy. RE in the 1930s; at North Walsham, the Corn Hall [1848] served. Whilst at Cromer there is no trace of any building ever being used by F Coy. 5th Bn. Norfolk Regiment, nominally based there in 1914, at Melton Constable, one of their drill stations, a drill hall is built onto the **Railway Institute** [1880]. Other pre-WWl drill halls survive at **Holt Road, Fakenham**, and **Queen's Close, Attleborough**. There were a number of new drill halls built in the 1930s to meet the changing needs and demands: **Aylsham, Dersingham, Swaffham, Loddon**, and **Wymondham**. The latter was re-built in the 1980s. Behind Loddon are the twin explosives and inflammables stores built for the Home Guard during WWll.

Drill Halls of the HIGHLAND DIVISION in 1914
A division of the Territorial Force [TF] in 1914 mirrored a regular army division and consisted of troops of all arms: infantry, cavalry, artillery, engineers and signallers, army service corps, and medical corps. In addition to the usual two field artillery brigades and one of howitzers, the Highland Division

contained mountain gunners. The infantry were the three brigades of volunteer battalions, thirteen in total, of the Seaforth & Cameron, Gordon, and Argyll & Sutherland Highlanders. The Shetland Companies of the Gordons served as divisional troops. The cavalry were the Fife & Forfar Yeomanry and Lovat's Scouts, a double regiment with eight squadrons, and their attached Inverness-shire Royal Horse Artillery. There was a RE Signalling Company attached to each infantry brigade, and an Army Service Corps Transport & Supply Column and a Field Ambulance attached to the Mounted Brigade, and another one of each to the Division. It should be noted that the Black Watch brigade and the RGA and fortress REs were assigned to coast defence duties, and the two regiments of Scottish Horse, and Highland Cyclist Battalion were unattached within Scottish Command.

Unlike TF units based in populous areas, most of Highland Division's troops were thinly spread across large tracts of sparsely-populated countryside. Only one of its thirteen infantry battalions, Aberdeen's 4th Bn. of the Gordons, was concentrated in one place, the other twelve having companies based in a total of 90 towns, most with additional drill stations, totalling a further 200 or so locations ranging from small towns such as Dollar, where part of F Company of the Argylls' 7th Bn. drilled, to isolated farmsteads such as Bower Madden [Caithness], where elements of H Company of the 5th Bn. of the Seaforths met. There are parallel differences between the bases of the Yeomanry, with the Fife & Forfar based in four large towns and a handful of smaller locations, whilst the Lovat's Scouts spread their eight squadrons across over 70 locations, clearly reflecting the difference in the demographic character of the areas from which they were recruiting.

In terms of the provision of drill halls, there seem to be no hard-and-fast rules. Virtually every base for squadron, company or battery, had a drill hall, but there were enormous differences across this provision, seldom easily explained. The grand baronial, often granite, piles still to be seen in **Inverness**, **Kirkcaldy**, **Dundee**, **Dunfermline**, and **Stirling**, for instance, are to be expected, reflecting these towns' importance and wealth. Less expected are the no-less grand structures which still stand in **Elgin**, **Castletown**, **Golspie** [p165], **Thurso** [2] [pp43,69],

Forres [p166] or Huntly [p36]. Whilst one might expect to find simple buildings in some of the more remote areas of the Highlands, and this is borne out at **Southend** [Kintyre] [p50], **Broadford** [Skye], and **Gairloch** [Wester Ross], each of these being best described as a hut. That which housed the HQ of E Sqdn. of the 2nd Lovat's Scouts at **Kyle of Lochalsh**, can hardly be described as impressive. It is difficult to explain the differences and contrasts, for example between the regulars' barracks at **Ballater** on Royal Dee-side, and the TF's hut, now the band's practice-room; or the splendid set of eight drill halls occupied by the Seaforths' 5th Bn., and the mixed bag of premises used by some of the other Highlander battalions. It must also be noted here, that some places which held only the status of drill stations, were nevertheless provided with drill halls, an example being **Achiltibuie**, one of nine drill stations used by E Sqdn. 2nd Lovat's Scouts. Another example is **Bonhill**, a satellite of Jamestown, used by E Company of 9th Bn. Argyll & Sutherland Highlanders.

Below is a sample of some of the Highland Division's units, showing the provision of drill hall accommodation.

HIGHLAND Division TF 1914; HQ: **2 Charlotte Street, PERTH;**

INFANTRY
Argyll & Sutherland Brigade; HQ: **Drill Hall, STIRLING;**

5th Bn; HQ, A-D, F & G Coys: Finnart Street, GREENOCK;
    E Coy: **2 King Street, PORT GLASGOW;**
    H Coy: Binnie Lane **GOUROCK;**

6th Bn; HQ, A B & C Coys: **66 High Street, PAISLEY;**
    D Coy: Campbell Street, RENFREW;
    E Coy: **Dimity Street, JOHNSTONE;**
    F & H Coys: **Auldhouse Road, POLLOCKSHAWS** [p164];
    G Coy: **Paisley Road, BARRHEAD;**

7th. Bn; HQ, A Coy: **Drill Hall, STIRLING** [p36];
    B Coy: Tryst Rd, STENHOUSEMUIR;
    C Coy: **Cow Wynd, FALKIRK** [p276];
    D Coy: Greenhead Road, LENNOXTOWN;

E & H Coys; **Ochil House, ALLOA** [*p40*];
F Coy: **77 Park Street, ALVA** [*p269*];
G Coy: **Swansacre, KINROSS**;

8th Bn; HQ, D Coy: DUNOON;
 A Coy: INVERARAY;
 B Coy: **Esplanade, CAMPBELTOWN** [*p99*];
 C Coy: **Main Street, SOUTHEND** [*p50*];
 E Coy: **Manse Brae, LOCHGILPHEAD**;
 F Coy: **BALLACHULISH**;
 G Coy: **BOWMORE**;
 H Coy: **EASDALE**

9th Bn. HQ & C Coy: **Hartfield House & Drill Hall, DUMBARTON**;
 A Coy: **East Princes Street, HELENSBURGH** [*p252*];
 B Coy: **KIRKINTILLOCH**;
 D Coy: Station Road, MILNGARVIE;
 E Coy: JAMESTOWN;
 F Coy: **158-60 Middleton Street, ALEXANDRIA**;
 G & H Coys: CLYDEBANK;

The drill stations maintained by each of the Argylls' battalions in 1914 were:
 5 Bn: one, 6 Bn: none, 7 Bn: ten, 8 Bn: thirty-two & 9 Bn: five

ARTILLERY
Highland RGA [Heavy]: HQ & Battery: **Elgin Road, DUNFERMLINE**;
4th Highland [Mountain] Bde. RGA:
 HQ & Buteshire Battery; Russell Street/**High Street, ROTHESAY**;
 Argyllshire Battery: **Esplanade, CAMPBELTOWN**;
 Ross & Cromarty Battery: **Main Street, LOCHCARRON**;
 Ammunition Column HQ: **Campeltown Road, TARBERT**;
1st Highland Bde. RFA: HQ & Batteries: North Silver Street, ABERDEEN;
2nd Highland Bde. RFA: HQ: **Dudhope Drill Hall, Brown Street, DUNDEE**:
 Forfarshire Battery: **Marketgate, ARBROATH** [*p99*];
 Fifeshire Battery: **North Street, LEVEN** [*p286*];

CAMPBELTOWN, the drill hall was damaged by a WWll bomb

ARBROATH, the massive, boat-shaped artillery drill hall

City of Dundee Battery & Ammunition Column: as above, **DUNDEE**;

3rd Highland [Howitzer] Bde. RFA:

HQ & 1 & 2 Renfrewshire Batteries: 8 South Street, **GREENOCK**;

Ammunition Column: **Earls Park Avenue, CATHCART**;

ENGINEERS

Divisional REs: HQ & 2 Field Coy: 80 Hardgate, ABERDEEN;

1 Field Coy: **21 Jardine Street, GLASGOW**; [*p31*]

Divisional RE Signals Coys: HQ & 4 Sections: 80 Hardgate, ABERDEEN;

CAVALRY

Highland Mounted Bde: HQ: Academy Street, INVERNESS [*p283*]; attached to Highland Mounted Brigade:

Army Service Corps Transport & Supply Column: Academy Street, INVERNESS;

Field Ambulance: HQ, A & B Sections: **Rose Street, INVERNESS**;

Inverness-shire RHA: HQ & Battery: Margaret Street, INVERNESS;

Ammunition Column: **Drill Hall, King Street, NAIRN** [*p286*];

Fife & Forfar Yeomanry: HQ: **Hunter Street, KIRKCALDY**;

A Sqdn: **Castlebank Road, CUPAR**;

B Sqdn: **Elgin Road, DUNFERMLINE**;

C Sqdn: **Dudhope Drill Hall, DUNDEE**;

D Sqdn: **Brechin Road, FORFAR**;

1st Lovat's Scouts: HQ & D Sqdn: Croyard Road, BEAULY;

A Sqdn: **Drill Hall, ROY BRIDGE** [*p28*];

B Sqdn: LOCHMADDY [North Uist];

C Sqdn: **Skeabost House [Hotel] SKYE** [*p39*];

E Sqdn: **Church Road, KYLE of LOCHALSH**;

F Sqdn: **The Square, DORNOCH** [*p42*];

G Sqdn: **38 Perrins Road, ALNESS**;

H Sqdn: Academy Street, INVERNESS;

If nothing else, this demonstrates what an enormous task it must have been to get these troops together to take part in the exercises which might develop their skills in working as a cohesive force at battalion, brigade, or indeed, divisional level.

The LONDON REGIMENT in 1914

In 1914, the London Regiment was the largest infantry regiment in the Territorial Force with 26 battalions, organised into six infantry brigades in two divisions. Each of these battalions was, for the most part, based in a single drill hall which met all its needs, and was local to the majority of its members. Many of these buildings still stand, and although a handful are still used for their original purpose, others have a variety of uses. The density of these buildings reminds us that the cities of London and Westminster were once heavily-populated residential areas, capable of generating the 15000+ men needed for 26 infantry battalions, and, at the same time, those who formed the other arms: cavalry, artillery etc. We are also reminded that what we now think of as the inner suburbs, places like Croydon, or Hampstead, or Stratford, were the recruiting grounds of other regiments entirely, the Royal East Surreys, the Middlesex, and the Essex, respectively. There appears to have been at least one successful venture into regimental imperialism, when territory of the Queens Royal West Surrey Regiment around Kennington and Bermondsey was taken over, probably in 1908, by the 21st Bn. [First Surrey Rifles], at Camberwell, and the 22nd Bn. [The Queen's], based in Jamaica Road.

The London Regiment's drill halls were:

1st Bn. **HANDEL STREET, Bloomsbury**: extensive complex including two large halls etc; still in use by London Universities' OTC

2nd Bn. **9 TUFTON STREET**, Westminster: now offices

3rd Bn. 21 EDWARD STREET, St Pancras: re-developed

4th Bn. 112 SHAFTESBURY STREET, Shoreditch: backing onto **Wenlock Street**, the former 1930s **Hackney TA Centre**

5th Bn. 130 BUNHILL ROW, Finsbury; demolished and re-developed

6th Bn. **57a FARINGDON ROAD**, Finsbury [*p101*]: archway with crests etc; hall behind & garages used by OTC

7th Bn. 24 SUN STREET, Finsbury Square: demolished and re-developed

8th Bn. 130 BUNHILL ROW, Finsbury: demolished and re-developed

9th Bn. **56 DAVIES STREET**, Westminster [*p102*]: still in use by TA

10th Bn. **HILLMAN STREET**, formerly 49 The Grove, Hackney: council offices

11th Bn. 17 PENTON STREET, Finsbury: demolished for Public Carriage Office

12th Bn. **CHENIES STREET**, Holborn: converted to arts centre

13th Bn. **IVERNA GARDENS**, Kensington: hall in mews off High Street

14th Bn. 59 **BUCKINGHAM GATE**, Westminster: re-developed; part of hall removed to the new London Scottish drill hall on Horseferry Road, Westminster

15th Bn. **SOMERSET HOUSE**, Strand: now art gallery/exhibition space

16th Bn. 58 **BUCKINGHAM GATE**, Westminster: frontage remains as offices

17th Bn. 66 TREDEGAR ROAD, Bow: demolished for Post Office sorting office

18th Bn. **DUKE of YORK'S HQ**, Chelsea: part-converted to luxury apartments

19th Bn. 76 HIGH STREET, Camden Town: demolished & re-developed as shops

20th Bn. **HOLLY HEDGE HOUSE**, Blackheath: still in use by TA

21st Bn. **4 FLODDEN ROAD**, Camberwell: rebuilt c1980s as TAC on same site

22nd Bn. **2 JAMAICA ROAD**, Bermondsey: original buildings incorporated into active drill hall for Royal Marine Reserve

23rd Bn. **27 St JOHN'S HILL**, Battersea [*p102*]: still in use by TA

24th Bn. **71-3 NEW STREET**, [now Braganza Street], Southwark [*p103*]: still a TAC

25th Bn. **FULHAM HOUSE, 87 HIGH STREET**, Putney Bridge [*p103*]: original house with added hall and garages etc. still in TA use

28th Bn. **DUKES ROAD**, St Pancras: the ornate facade of the Artists Rifles drill hall, with its terracotta medallions, is now The Place theatre

It may be that over half of the London Regiment's drill halls survive, but most of them have undergone significant changes. In Braganza Street, Southwark, for instance, more than the street name has changed. The 19th [Lambeth] Corps of the Surrey Volunteer Rifles, had their HQ at 10 South Place,

LONDON's 57a Faringdon Road drill hall's gateway; through the arch, the hall

LONDON's 56 Davies Street drill hall of Queen Victoria's Rifles, still a TAC

BATTERSEA, St Johns Hill drill hall, built for a battalion of the London Regt.

Kennington, where, in 1861 they built a drill shed, behind the four-storey house which accommodated their messes, offices and armoury. They also had premises at 51 Newington Place. In December 1867, the Inspector-General of Volunteers opened their brand-new drill hall in neighbouring New Street. This was a three-storey block of five bays, built as a pair of semi-detached houses, with a pediment over the projecting middle three. A large drill hall, a smaller hall, and parade-square lay behind. The main block held messes for officers, and for sergeants, canteen, and a club-house, provided with billiard and bagatelle tables. Shooting was a major activity, both indoor using Morris Tubes, and outdoors at Wraysbury and Bisley. An underground indoor rifle range had been built in 1890. In 1902 the strength of the 4th Volunteer Bn. The Queen's Royal West Surrey Regiment, whose HQ this was, numbered 1009 men in eleven companies, including one of cyclists, plus Maxim Gun, signalling, and medical sections, and two sections of mounted infantry. The mounted infantry's horses were stabled in Earls Court until 1904, when they were moved nearer to home in Camberwell Green. The battalion also supported three bands. When the TF came into being in 1908, the battalion was re-designated as the 24th Bn. the London Regt. There had for long been discussion of the problems of 20 year leases for the land on which the drill hall stood. Although re-building was desirable, it was always felt that the lease was too short to warrant the investment. In 1908, however, the County of London Territorial Association took over responsibility, buying the land outright in 1910. However it was not until 1937 that the drill hall was finally rebuilt. In 1939 a duplicate unit was formed, moving into a building at St George's Market, Elephant & Castle, formerly used as a dance-hall and gymnasium. By the start of WWll, both battalions had reverted to being part of the Queen's Royal Regiment [West Surrey] as 1/7th and 2/7th [Southwark] Battalions. After WWll another change came with conversion to anti-aircraft troops, as 622 [Queen's] HAA Regt. RA [TA]. The new role necessitated modifications to the buildings. A gunnery training building was constructed, along with garages and workshops, and a new miniature range, the underground one having been filled in to provide the base for new building. Little could be done regarding the access through the archway built in 1937. The kerb was eventually lowered to help on width, but, on occasions, trucks towing radars could only be got in by letting their tyres down. The 3.7" HAA gun with a shortened, weighted barrel enabled it to be used for training in the indoor training block. Many of these improvements were carried out in 1952. A REME unit was attached to 622 Regiment and used additional TA premises at Chapter Terrace, 300m from the drill hall. Following AA Command's stand-down in 1955, 622 Regiment was amalgamated with the neighbouring 570 LAA/SL Regiment whose drill hall was that of the old Surrey Rifles [once 21st Bn. London Regt.] in Flodden Road. The two units became 570 LAA Regt. with batteries in Braganza Street, Flodden Road, and with the HQ in the 1930s drill hall at Highwood Barracks in Dulwich opposite Hornimans Museum. In1961, the battery left Braganza Street for good. It is currently occupied by a volunteer medical unit, and by an ACF unit. The re-constructed drill hall at Flodden Road is base for an independent Royal Engineers field squadron This narrative has sought to demonstrate how drill halls have been forced to adapt to changes in the roles of their occupants, re-organisations by the War Office, technological innovation in weapons and equipment, and demographic change in their catchment areas. It also shows, incidentally, how complicated became the family trees of regiments, especially of those which began life as popular volunteer movements.

Drill halls of
the Territorial Army in NOTTINGHAMSHIRE 1950

By 1950, much of the inevitable contraction which followed the end of WWll had been worked through, but new conflicts were waiting to put pressure on manpower and equipment. The role and function of the County's TA units had changed, most notably, those of the Yeomanry. The county had always had two yeomanry regiments: the South Notts Hussars, and the Sherwood Rangers. Having started WWll as horsed cavalry in Palestine, the Rangers were re-trained as infantry, then as Coast Artillery, before finding their niche as an armoured unit. From 1947 they became part of the Royal Armoured Corps equipped with Comet tanks. After the end of WWl, the Hussars had been converted to field artillery, continuing in that role through WWll. In 1947 they were designated 307 Field Regt. RA [TA], equipped with Ram 25pdr. SP guns. The Hussars' duplicate regiment, raised in 1939, started life as a Field Artillery

KENNINGTON, Braganza St drill hall home to infantry, AA gunners & medics

FULHAM HOUSE, the original house of 1730s backed by the modern hall

103

SOUTHWELL, the drill hall of 1914 with its curved roof

SUTTON-in-ASHFIELD, the original drill hall, extended in the 1950s

Regiment, was re-organised, dissolved, then in 1947 re-formed as 350 Heavy Regt. RA [TA] equipped with 7.2" howitzers. One unit with a shorter history was 528 LAA [Mobile] Regt. formed in August 1939, and re-constituted in 1947, equipped with 40mm Bofors guns. An even newer unit was 48 Counter-Bombardment Troop RA [TA], consisting of a small number of specialist intelligence gatherers whose function was to select battle-field targets for the gunners. The County's infantry volunteers are remembered as the Robin Hood Rifles, becoming, as part of the TF in 1908, 7th Bn. of the Nottingham & Derby Regt, better known as the Sherwood Foresters. In 1936, they converted to Searchlight troops of the RE, and then, in 1940, to the RA. In March 1949 they became 577 LAA/SL Regt. RA [TA]. The 8th Bn. Sherwood Foresters served as infantry through both World Wars, re-forming in 1947 as motorised infantry. To look after the Yeomanry's tanks a REME unit was formed with a RAOC section attached. Also, in the County, were a Signals regiment, WRAC units, a squadron of a specialist signals unit and a RASC transport company, both specifically tasked with supporting the AA gunners. In addition, there was a RAuxAF squadron of LAA gunners for airfield defence.

To house these units, the County Territorial & Auxiliary Forces Association, with offices at **6 Clinton Terrace, Derby Road**, Nottingham, maintained a range of old and new buildings. Some were up to the tasks demanded of soldiers in the nuclear age, others would have been pushed to satisfy the demands of horse and musket. The tanks of the Sherwood Rangers lived at the old Militia Stores, then known as The Barracks, Albert Street, Newark, with detachments at **Cavendish Road, Carlton**, at **Sutton Road, Mansfield**, where a few huts and a pair of staff houses remain, and at the TAC off London Road, in Storcroft Road, Retford, re-developed as housing. The **Carlton** drill hall dates from 1939. The artillery units shared HQ at **6 Clinton Terrace**, with 48 Counter-Bombardment Troop next-door at number 5. Their batteries were over the road at the **Derby Road** drill hall, a magnificent neo-Baroque building of c1910, on four floors with a hall contained within, now used as offices; at the 1930s drill halls at **Broadgate, Beeston**, and **Hucknall Lane, Bulwell**; at both **Bath Street, Mansfield**, re-built in the 1980s to be re-opened by

Denis Thatcher, and **Sutton Road**; at **Arnot Hill Road, Arnold**, which appears to date from before WWl, has been a false-teeth factory, and is currently a print-works; and at **Scofton House, Park Street, Worksop**, another site later re-built in 1974, and still in TA use. The Signals units were at **Derby Road**, and **Beeston**. The drill halls at **Beeston** [1939], **Bulwell** [1938], and **Carlton** [1939], are built in a similar style with two-storey blocks, of brick with facings in stone and contrasting brick, ranged around courtyards with garages and workshops. Before its re-building, **Scofton House** comprised the old mansion and out-buildings. The Foresters were based at **Sherwood Avenue, Newark**, a neo-Georgian building with later additions, from 1938, behind; at **Bowbridge Camp, Newark**, some of whose surviving huts are now incorporated in a primary school; at **Shaw Street, Worksop**, a pre-WWl hall now in community use; at **Alfreton Road, Sutton-in-Ashfield**, another 1938 build ; and at **Newark Road, Southwell**, built in 1914. There are stylistic similarities between **Arnold, Southwell** [*p104*], and **Sutton-in-Ashfield** [*p104*], the most obvious one being the curved roof, quite an uncommon feature in drill halls anywhere. The REME/RAOC unit was based at Cromwell Camp, Chilwell, now either absorbed by Chetwynd Barracks or, more likely, replaced by the 1980s TAC next door. The RAuxAF LAA squadron was in **Upnah House, 22 Balmoral Road, Nottingham**, a large Victorian villa with hall behind, now part of Nottingham Girls' High School. Next to the government buildings in Chalfont Drive, soon to have a Regional Seat of Government buried on site, is **HMS Sherwood**, the Royal Naval Reserve centre, a mixture of brick buildings and hutting. The Nottinghamshire TA Handbook for 1950 lists the proposed new TAC on **Triumph Road,** next to the Raleigh factory, and to be provided in 1990 with an anti-terrorist blast-wall, but not the slightly later TACs in **Wigman Road, Bilborough** [1957], or **Hallcroft Road, Retford** [1956] [*p105*], found to be necessary for the development of increasingly sophisticated equipment which was to have far-reaching implications for the training of skilled personnel in appropriately-designed buildings.

RETFORD, the front block of the 1950s building, similar to Newark's extension

105

CHAPTER 5
The Fieldwork Survey

Introduction: background to the Survey

The impetus for the survey originated in the Defence of Britain Project, in which the present author had been involved as a volunteer co-ordinator. The Project was set up to record military structures from the twentieth century throughout Britain, and relied on individuals recording sites, and reporting them to a central clearing house for inclusion in a national database. A thesaurus of terms was compiled, but nothing remotely prescriptive was sent out. This meant that a wide range both of structures, and of building-functions was recorded. Contributors in several areas included drill halls in their returns, chiefly because of their secondary role as Home Guard bases in WWll. There appeared to be no literature on drill halls; conservation bodies, whilst having some interest in the topic, had little information, and it began to become apparent that, in many cases, their survival was threatened. This threat applied as much to active sites, quickly becoming redundant in the post-Cold War thaw, and to older, long-abandoned former drill halls. Many in both categories occupied prime building land, and, more-importantly, could be defined as brown-field sites. It seemed desirable that some record be made to record those that remained, to list those which had already gone, and to take some sort of snap-shot of the current situation in order to inform future decisions on preservation. The present author and his wife, therefore embarked on such a survey early in 2001, fortunately having little idea initially, of the scope. It has entailed travelling to almost every town in Britain over the last five years, a thoroughly delightful experience in itself, and has revealed a remarkable incidence of drill hall survival, but also apparently unaccountable instances of their sad demise. The Gazetteers list every example visited or for which references were discovered. The astute reader will notice that no end-date for the survey is ever registered, for it quickly became apparent that the process is endless. Fresh examples surface all the time, and are added to the list. This chapter and the Gazetteers can claim to be no more than depictions of the situation at a particular moment in time. More will be said about that later.

Methodology

No two drill halls, or later [post-1947] TA Centres are the same, although many share similar characteristics. They seldom feature in architectural guides, town-trails, military, especially regimental, histories, or Sites & Monuments Records [SMRs]. At some times in our history, notions of security have promoted a certain coyness about including them in directories, or even, on town maps. It was therefore decided to visit every likely location in order to find surviving structures, or to find out whether or not there had ever been a drill hall in a particular place, and if there had been, what had happened to it. The likely locations were initially identified in a number of ways:

1 **Ray Westlake's books** on the Rifle Volunteers, Volunteer Engineers & Artillery, cadet units, and others, all detailed in the Bibliography, have been useful in locating those places at which volunteer units were based. Added to these is the series on Yeomanry Regiments produced by the Army Museums Ogilby Trust. For the location of units at particular times during WWl, Brigadier James's book is invaluable.

2 The periodic **Territorial Force Lists** detail all the volunteer units, right down to individual company level, distinguishing between the base for such a unit, and outlying drill stations at which components or detachments, may have met to drill in smaller units. The TF List for 1914 has been used as it was at that moment that volunteer forces were at their most numerous. The premise that drill halls would most likely be found at those places designated as bases for squadrons of yeomanry cavalry, for companies of infantry, or for complete units of

engineers, gunners, army service corps or field ambulances became the single most important criterion for checking out a location. For the most part, this strategy worked. There were places which, for whatever reason, might have been expected to have had a drill hall, and did not. Conversely, there were drill stations which were not expected to have had drill halls, but did. Generally, however, in round about 99 cases out of 100, the premise held good.

3   A succession of re-organisations of the County Territorial Associations into small regions, and then, again into larger ones, has meant that many **TA Records** have disappeared. Nevertheless, approaches to the regional Reserve Forces & Cadets Associations [RFCAs] have proved extremely helpful, especially in identifying premises given up in the TA cuts of the 1950s and 1960s. Chief Executives, Secretaries, Administrative and Estates Officers have kindly often made information available where it existed.

4   The problem of TA records is clearly not a new one. In 1958, the War Office sent out a circular to County Associations in order to be able to compile a historical review of TA Centres. An incomplete record of the **Review** is held at The National Archive at Kew, and there are startling differences across associations, which reflect not only the pressure on over-worked County Secretaries, but also the evident lack of local knowledge, which is completely understandable when people were moving around the country. One secretary explains that his predecessor carried everything in his head, hardly surprising as he had another job, and ran the family business as well. Another complained about 'silly season tasks' being undertaken in the summer when there was so much more to be done with camps to organise and suchlike. Such reactions are reflected in the quality of the responses. Secretaries were asked to say how many TACs there were in each of their counties' locations in 1910 and in 1933. Much time must have been devoted to sorting out the places which rightly belonged in their lists, and those that appeared to have migrated across the country. The Derbyshire Secretary was mystified by the inclusion of

NEWMARKET, the Victoria Drill Hall

Coedpoeth in his list. No doubt, the Denbighshire Secretary would have been equally mystified, had he had the time to notice its omission from his own schedule. Thus places fell through the net. Some Secretaries simply wrote 'no knowledge' down the 1910 column, and completed the 1933 one to the best of their ability. Others went into enormous detail. Kent's return runs to nine pages with addresses and occupying units. Sussex completes the basic questionnaire quite adequately, and then appends four extra sheets with every range, indoor and outdoor, armoury, store, PSIs' quarters, vehicle shed, and saddle-room. If they used a room in a school once a week, then that is recorded with the amount of rent payable. So we learn, for instance, that the school at Hadlow Down cost the TFA 1/6 per night, from November 1909, but had been given up by 1933. This level of detail shows us that the TF had 17 separate premises in Brighton alone in 1910. On the other hand, information from Surrey is particularly sparse. Only four locations are admitted in 1910, and six in 1933, none with any detail. The column for comments contains only the words 'No Record' and twenty sets of ditto marks. The return for Leicestershire is no better. A similar range of returns can be seen for Scotland: Lanarkshire supplies enormous detail, Argyllshire lists all its drill stations, but Berwick, Selkirk & Roxburgh, would clearly rather not have been bothered. Whilst both Glamorgan and Monmouthshire included some very useful building dates and suchlike, Flint and Denbigh struggled to confirm the basic existence of centres. There are also, inevitably, a number of anomalies, and downright inaccuracies, which raise more questions than answers. Clearly there is so much scope for further research. One day we may know why Newmarket's Victoria Drill Hall, stylistically datable to the late nineteenth century, seems not to have existed in 1910 [*p107*], and is officially dated 1938, when there has been a company of the Suffolk Regiment based in the town from at least 1889. Or why it is that there is no local knowledge of there ever having been a drill hall in Porthcawl, when the 1958 Review records that the TA presence ceased only in 1928. A summary of the 1958 Review is shown in Table 1 below.

5   Norman Litchfield's comprehensive **The Territorial Artillery**, with its unit lineage has proved invaluable in tying down start dates for some 1930s drill halls as it logs both conversions to artillery, and the formation of new AA gun or searchlight units.

6   Some areas, with their own **local records**, on the other hand, were made much more straightforward. The Yorkshire & Humberside RFCA forwarded requests for information to Major Tony Podmore, who has already produced a family tree for Yorkshire's volunteer forces, unusually, it must be said, recording the locations of all units. Some TA/TF Associations have produced their own lists of units and venues at different times, notably 1908 and 1950. Some produced histories for the golden jubilee year, 1958. Perhaps more will appear in the forthcoming centenary year.

7   There were other useful sources which must be mentioned here. Copies of the **Territorial Magazine**, in its various forms, mention individual TACs, and their occupants. A number of other printed sources are listed in the Bibliography.

The major focus of the survey, however, was on the ground. Where addresses or clear locations were available, then enquiries were easier. Otherwise, then, a range of strategies came into play: Kelly's Directories, 25" OS maps, usually second editions dated around 1912-20, and local histories. Public Libraries and Museums were usually immensely helpful. If they, themselves, did not know then they usually knew someone who did. The list of acknowledgements must represent a roll-call of many of the nation's most knowledgeable local historians. Our last resort was often the most effective: stopping pensioners in the street and asking them if they remembered a drill hall in town. Many had joined up there in 1939, or their fathers had in 1914, or had enjoyed social occasions there. Even on quiet Sunday mornings there was usually a Last of the Summer Wine group sitting in the sun in an otherwise deserted market-place, only too happy to help, with a bit of nostalgia thrown in. In cities, of course, where populations are more transient, this last approach seldom bore fruit.

1958 War Office Historical Review of TA Centres in UK

	1910	1933	1958
ENGLAND			[comments]
Bedfordshire	6	8	
Berkshire	13	11	
Cambridgeshire	4	6	
Cheshire	30	18	
Cornwall	21	16	
Cumberland & Westmorland	28	23	
Derbyshire	2	10 + 6	5 in Derby
Durham	18	11	
Gloucestershire	16	6	
Hereford, Radnor & Brecon	6	6	
Hertfordshire	32	15	2 in St Albans
Kent*	61	48	
Leicestershire**	2	6	
Lincolnshire	4	17	
London	52	37	
Middlesex	18	17	
Northamptonshire***	2	10	
Northumberland	42	22	
Nottinghamshire	13	8	
Oxfordshire	17	9	
Shropshire	11	7	
Staffordshire	14	-2,+15=27	-2,+14 =39
Suffolk	12	12	
Surrey	4	6	
Sussex****	156	40	
Warwickshire	10	15	
Wiltshire	4	16	
Yorkshire ER	22	10	
Yorkshire NR	23	20	
Yorkshire WR	19	25	

missing: Bucks, Devon, Dorset, Essex, Hants & IoW, Isle of Man, Lancs, Norfolk, Somerset, Worcs;

* [only actual drill halls recorded]
** [1910 list not known]
*** [inc Huntingdon & Pboro]
**** [inc. ranges, sheds, houses etc]

SCOTLAND

Aberdeen, Banff & Kincardineshire	53	25
Angus	7	8
Argyllshire	30	23
Ayrshire	22	16
Berwickshire & Roxburghshire	2	2
Dumfries & Galloway	23	12
Dunbartonshire	12	11
Fife	20	14
Lanarkshire	17	12
Perthshire	20	17
Renfrewshire	6	6
Stirlingshire, Clackmannan & Kinross	17	1

missing: Caithness & Sutherland, Ross & Cromarty, Orkney & Shetland, Western Isles, Inverness;

WALES

Caernarvonshire & Anglesey	2	10
Cardigan, Carmarthen & Pembrokeshire	9	8
Denbigh & Flintshire	8	11
Glamorganshire	14	23
Merioneth & Montgomeryshire	20	4
Monmouthshire	9	15

Some thousands of such random encounters were bound to throw up the occasional, apparently serendipitous, bulls-eye. One evening in Wilton near Salisbury we stopped a gentleman to enquire about Wilton's drill hall. He was unable to help, but it turned out that many years previously he had been adjutant of a TA battalion of the Lancashire Fusiliers, and described how he paraded the entire battalion of 600 men inside the enormous drill hall at Bury. Similarly, we were surprised to be told by a school crossing-patrolman in Shotts that his son was the person who had bought the old drill hall, demolished it, and built a new house for his family on the site. Even television had its part to play. One edition of *Flog It* featured Eldred's, the auctioneers, selling antiques from their Auction House in the drill hall at Plympton, a site which the almost-completed survey had, hitherto, failed to identify. In many cases, as we have seen, librarians put us in touch with their local history expert, and it was these men and women who were often able to tell us of buildings which had been gone for two or three generations. For it would appear that many drill halls ceased operating in the years after WWl. The 1958 Review, incomplete as it was, showed that whilst some areas had actually increased numbers of locations over the years, on balance, a clear decrease from 951 active drill halls in 1910, to 648 in 1933, was evident. There are certainly towns where there has been no active drill hall in living memory.

Results

The data gathered in the fieldwork survey demonstrates just what a rich seam of architectural heritage has been mined. Of the two and a half thousand or so sites investigated around seven eighths yielded premises used by the volunteer forces, and two thirds of those are still standing. These results are shown in Table 2 below.

Nearly 500 drill halls were activated in the period up to 1900. Whilst around a third of these were adaptations of existing buildings, the rest were purpose-built, and, on average, around Britain, at least half of each of these categories survives. The middle period, from 1901 to 1945, with around 1300 examples, contains two specific building periods of particularly high productivity: the first around the establishment of the Territorial Force in 1908, and the other covering the re-armament period of the later 1930s. Differences are evident here between England on one hand with fairly equal representation across both phases, and Scotland and Wales, on the other, where very little new building appears to have taken place in the pre-WWll years. In fact, of the 114 drill halls built between 1900 and 1945 in Scotland, only six can be dated to the late-1930s, with a similar proportion in Wales. From this period, around two-thirds in England, and well over half in Scotland and Wales have survived. In the post-WWll period, with around 230 examples, there is an even higher survival rate: over 90% in England and Wales, and 100% in Scotland. Of the 300 or so sites additionally investigated, around 20% of them are barracks of the Regular Army, only included in the figures if specifically used by the TF, like High Wycombe, or by the TA, as at Lincoln or Reading. Premises used by the Militia, or by the Yeomanry prior to 1860, are included in the count. Another group included in the Gazetteers, but excluded from the totals will be those locations expected to have a drill hall but, for whatever reason, not doing so. Thus Cromer is not counted, but Melton Constable is. The balance of the 300 additional sites, however, about half, are those where there are references in the literature, but nothing proved on the ground. It is wholly conceivable that a good few of these, with deeper digging, may yet produce evidence of the existence of a drill hall, even one which may survive.

FIELDWORK SURVEY OF DRILL HALLS commenced 2001

	EXTANT	DEMOLISHED	TOTAL
ENGLAND			
PERIOD to 1900	309	167	476
PERIOD 1901-1945	584	397	981
PERIOD 1946-2000	168	8	176
TOTALS	1061	572	1633
ADDITIONAL SITES INVESTIGATED			230
			1863 TOTAL
SCOTLAND			
PERIOD to 1900	108	28	136
PERIOD 1901-1945	115	73	188
PERIOD 1946-2000	35	0	35
TOTALS	258	101	359
ADDITIONAL SITES INVESTIGATED			40
			399 TOTAL
WALES			
PERIOD to 1900	29	7	36
PERIOD 1901-1946	78	44	122
PERIOD 1946-2000	11	2	13
TOTALS	118	53	171
ADDITIONAL SITES INVESTIGATED			29
			200 TOTAL

GRAND TOTALS:	SITES EXTANT:	1437
	SITES DEMOLISHED:	726
	SITES INVESTIGATED:	2462

A number of factors such as unavailability of information, wholesale re-development on the ground, or the re-naming of streets and the re-numbering of houses, have sometimes made it impossible in the time available to verify a particular building's existence. Such instances add up to about one in twenty of the sites investigated. Another factor is the very short occupation-spans of some premises, set against the often long gaps between map revisions or official surveys. Many of the premises, for instance recorded in the 1958 Review as being in use in 1910 but not in 1933, will have, quite likely, ceased operation in 1918. Others, not in use by 1910, will have appeared, as many others did by 1914, and could well have gone out of use by 1920, thus appearing in neither snap-shot. There will, most probably, have been similar occurrences at other times throughout the last 150 years. It is, of course, impossible to say how many have been missed, as fresh examples continue to appear. Each fresh discovery is investigated, on the ground, and information as to current status is incorporated into the Gazetteers as soon as is possible. This is a continuous process which renders the Gazetteers instantly out-of-date, but only in regard to a tiny proportion of sites. At the time of publication, the Gazetteers are totally up-to-date, but some of the above statistics may not be, but may still be taken as reasonably accurate indicators of survival rates and building periods.

Analysis
National differences across England, Scotland and Wales with respect to building policy have already been referred to, but another aspect illuminated by the Survey has been differences across county associations. Some of the differences are obvious. Small, predominantly rural counties like Berkshire, Bedfordshire and Herefordshire, for instance, have small numbers of sites. Larger, but still sparsely-populated counties like Cambridgeshire or Norfolk will still have few sites, mainly located in the market towns, with a quarter of Norfolk's locations in Norwich itself. The conjunction of large area, low density of population in rural areas, and lack of large centres of population as well, results in large numbers of drill stations. The most obvious illustration of this is the Highlands of Scotland, where 45 confirmed drill halls, several of which were, incidentally, no more than huts, were, in 1914, supplemented by 115 drill stations, located in farms, village-schools, large houses

and so on. Only the presence of the city of Norwich, distinguishes Norfolk, with over fifty drill stations, from such an area in its lack of nodal points. The corollary to all this is the relative density of drill halls in urban areas, Liverpool being a good example of a provincial city with, in 1914, accommodation for six whole battalions of infantry, plus yeomanry cavalry, engineers, gunners, service corps and medical units. Other industrial cities sustained similar levels of provision.

Most of the above is entirely predictable. It is, perhaps, the inter-War years where there are some surprises to be seen. The invasion coast stretching from Dorset to Kent might have been expected to have undergone some modernisation in the years leading up to the outbreak of WWll, but barely a dozen new drill halls were built in the entire coastal strip in the decade 1931-40. During those years, roughly sixty new drill halls were built on Merseyside, in the Birmingham conurbation, and in London [defined as the area now within the M25]. In short, they were built where the right recruits could be found in numbers, and for an army which would fight wherever it was directed. Another factor was the new responsibility of the TA for air defence. If the bomber was to get through, as the prevailing wisdom maintained, it would be with a view to neutralising industrial production by destroying the factories, and undermining the morale of their workers. This meant attacking the cities, so that's where the new AA units were formed.

Findings with reference to survival are sometimes difficult to interpret. Shropshire seems to have been victimised, with 11 out of the sixteen pre-WWl drill halls gone. Cornwall, on the other hand, enjoys, over-all, a survival rate of over 85%. This may well prove to be related to rates of economic development, re-generation etc. and it may be only a matter of time before Cornish drill halls suffer the same fate as those of Shropshire. However, this appears not to be borne out in Kent, where one might expect rapid re-development to have swept away vestiges of Victorian life, but over 60% of Kent's drill halls survive. Cities are just as difficult to call. Whilst Bristol, Cardiff, Derby, Aberdeen and Plymouth have lost most of their drill halls for one reason or another, Southampton, Edinburgh, Norwich and

Birmingham have retained most of theirs. Whilst some particular losses may be attributed to specific agents: the Luftwaffe, T Dan Smith, or expanding supermarket chains, many of these disparities have no logical explanation outside the world of paranoia.

However rosy the situation may be painted by these findings, there is every indication that the future holds many threats to the continuing survival of these monuments. There appear to be few developers with the vision to re-cycle old buildings which present difficulties. For every Elsfield Hall, on the Oxford ring-road, imaginatively transformed into spacious, light, open-plan offices, there is a Trowbridge or a Stourport, flattened for new-build housing, because it's easier, but, above all, cheaper to start from scratch rather than to convert. At Elsfield Hall, the insertion of a mezzanine floor, and a large, stained-glass window in one gable end, do little to compromise the building's integrity, being well-nigh invisible from outside. The conversion of Lincoln's nineteenth-century drill hall to a high-quality performance venue, with public spaces for hire, has ensured that a building with important local significance, has gained a new lease of life, and a high-level quality of life at that. Examples at Yorkhill Parade, Glasgow, at Houghton-le-Spring, at Kings Heath, Birmingham, and, to a lesser extent, at Macclesfield, show that it is possible to convert many of these buildings into apartments. Other schemes from Fort Picklecombe to the Woolwich Arsenal have shown that military buildings do not automatically exclude themselves from such treatments. They may, just be a bit more demanding, but then may produce more worthwhile results. Let us hope that there are not too many spaces needing watching, in the near future.

GAZETTEER
Introduction

The GAZETTEER consists of three sections: England, Scotland and Wales. There are included, almost 1900 sites in England, nearly 400 in Scotland & just under 200 in Wales. These are listed alphabetically by town, with region, county or unitary authority in brackets. If the town-name is in *italics*, this means either that the building has been demolished, or there is no evidence of there ever having been a dedicated or even designated drill hall there. When a town with multiple sites has any surviving buildings at all, then its name will be in plain text.

If the site has been photographed by the author, this is shown by 'P'; if the site has been visited by the author, then a 'V' is shown; if a building has been demolished, but the author has archive photographs, then 'A' is shown; if there is a current Territorial Army Centre, then 'TAC' is shown, and 'ACF' or 'ATC' for a cadet centre.

In each entry, **bold** is used to denote buildings which were surviving when surveyed by the author since the start in 2001;

this is no guarantee of the building's continued survival. More information on this issue is in Chapter 5, where the reader may also find a discussion about the sources of information, and the dating of buildings.

Below each entry, marked ¶ is a schedule of Volunteer, TF or TA units stationed in that location at particular times. The 1914 date is universal as this appears to be the heyday of volunteer units. Additional dates are used in some cases, either to exemplify particular conditions or trends, such as pre-WWll or post-1947 re-organisations, or to clarify specific local arrangements. The 1914 schedule is complete, whereas the other dates are samples.

The term 'TAC' is used, following TA custom, for post-1947 buildings, and the generic 'drill hall' is used for all others.

It must be stated, once more, that this list, even with 2500 entries, cannot be complete, and the author is always delighted to be told of omissions and errors.

A-Z Gazetteer: England

A

Abingdon [Berkshire]; V
*1 Abbey Close, drill hall; demolished for supermarket, c1980s;
¶ In 1914, drill station D Sqdn. Berks Yeomanry; base F Coy. 4 Bn. R Berkshire Regt

Abridge [Essex]; V
there was never a dedicated building in the village;
¶In 1914, drill station for E Coy. 4 Bn. Essex Regt;

Accrington [Blackburn with Darwen]; PV [p115]
*1 Abbey St, Orderly Room of 5 Bn. E Lancs Regt. in 1914; no building traced;
*2 Argyle St, **Drill Hall**, pre-1900; large, 8-bay hall with timber trusses shaped gable over doorway; low indoor range at right-angles to hall; Nissen hut in compound; officers' mess demolished for new use as haulage yard;
¶ In 1914, base for F Coy. 5 Bn. East Lancashire Regt;

Acocks Green [Birmingham]; V
*1 Stockfield Rd; ex-TAC [RAMC]; site became Car Showroom, then Mecca Bingo;

Acton [Greater London]; PV ACF
*1 Horn Lane, Engineer House, Middlesex Yeomanry drill hall, pre-WWl; latterly REs; large detached Victorian house, demolished 2001; c1990s Cadet Centre;
*2 Ravenscourt Park, Stamford Brook Lodge; drill hall, demolished soon after 1920;
¶ In 1914, HQ+C-H Coys. 10 Bn. Middlesex Regt [Ravenscourt Park];

Aintree [Liverpool]; PV TAC [p115]
*1 Long Lane, Aintree Barracks, **TAC**, opened 1982 in a converted bakery; low, glass-fronted, yellow-painted, block with projections & turret; gabled sheds to rear;

Alderney [Channel Islands]; ACF
*1 Ollivier Street, Arsenal, HQ Royal Alderney Artillery & Engineer Militia in 1911; the Arsenal & Store Establishment within the defended perimeter of **Fort Albert** includes artillery gun-sheds, barracks and store-houses, part converted into flats;

Aldershot [Hampshire]; PV TAC
*1 Redan Road, drill hall; in 1914, Redan Hill; demolished c2002;
*2 Seeley House, Malta Barracks; **HQ RFCA South-east**; main block + yard with garages, c1980s;
¶ In 1914, drill station for B Sqdn. Hampshire Carabiniers, & for A Sqdn. Surrey Yeomanry; base for E Coy. 4 Bn. Hampshire Regt; Hampshire Bde. Coy. Wessex Divnl. Transport & Supply Column ASC [Redan Hill];

Alford [Lincolnshire]; PV
*1 **Corn Exchange**, 1856, in use by Rifle Volunteers 1892; in 1900 this was not a Company base;
*2 South St, ["South end" in 1913 Directory], **Drill Hall** c1900 cf Spilsby & Horncastle; hall with indoor range along one side, & 2-storey admin block across the back; not in use in 1933; now bric-a-brac dealers.
¶ In 1892, base for H Coy, 1 Vol. Bn. Lincolnshire Regt;
¶ In 1914, drill station for B Sqdn. Lincolnshire Yeomanry, [Louth]; & base for F Coy. 5 Bn. Lincolnshire Regt.

Alfreton [Derbyshire]; PV
*1 Hall Rd, group of government buildings- police, court etc; a 1937, drill hall-style building, very similar to Eckington; long front range, garages etc behind lateral hall; plaque records '9 Training Bn. RASC 1939-45'; recorded as TA in 1958 Review;
¶ In 1914, drill stations B Sqdn. Sherwood Rangers, E Coy. 5 Bn. Sherwood F'sters;

Alnmouth [Northumberland]; PV

Duke of Northumberland Bty, 1861, for Northumberland [Percy] Artillery Volunteers;

Alnwick [Northumberland]; PV TAC [*3] [p67]

*1 Bondgate Without, Militia Barracks, c1857; demolished for Playhouse cinema by early-1920s; formerly 3-storeyed, 4-bay, plain block;

*2 Fenkle St, **Drill Hall**, built as a bank c1840; obtained by the Duke in 1887, for 2 Northumberland [Percy] Artillery Volunteers; subsequently used by units of the Northumberland Fusiliers & their successors; imposing 3-storey house with Greek Doric porch, giant pilasters, balustrade etc;

*3 Lisburn Terrace/Clayport, **TAC**, c1980s; in use by infantry unit; 2-storey, split-level, brick main building with pitched roof; yard with garages etc;

¶ In 1914, drill station for C Sqdn. Northumberland Hussars; HQ+D & F Coys.7 Bn. Northumberland Fusiliers;

Altcar see Formby;

Alton [Hampshire]; PV

*1 56 The Butts, **Drill Hall Cottage**, now private residence, formerly caretaker's house; drill hall, pre-WWl, demolished c1960s; housing on site;

¶ In 1914, drill station B Sqdn. Hants Carabiniers; base H Coy.4 Bn. Hants Regt;

Altrincham [Trafford]; V

*1 Ashley Road, *Hale*, drill hall, in use 1914; demolished for supermarket;

¶ In 1914, base for A Coy. 5 Bn. Cheshire Regt;

Amble [Northumberland]; PV

*1 Percy Street, drill hall, c1860; the Primitive Methodists took over the old drill hall in Percy Street in 1885; this may be the present Trinity Methodists;

*2 Church St, drill hall, built as Old Assembly Rooms, taken over by the Volunteers around 1887; a gymnasium, reading-room & billiard room were included; this subsequently became Ballantyne's Workshop, & by 1985 had been demolished for housing;

¶ In 1914, base for E Coy. 7 Bn. Northumberland Fusiliers;

Ampthill [Bedfordshire]; PV ACF

*1 Woburn St, **Drill Hall**, in use 1910 & 1933; 2-storey front block with hall behind, brick with stone dressings;

ACCRINGTON, timber trusses and roof-lights in this substantial hall

AINTREE, the Mothers Pride bakery converted into a TAC in 1982

garages etc to rear; possible 1930s remodelling;

¶ In 1914, drill station C Sqdn. Bedfordshire Yeo; base E Coy. 5 Bn. Beds. Regt.

Andover [Hampshire]; V
*1 East Street [next to school, S end], drill hall, 1908; in 1976, in use as Country Bumpkins' Club; burned down, now car-park;

¶ In 1914, drill station for C Sqdn. Hampshire Carabiniers; base for D Coy 4 Bn. Hampshire Regt; HQ Coy. Wessex Divnl. Transport & Supply Column ASC; drill station 3 Wessex Divnl. Field Ambulances RAMC;

Arnold [Nottinghamshire]; PV
*1 Arnott Hill Road, **Drill Hall**, c1914; 2-storey front block & hall with curved roof; indoor-range behind; in use until 1980s, then dental laboratories, now printers;

¶ In 1914, drill st'n B Sqdn. S Notts Hussars; base F Coy. 8 Bn. Sherwood F'sters

¶ In 1949, base for one Bty. 528 [Notts] LAA [Mobile] Regt. RA, TA;

Arundel [Sussex]; PV
*1 Castle Gardens, **Drill Hall**, pre-1900; built by Henry,15th Duke of Norfolk; in 1914, recruiting office; 2-storey rectangular block, formerly with arched entrance on west; corrugated-iron roof; now terrace of four cottages;

¶ In 1914, base for F Coy. 4 Bn. Royal Sussex Regt;

Ashbourne [Derbyshire]; PV
*1 Cokayne Ave, **Drill Hall**, c1938; 2-storey front-block with little behind; 2-storey staff house up Hall Lane, appears earlier; in use during WWll; Bankcroft Centre;

¶ In 1914, drill station for C Coy. 6 Bn. Sherwood Foresters.

Ashburton [Devon]; PV ACF
Love Lane, **Drill Hall**, possibly post-WWll; no mention of location 1897 or 1935; small, single-storey, gabled hall in blockwork;

¶ In 1914, drill station for H Coy. 5 Bn. Devonshire Regt;

Ashby-de-la-Zouch [Leicestershire]; PV
*1 Range Road, **Drill Hall**, c1914, in use up to early 1950s; hall, indoor range, & offices fronted by semi-detached houses, one of which may have been the orderly room; barred sash windows appear original; now art rooms for High School;

¶ In 1914, base for A Coy. 5 Bn. Leicestershire Regt.

Ashford [Kent]; PV TAC
*1 Norwood St, drill hall, 1888; demolished c1960s for Police Station; on 1907 map but not on 1933; prior to provision of drill hall, drills held from 1860 in Railway Station Yard, with Armoury under Assembly Rooms in Park St, and Club-room in Elwick Rd opposite cattle-market; Yeomanry Drill Instructor resident in Sussex Ave. 1899;

*2 Newtown Rd, drill hall, 1910; used by PO as sorting office 1976-86, then demolished for housing; in use by Fortress REs + Buffs in 1911;

*3 43 Marsh St. in use 1910;

*4 Cattle Market recorded as base for Buffs 1910;

*5 Wellesley Hall recorded as base for RAMC 1910;

*6 Rowcroft Barracks, **TAC**, c1970s; square admin. block with extensive garaging to rear; island site in new Rail Link works;

¶ In 1899, base for H Coy. East Kent Volunteers

¶ In 1908, base for D Sqdn. Royal East Kent Yeomanry; HQ+E F & H Coys. 5 Bn. The Buffs; drill station for F Coy. Kent Cyclists Bn; HQ+B Section 2 Home Counties Field Ambulance RAMC;

¶ In 1914, base for D Sqdn. Royal East Kent Mounted Rifles; base for No.2 Works Coy. Kent RE Fortress; HQ+E F & H Coys. 5 Bn.E Kent Regt; drill station for F Coy. Kent Cyclists Bn; HQ+B Section 2 Home Counties Divnl. Field Ambulance RAMC;

¶ In 1933, base for 386 Bty. 97 [Kent Yeomanry] Field Regt. RA [TA];

¶ In 1939, base for 306 Bty. 75 HAA Regt. RA [TA];

Ashington [Northumberland]; PV TAC
*1 Back Woodhorn Road, **TAC**, in use by infantry unit; brick, 6-bay, 2-storey block c1970s; coloured royal coat-of-arms over door; entrance framed in stone; set in yard; may be on site of earlier building;

¶ In 1914, drill station for C Sqdn. Northumberland Hussars; base for B Coy. 7 Bn. Northumberland Fusiliers;

Ashton-in-Makerfield [Wigan]; PV [p117]
*1 Armoury Bank, **Armoury**, pre-1900; 2-storey main block, with hall cross-wing; additions to rear; stylistically could date back to 1870-80s; interesting window detail in hall: portholes, lancets etc. giving mediaeval flavour; now Indian restaurant [the *Lal Quilla* which is the local name of the Red

Fort at Delhi] & hairdressing salon;

¶ In 1914, base for A Sqdn. Lancashire Hussars;

Ashton-under-Lyne [Tameside]; PV TAC [*p35*]

*1 Old Street, **Armoury**, pre-1900; gabled, red-brick, two-storey front block with tower, oriel, semi-circular stair turret, shield over doorway etc; large hall behind, then smaller hall, & two staff houses to Cotton Street; garage block built onto side; plaque to ex-Terrier; in use by infantry & RAMC units;

*2 Audenshaw, in use 1941;

¶ In 1914, HQ+A-H Coys. 9 Bn. Manchester Regt;

¶ In 1941, base for 88 AT Regiment RA [TA] [Audenshaw, *Ardenshaw* in Litchfield]

Aspatria [Cumbria]; PV ACF

*1 Outgang Road, **Drill Hall**, by 1910; 2-storey front block hall, & garage, now undertakers', sideways on to road; beyond, 2-storey, detached house for drill instructor; all rendered & painted;

¶ In 1914, base for H Coy. 5 Bn. Border Regt;

Astley Bridge **[Bolton];** V

no evidence for dedicated building; Parochial Hall in Newnham St. [demolished] was built for ex-servicemen by Major Hesketh the owner of the large mill; in 1914 Captain Hesketh commanded F Coy. 5 Bn; probability that they drilled in Mill, then moved to Parochial Hall;

¶ In 1914, base for F Coy. 5 Bn. Loyal North Lancashire Regt;

Aston **[Birmingham];** V ACF

*1 Witton Lane, ex-TAC; disposed of 1970s; used by BT, then demolished; part of Aston Villa FC car-park;

*2 Aston Manor [begun 1618], used by TF; demolished;

¶ In 1914, HQ+A & C-H Coys.8 Bn. Warwickshire Regt; HQ+HQ Coy. South Midland Divnl.Transport & Supply Column ASC.

Atherton **[Wigan];** V

*1 Mealhouse Lane, drill hall, by 1908; demolished, car-park;

¶ In 1914, base for H Coy. 5 Bn. Manchester Regt;

Attleborough [Norfolk]; PV

*1 Queens Close, **Drill Hall**, pre-WWl; now flats; 2-storey front block with bow windows, flagpole over door; rear extensions; small-arms range destroyed;

¶ In 1914, drill station for A Sqdn. Norfolk Yeo; & base E

ASHTON-in-MAKERFIELD, the Armoury, now named for Delhi's Red Fort

BANBURY, the 1950 extension to the drill hall of 1857 & 1938

Coy. 4 Bn. Norfolk Regt;

Avonmouth [Glos]; V
*1 Ermine Way, drill hall on 1980s street map; demolished, now empty plot;

Axbridge [Somerset];
no known drill hall; Bromswald House; HQ of 13 [Somerset] Bn. Home Guard
¶ In 1914, drill station for B Sqdn. N Somerset Yeomanry;

Axminster [Devon]; PV
*1 Chard Street, **Drill Hall**, in use till 1935; 18C Meeting House, L-shaped with Gothic windows & blocked coach-arch; now Coopers Cottages;
*2 Silver Street, **Drill Hall**, 19C; built from stones from Newenham Abbey; 3-storey block with coach-arch; now carpet warehouse-Thos. Whitty House;
¶ In 1914, drill station B Sqdn. 1 Devon Yeo; base H Coy. 4 Bn.Devonshire Regt;

Aylesbury [Buckinghamshire]; PVA TAC
*1 Walton St, Lucas's Pawnbroker's shop, recruiting office for Bucks. Yeo 1914; reference to 'depot' in Walton Street 1914;
*2 **14 Temple Square**, HQ of Bucks. Reserve Bn. 1914; 2-storey house, of early-19C, with consoled doorcase, & dentillated frieze; now Dentist's;
*3 Kings Head PH used as billet for Yeomanry 1914;
*4 George Hotel [aka Bodega] acquired as TA HQ. 1921; demolished 1935;
*5 Oxford Road, **TAC**, 1934; imposing 2-storey, L-shaped office/ accommodation block round hall; another, smaller 2-storey block across yard with garaging; two staff houses; Buckingham Swan badge over main entrance; apparently about to be demolished for housing, 2005;
*6 Walton House, Walton Road, Home Guard HQ 1940; [24 Walton Street home of Col. Viney, CO of Bucks. Reserve Bn. 1930-4]; Walton Ho. was pulled down in 1945-6 for Technical School; site now housing;
¶ In 1914, base B Sqdn. Buckinghamshire Yeomanry; HQ+D Coy. Ox & Bucks. Ll;
¶ In 1947, base for 299 Field Regiment [Bucks Yeomanry] RA [TA]

Aylsham [Norfolk]; PV ACF
*1 Cawston Road, **Drill Hall**, c1930s; now offices &

community use; single-storey front block with hall behind, & garage to rear;
¶ In 1914, drill station for C Coy. 5 Bn. Norfolk Regt;

B

Bacup [Lancashire]; V
*1 Yorkshire Street, Corn Mill, drill hall; demolished for health centre;
¶ In 1914, base for H Coy. 5 Bn. East Lancashire Regt;

Bakewell [Derbyshire]; PV ACF
*1 Castle Street, **Cadet Centre** in part-demolished drill-hall complex in use until 1950; mainly single-storey building + garage remain;
¶ In 1914, base B Sqdn. Derbyshire Yeomanry, & D Coy. 6 Bn. Sherwood Foresters

Bamber Bridge [Lancashire]; PV
*1 School Lane, **Drill Hall**, pre-WWl; shell of ruinous building;
¶ In 1914, drill station for 11 Lancashire Bty. 2 West Lancashire Bde. RFA; drill station for C Coy. 4 Bn. Loyal North Lancashire Regt;

Banbury [Oxfordshire]; PV TAC [p117]
*1 Oxford Rd, **Drill Hall**, c1857 [stone], 1938 & 1950; stone barn & former-stabling of farm [Easington Hall, now hotel]; extensions of 1938 include large vehicle shed with single-storey offices, & garages attached to barn; new building 1950, 2-storey messes, offices, armoury etc. either end of hall, range alongside & garage-block;
¶ In 1914, base for D Sqdn. QOOH; base for C & G Coys. 4 Bn. Ox. & Bucks. LI;
¶ In 1971, HQ of QOOH;

Barking [Greater London]; PV
*1 Longbridge Rd, site of drill hall [marked on 1970 map]; double-fronted, detached,1930s/50s house on corner of Brixham Gdns; possibly staff house;
¶ In 1950, HQ+P & R Btys. 482 HAA Regt. [Essex] TA
*2 Queens Rd, site of drill hall, demolished for road widening;
¶ In 1914, D Coy. 4 Bn. Essex Regt;
¶ In 1950, detachment D Coy. 4 Bn. Essex Regt. & WRAC units;
*3 Ripple Rd, ex-**TAC**; 3-storey, L-shaped block

incorporating garages; c1930s;

¶ In 1950, 919 Coy. AA Command Transport.

Barnard Castle [County Durham]; PV ACF[***2**]

*1 South Durham Militia Barracks, 1864; taken over by DLI in 1870s, in use until 1930s, when sold to town; mostly demolished 1960s for re-building of Old Folk's Home; stone gatehouse, guardroom, & boundary wall remain; plaque records history of units occupying site;

*2, Stainton Camp, one mile NE of town; WWll buildings: guardroom, stores, Nissen huts & accommodation, now industrial estate; recently-built ACF residential centre;

¶ In 1914, base for F Coy. 6 Bn. DLI;

Barnet [Greater London]; PV TAC [***2**]

*1 Barnet Barracks, in use pre-WWl; demolished for Shires Shopping Centre;

*2 St Albans Road, **Drill Hall,** 1936 datestone; tethering rings for Yeomanry horses in situ; 2-storey front block with higher, glazed stair-tower; in use by RLC [V];

¶ In 1914, base B Coy. 7 Bn. Middlesex Regt.; & base D Sqdn. Hertfordshire Yeo;

Barnsley [South Yorkshire]; PV TAC [*p120*]

*1 Eastgate, **Drill Hall,** 1896; now military publishers' offices; ornate 2-storey front block in millstone grit with gable, crest & arched doorway; behind, large lateral hall; to rear, outbuildings, garages etc round courtyard;

*2 Wakefield Road, **TAC,** c1980s in use; large 2-storey hall & offices, separate garage block;

¶ In 1914, drill station for C Sqdn. Yorkshire Dragoons; and base for C & E Coys. York & Lancaster Regt.

Barnstaple [Devon]; PVA TAC

*1 Trinity Street, HQ+Stores, Yeomanry, in 1897; not traced;

*2 19 Bear Street, HQ Yeomanry [Royal North Devon Hussars], in 1910; 2-storey terraced property, now a Chinese restaurant;

*3 2 Castle Street, HQ Volunteer Bn. Devonshire Regt. 1897; still in use by 6 Bn. in 1923; later became fire station, then offices, now demolished for public garden;

*4 Tuly Street, HQ B Sqdn. R N Devon Hussars in 1914; shown in old photograph of building with inscription over door; no local knowledge, and impossible to locate this building in Tuly Street even prior to re-development;

*5 Oakleigh [and Ashleigh] Rd [now Barbican], Fortescue Lines, **TAC,** part in use by 1914, the rest pre-1935; two large 2-storey blocks, one with crest over entrance, & stair-tower in international modern style; the other, with pedimented windows, elaborate door-case, balustrades etc. figures in WWl photographs;

¶ In 1906, HQ 4 Volunteer Bn. Devonshire Regt. at 2 Castle Street;

¶ In 1914, HQ+B Sqdn. N Devon Hussars; HQ+A & H Coys. 6 Bn. Devonshire Regt;

¶ In 1930, 384[South Molton] Bty. [Howitzer], 96 Royal Devon Yeomanry Field Bde. RA [TA], & 6 Bn. Devonshire Regt. both based at Oakleigh Road;

¶ In 1947, 628 Heavy Regt. RA [TA];

Barrow Gurney [Somerset]; PV

*1 behind Fox & Goose PH on main road [A38]; **Drill Hall;** single-storey, flat-roofed building now in use for accommodation, but traces of range found on conversion; adjacent garage in similar style, recent & non-military;

¶ In 1914, drill station for D Sqdn. North Somerset Yeomanry;

Barrow-in-Furness [Cumbria];

*1 The Strand, drill hall, in use by 1891; demolished, site redeveloped as a super-market;

*2 Holker Street; **Drill Hall,**1927; inscription on door-case: "Company Headquarters 4th Battalion The Kings Own Regt."; 2-storey front block with gables, pediment over archway, rusticated brickwork, & stone facings; behind, large, lateral hall, yard & garages etc; in use by infantry unit

¶ In 1914, drill station C Sqdn. Westmorland & Cumberland Yeo; base Nos.7 & 8 Coys. Lancashire & Cheshire RGA-Defended Ports; base for C-F Coys. 4 Bn. Royal Lancaster Regt; drill station for 3 West Lancashire Divnl. Field Ambulances RAMC;

Barton-upon-Humber [North Lincolnshire]; PV

*1 Market Place, in use by volunteers,1892; not identified;

*2 Butts Road, drill hall demolished, gate-piers remain; in use 1933; also mentioned in connection with Home Guard in WWll; ACF huts in use 1961;

¶ In 1914, drill station D Sqdn. Lincolnshire Yeomanry, & base E Coy. Lincs. Regt; ¶In 1933, base for machine-gun platoon, 5 Bn. Lincolnshire Regt;

BARNSLEY, the drill hall is now offices of a military publishing company

BATH, the drill hall of the Somerset Light Infantry in the Lower Bristol Road

Basingstoke [Hampshire]; PV ACF
*1 Sarum Hill, drill hall, on 1896 map; demolished, but possible garage block still stands, fronting Flaxfield Road; ***2** Goat Lane, **Drill Hall**, pre-WWl; 2-storey front block + basement, hall behind; indoor range along W side; back of hall now adapted to use as garage; original roof-trusses & pendant lights; used by infantry, 1930s;
*3 Penrith Road, **Drill Hall**, pre-WWl; 3-storey admin. block with hall alongside [cf Camberley]; used by artillery, 1930s; ¶ In 1914, drill station for B Sqdn. Hampshire Carabiniers; base for Ammunition Column, Hampshire RHA; base for G Coy. 4 Bn. Hampshire Regt; base for G Coy. 9 [Cyclist] Bn. Hants Regt; drill station 3 Wessex Divnl. Field Ambulances RAMC;

Bath [Glos]; PV TAC
*1 Upper Bristol Road, Albion Buildings & drill hall in use 1897; site cleared for redevelopment as garage;
*2 Upper Bristol Rd, Ivy Lodge, **Drill Hall**, RAMC HQ in 1914; square 19C house; hall behind with stepped facade, ventilators & roof-lights; recently in use as a garage; stone perimeter wall around site;
*3 Upper Bristol Rd. Victoria Drill Hall, in use by REs in 1914; no trace, but Victoria Business Centre may occupy site;
*4 Upper Bristol Road, Harding House, **TAC**, in use by Signals unit; refurbished, 4-storey, stone-built, 19C Albion Cabinet Works;
*5 Lower Bristol Road, **Drill Hall**, HQ SLI in 1897; corner of Brougham Hayes, large stone-built hall,10 bays long, with side doors, & half-moon windows at each end; currently derelict [*p120*];
*6 16 York Street, Recruiting Office in 1914;
¶ In 1914, HQ+A Sqdn. N Somerset Yeomanry; HQ+1 Field Coy. Wessex Divnl. REs. [Upper Bristol Road]; HQ+A & B Coys. 4 Bn. Somerset LI. [Lower Bristol Rd]; base for A Section 2SW Mounted Bde.Field Ambulance RAMC;

Batley [West Yorkshire]; PVA TAC
*1 Bradford Road, drill hall, 1870; demolished 1992; formerly 2-storey stone-built front block with tower; large, lateral hall behind; closed 1965; later Fire Museum; Harrison House, now church, possibly former PSI's house;
*2 Intake Lane, **TAC**; apparently late 19C village school, Z-plan with new block to side, & garages to rear;

¶ In 1914, base for G Coy. 4 Bn. KOYLI

Battersea [Greater London]; PV TAC [2] [*p102*]
*1 15 Battersea Square, no such address now;
¶ In 1914, D & E Coys. 1 Bn. London Regt. [Royal Fusiliers] cf Handel St.
*2 27 St Johns Hill, Battersea, **Drill Hall**; ornate, castellated, red brick & stone, 3-storey front block with arch to courtyard and garages etc;
¶ In 1903, HQ 4 Vol. Bn. East Surrey Regt.
¶ In 1914, HQ 23 Bn. London Regt
*3 St Johns College, Battersea; no longer in existence;
¶ In 1914, A Coy. 10 Bn. Middlesex Regt;

Battle **[Sussex];** V
*1 North Trade Road, drill hall, by 1909; used as recruiting office in WWl; demolished for Telephone Exchange;
¶ In 1914, base for B Coy. 5 Bn. Royal Sussex Regt.

Beaminster [Dorset]; V ACF
*1 Barrowfield Road, **Cadet Centre**; no location given in 1911; the drill hall may have occupied this site; a house, currently being built [2004] may now occupy this plot;
¶ In 1914, drill station for A Coy. 4 Bn. Dorsetshire Regt;

Beamish **[County Durham];** V
there appears never to have been a dedicated building here;
¶ In 1914, base for E Coy. 8 Bn. Durham LI;

Beccles [Suffolk]; PV ACF
*1 Peddars Lane, **Drill Hall**, pre-WWl; house, small hall, garage & orderly room along road frontage, backed by large, lateral hall;
¶ In 1914, base for D Sqdn. Suffolk Yeomanry; drill station for 1 Suffolk [Howitzer] Bty. 3 East Anglian [Howitzer] Bde. RFA; base for B Coy. 5 Bn. Suffolk Regt; & drill station for F Coy. 6 [Cyclist] Bn. Suffolk Regt.

Beckenham **[Kent];** V
*1 Elm Cottage, High Street, in use 1908; in 1910, Instructor's house & drill ground;
*2 87 Charleville Road, [Village Way by 1915], drill hall became Pavilion Picture Theatre, still in existence on 1933 OS map;
¶ In 1908, base for D Coy. 5 Bn. Royal West Kent Regt;
¶ In 1914, base D Coy. 5 Bn. Royal West Kent Regt; base C Coy. Kent Cyclist Bn;

Bedale [North Yorkshire]; PV
*1 Bridge Street, **Drill Hall**, pre-1900; now furniture store; gabled hall onto street;
*2 Black Swan Yard, reported by RFCA, no trace;
*3 Benkhill Drive, Cadet Centre at school;
*4 Leeming Bar, cadet centre reported by RFCA;
¶ In 1883, base for B Coy, 1Vol. Bn. PoW Yorkshire Regt;
¶ In 1908, drill station for H Coy. 4 Bn. PoW Yorkshire Regt;

Bedford [Bedfordshire; PVA TAC
*1 Kempston Barracks,1875 Cardwell depot of Bedfordshire Regt; Keep/Armoury & front range in yellow brick & stone dressings; Freemasonry HQ + offices;
*2 Ashburnham Road [west side], drill hall, 1911; demolished when replaced by ***5** incorporating stone crest;
*3 Ashburnham Road [off east side, Woburn Road]; **Drill Hall**, brick & stone T-shaped front block with Bedfordshire Regt. crest on gable; hall behind; yard with stabling, garages etc. to rear; c1930s; now religious centre;
*4 Gwyn Street, [corner of Greenhill, Hassett & Gwyn Streets] drill hall in use by 1914, demolished 1963 for bus station redevelopment; 2-storey front block with hall behind; arched entrance in side to Greenhill Street, immediately behind front block;
*5 Kempston Rd, **TAC** 1983; in use; two new TACs in 1933 in 1958 Review [***3**&?];
¶ In 1914, HQ & A Sqdn. Bedfordshire Yeomanry, [Ashburnham Road]; HQ & 1 Field Coy. Divisional. RE , [Ashburnham Road]; HQ & Nos 1 & 2 Sections East Anglian Divisional. RE Signal Coy. [Ashburnham Road]; HQ & A Coy. 5 Bn. Bedfordshire Regt. [Gwyn Street]; B Section Eastern Mounted Bde. Field Ambulance RAMC;

Beeston [Nottinghamshire]; PV TAC
*1 Broadgate, **Drill Hall**, 1939; square, 2-storey block, with garages etc. to rear; in use by EM Universities OTC; similar in style to Bulwell & Carlton;
¶ In 1949, base for one Bty. 577 LAA/SL Regt. [The Robin Hoods, Foresters]; HQ + Sqdn. 5 AA Group [Mixed] Signal Office Sqdn. Royal Corps of Signals;

Belford **[Northumberland];** V
no location identified; it may be, in the absence of a dedicated drill hall, that the late-17C Blue Bell Hotel served

BERWICK-upon-TWEED's Ravensdowne drill hall

the purpose; alternatively, the main focus was **Wooler**;

¶ In 1914, base for C Coy. 7 Bn. Northumberland Fusiliers;

Bellingham [Northumberland]; M

*1 Main Street, **Armoury House**; late-Victorian 2-storey terraced cottage used as Armoury; rifles were issued from here to TF troops; drilling probably took place in Town Hall or at Hesleyside Hall, where the Charltons were squires;

¶ In 1914, base for B Coy. 4 Bn. Northumberland Fusiliers;

Belper [Derbyshire]; PV ACF

*1 Clusters Road, **Drill Hall**,1902; 2-storey gabled office/stores, house & hall;

¶ In 1914, drill station A Sqdn. Derbys Yeo, & base F Coy. 5 Bn. Sherwood F'sters;

Benenden **[Kent];**

*1 Instructor's House, Armoury & rifle range in 1910; not traced;

Bermondsey [Greater London]; PV TAC [RMR]

*1 2 [Old] Jamaica Road, **Drill Hall**; 3-storey Edwardian house, & 4-storey pre-WWl admin block, joined by c1970s residential block; garages/other outbuildings to side & rear; War Memorial to Queen's Royal West Surreys; now RMR, London;

¶ In 1914, 22 Bn. London Regt. [The Queen's]

Berwick-upon-Tweed [Northumberland];

*1 Ravensdowne, **Drill Hall**, pre-1900; in use RLC unit; 5-bay, stone front block, with central square 3-tier gate-tower; to left of tower, 2-storey house with bow-window to side; to right of tower, single storey orderly room; behind, long hall with buttresses along sides [*p122*];

*2 Magdalene Fields, site of hutted & tented training camp from 1909; now holiday village;

¶ In 1914, drill station for A Sqdn. Border Horse; base for G & H Coys.7 Bn. Northumberland Fusiliers;

Bestwood Village [Nottinghamshire]; PV

*1 Bestwood Lodge, 1862-5 by Teulon; **Drill Hall** added to side of main house for use by the Volunteers; 7 bays, single-storey, with stepped gable; now a hotel; 25 yard Range in Park, 1914;

Beverley [East Yorkshire]; PVA TAC [*1]

*1 Norwood Far Grove, Wolfe Armoury, **TAC**, c1990; pagoda-style hall + garages;

*2 Victoria Barracks, built c1870 as Cardwell depot of East

Yorkshire Regiment + militia; formerly had Keep; in use until 1961, demolished 1981 for supermarket;

*3 Railway St, in use 1914 as Yeomanry HQ;

*4 Albert Terrace, **Drill Hall**, now Health Centre; built as Foundation School, & taken over by 2 Vol. Bn. East Yorks. Regt. in 1890; house & lateral hall behind; later adapted as fire-station;

*5 Wilbert Lane, drill hall, 1862; in use until 1890;

*6 Toll Gavel, drill hall in 1878;

*7 Walkergate, drill hall in late 19C;

¶ In 1914, HQ & B Sqdn. East Riding Yeomanry; base for F Coy. 5 [Cyclist] Bn. East Yorkshire Regt; & base for C Coy. 5 Bn. Princess of Wales Own Yorkshire Regt.

Bexhill-on-Sea; PV ACF

*1 The Downs, [Down Road], **Drill Halls**, by 1909; two similar castellated 2-storey front blocks, each with a large hall behind; that on the west has a Royal Sussex Regt. badge over the archway; both front blocks are turreted, provided with arrow-slits, battlements, etc; each with annexe along the side, that on the east being two-storey; behind the halls are further two-storey blocks; adjoining is a leisure centre; the west hall is a cadet centre; all in red brick with stone dressings [pp166,124];

¶ In 1914, drill station for D Sqdn. Sussex Yeomanry; base 6 Sussex Bty. 2 Home Counties Bde. RFA; drill station for 2 Field Coy. Home Counties Divnl. RE; drill station for B Coy. 5 Bn. Royal Sussex Regt.

Bexleyheath [Kent]; PV TAC [*2]

*1 96 Broadway, drill hall in use 1933; demolished for re-development c1970s;

*2 80-104 Watling St, **TAC,** opened 1984 by Princess Anne**;** two-storey block; over door, crest of Royal West Kent Regt; signals units;

¶ In 1933, 207 Bty. 52 [Kent] Medium Bde. RA [TA];

Bicester [Oxfordshire]; V

*1 Chapel Street, drill hall; not in use 1933; demolished for housing: Bryan House;

¶ In 1914, drill station for B Sqdn. QOOH; and for G Coy. 4 Bn. Ox & Bucks. LI;

Bideford [Devon]; PV ACF

*1 Torridge Hill, **Drill Hall**, by 1897; two-storey front block with hall behind; in use as warehouse;

*2 Abbotsham Road, ACF Centre;

¶ In 1914, drill station D Sqdn. N Devon Hussars; base C Coy. 6 Bn. Devonshire R;

Biggleswade [Bedfordshire]; PV

*1 Shortmead St, 1930s; 2-storey front block, United Services club- 'Millennium House'; to rear, earlier hall + large garage/workshop demolished 2004;

¶ In 1914, base B Sqdn. Bedfordshire Yeomanry, & D Coy. 5 Bn. Bedfordshire Regt.

Bilborough [Nottinghamshire]; PV TAC

*1 Wigman Road, **TAC**, 1957; T-shaped, two-storey, block, with garages etc;

Billingborough [Lincolnshire]; V

*1 Public Hall in use 1892; TA in Old Village Hall in 1961; demolished; ACF in Birthorpe Road until 1984, moved to The Hut, Buckminster House, 1984;

*2 indoor range built by volunteers in cellar of Ringston Hall, [Manor Farm] 1913;

¶ In 1892, base for H Coy. 2 Vol. Bn. Lincolnshire Regt;

Bilston [Wolverhampton]; PV [*p124*]

*1 Mount Pleasant, **Drill Hall** in use by 1912, until c1962; 2-storey, 3-bay, front block with elaborate stucco decoration & pediment; large arched windows & door, all with key-stones; gabled roof with two dormers to front; hall behind; now night-club;

¶ In 1914, base for G Coy. 6 Bn. South Staffordshire Regt

Bingham [Nottinghamshire]; V

only tentative identification of location; probably former school;

¶ In 1892, officer + 30 men of E Coy. 4 Vol. Bn.

¶ In 1914, base for A Sqdn. South Nottinghamshire Hussars; drill station for E Coy. 8 Bn. Sherwood Foresters;

Bingley [West Yorkshire]; PV ACF

*1 Hillside Road, **Cadet Centre**, former TA hut; only ever huts on site since 1930s;

¶ In 1914, base for H Coy. DoW West Riding Regt.

Birchington [Kent];

*1 Drill Hall recorded 1910 in use 5 Bn. Buffs; recorded 1914 as drill station 4 Bn;

Birdwell [South Yorkshire]; PV ACF

[Hoyland Common to WO]

*1 Sheffield Street, **Drill Hall**, by 1910; now shooting club,

BEXHILL-on-SEA's second drill hall used by the artillery and engineers

BILSTON's Mount Pleasant drill hall, now a night-club

with underground range, & cadet centre in new hut to rear; hall to road frontage with turrets; orderly room, armoury etc. as annexes to hall; cf Treeton

¶ In 1914, base for H Coy. 5 Bn. York & Lancaster Regt.

Birkenhead [Wirral]; PV TAC

*1 Harrowby Road, **Drill Hall**, RE unit; 59a & 79a in use 1914; long, 2- & 3-storey, brick front block, with lateral hall behind; in front a parade-ground, behind, a large yard with modern garages; the whole is on an island site surrounded by Victorian terraced housing on all four sides;

*2 Grange Road West, **Drill Hall**, c1900; large hall to street frontage, with symmetrical facade: 2-storey house/office buildings at each end, then square, castellated towers, then gable-end of hall with central porch; hidden by modern sign-board is badge of 1st Volunteer Bn. Cheshire Regt; indoor range along back wall; small yard with two garages- one now Boxing Club; main hall now Sports & Fitness Centre; staff recall recent Centenary, c2000;

¶ In 1901, six Coys. of 1 Volunteer Bn. Cheshire Regt. at Birkenhead;

¶ In 1914, base D Sqdn. Denbighshire Hussars; base Cheshire Field Coy. Welsh Divnl. REs [59a Harrowby Road]; HQ+A-D Coys. 4 Bn. Cheshire Regt. [Grange Rd]; base Welsh Border Mounted Bde. & Welsh Divnl. Transport & Supply Columns ASC [both 79a Harrowby Road];

Birmingham [see also Acocks Green, Aston, Handsworth, Harborne, Kings Heath, Saltley, Sheldon, Sparkbrook & Sutton Coldfield]

Birmingham city centre; PV

*1 Great Brook Street, barracks, demolished;

*2 Thorp Street, **Drill Hall**, pre-1880; long front block to street with two castellated gate-towers; one is now part of Chinese Restaurant, other leads into shell of hall now car-park; walls of hall open to sky; on gate-tower legend: "1st Warwickshire Rifle Volunteers"; sold 1970s [p125];

¶ In 1914, base for A Sqdn. Warwickshire Yeomanry; Southern Command Signal Coys. RE [Gt. Brook St]; HQ+A-H Coys. 5 & 6 Bns. Warwickshire Regt.[Thorp St]; HQ+A & B SWections, 1 South Midland Mounted Bde. Field Ambulances RAMC [Gt Brook St]; HQ+A-C Sections, 2 South Midland Divnl. Field Ambulances RAMC [Gt Brook St]; 1 Southern General [Gt Brook St] & South Midland

Clearing Hospitals RAMC; drill station for B Sqdn. Worcestershire Yeomanry;

Birstall [**West Yorkshire**]; V

*1 reference to drill-shed 'returned to industry & ND Vols. in James Hall';

¶ In 1860, the 30th Corps of West Yorkshire Rifle Volunteers formed at Birstall, but had disappeared by 1873;

Birtley [**County Durham**]; PV ACF

*1 Birtley Lane, drill hall, by 1896, demolished in 1970s to build sheltered housing; cadet hut & modified, original indoor range on site still; maps show that a range of buildings including a cottage, fronting the street, was extended, between 1919 & 1939, to form an L-shape, by the addition of a large hall;

¶ In 1914, base for D Coy. 8 Bn. Durham LI;

Bishop Auckland [**County Durham**]; PV TAC

*1 St Andrews Road, **Eden Armoury**, c1930s; 2-storey front block with hall behind; yard with garages etc; early CO's arms over door,+ other relics of DLI past;

¶ In 1914, HQ+A & B Coys. 6 Bn. DLI;

Bishops Stortford [**Hertfordshire**]; PVA

*1 Silver Leys, Hadham, **Barracks** of 1 Herts. Light Horse; the building is a car-stereo workshop; a long, low single-storey hall, with pillared porch; the portion to the right was stabling & retains tethering rings;

*2 Market Square, **Drill Hall**, 1906; health centre; large hall with arched doorway; inscription "Drill Hall" & datestone; single-storey extensions behind; possible staff house: "The Lodge";

¶ In 1860, 6 Corps. Hertfordshire Rifle Volunteers, re-designated C Coy. 1 Volunteer Bn. Hertfordshire Regt. 1887.

¶ In 1914, drill station for C Sqdn Essex Yeomanry [based at Waltham Abbey] base for C Coy. 1 Bn. Hertfordshire Regt.

Bishops Waltham [**Hampshire**]; PV ACF

*1 Victoria Road, **Drill Hall**, 1914; hall of six bays on one side, & four on other; foundation stone, March 1914, built for Hampshire RGA;

¶ In 1914, drill station for B Sqdn. Hampshire Carabiniers; drill station for No.3 Coy. Hampshire RGA-Defended Ports; drill station for C Coy. 4 Bn. Hampshire Regt;

BIRMINGHAM's Thorp Street drill hall, whose empty shell is a car-park

Blackburn [Blackburn with Darwen]; PV TAC
   *1 50 King Street, in use 1914; street derelict;
   *2 Canterbury St, **Drill Hall**, pre-1889; in use by RAMC & signals units; stone-built, 2-storey, 5-bay front block with central doorway with gable above, backed by castellated tower; badge of 2 Lancs Rifle Volunteers set in gable; hall sideways on to street; yard with garages etc. to rear;
   *3 Moss Street, Somme Barracks, **TAC**, in use by infantry unit; rectangular block with hipped roof; set in yard with garages etc; cf Bolton, Nelson Street;
   ¶ In 1859, 2 Corps Lancs Rifle Volunteers formed; 1 Vol Bn. E Lancs Regt. in 1889;
   ¶ In 1914, HQ+4 Lancashire Bty. 1 East Lancashire Bde. RFA [King Street]; HQ+A-E Coys. 4 Bn. East Lancashire Regt;

Blackpool [Blackpool]; PVA TAC
   *1 Yorkshire Street, **Drill Hall**, pre-1914; in use by 208 Field Ambulance RAMC; island site with 2-storey, bow-fronted orderly-room block, alongside large hall; on other side of hall, 2-storey front block with garage-block behind; all in red brick; half-moon window & pedimented doorway in front wall of hall; similar in rear;
   ¶ In 1914, drill station D Sqdn. Duke of Lancasters Own Yeo; base for 11 Lancs Bty. 2 West Lancs Bde. RFA [Yorkshire Street]; drill station G Coy. 5 Bn. R Lancaster R;

Blandford Forum [Dorset]; PV ACF
   *1 Market Place, **Town Hall/Corn Exchange**, 1734, in use as drill hall 1911; classical front with large hall behind;
   *2 Kingstone Close, ACF Centre;
   ¶ In 1914, base for C Sqdn. Dorset Yeomanry; base for H Coy. 4 Bn. Dorset Regt;

Blaydon [Tyne & Wear]; PV ACF
   *1 Blaydon Bank, **Drill Hall**, pre-WWl; stone-built, gabled hall to road; decorative details on pillars and gables; cadet hut to side over range; has been office/factory;
   ¶ In 1914, base for G & H Coys. 9 Bn. Durham LI;

Bletchley [Buckinghamshire]; PV TAC
   *1 Water Eaton Road, **TAC**, c1930s; 2-storey front block, with Buckingham Swan badge over main door; later garage/workshop blocks & staff house;
   ¶ In 1914, drill station for A Sqdn. Buckinghamshire Yeomanry;

Bloxwich [Walsall]; PV
   *1 1 Wolverhampton Road, Armoury, **Public Hall**, built 1857 [date-stone]; in use by Volunteers, referred to as Music Hall, 1900; large hall with annexes on each side, & single-storey block to rear; now gymnasium;
   ¶ In 1914, base for D Coy. 5 Bn. South Staffordshire Regt.

Blyth [Northumberland]; PV TAC
   *1 Quayside, **Drill Hall**, pre-WWl; 2-storey, 9-bay by 8-bay L-shaped front block with gablet over central arched doorway; hall within angle, with large, leaded ventilator in roof; then 2-storey house & extensive garaging; site fills whole block; at front, a garage/stable & outbuildings; now centrepiece of waterfront regeneration programme & called: Spirit of the Staithes;
   *2 Cowpen Rd, **TAC**, c1970s; square, steel-framed, 2-storey block with grey brick & glass infill; large brick & steel hall to side, & large yard with garages/gun-sheds; in use by RA unit;
   ¶ In 1914, base for No.4 Coy. Tynemouth RGA-Defended Ports; base for F Coy. Northern Cyclist Bn;

Bodmin [Cornwall]; PV TAC [***3**]
   *1 Militia Armoury in French chateau style, c1857; in use as Light Infantry Office & regimental museum;
   *2 Barracks, c1880, built as Cardwell depot of DCLI; currently [2004] being renovated as apartments;
   *3 7 Castle Canyke Road, **TAC**, 1958; two-storey front block with other buildings including garages, indoor-range etc;
   ¶ In 1914, base for D Sqdn. 1 Devon Yeomanry; HQ+E Coy. 5 Bn. DCLI;

Bognor Regis [Sussex]; V ACF
   *1 24 Bedford Street, drill hall, in use by 1931; demolished;
   *2 391 Chichester Rd. house, now extended & sold as private residence; ACF/ATC huts in use;
   ¶ In 1914, drill station C sqdn. Sussex Yeo; drill station G Coy. 4Bn. Sussex Regt;
   ¶ In 1931, 227 [FA] Signals Section & 4 Bn. Sussex Regt;
   ¶ In 1947, detachment 605 HAA [Mobile] Regt. RA TA;
   ¶ In 1950, C Coy. 7 [Cadet] Bn. Sussex Regt;

Bolton [Bolton]; PV A [***2** & ***3**] TAC [***5**]
   *1 The Haugh, off Bromwich Street, drill hall in 1909; road gone;

*2 Fletcher St, Workhouse, was HQ 2 Volunteer Bn. Loyals, in 1881; referred to as the Barracks, Fletcher Street, in 1914; long 2-storey block to street with pediment over entrance & archway through to yard behind; replaced by

*3 **Derby Barracks**, Fletcher St, 1937; one L-shaped, & one rectangular, larger, 2-storey block, set in a yard with garages to rear; the larger block has an off-centre, stone doorcase with inscription above: "5th Bn. The Loyal Regt. Derby Barracks 1937";

*4 Silverwell Street, artillery drill hall, built late-1880s; the complex included offices, canteen, messes, stores, a large drill hall, riding-school, stabling, & underground range; subsequently, after 1967, a sports centre, then demolished for housing & offices;

*5 Nelson Street, **TAC**, c1970s; in use by RA unit; large rectangular block with hipped roof, set in yard with garages etc; cf Blackburn, Moss St;

*6 Orlando Street, drill shed reported 1867;

¶ In 1914, base B Sqdn. Duke of Lancasters Own Yeo; HQ+18-20 Lancs. Btys. & Ammunition Column 3 E Lancs Bde. RFA [Drill Hall]; HQ+A-C & E Coys. 5 Bn. Loyal North Lancs Regt; base C Section 1 E Lancs Divnl. Field Ambulances RAMC;

¶ In 1947, base for 253 Field Regt. [Bolton] RA [TA]

Booker [Buckinghamshire]; PV TAC

*1 Old Horns Lane, **TAC**, 1980s; 2-storey Z-plan offices; workshops, garages etc. in yard; in use by infantry & signals units; backs on to Wycombe Air Park;

Bootle [Sefton]; PV A[*3] TAC [*2]

*1 99 Park Street, drill hall in use 1914 & 1947; demolished for housing;

*2 Strand Road, **TAC**, c1970s; 2-storey square block + garages;

*3 105 Fernhill Road, in use as staff housing in 1930s;

¶ In 1914, HQ+A-D & F Coys. 7 Bn. Kings Liverpool Regt; [Park Street]

¶ In 1947, 40 [The Kings] Bn. Royal Tank Regt;

Boston [Lincolnshire]; PV ACF

*1 **Corn Exchange**,1772, HQ rifle volunteers in 1892;

*2 Main Ridge, **Drill Hall**, built 1869 for artillery volunteers, now snooker-hall; Dutch-gabled roof to hall + tall gun-store the length of the hall;

*3 Main Ridge, **Drill Hall**, 1913, 2-storey front block & hall behind, very similar [mirror-image] to Spalding; designed by Scorer & Gamble; single-storey lean-to, & garages to rear; opened by General Bethune [DG TF];

¶ In 1892, base for C Coy. 2 Vol. Bn. Lincolnshire Regt [1]; base for 1 Position Bty. Vol. Artillery [*2];

¶ In 1914, drill station B Sqdn. Lincs Yeo, & base C Coy. 4 Bn. Lincs Regt. [*3];

Botley [Hampshire]; V

local information suggests no dedicated location; Market Hall, 1848; RBL tin hall built 1923, rebuilt 1984; maybe a public house; all are possibilities;

¶ In 1914, base for C Coy. 4 Bn. Hampshire Regt;

Bourne [Lincolnshire]; PV

*1 North St, drill hall in existence late 19C, provided with gymnasium & recreation room; early in 20C it was a skating rink; possibly the hall behind the British School, used as WWl hospital;

*2 Cavalry House, South St, home of Thomas Rawnsley, wool-merchant, who raised a troop of Yeomanry Cavalry in Napoleonic times; 2-storey, stone-built 18C house;

*3 St Peters Rd, Bourne Institute, founded 1896; the basement rifle-range used by Bourne Volunteer Training Corps during WWl; now Pyramid billiards club;

*4 West St, Recruiting Office for 2 Volunteer Bn. Lincs Regt; now shop [sign remains];

*5 Manor Road [sic] in use by 4/6 Lincolns & ACF in 1961;

*6 Church Lane, St Peter & St Paul Church Hall rented by ACF, c1980s;

¶ In 1860-73, 15 Corps of Lincolnshire Rifle Volunteers formed in Bourne;

¶ In 1914, drill station A Sqdn. Lincolnshire Yeomanry, & F Coy. 4 Bn. Lincs. Regt;

¶ In 1961, base for 1Plat. A Coy. 4/6 Royal Lincolns, & ACF [Manor Road];

Bournemouth [Dorset]; PVA ACF/ATC [*5 & *8] [pp35,37]

*1 177 Holdenhurst Rd, **Drill Hall**,1895; built for HQ 4 Volunteer Bn. Hampshire Regt; later inscription on front of building reads HQ 5/7 Bn; large brick & stone, double-fronted block with bow-windows, arched entrance & oriel over; behind, large hall, & behind that, 2-storey cross-wing with garages, workshops etc; now used as auction house;

2 Lansdowne Rd, Victoria Drill Hall,1902; demolished for road-building & re-development; used by Artillery Volunteers;

3 Verulam Place orderly room of Hampshire Carabiniers, c1896;

4 Old Christchurch Road, Artillery Volunteer HQ in use c1870; demolished; marked on 1870 OS map as HQ 4 Hants. Artillery Volunteers;

5 Portman Road, Boscombe, Victoria **Drill Hall**, 1891; built as part of estate but adopted as a drill hall for G Coy. from the start; chapel-like building with elaborate pediment over entrance; possible indoor range along side;

6 Wimborne Rd, Winton, drill hall, 1869; built as mission hall & British School; used by Artillery Volunteers, 1896-1906; site now Old Fire-Station;

7 Bingham/ Wycliffe Roads, Winton, **Drill Hall**, 1906; used by Artillery Volunteers; then Boys Brigade HQ; gabled hall with gun-store built on corner;

8 Willsdown Road, ACF;

¶ In 1914, base D Sqdn. Hampshire Carabiniers; base 6 Hampshire Bty.3 Wessex Bde. RFA [Victoria Hall]; HQ+E-H Coys. 7 Bn. Hants Regt. [177 Holdenhurst Road];

Bovey Tracey [Devon]; PV ACF

1 High Street, **Town Hall**, used as drill hall,1910;

2 Station Rd, **Cadet Centre**; small hall & indoor range, post-WWll; on adjacent plot housing on site of Phoenix Hall, former drill hall;

¶ In 1914, drill station C Sqdn. Royal Devon Yeo; & for G Coy. 5 Bn. Devonshire R;

Bradford [West Yorkshire]; PV TAC

1 Manningham Lane, Drill Parade, **Bellevue Barracks**; early buildings +1960s; 1 & 2-storey blocks of modern offices etc + garages; 2-storey block backed by hall of c1910 vintage;

2 Valley Parade, drill hall marked on 1932 OS map; 1959 map marks this as TA Centre + further **TA building** on Burlington Terrace; in use by RA units until 1955, when sold; drill hall demolished for Sunwin Stand of football stadium; other building survives as garage;

3 Bradford Moor Barracks, vacated by regulars 1920, used by 70th [WR] Field Bde. RFA who added a riding-school, but returned to Valley Parade 1930s;

¶ In 1914, drill station for Yorkshire Hussars; HQ, 4 West

Riding Bty. & Ammunition Column, 1 WR Bde. RFA, [Valley Parade]; HQ, + A-H Coys. 6 Bn. Prince of Wales Own West Yorkshire Regt. [Belle Vue Barracks]

Bradford-on-Avon [Wiltshire]; PV [*p67*]

1 Silver St, **Armoury** in 1911; castellated, stone-built, front block dated 1881; it was used by the Volunteers & also by G & T Spencer's as an Ale & Porter Store;

¶ In 1914, base for G Coy. 4 Bn. Wiltshire Regt;

Braintree [Essex]; PV ACF [**3**]

1 Corn Exchange used prior to 1911, demolished;

2 Victoria St, **Drill Hall**, 1911; two-storey, T-shaped front block with hall attached; sold in 1963 & now community centre; nos. 18 & 20, opposite with Essex crests, were staff houses;

3 Coggeshall Road, acquired 1939 for site of new TAC, never built; hutted camp used by TA after 1963; now demolished for Kilkee Lodge nursing home; ACF uses garage [1980] & Nissen hut small-arms range on site;

¶ In 1914, base B Sqdn. Essex Yeomanry; F Coy. 5 Bn. Essex Regt.; & drill station C Coy. 8 [Cyclist] Bn. Essex Regt.

¶ In 1950, R Bty. 646 LAA Regt. [5 Bn. Essex Regt.]+ WRAC [Victoria Street]; 313 Sqdn., 134 [Essex] Construction Regt. RE [Coggeshall Road].

Brampton [Cumbria]; PV

1 35 Carlisle Road, **Drill Hall/Armoury**, in use by 1897; small hall sideways to street; now garage/workshop;

2 Crow Hall apparently used by Rifle Volunteers for social/fundraising events; connected with "Belted Will" masonic lodge;

¶ In 1860, 4th Corps Cumberland Rifle Volunteers formed here;

¶ In 1880, base for F Coy. 1 Cumberland Rifle Volunteers;

¶ In 1887, base for F Coy. 1 [Cumberland] Vol. Bn. Border Regt;

¶ In 1914, drill station for C Coy. 4 [Cum'land & West'land] Bn. Border Regt;

¶ In 1929, detachment of 4 Bn. still present

Brandon [Suffolk]; V

no location identified; possibly *Thetford* was used;

¶ In 1914, base for G Coy. 4 Bn. Norfolk Regt.

Brentford [Greater London]; V

1 The Butts, possibly site of drill hall;

¶ In 1914, base for B Coy. 8 Bn. Middlesex Regt.

Brentwood [Essex]; V

*1 Chestnut Grove, drill hall, 1935; sold for redevelopment, 1985; see **Warley** TAC;

¶ In 1914, drill station for D Sqdn. Essex Yeomanry; HQ 4 Bn. Essex Regt. & base for G Coy. 8 [Cyclist Bn.] Essex Regt.

¶ In 1950, Q Bty. 304 Fd. Regt. RA [Essex Yeo.]; HQ & R Bty. 563 LAA/SL Regt;

Bridgnorth [Shropshire]; V

*1 St Mary's Street, drill hall, demolished for housing- St Mary's Court, late-1960s to early-1970s; it was of two-storeys, brick & probably dated pre-1900; prior to demolition, used by ATC & as Boxing Club;

¶ In 1914, drill station D Sqdn. Shropshire Yeomanry; base F Coy.4 Bn. KOSLI

Bridgwater [Somerset]; PV TAC [*4]

*1 70 Friar Street, drill hall of SLI in 1914; demolished for housing, c1980s;

*2 Clare Street, drill hall of Yeomanry & ASC in 1914; redeveloped c1980s;

*3 Waverley Road, **Drill Hall**, c1935; now TS Blake- Sea Cadets; large hall; indoor range, & single-storey annexes, all within a compound;

*4 Carvers Road, **Drill Hall**, c1935 and later; HQ of Home Guard until March 1943; in use; 2-storey, gabled, front block with stone portico; 2-storey, flat-roofed front block with hall behind; two further halls + extensive garages, huts etc;

¶ In 1914, base for C Sqdn. West Somerset Yeomanry; base for C Coy. 5 Bn. Somerset LI; base for SW Bde.Coy. ASC Divnl. Transport & Supply Column;

Bridlington [East Yorkshire]; PV ACF

*1 Swindon Street, **Drill Hall**; pre-WWl, in use 1944; 2-storey front block with hall behind; garage doors at rear open onto Swindon Street;

¶ In 1914, base for B Coy. 5 Bn. Princess of Wales Own Yorkshire Regt; base for G Coy. 5 [Cyclist] Bn. East Yorkshire Regt.

Bridport [Dorset]; PV ACF

*1 Gundry Lane, **Drill Hall**, by 1911; now youth centre & ACF; 2-storey front block with hall behind, & yard to side

with garages etc;

¶ In 1914, drill station for A Sqdn. Dorset Yeomanry; base for Dorset Bty. 3 Wessex Bde. RFA; base for A Coy. 4 Bn. Dorset Regt.

Brierley Hill [Dudley]; V

*1 Hall Street, Armoury in 1900; demolished for Moor Shopping Centre, c1958;

*2 Temperance Hall recorded as HQ of Cadet Corps in 1914;

¶ In 1914, base for E Coy. 5 Bn. South Staffordshire Regt.

¶ In 1950, base for one battery of 643 LAA Regt;

Brigg [North Lincolnshire]; PV ACF

*1 Scawby Road, **Cadet Centre**,1993, on site of earlier drill hall, listed in 1961, probably dated back to WWl;

¶ In 1914, drill station for D Sqdn. Lincolnshire Yeo, & G Coy. 5 Bn. Lincs. Regt;

Brighouse [West Yorkshire]; PV

*1 84 Wakefield Rd, **Drill Hall**, pre-WWl; hall + mess block, & decorative baroque arch, [brought from redundant chapel] with inscription: '4 Bn. DoW West Riding Regt.'; adjacent garages ex-TA; all existed in 1996; since then, building encased in steel sheeting, and arch no longer visible;

¶In 1914, base for D Coy. 4 Bn. DoW West Riding Regt;

Brightlingsea [Essex]; PV

*1 Sydney Street, **Foresters' Hall,** in use c1914; gabled, brick hall, 2-storey cross-wing to Tower Street; this rear portion of structure now sailmakers; front two-thirds, still Foresters' Hall;

*2 High Street, **Drill Hall**, pre-WWl; cruciform hall & wings, with additions to rear; lately YMCA hall;

Brighton [Sussex]; PV TACs [*1 & *7] also see **Hove** [pp81,82];

*1 Lewes Road, Preston Cavalry Barracks, 18C-20C; hospital of 1793 extant; long pre-WWl range not on 1912 map, appears to be officers' mess-type building; 1980s **TAC** still in use; large yard with garages etc;

*2 117 Gloucester Rd, artillery **Drill Hall**, 1869; built for Sussex Volunteer Artillery; 2-storey central block with castellated parapet, flanked by, on one side a 2-storey house with eaves cornice; on the other side, an arched opening into the hall, now garaging, with large gates & similar eaves cornice to the house; Gloucester Mews, residential;

*3 Church St, **Drill Hall**, 1890; built for Sussex Rifle Volunteers; badge with Sussex martlets on front wall; elaborate stone, pedimented doorway; 2-storey, 11-bay symmetrical facade with 5 dormers in roof; large hall behind; now antiques warehouse;

*4 18 Montpelier Place, **HQ**, in use 1913; 18-19 stand as 19C semi-detached mansions;

*5 23 Gloucester Place, in use 1914;

*6 Queens Sq. **Drill Hall**, in use 1939; now Sussex Ice Rink, with adjoining house;

*7 198 Dyke Road, **TAC**, c1930s; large, 3-storey front block of 9 bays either side of a central entrance bay with elaborate stone porch; 19C villa to rear, with garages etc;

*8 85 Queens Rd. HQ from 1912;

¶ In 1914, HQ+A Sqdn. & drill station for B Sqdn. Sussex Yeomanry [Church St.]; HQ+1 & 2 Btys. 1 Home Counties Bde. RFA [Church Street]; HQ+1 Coy. Sussex RGA Defended Ports [117 Gloucester Road]; drill station for Home Counties Divnl. RE; HQ+1 Section Home Counties Divnl. Signals Coy. RE [23 Gloucester Place]; HQ+A-H Coys. 6 [Cyclist] Bn. Royal Sussex Regt. [18 Montpelier Place]; HQ+HQ Coy. Home Counties Divnl. Transport & Supply Column ASC [117 Gloucester Rd.]; 2 Eastern General Hospital RAMC [117 Gloucester Road];

Bristol City Centre; PV TACs [***7**, ***10**, ***11** & ***14**] [*pp63, 131,328*]

*1 St Michael's Hill; St Michael's Hill House, drill hall, in use by 1900, demolished after WWll bomb-damage, the site becoming part of the hospital; 3-storey brick private house with hipped roof & lantern, on E side of hill, & S side of Southwell St. with walled garden, taken over by Glosters between 1883 & 1900;

*2 Queens Road, Clifton; drill hall, in use 1914; rectangular hall 45x28m; demolished in early-1920s for Wills Memorial Building;

*3 32 Park Row; in use 1914; demolished, petrol station on site;

*4 St Georges; in use 1914; not found;

*5 Colston Fort, Montague Place, Kingsdown; in use 1914; earthen Civil War fort replaced by Colston's Fort House in 1823; plaque on flats records mobilisation of Gloucestershire Hussars in 1939, & destruction of fort [house] by bombing, 1940; now 1950s block of flats on site;

*6 57 Old Market Street, **Drill Hall**; imposing facade with Baroque gateway, coat-of-arms; large hall with clerestory windows & miniature range alongside; armoury at right-angles, fronts Jacob St; threatened with radical alteration for conversion to housing [*p131*];

*7 Horfield **TAC** 1930s; long, 3-storey front block with lateral hall behind; extensive yard with sheds & garage compound, huts & pair of staff houses;

*8 Whitefield Rd, Speedwell, ex-**TAC**, 1940; part-demolished & part converted for housing development; new, 2-storey Cadet Centre adjacent; surveyed by city archaeologist, prior to work commencing;

*9 2 Beaufort Road, Clifton; former **TAA Office**; 3-storey, double-fronted, Victorian house, now apartments; to rear, a block of apartments, possibly replacing TA buildings;

*10 Whiteladies Road, Artillery Ground **TAC**, in use RE unit + BU OTC; 2-storey, 1930s front block with RA badge over stone-dressed doorway; large lateral hall behind, with four annexes behind that; to one side, earlier drill hall now garages; range of later garages on opposite side of courtyard; original gate-piers with 'Artillery' on one & 'Ground' on other; attached to the earlier building, a 3-storey, gabled building with coach-arch to road;

*11 Winterstoke Rd [A3029] Bedminster, **TAC** in use by TA & RNR; imposing, 3-storey, 9-bay front block with Glos. Regt. crest, 1940 datestone, & two stone pilasters surmounted by Sphinxes; behind, large hall, yard with extensive garages, workshops & staff houses [now RNR];

*12 Headley Lane, Headley Park; TAC; demolished for housing, cadet hut;

*13 Bath Road, Brislington, Cadet Centre;

*14 Litfield Place, Dorset Ho. **Drill Hall**, in use by Royal Marine Reserves, built c1820-30; grand, 3-storey, stone house with recessed colonnaded front in unusual 1:2:3:2:1 pattern; RM crest over central column; brick-built drill hall & garages, below to side;

*15 Tackley Road, Purdown, hutted **Cadet Centre** & former TA Workshops; large 7-bay, range of shuttered garages, with hipped roof; now in private use;

¶ In 1914, base D Sqdn. N Somerset Yeo; base D Sqdn. Royal Glos Hussars [drill station at Horfield Barracks];

HQ+1 & 2 Glos. Btys. & Ammunition Col 1 S Midland [Glos] Bde RFA [Clifton]; HQ+1 & 2 Field Coys.S Midland Divnl. REs. [32 Park Row]; HQ+No.1Section S Midland Divnl. Signal Coys. REs. [32 Park Row]; HQ+A-E, G&H Coys. 4 Bn. Glos. Regt. [Clifton]; F Coy 4 Bn. Glos Regt. [St George]; HQ+A-H Coys. 6 Bn. Glos. Regt. [St Michaels Hill]; HQ+A B & C Sections 3 S Midland Divnl. Field Ambulances RAMC [Colston Fort]; 2 South Gen Hospital RAMC [Kingsdown];

¶ In 1947, base for re-constituted 312 Medium Regiment RA [TA];

Brixham [Devon]; ACF

*1 New Road, **New Market Buildings**, built 1886, used as drill hall;

2* 13 New Road, now shop, artillery HQ; 3* Mount Pleasant Quarry, ACF Centre;In 1902, base for 2 Coy. 1st Devon Vol. Artillery;

Brixton [Greater London]; PV TAC

*1 105 Holland Rd, became 105 Minet Rd; in use 1910; demolished for housing;

¶ In 1914, HQ, 15-17 Btys. Ammunition Column, 6 London Bde. RFA;

*2 132 Upper Tulse Hill, Brixton, **Drill Hall,** c1930s in use by RMP [V]; small square, Georgian HQ building; 2/3-storey c1930s admin & hall block;

¶ In 1914, base for A Coy. 5 Bn. East Surrey Regt .recorded as at Streatham;

Brocklesby Park [Lincolnshire]; V

*1 base for Earl of Yarborough's Lincolnshire Light Horse Volunteers [1867-87]; the Park was venue for exercises; the house had extensive 18C stabling etc;

Bromley [Greater London]; PV [p33]

*1 Beckenham Lane, Hill House, ex-**TAC**; former base of London Scottish; 2/3-storey Edwardian villa with conservatory & outbuildings; now converted to flats;

*2 East Street, **Drill Hall**; large hall, 1872 & 1890; attached 2-storey house/office with Dutch Gable end profile to one side, & 2-storey rectangular block across end; now PH;

*3 **Town Hall**, in 1906, basement used as drill hall; whole block converted to shops & housing;

*4 88 Tweedy Rd. recorded as 1910 base for A Sqdn. West Kent Yeomanry; home of drill instructor; demolished 1970s;

BRISTOL, the Old Market Street drill hall of the Gloucestershire Regiment

BRISTOL, Old Market Street prior to undergoing conversion to apartments

*5 3 West St. recorded as 1910 base for 5 Bn. Royal West Kent Regt; demolished for supermarket;

*6 Bromley Common, Yeomanry House recorded for 1933 in 1958 Review; possible location on Magpie Hall Lane where Slough Farm included West Kent Riding School, recorded in 1930 Directory & on 1933 OS map;

¶ In 1914, 5 Bn.HQ+A & B Coys. Royal West Kent Regt. [East Street]

¶ In 1933, HQ + A Coy. 5 Bn. Royal West Kent Regt; 314 AA SL Coy. RE [TA]; [East Street]; 387 Bty. 97 [KY] Bde. RFA [TA] [Yeomanry House];

Bromsgrove [Worcestershire]; PV

*1 Market Street, **Drill Hall**, pre-WWl; two-storey, red brick with stone dressings; castellated entrance with Worcestershire Regt. crest on gable; hall behind, + yard with garages etc; sold to local authority for Arts Centre, in early 1990s;

¶ In 1914, drill station B Sqdn. Worcestershire Yeo; base G Coy. 8 Bn. Worcs. Regt

Bromyard [Herefordshire]; PV ACF

*1 near church, **Drill Hall**, pre-WWl; two-storey, red-brick rectangular block;

¶ In 1914, drill station for F Coy. 1 Bn. Herefordshire Regt;

Brunswick [Manchester]; PV TAC

*1 Hyde Road, Ardwick Green, 1886, by Booth; **Drill Hall** in use by infantry unit; in stone, 3-storey symmetrical front with Norman details; tower with higher turret to left, large hall behind; later garages on one side; "Always Ready" legend over arch;

¶ In 1860, 20 Corps [4 Manchester] Lancashire Rifle Volunteers formed here;

¶ In 1888, 20 Corps became 5 Volunteer Bn. Manchester Regt; in 1908, 8 Bn;

¶ In 1914, HQ+A-H Coys. 8 Bn. Manchester Regt; HQ+15-17 Lancashire Btys. & Ammunition Column, 2 East Lancashire Bde. RFA;

*2 Belle Vue Street, **TAC**, c1930s; in use by RA unit; 2- & 3-storey front block with two stone doorcases; garages & gun-sheds, & then, beyond those, a detached hall;

Buckhurst Hill **[Greater London];** V

no location identified;

¶ In 1950, detachment of C Coy. 4 Bn. Essex Regt.

Buckingham [Buckinghamshire]; PV

*1 Hunter St, **Yeomanry House**, pre-1800; 3-storey early Georgian house with early 19C porch, & 2-storey extensions behind; to side, a 19C drill-hall or riding-school, & behind that, a courtyard with balcony over stabling etc; there was a barracks pre-1805; now university college;

*2 West St, **Volunteer Barracks**, early-19C; double-pile, stone-built domestic block, with stabling, cart-sheds etc.

¶ In 1914, HQ+A Sqdn. Buckinghamshire Yeomanry; base C Coy. Ox & Bucks LI;

Bude [Cornwall]; PV

*1 Neetside Centre, **Drill Hall**, pre-1900; now CAB Centre; large granite church-like hall with castellated porch;

¶ In 1914, base for H Coy. 5 Bn. DCLI;

Budleigh Salterton [Devon]; PV ACF

*1 Moor Lane, **Drill Hall**, pre-WWl; large, single-storey, corrugated-iron-clad hall, with porch, & indoor range;

¶ In 1914, drill station for D Coy. 4 Bn. Devonshire Regt;

Bulwell [Nottinghamshire]; PV TAC

*1 Hucknall Road, **TAC**; 1938; cf Beeston; 2-storey main block plus garages etc;

¶ In 1949, base for one Bty. 307 S Notts Hussars Yeomanry, Field Regt. RA, TA; base for one Bty. 350 [S Notts Hussars Yeomanry] Heavy Regt. RA,TA; base for one Coy. 307 [Northern Command] Bn. WRAC, TA;

Bungay [Suffolk]; PV

*1 The Castle armoury, base of Rifle Volunteers pre-1900;

*2 The **Armoury**, Nethergate/Broad St, in use to 1906; 3-storey house fronting Nethergate St. shows blocked archway, & outside stair to upper level; Broad St front timbered, & double-height bow window; private residence;

*3 Scales St, **Drill Hall**, 1906 [datestone]; now Garage; hall with gable end to road, porch, offices/ garaging to side;

¶ In 1914, drill station for D Sqdn. Suffolk Yeomanry; base for F Coy. 6 [Cyclist] Bn. Suffolk Regt; & drill station for B Coy. 5 Bn. Suffolk Regt.

Burnham-on-Crouch [Essex]; PV

*1 High St, **Drill Hall**, built as chapel, mid-19C; subsequently drill hall, auction house, snooker club, now sailmaker; floor inserted; classical front with pediment, later foyer, now shops; used by HG in WWll;

¶ In 1914, drill station for F Coy. 4 Bn. Essex Regt;

132

¶ In 1950, detachment of B Coy. 4 Bn. Essex Regt.

Burnham on Sea [Somerset]; V   ACF [Highbridge Road];

Burnley [Lancashire]; PV ACF

*1 Kingsway/Edward Street, **Drill Hall**, 1914; converted to Corporation depot & TA/CD Centre, 1966 by Major Birtwistle; in use by TA in 1983; now ACF hut on site; large, stone-built hall with gabled end; datestone over door; now snooker-club;

¶ In 1914, base for 6 Lancashire Bty. 1 East Lancashire Bde. RFA; HQ+A-D Coys. 5 Bn. E Lancs Regt; base for C Section 2 E Lancs Divnl. Field Ambulances RAMC;

Burslem [Stoke-on-Trent]; PV [*p134*]

*1 Newcastle Street, **Drill Hall**, 1902; imposing castellated front with arched doorway with arms of North Staffordshire Regt. over; large hall behind; yard with garages etc; now Stoke-on-Trent Gymnastics Centre.

Burton-on-Trent [Staffordshire]; PV TAC

*1 High Street in use 1912;

*2 Horniglow Street, drill hall, closed late 1980s; now Car-park;

*3 Hawkins Lane/Wharf Road. Coltman House **TAC** late 1980s; two-storey block & garages etc; in use by West Midlands Regt.

¶ In 1914, base C Sqdn. Staffordshire Yeomanry; HQ+A B & H Coys.6 Bn.N Staffs R

Bury [Bury]; PV TAC [*3] [*p72*]

*1 Bolton Road, **Wellington Barracks**, 1842; QM stores, one other building [now Fusiliers' Assoc'n] & Gateway remain as museum of Lancashire Fusiliers; all in local stone; rest demolished for housing;

*2 Bolton Road, Elton Square, Militia Barracks, 1859; still there 1969; demolished for old people's housing;

*3 Castle St **Armoury**, 1868; extensive, castellated, Norman 2-storey front block with tower & turrets; vast hall behind; extended 1907; large Lancs Fusiliers crest above balcony on tower; capacity for entire battalion to drill inside; garages to rear;

¶ In 1914, HQ+A B E F & H Coys. 5 Bn. Lancashire Fusiliers; drill station C Section 3 East Lancashire Divnl. Field Ambulances RAMC;

Bury-St-Edmunds [Suffolk]; PV TAC [*3]

*1 Newmarket Rd, **Barracks**, c1880; Suffolk Regt. Cardwell

depot; Keep/Armoury, gate-piers & boundary walls with loopholed corner bastions; FE College.

*2 Kings Rd, **Drill Hall**, 1857; built as barracks for Suffolk Yeomanry; subsequently home of TA artillery unit until 1977; in chequerwork brick, converted to housing-*Yeomanry Close* ;

*3 Newmarket Rd, Blenheim Camp,**TAC**, 1977; two 2-storey blocks at right-angles to each other, within compound with garages etc;

¶ In 1914, HQ Suffolk Yeomanry; HQ, E & F Coys. 5 Bn. Suffolk Regt; & base for H Coy. 6 [Cyclist] Bn. Suffolk Regt.

Buxton [Derbyshire]; PV ACF

*1 Silverlands, **Drill Hall**, 1937; 2-storey front block with hall behind; yard with garaging to rear; closed as TAC c1999;

¶ In 1914, drill station B Sqdn. Derbys Yeo; base C Coy. 6 Bn. Sherwood Foresters;

C

Calderstones [Liverpool]; PV TACs [*1 & *2]

*1 35-101 Mather Avenue, **TAC**, opened 1938; in use by RLC unit; 2-storey front block with two semi-circular projections; balcony over main door with royal arms of George Vl on RE badge; lateral hall & yard with garages, workshops;

*2 Crawford Hall, in use by LU OTC; 1980s pagoda-style building with garages etc. in yard;

¶ In 1947, 573 [M] HAA Regt. [Kings];

Calne [Wiltshire]; PV ACF

*1 **Town Hall** [1884-6] used as Armoury & Drill Hall in 1911; imposing Tudor/Gothic structure with tower; armoury in yard to rear;

*2 Bryans Close, ACF Centre in huts;

¶ In 1914, drill station for C Sqdn. Wiltshire Yeomanry; drill station for D Coy. 4 Bn. Wiltshire Regt; drill station for 1 SW Mounted Bde. Field Ambulances;

Camberley [Surrey]; PV TAC [*1]

*1 London Road, Braganza TAC [*p134*]; pre-WWl **Drill Hall**; tall 2-storey block with detached staff house to left, & attached hall to right; used by Home Guard in WWll; in use by Queens Royal Surrey/Prince of Wales Regt; adjacent huts for ACF, ATC;

BURSLEM, this typically castellated drill hall is a gymnastics centre

CAMBERLEY shows an alternative lateral layout of house, orderly-room & hall

*2 London Road, York Town, drill hall, in use 1913; now industrial estate;

¶ In 1914, drill station for B Sqdn. Surrey Yeomanry; base for B Coy. 5 Bn. Royal West Surrey Regt.

Camborne [Cornwall]; PV TAC [***3**]

*1 Wheal Gurry, armoury in use 1897; not traced;

*2 corner North Roskear & Park Roads, **Drill Hall**, pre-1900; built in granite & now in use as flats; two large buildings + smaller ones within an enclosure;

*3 North Roskear Road, **Drill Hall**, c1935; single-storey front block with hall behind; garages etc. across yard;

¶ In 1914, base for B Coy. 4 Bn. DCLI;

Cambridge [Cambridgeshire]; PVA TACs

*1 196 East Road, drill hall, 1914; built to house the three units of the TF based in Cambridge; entrances on East Road led into orderly rooms, offices, canteen, stores, lecture room & armoury with gallery above for the Yeomanry's saddlery; then came the large drill hall, entered directly through the middle archway, & miniature range; converted from the technical schools, by Talbot, Brown & Fisher of Wellingborough; the two frontages flanking the archway, surmounted by gables; passages down each side lead to Adam & Eve Lane; taken over by GPO in 1967, & demolished 1983 for redevelopment; the crest is preserved in TAC at Cherry Hinton Road [***8**];

*2 14 Corn Exchange St, in 1914 & through to 1970s redevelopment of Lion Yard, HQ of Cambridgeshire Regt;

*3 Grange Rd, HQ of CU OTC from 1860-1971, with armoury, 1250 yard range, NCO's house, forge, magazine, orderly room etc; in 1938, garaging for 14 vehicles added; no trace remains;

*4 22 Market St, HQ of CU OTC in 1914; building now shop;

*5 39 Green St, Eastern District [military] General Hospital in 1913, but moved by 1915; present 1920s building post-dates rest of street; actual hospital was on site now occupied by University Library [built 1931-4 in Queens Rd].

*6 Quayside, HQ of CU OTC, on upper floors sharing with sports facilities; building, in altered state in retail, leisure & residential use;

*7 Coldhams Lane, **TAC**, cement works converted 1947, rebuilt 1988; in use by CU OTC + signals unit;

*8 450 Cherry Hinton Road, **TAC**, 1987, in use by RAMC unit;

¶ In 1914, base for A Sqdn. Suffolk Yeomanry; base for HQ & A-D Coys.1 Bn. Cambridgeshire Regt.; & 1 Eastern General Hospital RAMC.

Camelford [Cornwall]; PV

*1 The Clease, **Drill Hall**, 1911; now renovated as Millennium Hall; single-storey hall with side projections, porch & indoor range;

¶ In 1914, drill station for D Sqdn. 1 Devon Yeomanry; base for F Coy. 5 Bn. DCLI;

Canley [Coventry]; PV TAC

*1 Sir Henry Parkes Rd, St Georges House **TAC**, 1990s; in use by West Midlands Regt. & Signals Unit; extensive site with modern, pavilion style buildings & garages;

Cannock [Staffordshire]; PV TAC [***2**]

*1 Norton Canes, Norton Hall; in use 1914, given up 1931; demolished;

*2 Walsall Rd, Bridgtown, **Drill Hall**, pre-WWll; 2-storey front block with lateral hall behind, later office/accommodation block behind that; to rear, garages etc; staff house to one side + earlier garage;

¶ In 1914, HQ+2 Field Coy. N Midland Divnl. RE; drill station B Sqdn. Staffs. Yeo.

Canterbury [Kent]; PV TAC [***5**]

*1 10 St Margarets St, Yeomanry HQ in 1908; probably the Old Militia Barracks recorded in 1910 as base for Buffs, Yeomanry & Cyclists; site re-developed;

*2 3 **Adelaide Place**, RAMC base 1908; house/restaurant;

*3 66 **Northgate**, drill hall, in use 1908; 3-storey building is shop; previously Old City Arms PH; in use by 1899;

*4 Rose Lane, drill hall, in use 1908; site completely re-developed;

*5 Sturry Road, **Drill Hall**, c1930s; at least three large sheds, plus office and accommodation blocks;

*6 RAMC recorded in Castle St. in 1910;

*7 St Peters Lane, **Drill Hall**, recorded in 1933; very large hall, behind 2-storey, 18-bay front-block, with single-storey wing at one end; now in use as Westgate Hall;

¶ In 1899, base for B & C Coys. East Kent Volunteers;

¶ In 1908, HQ Royal East Kent Yeomanry [St Margarets]; base for B Coy.4 Bn. The Buffs [Northgate]; base for F Coy.

Cyclist Bn. [Rose Lane]; base 2 Home Counties Field Ambulance RAMC [Adelaide Place];

¶ In 1914, HQ Royal East Kent Mounted Rifles + drill station B Sqdn; HQ+B & C Coys. 4 Bn. East Kent Regt; base F Coy. Kent Cyclist Bn; base A Section 2 Home Counties Divnl. Field Ambulance RAMC;

¶ In 1933, 385 Bty. 97 [KY] Field Bde; & HQ+B Coy. 4 Bn. Buffs; [St Peters Lane];

Canvey Island [Essex]; V ACF

*1 Runnymede Road, TAC, demolished 1987, new ACF Centre;

¶ In 1950, P [Essex] Bty. 415 Coast Regt. RA [TA];

Carlisle [Cumbria]; PV TAC

*1 The Castle; HQ Kings Own Borderers + **TAC**; still in use by infantry unit; **Militia Armoury**, 2-storey, stone-built block with 1881 datestone; armoury later transferred to a barrack-block; TA currently use *Burma* block, & ACF occupy *Ypres*;

*2 Strand Road, **Drill Hall**, pre-1914; 2-storey, polychrome brick, 8-bay front block, with 3-storey, off-centre gate-tower with saddle-back roof; behind, a large hall; to side, a later garage-block facing back into yard; now used by FE college;

*3 Eastern Road, Harraby, ex-**TAC**, 851 Westmorland & Cumberland Yeomanry in 1965; presents as 1960s curtain-wall, brick & glass office building; symmetrical, 11-bay 2-storey L-shaped front block; to one side, older staff house & indoor range still in use by ACF; to rear, extensive garaging; now owned by plant hire firm & leased to construction company;

*4 Well Lane, c1920s house reportedly used as drill hall, then Border Regt. almshouses; now Care Home as part of Lonsdale Trust;

*5 ex-**TA Camp** at Stanwix on Brampton road, now official Travellers' Site;

¶ In 1914, base D Sqdn. Westmorland & Cumberland Yeo; base 1 Cumberland [H] Bty. 4 East Lancashire [Howitzer] Bde. RFA; HQ+A & B Coys. 4 Bn. Border Regt;

Carlton [Nottinghamshire]; PV TAC [***2**] [*p64*]

*1 Station Rd, drill hall in use 1912; no trace; possible building corner of Conway Rd, now RBL social club; late Victorian house next to long hall to road with coach-arch; later additions;

*2 Cavendish Drive; **Drill Hall**,1939; 2-storey square plan +

wings; in use, HQ Sherwood Rangers Sqdn. of Royal Yeomanry;

¶ In 1914, base for E Coy. 8 Bn. Sherwood Foresters, & drill station for A Sqdn. South Nottinghamshire Hussars.

¶ In 1949, base for one Sqdn. The Notts. [Sherwood Rangers Yeomanry] RAC; base for one Bty. 577 LAA/SL Regt. [The Robin Hoods, Foresters]; HQ + Coy. 905 [AA Command Mixed] Transport Coy. RASC, TA;

Carnforth [Lancashire]; PV A [*2]

*1 Market St/Haws Hill, [Royal] **Station Hotel**, drill hall in 1914;

*2 Lower North Rd, **Drill Hall**, pre-WWl; 2-storey orderly-room block, ornate, rusticated stone porch alongside, & single-storey, bow-fronted cottage; large, first-floor hall 55'x 32' behind; also small committee-room, store, cloaks etc; 25 yard indoor range in basement; sold by TA in 1965 as Civic Hall;

¶ In 1914, base for F Coy. 5 Bn. Royal Lancaster Regt;

Castle Cary [Somerset]; PV ACF [*p49*]

*1 Church Road, **Drill Hall**, pre-WWl; 2-storey front block in stone & brick; hall behind, & then house in line; indoor range & other annexes;

¶ In 1914, drill station for C Sqdn. N Somerset Yeomanry; base for F Coy. 4 Bn. SLI;

Castle Eden [County Durham]; V

*1 site of drill shed next to 'Toll Cottage'; demolished for construction of 2 houses;

¶ In 1914, base for F Coy. 5 Bn. Durham LI;

Castleford [West Yorkshire]; PV TAC

*1 Maltkiln Lane, **Drill Hall**, in use; pre-WWl block, 2-storey brick with stone doorway, & hall behind; 1990s block to side, with garages;

¶ In 1914, base for H Coy. KOYLI;

Castor [Cambridgeshire]; V

*1 25a Peterborough Road, site of Old Village Hall, 1921-56, base for Home Guard; hall was ex-Luton YMCA timber hostel, 65'x 35';

Caterham [Surrey]; PV

*1 Godstone Road, **Drill Hall**, pre-WWl; 2-storey front block, half-timbered with projecting porch; behind, 2-storey accommodation/orderly room/QMS etc block, alongside hall; to rear, garage block; now Youth Centre;

¶ In 1914, base for E Coy. 4 Bn. Royal West Surrey Regt.

Catterick [North Yorkshire]; V

*1 Militia drill hall reported, and TF drill hall, in use by 1910, in 1958 list; no local knowledge; Booth Hall built c1900 or .....*2 Catterick Garrison, begun c1900;

¶ In 1914, drill station for B Coy. 4 Bn. Princess of Wales Own Yorkshire Regt.

Causeway Green [Sandwell]; PV TAC

*1 Wolverhampton Rd, Oldbury, Gundolph House **Drill Hall**, c1930s; in use by RE unit; large 2-storey L-shaped block with hall; yard with extensive garages, workshops etc. & staff house;

¶ In 1914, base for E Coy. 7 Bn. Worcestershire Regt.

Chapel-en-le-Frith [Derbyshire]; PV

*1 National School was the drill station for 7 Corps of Derbyshire Rifle Volunteers, known as the Chatsworth Rifles, formed at Chapel in 1860;

*2 Market St, drill hall, in use until after WWl; built of corrugated iron; it was demolished for the building of a new road off Market St;

*3 Market St, **Drill Hall**; appears to be an adapted 2-storey, early 19C house, with a large arch cut into the front wall; very little accommodation behind; now a pet supplies shop; local residents assert that what stands represents all there ever was; it was used by HG & CD in WWll;

¶ In 1914, base for B Coy. 6 Bn. Sherwood Foresters;

Chard [Somerset]; PV ACF

*1 Fore St, drill hall in use 1914; not found;

*2 Furnham Rd, **Drill Hall**, pre-WWl; 2-storey front block in brick & render, with gable over entrance; hall behind with indoor range, garage, & other annexes [*p138*]; [cf Castle Cary];

¶ In 1914, drill station for D Sqdn. W Somerset Yeomanry; base H Coy. 5 Bn. SLI;

Charlestown [Cornwall]; PV

*1 **Drill Hall**, 250yds. from harbour, late 18C; in use by army & Home Guard until post-WWll; commercial; 2-storey, T-shaped granite block, outbuildings & gunstore;

¶ In 1914, drill station for No.1 Heavy Bty. Cornwall RGA-Defended Ports

Chatham & Old Brompton [Kent]; PVA ACF [*7]

*1 New Road [now New Road Avenue], in use 1908; drill

hall marked 1909 map; demolished for housing;

*2 Fort Pitt Rd/Boundary Rd, drill hall, in use1908; marked 1909 map; built with Hennebique method of re-inforced concrete; demolished for housing, Cressey Court;

*3 31 High St, Old Brompton, in use 1908; not found;

*4 Garden St, Old Brompton, in use 1908; no trace on 1909 map;

*5 Dock Rd, drill hall, in use 1933, HQ HG 1940; referred to as RAFA club in 1990 reminiscence; no trace;

*6 Barrier Rd, HQ Home Guard 1952; marked as **Drill Hall** 1932 map; built as school 1879 [datestone]; imposing, ornate 2-storey front block, with halls behind; now Armed Forces Careers Centre;

*7 Khyber Rd, ACF Centre in use, no access;

¶ In 1908, base A Sqdn. Royal East Kent Yeomanry [New Rd]; HQ+half bty. Home Counties Kent RGA Heavy Bty. & Ammunition Column [Fort Pitt Rd]; HQ Kent RGA [31 High St]; 1 Coy. Kent RGA [Garden St]; base F & G Coys. 5 Bn. Royal West Kent Regt. [Fort Pitt Rd]; base for C Coy. Kent Cyclist Bn; base for Section C 1 Home Counties Field Ambulance RAMC;

¶ In 1914, base for A Sqdn. Royal East Kent Mounted Rifles; drill station for Kent Bty. & base for Ammunition Column, Home Counties RGA -Heavy; base for F & G Coys. 5 Bn. Royal West Kent Regt; drill station D Coy. Kent Cyclist Bn; base C Section 1 Home Counties Divisional Field Ambulance RAMC;

¶ In 1933, HQ+205 Bty. 52 [K] Med Bde; 203 Med Artillery Signal Section; D Coy. 5 Bn. Royal West Kent Regt. [Boundary Rd]; 313 AA SL Coy RE; & 44 [HC] Div Ordnance Coy. [Dock Road];

Chelmsford [Essex]; PVA TAC

*1 Market Road, militia storehouse built c1855 for West Essex Militia, superseded by drill hall 1902; demolished for APU expansion 1994; a sign is incorporated into APU gate; foundation stone re-sited at Springfield Lyons;

*2 London Road, RE **Drill Hall**, c1930s; used by GPO into 1980s, now church; front block with porch, hall behind; large yard, whose east wall was the inner wall of the indoor range, [lead staining]; 1950s garages in commercial use;

*3 Broomfield Rd, RE unit here 1947-61; pair of PSIs' houses now private dwellings;

*4 Springfield Lyons, **TAC**, built 1994; two large, linked blocks of two storeys & garage block; main facade has elements of traditional drill hall; display of original foundation stones by gate [p138];

*5 250 Springfield Road, **Springfield Tyrells**, 1888; HQ RFCA East Anglia; large, 3-storey detached mansion, built as home for Ridley, the brewer, [datestone]; surrounded by temporary government office buildings cWWll;

*6 Pitfield Estate near Army & Navy roundabout; Pitfield House c1900, last used by RN Reserve; two detached officers' houses; bungalow last used as cadet centre; all now private dwellings with new houses interspersed;

¶ In 1914, drill station B Sqdn. Essex Yeo; HQ & Bty.+sub-section Ammunition Column, Essex RHA; HQ No.1 Electric Lights Coy. RE [Fortress]; HQ, A & B Coys. 5 Bn. Essex Regt. [+drill station at Broomfield]; Eastern Mounted Bde. Transport & Supply Column ASC;

¶ In 1950, HQ & P Bty. 646 LAA Regt+Workshop units; 855 FC Bty.[Essex Fortress]; 1563 Tipper Coy. RASC; 3 Essex Platoon, WRAC; [Market Rd]; 304 Fd. Regt. Essex Yeo. [London Rd]; 313 Fd. Sqdn. [one troop] of 134 Construction Regt. RE [Broomfield Rd];

Cheltenham [Glos]; PV TAC

*1 Arle Road, **TAC**; similar in style to Cinderford [1957]; 2-storey front block in brick & glass, with tower; yard with garages etc;

¶ In 1914, drill station for A Sqdn. Glos Hussars; base for E-F Coys. 5 Bn. Glos Regt;

¶ In 1947, HQ 498 HAA Regt. RA TA;

Chertsey [Surrey]; PV ACF

*1 Drill Hall Road, **Drill Hall**,1902; in use by Home Guard in WWll; rectangular block with central entrance, & hall behind; Drill Hall Cottage, home of PSI, adjacent; members of 15 Corps Surrey Rifle Volunteers bought shares in the Drill Hall Co;

¶ In 1914, base for G Coy. 6 Bn. East Surrey Regt;

Chesham [Buckinghamshire]; PV ACF

*1 Berkhampstead Rd, [A416], **Drill Hall**, pre-WWl; part youth centre, part ACF Centre/TS, Townsend House; long 2-storey block linked to 2-storey 'cottage'; across yard, shorter block, possibly former stabling, indoor-range, & garage; over the main door, the Buckinghamshire swan badge;

CHARD, one of a group of Somerset drill halls sharing many characteristics

CHELMSFORD's 1994 Springfield Lyons TAC, drawing on traditional elements

¶ In 1914, base D Sqdn. Buckinghamshire Yeo; drill station C Coy. Ox & Bucks LI;

Cheshunt [Hertfordshire]; PV [*p62*]

*1 Crossbrook St, **Drill Hall**, c1938; 2-storey front block, semi-circular projection, porch with crest of Hertfordshire Regt. over; hall behind; garage & staff house [no. 180] to rear; now in community use;

¶ In 1914, drill station for H Coy. 1 Bn. Hertfordshire Regt.

Chester [Cheshire]; PV TAC [*7] ACF [*2]

*1 Eastgate, **Old Bank Buildings**, 1895 by Lockwood; half-timbered black & white 3-storey Elizabethan style offices & shops;

*2 **Castle**, barracks, 1800-04, by Harrison; one wing is the Officers' Mess of the Cheshire Regt; the other, formerly the Armoury, now Regimental HQ & Museum; the Armoury wing has a semi-circle of buildings behind, enclosed by high wall with gate;

*3 Old Prison Yard, Shipgate St, artillery drill hall, in use 1914; re-developed for housing under Civic Trust scheme;

*4 Volunteer St, **Drill Hall**, 1865; 3-storey castellated gatehouse tower with higher circular stair-turret; 2-storey front block with square, machicolated turret at corner; hall demolished for parking; now flats;

*5 Thomas St in use 1914; street no longer exists;

*6 Eastgate, **Grosvenor Hotel**, 1863-6; used as Yeomanry officers' mess;

*7 The Dale, Fox Barracks, **TAC**, 1970s;

¶ In 1914, HQ + drill station for B Sqdn. Cheshire Yeomanry [Old Bank Buildings]; HQ+ 1&2 Btys.& Ammunition Column, Cheshire RFA [Old Prison Yard]; HQ+B & E Coys. 5 Bn. Cheshire Regt. [Volunteer Street]; HQ+A & B Sections, Welsh Border Mounted Bde. Field Ambulances RAMC, [Thomas Street];

Chesterfield [Derbyshire]; PV TAC [*3]

*1 Ashgate Road, drill hall demolished;

*2 10 Corporation St, HQ & A Coy. 6 Bn. Sherwood Foresters in 1914; the building is occupied by a betting shop & a barber; it was built in 1875 as the end of a terrace;

*3 Wallis Barracks, Boythorpe Rd, 1938 **Drill Hall** in use by RE unit; recorded as 'additional' in 1958 Review;

¶ In 1914, base A Sqdn. Derbys Yeo, drill station B Sqdn. Sherwood Rangers, base HQ & A Coy. Sherwood Foresters,

set in yard with garages, outbuildings etc; stone relief of Queen's Regt. lamb & flag over doorways;

Coventry [Coventry]; PVA TAC [***1**]

*1 Radford Road, Westfield House **TAC**; in use by Signals & REME units; large 1990s block replaced old house; garages to rear;

*2 Queen Victoria Rd, drill hall, sold 1970s, post-1973 demolished;

*3 Quinton Rd, drill hall, demolished for re-development;

*4 Barracks Way, early-18C barracks converted from public house, later updated as Cavalry Barracks, included riding school; mention also made of factory conversion in mid-19C, possibly for anti-Chartist operations; for a while served as market-place; now demolished;

*5 reference to Stevens Memorial Hall as HQ 2 Cadet Bn. Warwickshire Regt. In 1914;

¶ In 1914, base for C Sqdn. Warwickshire Yeomanry; drill station for Warwickshire RHA; HQ+4 Warwickshire [Howitzer] Bty. & Ammunition Column 4 South Midland [Howitzer] Bde. RFA [Quinton Road]; HQ+A-D Coys. 7 Bn. Warwickshire Regt;

Cowes [Isle of Wight]; PV [*p47*]

*1 Denmark Rd, **Drill Hall**, 1912; 2-storey, brick, 9-bay, front block with pediment over central archway; hall behind parallel to street; house behind hall at NE end; adjoining front block at SW end, a linking block, then a 2-storey building with oriel; in use Home Guard WWll; foundation stone laid by Princess Henry of Battenberg, 4 May, 1912; now in commercial use;

¶ In 1914, base for H Coy. 8 Bn. Hampshire Regt;

Cramlington [Northumberland]; PV TAC

*1 High Pit Rd, **Fox Barracks TAC**, c1980s; factory-style buildings, sheds/offices;

Cranbrook [Kent]; PV ACF

*1 Causton Rd, **Drill Hall**, pre-1908; small gabled hall with dormers & cross-wing; detached staff house, timber hut, & indoor range; similar hall to Tenterden;

¶ In 1908 & 1914, base for A Coy.5 Bn. The Buffs;

Craven Arms **[Shropshire]**; V

no location identified; no drill hall necessarily existed;

¶ In 1914, drill station for C Sqdn. Shropshire Yeomanry, & for G Coy. 4 Bn. KOSLI

COCKERMOUTH, a drill hall of the Border Regiment

CREWE's Myrtle Street drill hall dates from 1937

143

Crawley [Sussex]; PV   TAC

*1 Kiln Mead, **TAC** in use by REME unit, post-WWll; 2-storey front block; large yard with garaging to rear;

¶ In 1914, drill station for C Coy. 4 Bn. Royal Sussex Regt.

Crediton **[Devon];** V ACF/ATC [*2]

*1 Bowden Hill, drill hall, by 1910; demolished for housing;

*2 Charlotte St, huts;

¶ In 1914, drill stationA Sqdn. 1 Devon Yeo; base for Ammunition Column 4 Wessex Bde. RFA; drill station F Coy. 6 Bn. & base for E Coy. 7 [Cyclist] Bn. Devonshire R;

Crewe [Cheshire]; PV TAC [*p143*]

*1 Myrtle Street, **Drill Hall**, 1937; 2-storey front block in rusticated brick-work;hall behind with two entrances fronting Myrtle St, & a garage beyond; indoor range runs along back of hall; in use by TA infantry unit;

¶ In 1914, drill station for C Sqdn. Cheshire Yeomanry; base for 3 Cheshire Bty. Cheshire Bde. RFA; drill station for F Coy. 7 Bn. Cheshire Regt;

Crewkerne **[Somerset];** V

*1 behind 17 Market Street, Armoury of SLI in 1914; drill hall, demolished mid-1970s for Falkland Square shopping precinct;

¶ In 1914, drill station D Sqdn. W Somerset Yeomanry; base for F Coy. 5 Bn. SLI;

Cromer **[Norfolk];** V

no dedicated building; in Napoleonic times the militia drilled on The Marrams, & kept their arms & equipment in the church; probably used **Melton Constable;**

¶ In 1914, drill station B Sqdn. Norfolk Yeo; & base for F Coy.5 Bn. Norfolk Regt;

Crook [County Durham]; PV

*1 North side of Market Square, **Drill Hall**, pre-WWl; Crofts Social Club; 7-bay hall on end of L-shaped 2-storey block with lean-to; garages etc in yard to rear;

¶ In 1914, base for D Coy. 6 Bn. Durham LI;

Crosby [Sefton]; PVA

*1 Coronation Road, **Drill Hall**, c1910; 2-storey front block with hall behind; arched entrance with double doors;

¶ In 1914, base for E Coy. 7 Bn. Kings Liverpool Regt;

¶ In 1947, 390 LAA Regt. RA TA [Kings Own];

Crowborough [Sussex]; PV

*1 Fermor Road, **Drill Hall**, in use 1914 onwards; 2-storey

front block; traces of inscription along the top; hall behind with single-storey annexes; Nissen-type garage to side; has been in educational use;

*2 training camp in use by ACF etc;

*3 Oddfellows Hall referred to as drill hall from 1909, in 1958 Review; not traced;

¶ In 1914, base for G Coy. 5 Bn. Royal Sussex Regt.

¶ In 1934, base for 5 Bn. Royal Sussex Regt;

Croydon [Greater London]; PV TACs [*2 & *3]

*1 Tamworth Road, drill hall in use 1913; whole street re-developed;

*2 Mitcham Road, **Barracks**, pre-1900; drill sheds, other early buildings; 2-storey, L-shaped block with cupola represents 1930s improvement; also 1960s block, in yard with garages, WWll explosives stores etc;

*3 Sydenham Rd, **Drill Hall**, c1930s; large 2-storey, L-shaped block encasing hall; yard with garages etc. TA Association badges;

¶ In 1903, HQ 1 Vol Bn. The Queen's [Royal W Surrey] Regt. [Mitcham Rd.Barracks]

¶ In 1913 & 14, HQ+A B D F & H Coys. 4 Bn. Queens Regt; base for South East Mounted Bde. Transport & Supply Column [Mitcham Road Barracks];

¶ In 1913 & 14, base for C Sqdn. Surrey Yeomanry [Tamworth Road];

Crystal Palace [Greater London]; PV   ACF

*1 64 High Street, Penge, **Drill Hall**; Victorian villa with outbuildings & ACF hut to rear; marked "drill hall" on 1970s street atlas;

¶ In 1913 &14, base for C Coy. 4 Bn. Royal West Surrey Regt;

Cuckfield [Sussex]; PV

*1 High Street, **Drill Hall**, mid-19C or earlier; building variously described as Court-house, drill hall etc; drill hall was recruiting office 1914; long brick 2-storey range of 9 bays, with pediments over two at each end & three in the centre; now split into three dwellings; to rear, 1 & 2 Drill Cottages;

¶ In 1859, 2 Corps Sussex Rifle Volunteers formed here;

¶ In 1880, base for A & B Coys. 2 Sussex Corps/Volunteer Bn. Sussex Regt;

¶ In 1914, drill station for A Coy. 4 Bn. Royal Sussex Regt;

Cullompton [Devon]; PV

*1 High Street, armoury of Rifle Volunteers; Town Hall on site;

*2 The Green, 19C Workhouse taken over as **Drill Hall** by 1910; used by RBL & local shooting club; L-shaped, brick, 2-storey block, with hall to side, & indoor range behind;

¶ In 1914, drill station for A Sqdn. 1 Devon Yeomanry; base for G Coy. 4 Bn. Devonshire Regt; base for D Coy. 7 [Cyclist] Bn. Devonshire Regt;

D

Dagenham [Greater London]; PV

*1 Halbutt Street, Becontree; **Drill Hall**; 2-storey front block with hall behind; garages & indoor range to rear; c1930s; now Social Services Dept;

¶ In 1950, A Coy. 4 Bn. Essex Regt.

*2 Rectory Road, **Drill Hall**; c1930s, hall, flats, staff house; now Day Centre;

¶In 1950, detachment A Coy. 4 Bn. Essex Regt.

*3 Wood Lane, **Drill Hall**; 2-storey L-shaped block with large hall behind; c1930s; now Leisure Centre.

¶ In 1950, HQ+P & R Btys. 517 LAA Regt.; & 161 Inf. Workshops REME [Essex] TA;

Dalton-in-Furness [Cumbria]; PVA

*1 Ulverston Rd, **Drill Hall**, in use 1914; 2-storey, gabled stone block, possibly adapted from previous use, now joinery workshop;

*2 Nelson St, **Drill Hall**, 1928; 2-storey front block, consisting of 3-bay house, gabled projecting porch with stone archway, 3-bay front to hall with blocked access; inscription on archway: "4TH Bn. The Kings Own Royal Regt.Company Quarters, 1928"; hall behind with indoor range & garage; now offices for voluntary organisations etc;

¶ In 1914, base for G Coy. 4 Bn. Royal Lancaster Regt;

Darlaston [Walsall]; PV

*1 57 Pinfold Street, in use 1900; demolished; adjacent site occupied by PH *The Staffordshire Knot*.

*2 61-62 Church Street, **Drill Hall**, in use 1912-1971; two-storey front block with hall parallel, & indoor range behind; 24' Nissen & garage-block in yard; in commercial use as workshop;

¶ In 1914, base for F Coy. 6 Bn. South Staffordshire Regt.

Darlington [County Durham]; PV TAC [*2]

*1 Larchfield St, **Drill Hall**, 1897; used as a cinema, now FE College sports hall; large hall to frontage with Dutch-gabled facade, incorporating 2-storey office wing; smaller hall behind; courtyard lined by stores, garages etc;

*2 Neasham Rd, **Drill Hall**, c1930s; 2-storey U-shaped block with hall and garages etc. to rear; similar to Newton Aycliff, Greenwell Rd, with glazed, 2-storey oriel at each front angle;

¶ In 1914, drill station B Sqdn. North'land Hussars; base D E & H Coys. 5 Bn. DLI; HQ+A & B Sections 2 Northumbrian Divnl. Field Ambulances RAMC [Larchfield St];

Dartford [Kent]; PV

*1 Lowfield St, **Drill Hall**, pre-1908; large hall with two-storey front block & single-storey aisles, with dormers over; across a small yard, a stables/garage block, also with dormers, & a store, all in yellow brick; former entrance in facade; Judokwai;

¶ In 1908, drill station B Sqdn. W Kent Yeo; base C Coy. 5 Bn. Royal W Kent Regt;

¶ In 1914, base B Sqdn. West Kent Yeomanry; base C Coy. & drill station for E Coy. 5 Bn. Royal W Kent Regt; drill station for 4 London Divnl. Field Ambulance RAMC;

¶ In 1933, 206 Bty. 52 [K] Med Bde; & C Coy. 5 Bn. Royal West Kent Regt;

Dartmouth [Devon]; V

*1 Clarence Hill, Mount Galpin [House], **Drill Hall**, by 1906, until at least 1954; 3-storey, grand Regency house built by prominent local family; half-hexagonal bay window to street, white stucco, hall etc behind dug into hill-side; now apartments & terraced garden;

*2 Crowther Hill, drill hall, by 1906; No 8 is a new house, dated 1987, but may be a conversion of the older building;

*3 South Parade, HQ, 1910; no known address;

¶In 1914, drill station C Sqdn. 1 Devon Yeomanry; drill station 2 Devon Bty. 4 Wessex Bde. RFA; base for F Coy. 7 [Cyclist] Bn. Devonshire Regt;

***Darwen* [Blackburn with Darwen]; V**

*1 Everton Street, drill hall, demolished;

¶In 1914, base for F & G Coys. 4 Bn. East Lancashire Regt;

Daventry [Northamptonshire]; PV ACF [*2]
*1 New Street, Assembly Hall served as drill hall; building demolished 1970s;
*2 Waterloo, ex-**TAC**, c1980s; small L-shaped block & garage;
¶ In 1914, base for D Sqdn. Northamptonshire Yeomanry, & drill station for B Coy. 4 Bn. Northamptonshire Regt.

Deal [Kent]; PV ACF [*1] ATC [*2]
*1 Middle Deal Road, drill hall, in use 1908; demolished for housing; ACF hut & buried indoor range;
*2 Hope Road, **Drill Hall**, 1878; built for 5 Cinque Ports Artillery Volunteers [inscription]; long hall with central arched entrance under gable with shield; at one end a two-storey cross-wing with curved corner to street;
*3 1958 Review cites Grove Terrace as Drill Hall; Grove Rd opposite Cavalry Bks;
¶ In 1908 & 1914, drill station for C Sqdn. Royal East Kent Yeomanry; base for Ammunition Column 3 Home Counties [CP] Bde. RFA [Grove Terrace];

Delabole [Cornwall]; PV
*1 Pengelly, **Drill Hall**, pre-WWl; converted to flats; gabled hall to road, with staff house alongside;
¶ In 1914, drill station for F Coy. 5 Bn. DCLI;

Denaby Main [South Yorkshire]; PV
*1 Fairway Buildings, **Drill Hall**, 1908; double-pile hall with annexes on each end; blank wall along back may represent indoor range; now flooring shop; plaque records units based here;
¶ In 1914, base for G Coy. 5 Bn. KOYLI; [1908-38]
¶ In 1938, base for 159 & 171 Btys. 53 & 57 LAA Regt; [1938-46]
¶ In 1940, 43 West Riding Bn. Home Guard; [1940-45]
¶ In 1946, 7 Bn. York & Lancaster Regt; [1946-60]

Denton [Northamptonshire]; PV ACF
*1 Horton Road, **Cadet Centre**; guardroom of explosives storage site, and other neighbouring admin. site buildings used for outdoor pursuits activities;

Derby [Derbyshire]; PV TACs [*2 & *7] ACF [*6]
*1 Sinfin Lane, Normanton Barracks, built 1880 as depot for Sherwood Foresters; demolished 1984;
*2 Sinfin Lane, **TAC** [RAMC] 1981, with gates from barracks;

*3 Uttoxeter New Road, **Rowditch Barracks**, built 1859 for Derbyshire Militia; two barrack blocks + guardrooms survive;
*4 91 Siddalls Road, drill hall of Derbyshire Yeomanry, RAMC, & RFA; now site of Bus Station;
*5 Newlands Road/ Beckett Road, drill hall; demolished for redevelopment, referred to as "Royal Drill Hall";
*6 Phoenix Street, **Drill Hall**, smithy with stabling built 1891-1900, bought by TA in 1920; house demolished, outbuildings & entrance remain;
*7 Kingsway, **Drill Hall**, 1939, in use; extensive garaging etc around 2-storeyed front block, lateral hall behind; 1958 Review records five TACs in 1958;
¶ In 1914, base HQ, C & D Sqdns. Derbyshire Yeo; 4 North Midland Howitzer Bde. RFA; HQ+1 Bty.+Ammunition Column; HQ+ A B & C Coys. 5 Bn. Sherwood Foresters; 1 North Midland Divnl. Field Ambulance, HQ+ A B & C Sections.

Dersingham [Norfolk]; PV ACF
*1 Doddshill Rd, **Drill Hall**, c1930s; 2-storey front block with hall behind, & single storey offices etc; projecting front porch, & side door with blank stone for crest;
¶ In 1914, drill station for C Sqdn. Norfolk Yeo; & for E Coy. 5 Bn; Norfolk Regt.

Desborough **[Northamptonshire];** V
*1 Beech Close, drill hall, at least pre-WWll; demolished for old people's home;
¶ In 1914, base for G Coy. 4 Bn. Northamptonshire Regt;

Devizes [Wiltshire]; PV ACF [*1]
*1 London Road, **Le Marchant Barracks**, 1880s; Cardwell depot of Wiltshire Regt; Keep, barrack-blocks etc;
*2 Militia Barracks, 1856; four ranges around a drill square; handed over to Police in 1879; demolished 1964;
*3 32 St John St, **Orderly Room** of 2 Wiltshire Vol. Bn. in 1907 & 1911; 3-storey, 18/early 19C house with rear extension; now offices;
*4 **Town Hall** [1806], HQ & Armoury of 2 Wiltshire Vol. Bn. in 1907 & 1911;
*5 10 High St, **HQ** of RAMC Field Ambulances; street re-numbering and re-development suggests number 10 was the Four Seasons PH; 2-storey double-fronted house with outbuildings to rear;

Leslie Hore-Belisha, for RE Searchlight unit; 3-storey front block with Middlesex Regt. & RE crests over door, & relief of searchlights with beams; large block of buildings with garages;

¶ In 1938, base for 317 Coy. 36 [Middx] Regt. RE.

Egham [Surrey]; PV

*1 High Street, **The Institute**, in use as drill hall 1913; large 3-storey front block with hall and outbuildings behind;

*2 Kings Road, drill hall, c1914; demolished for houses- nos. 16a-c; drill hall hand-drawn onto 1914 map in Library;

¶ In 1914, base for H Coy. 6 Bn. East Surrey Regt;

Egremont [Cumbria]; PV

*1 North Road, **Armoury**, by 1914; 2-storey block now three houses, still known as "The Armoury"; behind, 2-storey, stone-built barn;

¶ In 1914, base for E Coy. 5 Bn. Border Regt;

Elland [West Yorkshire]; PV

*1 Jepson Lane, **Drill Hall**, pre-1900; Wainwright Hall, community centre; single-storey hall, parallel to street frontage, with pediment over door & modern porch; attached is 2-storey staff house; all in stone;

¶ In 1914, base for G Coy. 4 Bn. DoW West Riding Regt;

Ellesmere Port [Cheshire]; PV TAC

*1 Stanney Lane, **Drill Hall**, c1936; 2-storey front block with hall & garages etc;

¶ In 1914, drill station for Welsh Border Mounted Bde.Field Ambulance RAMC;

Eltham [Greater London]; V

*1 no specific location, but drill hall marked on what is now Mottingham Road on 1898 map; demolished for parade of shops c1930s;

¶ In 1914, 6 Bty. 2 London Bde. RFA;

Ely [Cambridgeshire]; PV

*1 Silver Street, **Militia Barracks**, mid-19C; armoury & orderly room, Masonic Hall; permanent staff quarters, terrace of 2-storey cottages, now, 1-12 The Range, with WD marker [1] on corner; terrace of Sergeants' Quarters with outhouses, now 13-20 Parade Lane; further block, double-pile with single-storey cells block behind, now 39-45 Silver Street, WD marker at each corner, [2 & 17]; Hospital at top of The Range, formerly RBL Club, three storeys, T-shaped with gables; everything in local yellow/grey brick; HQ of

DORKING's drill hall of 1889 for years hosted the Vaughan-Williams Festival

EASTBOURNE, The Goffs drill hall is now a veterinary surgery

151

Cambridgeshire Militia till 1880;

*2 Barton Road, **Drill Hall**, by 1910; 2-storey front block in brick with stone dressings & crests; garage attached & hall behind; now offices; [p154]

¶ In 1914, drill station A Sqdn. Suffolk Yeomanry, & base H Coy. 1 Bn. Cambs. Regt

Enfield [Greater London]; PV

*1 Carterhatch Lane/Cambridge Road junction, ex drill hall; demolished1965; former WWll PoW camp; used as REME workshops;

*2 Enfield Lock, no specific location;

¶ In 1914, drill station for B Sqdn. Hertfordshire Yeomanry; & base for F Coy. 7 Bn. Middlesex Regt. with a drill station at Enfield Town.

*3 Old Park Avenue, **Drill Hall**; pre-1914; ornate red-brick facade with turrets, stone dressings, arched doorway; staff house to side; now 'Drill Hall Social Club' [p167]

¶ In 1914, 5/7Bn. Middlesex Regt. recruited from Small Arms Factory;

Epping [Essex]; PV ACF

*1 Hempnall Street, **Drill Hall**; hall demolished, garage remains as cadet centre;

¶ In 1914, drill station for G Coy. 4 Bn. Essex Regt.

¶ In 1950, base for C Coy. 4 Bn. Essex Regt.

Epsom [Surrey]; V

*1 60 East Street, drill hall, in 1934; demolished for offices; drill hall at 2 Hawthorne Place in 1913; NB *Yeomanry Close* in vicinity;

¶ In 1914, base for H Coy. 5 Bn. East Surrey Regt;

Erith [Kent]; V

*1Bexley Road, 'Trevethan House', drill hall; destroyed for housing;

¶ In 1914, HQ 4+5 Kent [H] Btys.+Ammunition Column, 4 Home Counties [Howitzer] Bde. RFA; drill station 4 London School of Ambulance RAMC;

¶ In 1933, HQ+206 & 207 Btys. 52 [K] Medium Bde. RA [TA];

Esher [Surrey]; PV

*1 West End, Armoury, in use 1913;

*2 High St, **Drill Hall**; backs onto Library; until recently a squash-club; small, gabled, timber shed, range of garages to side;

¶ In 1914, base for A Coy. 6 Bn. East Surrey Regt.

Everton [Liverpool]; PV A[*2]

*1 50-52 Everton Brow, in use 1880; completely redeveloped;

¶ In 1880, new HQ 5 Volunteer Battalion Kings Liverpool Regt;

*2 57-61 Everton Road, **Drill Hall**, in use 1914 & 1947; terrace of early-Victorian houses, with central arch through to lateral hall, garages, sheds etc. at rear; currently derelict; 1930s photo shows 6" CA gun in hall, with practice equipment;

¶ In 1914, HQ+A-E & G Coys.9 Bn. Kings Liverpool Regt;

¶ In 1947, 420 Coast Regt, RA;

*3 Netherfield Road North, drill hall; street cleared away;

¶ In 1881, HQ 18 Lancashire Volunteer Rifles, then 5 Volunteer Bn. Kings Liverpool Regt; [see Everton Brow **1** above]

Evesham [Worcestershire]; PV

*1 Coronation St, **Drill Hall**, pre-WWl; brick hall flanked by 2-storey house on one side, & garage on other; decorative features: windows, stone dressings, chequer-board brickwork etc; now ex-Servicemen's club;

¶ In 1914, base for D Coy. 8 Bn. Worcestershire Regt.

Ewell [Surrey]; W

*1 Welbeck Close, London Road, 1938; Mercator House, **Drill Hall**; Home Guard base in WWll; 2-storey front block, & three single-storey blocks are wrapped around central hall with cupola; two further 2-storey blocks, large garage block, & detached house for staff; all set in yard with outbuildings;

¶ In 1939, base for 318 Coy. 30 Surrey Searchlight Bn;

Exeter [Devon]; PV TACs [*2 & *14]

*1 New North Road, Higher [Cavalry] Barracks aka "Town" or "New", 1792, extended 1867; now developed as housing with some modern blended in-filling;

*2 Barrack Road, Wyvern [Artillery] Barracks aka "Topsham", 1804; incorporating adjacent **TAC** ;

*3 Barrack Road, TAC, demolished for housing;

*4 9 Dix's Field, in use by 1897-1935; demolished for car-park;

*5 Colleston Cres, The Priory, in use 1914; not found;

*6 14 Oxford Road, in use 1914; 3-storey 19C terraced house stands;

*7 71 Holloway Street, in use 1914; no such number;

*8 19 Cathedral Close, in use 1914; not found, no such number;

*9 Goldsmith Street, Lennards Buildings, in use 1914; re-developed as shops;

*10 10 Bystock Terr. HQ 1 Devon Yeomanry, 1897;

*11 16 James Street, HQ Devon & Somerset REs, 1897;

*12 7 Well Street, HQ 4 Bn. Devonshire Regt. 1897;

*13 Bedford Circus, drill hall, HQ 4 Bn. Devonshire Regt. 1910; destroyed;

*14 Dryden Road, Pellew House, **TAC**, in use; 1980s offices; ACF HQ;

*15 Butts Road, **Drill Hall**, 1930s; now Red Cross HQ, Ermen House; 2-storey L-shaped block with stair-tower, enclosing hall; garages & four pairs of staff houses to rear;

*16 Normandy Road, **Drill Hall**, in use 1935; rectangular, 2-storey block, now converted to six houses;

17* 4 Leighton Terrace, York Road, HQ of Cyclists Bn. 1914;

¶ In 1914, HQ+ drill station for B Sqdn. 1 Devon Yeomanry [Dix'sField]; HQ Devon & Cornwall Infantry Bde; HQ 2 SW Mounted Bde. [Goldsmith Street]; HQ Wessex Div. [Cathedral Close]; HQ+1 Devonshire Bty.4 Wessex Bde. RFA; HQ+No. 1 Section Wessex Divnl. Signals Coys. REs. [Priory]; base Nos. 2&3 Works Coys. Devonshire REs-Fortress; HQ+A-C Coys. 4 Bn.Devonshire Regt; HQ+B & C Coys. 7 [Cyclist] Bn. Devonshire Regt; HQ Wessex Divnl. Transport & Supply Column ASC [Oxford Rd]; HQ+A & B Sections 1 Wessex Divnl. Field Ambulances RAMC [Holloway Street]; Wessex Clearing Hospital RAMC;

Exmouth [Devon]; PV ATC [*3]

*1 Imperial Road, **Drill Hall**, pre-WWl; Leisure Centre; large gabled hall, much adapted & expanded;

*2 St Andrews Rd, in use 1910;

*3 Phear Park, ATC;

¶ In 1914, drill station for B Sqdn. 1 Devon Yeo; drill station for 1 Devonshire Bty. 4 Wessex Bde. RFA; base for D Coy. 4 Bn. Devonshire Regt

F

Failsworth [Manchester]; PV TAC

*1 Oldham Road, **Drill Hall**, c1938; in use by RE units; 2-storey front block with extensive garages/workshops etc to rear in yard;

¶ In 1938, 71 [E Lancs] Searchlight Regt. formed as new unit;

Fakenham [Norfolk]; PV

*1 Holt Road, **Drill Hall**, pre-WWl; subsequently a cinema, now antique market & car dealer; low, long hall, & 2-storey administration & accommodation block across back end; garage alongside at rear;

¶ In 1914, base for C Sqdn. Norfolk Yeomanry; base for C Coy. 5 Bn. Norfolk Regt; & base for E Coy. 6 [Cyclist] Bn. Norfolk Regt;

Falmouth [Cornwall]; PV

*1 Pendennis Castle, Militia Stores & Armoury, c1849 in upper gun-room of keep; 1849-1866 the keep accommodated the Militia Orderly Room and Officers' Mess; in 1902 a pastiche Tudor extension to the Henrician keep guard-house was built for the Cornwall & Devon Miners' RGA [Militia]; when the Army left in 1921, these offices were demolished;1902 **RGA Barracks** + further military buildings on site;

*2 Brook St/Berkeley Vale, **Drill Hall**, 1874; built as chapel, converted to military use; now a market; ecclesiastical features overlain by inscriptions: 'Drill Hall, 1874, B Coy. 4/5 Bn. DCLI';

*3 Bar Rd/Grove Place/Harbour, drill hall, 1892; 2-storey/single storey front block, with small hall to rear; adjacent, large hangar-like geodetic structure, known locally as the 'Dome'; demolished 2002 for housing development;

¶ In 1914, HQ+No.6 Coy. Cornwall RGA-Defended Ports; HQ+No.1 Electric Lights Coy. REs-Fortress; base for C Coy. 4 Bn. DCLI;

¶ In 1935-9, 202 AA Bty. 56 HAA Regt.

Fareham [Hampshire]; PV ACF

*1 149 West St/Osborne Rd South, Connaught Drill Hall, 1898 & 1905; extended 1918; large hall in use into 1960s; demolished for re-development c1980s;

*2 Kings Rd, **Drill Hall**; marked on 1962 map as TAC; hall behind, brick with stone dressings, archway in end wall, stylistically c1914; on Kings Road a 2-storey front block of brick & stone, with pediment, hall behind, now known as Assembly Hall, night shelter; design etc. points to this being

ELY's drill hall lies alongside the parade-ground of the old Militia barracks

FARNHAM, the post-WWll AA TAC with extensive technical training facilities

a drill hall of c1914;

¶ In 1914, drill station Cosham Bty. Wessex RGA- Heavy; base H Coy. 6 Bn. Hants

Farncombe [Surrey]; PV ACF

*1 Hallam Road, Queens House, **Cadet Centre** on former drill hall site; buildings c1980s, replaced earlier, possibly1914; see **Godalming**;

Farnham [Surrey]; PV TAC [*2]

*1 Bear Lane [aka Park Lane], drill hall, c1908; 2-storey front block with lateral hall behind; used by HG in WWll; demolished c1988 for St Georges Yard;

*2 Guildford Rd, **TAC**, 1953; built for AA unit; 2/3-storey quadrangular block with hall within; AA dome-trainer incorporated; large yard with garages etc; [p154]

¶ In 1914, base for E Coy. 5 Bn. Royal West Surrey Regt.

¶ In 1950, base for R Bty. 536 LAA Regt. RA TA. [Bear Lane]

Farnworth **[Bolton];** VA [p156]

*1 James Street off Church Road, drill hall, demolished; low hall with indoor range along one side & offices along the other; screen-wall façade; cWWl & in use 1930s;

¶ In 1914, base for D Coy. 5 Bn. Loyal North Lancashire Regt;

Faversham [Kent]; PVA ACF

*1 **8 The Mall**, Yeomanry HQ in 1908; terraced Victorian house;

*2 Preston St. **Drill Hall** for RGA, built by Bulmer & Ware [plaque], 1849 as Assembly Rooms; used as drill hall since 1869; still used by ACF; 3-bay hall with door to street to one side; yard behind with 2-storey orderly-room block, house, gun-shed etc; rusticated quoins on main building, green & white wash;

*3 West St, Stonebridge Lodge built as school for employees of Gunpowder Factory; in 1859, converted into drill-room by Commandant of Artillery Volunteers; when school moved to purpose-built premises in...

*4 Tanners St, ground-floor room fitted out as an Armoury;

¶ In 1908, base B Sqdn. Royal East Kent Yeomanry; half-bty. Kent Home Counties RGA Heavy Bty.+Ammunition Column;

¶ In 1914, base for B Sqdn. Royal East Kent Mounted Rifles; HQ+Kent Bty. Home Counties RGA-Heavy;

Featherstone [West Yorkshire]; V
no location identified; probably met at nearby **Pontefract**;
¶ In 1914, base for E Coy. 5 Bn. KOYLI;

Felixstowe [Suffolk]; PV
*1 Garrison Lane, **Drill Hall**, 1901; 2-storey admin block alongside hall with Dutch gable on facade; garages & sheds to rear [*p156*];
*2 Landguard Fort, Submarine Mining Establishment in former Ravelin Battery; single-storey pentagonal block; datestone 1878 over doorway; now museum;
¶ In 1914, drill station for C Sqdn. Suffolk Yeomanry; & for 1 Coy. Essex & Suffolk RGA- Defended Ports.

Felling [Tyne & Wear]; V
*1 Coldwell Street, drill hall, demolished for housing c1970s;
¶ In 1914, base for E Coy. 9 Bn. Durham LI;

Fleet [Hampshire]; V
Extensive barracks but no known drill hall;
¶ In 1914, drill station for E Coy. 4 Bn. Hampshire Regt;

Fleetwood [Lancashire]; PV A[***3**] ACF [***3**]
*1 Esplanade, **North Euston Hotel**, built 1843 by Decimus Burton, used as School of Musketry 1860-99, referred to as the "Barracks"; 3-storey arc with central porte cochere, another porch towards each end of the building;
*2 Lord St, London House, **HQ** of TF unit, in 1912; 3-storey Victorian house on corner of London St;
*3 Preston St, drill hall, 1934; demolished; formerly 3-bay front block with turreted porch; indoor range & ACF hut remain; [*p158*]
¶ In 1914, base for G & H Coys. Royal Lancaster Regt;

Folkestone [Kent]; PV
*1 HQ of Volunteers in large hall in Pleasure Gardens by 1896;
*2 Shellon[s] St. drill hall, in use 1908; in use by 232 Bty. 75 AA Regt. 1938-45; demolished;
*3 Foord Road, drill hall; demolished along with neighbouring Gas-works;
¶ In 1899, base for D Coy. East Kent Volunteers;
¶ In 1908, drill station for D Sqdn. Royal East Kent Yeomanry; base for D Coy 4Bn. The Buffs; base for 2 Kent Bty. 3 Home Counties [CP] Bde. RFA;
¶ In 1914, drill station for D Sqdn. Royal East Kent Mounted Rifles; base for 2 Kent Bty. 3 Home Counties Bde. RFA; drill station No. 3 Coy. Kent RGA Defended Ports; base for D Coy. 4 Bn. East Kent Regt; drill station for H Coy. Kent Cyclist Bn;

Formby [Sefton]; PV
*1 Harrington Barracks, 1939; camp to service Altcar Ranges; levelled in 1960s for housing; some married quarters remain in Larkhill Lane;
*2 Green Lane, The Grapes, PH, served as drill hall; extensive early-19C building stands; formerly stable-yard & assembly hall used as drill hall, stood where car-park now is; premises subsequently used as cinema & ice-rink prior to demolition;
*3 Victoria or **Jubilee Hall** [on Timms Lane], is listed in Kelly's 1914 as base of part of H Coy. but located in Church Road;
*4 Gild [sic] Hall on Church Road, may have been used;
¶ In 1914, drill station for H Coy. 7 Bn. Kings Liverpool Regt;
¶ In 1947, base for 390th LAA Regt. RA [TA] at Altcar Ranges;

Fowey [Cornwall]; V
*1 Rawlings Road, drill hall; demolished, Ambulance Station on site;
¶ In 1914, base for No.2 Works Coy. REs-Fortress;

Framlingham [Suffolk]; PV
*1 New Road, **Drill Hall**, c1930s; single-storey offices etc. round central hall;
¶ In 1914, drill station for C Sqdn. Suffolk Yeo; & base G Coy. 4 Bn. Suffolk Regt;

Freshwater [Isle of Wight]; PV
*1 Drill Hall, 1899; built as a drill hall but always known as the [Cameron] "Memorial Hall", in memory of the photographer, Mrs Cameron's son; in use until 1961; now public hall; hall to street with castellated stepped facade to gable-end; 2-storey orderly-room block adjoining, with double-pile, gabled block behind; all in red brick; opened by Lord Tennyson, January 1899 [foundation-stone];
¶ In 1914, base for No. 5 Electric Lights Coy. REs-Fortress; drill station for A Sqdn. Hampshire Carabiniers; base for 5 Hants [H] Bty. 2 Wessex [Howitzer] Bde. RFA;

FARNWORTH, a 1930s picture of this demolished drill hall [photo: NW RFCA]

FELIXSTOWE, a fine example of the side-by-side layout

Frizington [Cumbria]; V
   *1 Yeatshouse Lane, drill hall demolished, school on site;
   ¶ In 1914, base for G Coy. 5 Bn. Border Regt;

Frodsham [Halton]; PV ACF
   *1 Main Street, **Drill Hall**, by 1887; sandstone arch, flanked by small, castellated towers & big, double gates, form frontage to hall; inscription over arch: 'I Company, 2nd E C V B : CR'; [Earl of Chester's Volunteer Battalion Cheshire Regt];
   ¶ In 1914, base for F Coy. 5 Bn. Cheshire Regt;

Frome [Somerset]; PV ACF
   *1 King Street, **Angel Hotel**, Yeomanry HQ in 1894;
   *2 Christchurch St. East, **Lamb Hotel**, Yeomanry HQ in 1910;
   *3 Gentle St, **HQ** & **Armoury** of SLI in 1894; imposing 19C house & outbuildings, latterly RBL;
   *4 Keyford St, **Drill Hall**, by 1914; 2-storey front block with gable over entrance; hall, indoor range, other annexes etc. behind; house to rear; in 1940 HQ of 4 [Somerset] Bn. Home Guard;
   ¶ In 1914, drill station for A Sqdn. N Somerset Yeomanry; base D Coy. 4 Bn. SLI; HQ 2SW Mounted Bde. Field Ambulances RAMC;

Fulham [Greater London]; PV TAC [*2] ACF [*4] [p103]
   *1 69 Lillie Road, drill hall, disappeared in redevelopment;
   ¶ In 1903, HQ 26 Middlesex [Cyclists], part of 2 Vol. Bn. KRRC
   *2 87 Fulham High Street, Fulham House, **Drill Hall**; in use by Royal Green Jackets; substantial yellow-brick 3-storey house of 1730s, with ornate, reconstructed pedimented gateway, & railings; behind, 1980s hall & garages etc.
   ¶ In 1903, 2 Middlesex, part of 2 Vol. Bn. KRRC
   ¶ In 1914, HQ+A-H Coys. 25 [Cyclist] Bn.London Regt.; & HQ 18 & 20 County of London Bty. & Ammunition Column, 7 London Bde. RFA.
   *3 67 College Street, Fulham; now re-named Elystan Place, but no No 67; built with revolutionary laminated timber roof trusses, by Fowke; NB "Ranelagh House", a modern re-development at <u>East</u> end of street;
   ¶ In 1903, 1 Middlesex RE;
   *4 190-2 Hammersmith Road, **Drill Hall**, pre-WWl; 4-storey front block with hall behind; lettering on front: 'Princess

Louise's Kensington Regiment', a title granted 1914; this was 13 Bn. Middlesex Regt; vacated by TA; Cadet Centre remains;

*5 Grove House, Hollywood Rd. in use 1910 but not in 1933; no such building now exists;

*6 36 Elm Grove, Hammersmith in use 1914 by D & E Coys. 7 Bn. London Regt; no such address; there is an Elm Grove Rd. south of Hammersmith Bridge in Barnes; NB also Harrow;

*7 Parsons Green Lane in use 1939;

¶ In 1939, base for 117 Field Regiment RA [TA] [Parsons Green Lane]

G

Gainsborough [Lincolnshire]; PV ACF [*2]

*1 Spital Terrace, **Public Hall** in use 1892; known as Temperance Hall; 1921 map shows Hall in angle of Drill Hall Lane; referred to as Public Hall in 1913; in use by TA in 1933; large hall with St John Ambulance inscription over ornate front; garage added to rear, may be recent, and for ambulances as is still used by St John Ambulance;

*2 Ropery Road, **Drill Hall**, 1939; 2-storey front block with stone doorway, with 'Egypt' & 'X' crest; hall and garages etc. behind; cf Frodingham;

¶ In 1892, base for J Coy. 1 Vol. Bn. Lincolnshire Regt;

¶ In 1900, base for E & F Coys. 1 Vol. Bn. Lincolnshire Regt;

¶ In 1914, drill station C Sqdn. Lincs Yeomanry; & base H Coy. 5 Bn. Lincs Regt;

¶ In 1933, base for C Coy. 5 Bn. Lincolnshire Regt;

Garston [Liverpool]; PV

*1 1 Earp Street, **Drill Hall**, in use 1914; two, parallel, gabled halls with roofed area between entered through shuttered gate; machicolation detail on outside wall in front; now carton & transport depot;

¶ In 1914, base for 13 Lancashire Bty. 3 West Lancashire Bde. RFA [Earp St];

Gateshead [Tyne & Wear]; PVA TAC [*4]

*1 Burt Terrace, Alexandra Road, drill hall, built by 1896; demolished by 1970s for housing development; E side of N end of road;

*2 Liddell Terrace, Angus Hall, **Drill Hall**, built 1899 for 1st

Newcastle-upon-Tyne Volunteer Artillery; refurbished at a cost of £500,000+ as part of a Community re-generation project; long hall front to road with Hanseatic-type gables, elaborate doorways & datestone over main door; at one end, 2-storey admin block & armoury; [p158]

*3 Alexandra Road, drill hall, 1898, demolished for 4; shown on 1919 map; W side of S end of road;

*4 **Napier Armoury**, Alexandra Rd, in use by RA & MI units; small hall, c1970s, with reset 1898 datestone, in use as cadet centre; long, 2-storey blocks, parallel to street, with yards in between; at one end, pair of staff houses;

*5 Elmgrove St. in use 1947; no such road by 1988;

¶ In 1907, 5 Volunteer Bn. DLI [Burt Terrace]; 1 Durham Volunteer REs. [Alexandra Road]; 1 Newcastle Volunteer RGA [Angus Hall];

¶ In 1914, base No.3 Works Coy. Durham REs-Fortress; HQ+A-D Coys. 9 Bn. DLI [Burt Terrace]; base for HQ Coy. Northumberland Bde. Coy. Northumbrian Divnl. Transport & Supply Column ASC [Angus Hall];

¶ In 1947, HQ 377th Observation Regt. RA [Durham] TA at Elmgrove Street;

Gillingham [Dorset]; PV ACF

*1 [now] Cemetery Rd, **Drill Hall**, by 1901; hall with cross-wing fronted by later 2-storey house; double garage & cadet hut; all in red brick; community centre;

¶ In 1914, base for D Sqdn. Dorset Yeomanry; base for E Coy. 4 Bn. Dorset Regt;

Gillingham [Kent]; PV

*1 Sub-Marine Mining School, at RE school, Brompton Barracks; moved to Pier Rd 1896;

*2 Trinity Cottage, Old Brompton recorded as in use 1910;

*3 Watling St, **Drill Hall**, post 1933, as no TA units in town at that date; 2-storey front block with later additions; White horse badge on front of building;

¶ In 1908, HQ+3-5 Coys. Kent Fortress RE, [Submarine Mining School];

¶ In 1914, HQ+3-6 Coys. Kent REs Fortress;

Glastonbury [Somerset]; PV ACF

*1 45 High St, Armoury of SLI in 1914; demolished for Woolworths;

*2 Street Road, **Drill Hall**, pre-WWl; 2-storey front block & adjoining house, both with brick details- keystones,

FLEETWOOD, the range survives of this former drill hall [photo: NW RFCA]

GATESHEAD, Angus Hall, once HQ of the 1st Newcastle Volunteer Artillery

dentillation; hall behind with indoor range; outbuildings, garages & huts;

¶ In 1914, drill station for C Sqdn. W Somerset Yeomanry; drill station for [Taunton] Bty. Somerset RHA; base for H Coy. 4 Bn. Somerset LI;

Glossop [Derbyshire]; PV

*1 Market Place, **Market Hall**, built 1838; the front part, the Town Hall; behind this was a large space which was split longitudinally by a timber screen, with half serving as drill hall of 4 Cheshire Rifle Volunteers; the market reclaimed the whole space in 1958; at the back, a 2-storey part of the block is municipal offices;

*2 Dinting Lane, **Drill Hall**, 1939; huts: mess & drill hall; curved corrugated iron-clad double garage; other huts for stores etc; in use in 1950s & 1960s by signals unit; industrial estate;

¶ In 1914, base for D Coy. 6 Bn. Cheshire Regt;

Gloucester [Gloucestershire]; PV TAC [*3] ACF [*4]

*1 Commercial Road, Barracks/Armoury of S Gloucestershire Militia, 1854-7; most demolished 1960 for County Buildings extension; gate-tower with turret & oriel survived, next to Gaol until 1970, since demolished.

*2 31 Commercial Road, Custom House, HQ Glos. Berks & Wilts Regt; 19C classical, two storeys, with royal coat-of-arms; now military museum;

*3 Eastern Avenue, **TAC**, 1950; in use by Yeomanry; 2-storey brick & glass front block; entrance porch with large window etched with 'Territorial Army'; yard with long range of garages etc;

*4 Clyde Cres. Brockworth, ACF Centre;

¶ In 1914, HQ+A Sqdn. Royal Glos Hussars [Barracks]; base for 3 [Glos] Bty. 1 S Midland [Glos] Bde. RFA [Barracks]; HQ+A &B Coys. 5 Bn. Glos Regt. [Barracks];

¶ In 1947, HQ 72 AA Bde; Royal Glos. Hussars; 5 Bn. Gloucestershire Regt;

Godalming [Surrey]; PV

*1 Bridge Street, **Borough** [public] **Hall**, 1906; in use as drill hall 1913;

¶ In 1913, base for F Coy. 5 Bn. Royal West Surrey Regt;

Godmanchester **[Cambridgeshire];** V

no trace of drill hall ever; may have used **Huntingdon**, only half-a-mile away;

¶ In 1914, base for D Sqdn. Bedfordshire Yeomanry; A & B Coys. Hunts. Cyclist Bn. drawn from Huntingdon & Godmanchester.

Golborne [Wigan]; PVA

*1 Bank Street, **Drill Hall**, c1936; single-storey hall with porch & offices in front, & wings to each side; now Bank Street Social Club;

¶ In 1947, 644 LAA/SL Regt;

Goole [East Yorkshire]; PV ACF

*1 Pasture Rd, **Drill Hall**, pre-1907; 2-storey red-brick front block with hall behind; yard with later garages etc; on 1907 map prior to adjacent church being built;

¶ In 1914, drill station for C Sqdn. Yorkshire Dragoons; base D Coy. 5 Bn. KOYLI;

Gosforth [Tyne & Wear]; V TAC [*2]

*1 Knightsbridge drill hall, in use 1914; demolished for housing;

*2 Airport Industrial Estate, Kingston Park, **TAC**, in use by RA & REME units; extensive factory-type buildings & offices replacing *1.

¶ In 1914, base for G & H Coys. 5 Bn. Northumberland Fusiliers;

Gosport [Hampshire]; VA

*1 Walpole Road, drill halls, both on 1910 map; both demolished for Library [Connaught DH, 1902] & supermarket;

*2 Haslar Street [now Road], drill hall on 1910 map & 1970s aerial photograph; almost all demolished for Marina;

¶ In 1914, base for 3 Hampshire Bty. 1 Wessex Bde. RFA [Walpole Road]; No.6 Electric Lights Coy. Hampshire Fortress RE; base for E Coy. 6 Bn. Hampshire Regt; 5 Southern General Hospital RAMC;

Grantham [Lincolnshire]; PV ACF [*pp46,66*]

*1 St Catherines Road, **Militia Barracks** of c1858 & 1872 built for South Lincs militia; castellated mediaeval style with gatehouse & angle towers; the drill shed, added 1913, & other offices are arranged around a central court; built of stone; now antiques centre & CPS office;

*2 Wharf Road, drill hall, on 1902 map; in use 1892;

*3 Prince William of Gloucester Barracks, ex RAF Spitalgate, expansion-period airfield; **TAC** in use, [TA Transport HQ];

¶ In 1880, base for A & B Coys. 2 Vol. Bn. Lincolnshire Regt;

¶ In 1914, base for A Sqdn. Lincolnshire Yeomanry, & B Coy. 4 Bn. Lincs Regt;

Gravesend [Kent]; PV ACF [*4]

*1 89 **Windmill St**, in use 1908; large detached house on corner site;1932 map shows evidence of substantial outbuildings;

*2 Wrotham Rd, in use 1908; no trace;

*3 Milton Road, in use 1908; large drill hall shown on 1932 map beside railway bridge; also referred to as Pelham Rd; now demolished for housing;

*4 Grange Rd, ex-TAC, c1930; main building demolished for housing, but ACF hut, Nissen-type indoor range, & two staff houses stand;

¶ In 1903, base for 1 Kent RGA, [Windmill Street];

¶ In 1908, base for B Sqdn. West Kent Yeomanry [Wrotham Road]; base for 4 Coy. Kent RGA [Milton Road]; drill station for No. 5 Coy. Kent Fortress RE;

¶ In 1914, drill station for B Sqdn. West Kent Yeomanry; base for No. 2 Coy. Kent RGA Defended Ports & for No. 5 Electric Lights Coy. Kent Fortress RE;

Grays [Essex]; PV TAC [*1]

*1 Brook Road, drill hall, in use WWl; 1960s replacement **TAC** on site;

*2 2 High Street in use 1950;

¶ In 1914, drill station for D Sqdn. Essex Yeomanry; 3 Essex Bty. 2 E Anglian Bde. RFA [Artillery Drill Hall]; drill station for H Coy. 6 Bn. Essex Regt;

¶ In 1950, 534 Coy. RASC, [2 High St]; R Bty. 285 Airborne Light Regt;[Brook Road]

Great Bardfield [Essex]; PV

*1 Dunmow Road, house, c1950, called 'Drill Hall House', hall demolished;

¶ In 1914, drill station for F Coy. 5 Bn. Essex Regt.

Great Yarmouth [Norfolk]; PV ACF

*1 Southtown Rd, **Barracks**, 1806 & 1855; armoury, officers' mess, HQ building, and quadrangle of single-storey barrack-blocks remain; Cardwell depot of Norfolk Regt. now in maritime/industrial use;

*2 Southtown Road, c1930s, **Drill Hall**; single-storey offices & garages etc. wrapped around hall with green lantern on ridge; currently in commercial use by printing firm;

*3 80 Southtown Road, Hampstead House, large 19C house, with mid-20C staff house behind; part of adjacent TAC;

*4 Nelson Road **Drill Hall**, 1867; brick & flint 2-storey entrance block with arched doorway; stepped gables on large hall behind; now youth centre;

¶ In 1914, drill station for B Sqdn. Norfolk Yeomanry; base for 1 Norfolk Bty. 1 East Anglian Bde. RFA [Nelson Road]; & for G & H Coys. 5 Bn. Norfolk Regt base for B Coy. & drill station for H Coy. 6 [Cyclist] Bn. Norfolk Regt.

Greenwich [Greater London]; PV TAC [2]

*1 159 Greenwich [High] Road; re-developed as industrial units;

¶ In 1914, HQ+A-C Sections, 5 London Divisional Field Ambulances RAMC;

*2 Wat Tyler Road, Blackheath, Holly Hedge House, **Drill Hall**; late-19C block; c1930 neo-Georgian block; accommodation block; large hall; + garages etc. all enclosed by fences on heathland;

*3 Randall Place, in use 1910; re-developed;

¶ In 1903, HQ 2Vol. Bn. The Queen's Own [Royal West Kent Regt.]

¶ In 1914, HQ+A-H Coys. 20 Bn. London Regt. [Blackheath & Woolwich]

Grimsby [North-East Lincolnshire]; PV TAC

*1 Victoria Street North, **Drill Hall**, 1891; originally 77 Victoria Street; built for the artillery volunteers of 1 Lincolnshire RGA; the 2-storey front block is castellated with an oriel window over the main door & a tower above; built in brick with stone dressings; the hall is behind; now a printers; in use until 1939; ref to Central Market in 1892 [p170];

*2 Bull Ring, Armoury, in use 1892; no specific site; re-developed;

*3 Corn Exchange, in use 1892; demolished;

*4 Westward Ho, Bargate, **Drill Hall**, 1939; in use by infantry & medical units; large L-shaped admin. block containing hall; garages to rear across yard & huts beyond; staff house to side; opened 17 January 1939 by Field-Marshall Sir Archibald Montgomery-Massingberd for ex 5 Bn. Lincs Regt; coat-of-arms over door, & corbels carved

with RE & Lincs' crests;

*5 Ainslie St/Doughty Rd, drill hall, built by 1907, used by Lincolns as depot & recruiting office WWl; in use by RASC unit WWll, & by 4/6 Lincolns until at least 1961; Bellamy's Garage; then demolished for car-park;

*6 Augusta St. drill hall, in use WWll, & by RASC, REME & WRAC units until at least 1961; used for a while for sports [tennis] coaching & trade exhibitions; demolished by 1980 for Eaton Court;

¶ In 1914, base for D Sqdn. Lincolnshire Yeomanry; 1 North Midland Bde. RFA, HQ, 1 & 2 Lincs Batteries; HQ, A & B Coys. 5 Bn. Lincolnshire Regt.; and B Section, Notts & Derby Mounted Bde. Field Ambulance;

¶ In 1892; base for E Coy. 1 Vol. Bn. Lincolnshire Regt [***2** & ***3**]; base for 1 Bde. Position Artillery + 3 batteries [***1**];

¶ In 1933, base for unit of 5 Bn. Lincolnshire Regt; base for 238 Bty.60 North Midlands Bde. RA [**5**];

¶ In 1939, base for 382 AA Searchlight Coy. RE, TA [***4**];

Grove, Isle of Portland [Dorset]; PV ACF [p69]

*1 Easton Lane, Isle of Portland, **Drill Hall**, 1874 & 1901; castellated, mediaeval castle-style front block with large hall behind; house with crow-stepped gables to side, all in Portland stone; another, later hall to rear, & ACF Hut to side;

¶ In 1914, base for No.3 Coy. Dorset RGA- Defended Ports; drill station for No.1 Electric Lights Coy. Dorsetshire REs-Fortress;

Guernsey [Channel Islands]; St Peter Port;

*1 Monument Road, Town Arsenal, HQ of Light Infantry, 1911;

*2 Anns Place, Militia HQ in 1911;

*3 Naftiaux Arsenal, HQ in 1911;

Guildford [Surrey]; PV

*1 Stoughton Barracks, 1870s; Cardwell depot of Queens Own Royal West Surrey Regt; Keep, gateway & barrack-blocks now converted to housing;

*2 Haydon Place, drill hall, 1886, bought from Edinburgh International Exhibition, and its re-erection paid for by money raised from officers; it was a glass-house, 122 feet [58m] x 60 feet [28m], and still in use in 1913; probably replaced by ***3**; on same block, with entry in adjacent street was

HAYLE, more like the village school, one of several Cornish drill halls c1911

ALNESS, built for the Lea & Perrins workforce, 1903, but bought by TA in 1938

MOLD, the office of the Flintshire Territorial Force Association

LINCOLN, the Broadgate drill hall, was known as "Bread & Cheese Hall"

CARDIFF's Ty Llewellyn TAC replaced a drill hall demolished for the Stadium

PORTSMOUTH's Connaught drill hall in Stanhope Street replaced an earlier one

GLASGOW's Gilbert Street Highland Light
Infantry drill hall is now apartments

POLLOCKSHAWS, the drill hall of the 6th
Bn. Argyll & Sutherland Highlanders

164

NORWICH, 44 Bethel Street, once HQ of a Field Ambulance

GOLSPIE, an unusual timber & corrugated-iron construction

FORRES, the front block of the Seaforth Highlanders' drill hall

BEXHILL-on-SEA has twin side-by-side drill halls; this one of the Sussex Regt.

ENFIELD, the unusually fancy drill hall and much plainer house

HALIFAX, the Prescott Street drill hall, covering a whole block

CHORLEY's Lancaster House TAC, still in use

HAMPSTEAD, the Henry Street [now Allitsen Rd] drill hall of the Sharpshooters

*3 Sandfield Terrace, TAC, 1953; 2-storey front block with lateral hall behind; demolished June 2001;

*4 58 Denzil Rd, drill hall, in use 1913; imposing double-fronted 19C house, now home;

*5 Leapale Lane, Drill Hall, acquired 1927; 3-storey orderly room block with double hall to side, & 3-bay, gabled lobby fronting hall; built as Webber's 'Churchacre' ironworks, bankrupted in Depression; now BellerbyTheatre; adjacent Telephone Exchange was HQ for B Coy. 39 GPO Bn. [11 Sussex Bn.] HG;

*6 Stockton Close, drill hall; demolished & redeveloped as Auto Services; some buildings may remain, adapted or altered; ACF hut on site;

*7 Artillery Rd & Artillery Terrace are named for Artillery Fields, mid-19C camping grounds for Surrey Militia;

¶ In 1914, base for B Sqdn. Surrey Yeomanry, [Denzil Road]; HQ+D Coy. 5 Bn. Royal WestSurrey Regt. [Haydon Place];

¶ In 1927, base for HQ+318 SL Coy. RE[TA] until 1939 [Leapale Lane];

Guisborough [North Yorkshire]; PV
*1 Park Lane, Drill Hall, pre-WWl; fitness centre; 2-storey front block with hipped roof & stone detail, hall behind; garage to side;
¶ In 1914, base for D Coy. 4 Bn. Princess of Wales Yorkshire Regt;

Guiseley [West Yorkshire]; PV
*1 Victoria Road, Drill Hall, pre-1900; now apartments & vacant hall; 2-storey front block, with pediment over door, similar to Morley; lateral hall behind;
¶ In 1914, base for C Coy. 6 Bn. DoW West Riding Regt.

H

Hackney [Greater London]; PV
*1 Grocers' Company's School, Clapton, drill hall [100'x40'], armoury, etc.
¶ In 1903, HQ 4 London, 10 Vol. Bn. KRRC
*2 1 Hillman Street, Drill Hall, pre-WWl; single-storey entrance to large hall; gunstore, garages, workshops etc attached; large admin. block now health centre may represent orderly-room, messes etc; currently unoccupied, but outbuildings form part of council depot; in military use 1947 & 1965; formerly 49-51 The Grove;

¶ In 1914, HQ 10 Bn. London Regt. [Hackney];
¶ In 1965, 114 Engineer Regt. TA;
*3 208 Mare Street, Hackney; 19C terrace, now shops;
¶ In 1903, orderly room, sergeants' mess, range etc. of 4 Vol. Bn. Essex Regt

Hadleigh [Suffolk]; PV ACF
*1 George St, Drill Hall, pre-WWl; hall, house, [datestone 1914] & later garage;
¶ In 1914, base for C Coy. 5 Bn. Suffolk Regt.

Hailsham [Sussex]; PV ACF[*3]
*1 Sturton Place, Drill Hall, pre-WWl; in use into 1930s by infantry; hall with arched doorway to road, extensions of different later periods to side; now clinic;
*2 London Rd, Drill Hall, by 1933; 2-storey, 11-bay front block with hall behind, to one side, & garages/gun-stores to other; in use by artillery unit from 1930s on; in use as county ambulance HQ;
*3 Victoria Rd, former 19C school building in use as Cadet Centre; tile-hung, gabled, T-shaped building with porch in one angle;
¶ In 1914, base for Ammunition Column, & drill station for 4 Sussex Bty. 2   Home Counties Bde. RFA;

Halesowen [Dudley]; PV ACF
*1 Grammar School Lane/Furnace Lane, Drill Hall, by 1904; long 10-bay, aisled hall with 2-storey block at one end; garage beyond; yard with further garaging & single-storey red-brick orderly-room block; cadet centre on adjacent site;
¶ In 1914, base for F Coy. 7 Bn. Worcestershire Regt.

Halesworth [Suffolk]; PV [p170]
*1 Ipswich Rd, Drill Hall ['Rifle Hall'], 1889; imposing hall built of brick with stone dressings; possible former small-arms range down one side; now public hall;
¶ In 1860, 7th. Corps of Suffolk Rifle Volunteers formed at Halesworth, also location for HQ of 3 Admin. Bn. [12.xi.1860]
¶ In 1881, F Coy. 1 Volunteer Bn. [late 1 Corps] Suffolk Regt;
¶ In 1914, drill station for D Sqdn. Suffolk Yeo; & base for F Coy. 4 Bn.Suffolk Regt;

Halifax [West Yorkshire]; PV
*1 Wellesley Park, Barracks; 1870s Cardwell depot of Duke of Wellington's West Riding Regt; almost complete; currently

GRIMSBY, the drill hall of the volunteer artillery, first RGA, then RFA

HALESWORTH, Rifle Hall of 1889

social services offices, & outdoor education facilities; all built in yellow brick with stone dressings;

*2 Prescott Street, **Drill Hall**, c1880s [*p167*]; very elaborate ecclesiastical style complex of halls, offices, and housing; currently vacant but for Armed Forces Careers in house adjoining main hall; very fine standard of building with highly decorative finish; all built in yellow brick with stone dressings; in use through 1950s & 1960s;

*3 Arden St, **Drill Hall**, c1880s; built as roller-skating rink, & later used as cinema; pre-WWI became artillery drill hall until sold in 1967; now Social Club; large, long, hall, with house at one end, & T-shaped crosswing for orderly-room, mess, offices etc at other;

¶ In 1914, drill station for D Sqdn. Yorkshire Dragoons; base for 5 West Riding Bty. 2 WR Bde. RFA; HQ, A-C+F Coys. 4 Bn. DoW West Riding Regt; B Section Yorkshire Mounted Bde. Field Ambulance RAMC;

Halstead [Essex]; PV

*1 Pretoria Road, **Drill Hall**, c1930s; single-storey block with hall to rear; now Jehovah's Witnesses' Hall, [Kingdom Hall];

¶ In 1914, drill station for B Sqdn. Essex Yeomanry; base E Coy. 5 Bn. Essex Regt.

¶ In 1950, detachment of R Bty. 646 LAA Regt.

Haltwhistle [Northumberland]; PV

*1 Banks Terrace, **Drill Hall**, pre-WWI; long hall & house to street; Masonic Lodge;

¶ In 1914, base for F Coy. 4 Bn. Northumberland Fusiliers;

Hampstead [Greater London]; PV TAC [2]

*1 444 Finchley Road, drill hall, c1930s; large 2-storey block wrapped around hall; RA crest over doorway; recently vacated by 10 Para [V] TA; demolished 2004;

¶ In 1935, 61 AA Bde. formed by conversion of 11 London Regiment

*2 1 Fitzjohns Avenue, Edinburgh House, **TAC;** c1980s; in use;

*3 Mansfield Road, Gospel Oak; temporary quarters, see Pond Street, [***4**]

¶ In 1903, 1 Cadet Bn. Royal Fusiliers;

*4 Pond Street, **Drill Hall**; referred to as 'Harben Armoury' in 1914; c1880, with elaborate detail: ironwork, traceried windows, stepped gable, coat-of-arms over door, balconies etc; next door 4-storey castellated house, attached; behind, hall; now leisure centre called: 'The Armoury'; [*p172*]

¶ In 1903, 1 Cadet Bn. Royal Fusiliers

¶ In 1914, A Coy. 7 Bn. Middlesex Regt.

*5 137 Park Road, Regents Park; site occupied by block of c1930s flats;

¶ In 1903, HQ 5 Middlesex, [West Middx];

*6 Henry Street [now Allitsen Road] St Johns Wood, **Drill Hall**, tall 6-storey house with oriels & tower, in brick with stone dressings,& plenty of detail: turrets, finials, balconies etc. c1880s; now residential; [*p168*]

¶ In 1914, HQ+A-D Sqdns. 3 County of London Yeomanry [Sharpshooters]

¶ In c1965, billet for US Marine guards from Grosvenor Square embassy.

Hamsteels [County Durham]; PV [*p173*]

*1 main street of Quebec village, **Drill Hall**, pre-WWl; stone-built long hall with 3-bay, projecting, Dutch-gabled entrance lobby; inscription: 'DRILL HALL' over door; now Quebec Village Hall; out-of-use by 1933;

¶ In 1914, base for H Coy. 8 Bn. Durham LI;

Hampton [Greater London]; PV

*1 High Street, **Drill Hall**,1914, probably closed 1959; 2-storey square block, with rusticated brickwork; datestone over pedimented doorway; coat-of-arms: three scimitars & legend, 8 Bn. DCO Middlesex Regt; adjoining range with cupola and corresponding wing in sympathetic brickwork, now office building, *Network House*.

¶ In 1914, base for G Coy. 8 Bn. Middlesex Regt;

Handsworth [Birmingham]; V

*1 59 Soho, drill hall, late Victorian double-fronted, 3-storey house;

*2 Thornhill Road, drill hall in use pre-1914 up until 1950; demolished for housing, probably Midland Close; 3-storey, double-fronted house on N corner of close may represent front block of hall and drill instructor's house;

¶ In 1914, base for G Coy. 5 Bn. South Staffs. Regt; base HQ & StaffordshireBde. Coys. Divnl. Transport & Supply Column, ASC; HQ+A Section North Midland Mounted Bde. Field Ambulance RAMC.

Hanley [Stoke-on-Trent]; PV TAC

*1 Bucknall New Road, **Drill Hall**, c1930s; single/2-storey

front block, symmetrical 11 bays with wings; garages etc. to rear; in use by West Midland Regt. TA;

¶ In 1914, HQ+ B Coy. 5 Bn. North Staffordshire Regt;

Harborne [Birmingham]; PV [*p78*]

*1 Tennal Grange, now **HQ RFCA**; house built 1904 [datestone]; probably not a TAC, but OTC has been based here; large Edwardian mansion on site of *Welsh Farmhouse* militia camp; garages, Nissen hut small-arms range, explosives/ inflammables store, 1960s training block;

*2 Court Oak Rd; Court Oak House: ex-**Drill Hall** sold c1960s; late-Victorian 3-storey mansion with stable-block; the house has decorative, non-military features; residential, with commercial use of stables;

¶ In 1914, Warwickshire Bde. Coy. South Midland Divnl. Transport & Supply Column ASC [Court Oak House];

Haringey [Greater London]; PV TAC[***3**]

*1 Harringay, no specific location; possibly PH with saddle-room;

¶ In 1914, drill station for D Sqdn. Hertfordshire Yeomanry.

*2 North Road, Highgate, drill hall, converted to flats 1965; on corner of Castle Yard & North Road, now occupied by replacement housing;

¶ In 1914, D Coy. 7 Bn. Middlesex Regt.

¶ In 1964, detachment of 300 LAD Regt. RA, TA;

*3 2 Priory Rd, Hornsey, **Drill Hall**, c1930s; 2-storey front block with crests over door; square house round corner & hall behind; range of sheds & garages to side;

¶ In 1903, HQ 1 Vol. Bn. Middlesex Regt.

¶ In 1914, HQ+C & H Coys. 7 Bn. Middlesex Regt.

*4 Church St, Edmonton/Cambridge Rd junction, ex drill hall in WWll hutted camp; used by 11 Bn. Paras, [8 Bn. Middlesex Regt.] demolished;

*5 High Road, Tottenham, **Drill Hall**, c1930s now Tottenham Sports Centre; 2-storey block wrapped around hall; integral house to side; garage block alongside, RE crest over main door;

¶ In 1914, base for E & G Coys. 7 Bn. Middlesex Regt.

*6 Park Lane, Tottenham, RE drill hall; demolished c1970;

Harleston [Norfolk]; VA

*1 Station Road, drill hall, pre-WWl; 2-storey front block, large hall behind; used by Pye Communications prior to demolition 1990s.

HAMPSTEAD's Pond Street drill hall, now a community centre

¶ In 1914, drill station for A Sqdn. Norfolk Yeomanry; & D Coy. 4 Bn. Norfolk Regt;

Harlow [Essex]; PV TAC
*1 Old Road, **Drill Hall,** 1947; 2-storey offices on right of yard; hall & garages etc.
¶ In 1914, drill station for G Coy. 4 Bn. Essex Regt.
¶ In 1950, R Bty. 304 Field Regt.[Essex Yeomanry].

Harpenden [Hertfordshire]; PV
no identified dedicated building, but Victoria Street School, [1896-c1930] used by Home Guard & first aid personnel WWll; in 1914 the North Midlands Territorial Infantry Bde. was posted to Harpenden, & used the Institute, the Gymnasium [Vaughan Road] & the Public Hall.
¶ In 1914, drill station C Sqdn. Hertfordshire Yeo; & B Coy.1 Bn.Hertfordshire Regt.

Harrogate [North Yorkshire]; PV ACF [*p174*]
*1 Commercial Street, Strawberry Dale, **Drill Hall,** 1894; part Cadet Centre & part commercial use; imposing late 19C stone-built house & hall, with tall tower; crest of WR Regt. above entrance arch; foundation stone;
*2 Duchy Rd. in use 1947;
¶ In 1914, drill station for C Sqdn.Yorkshire Hussars; base for E & F Coys. 5 Bn. Prince of Wales Own West Yorkshire Regt;
¶ In 1947, base for 491 [M] HAA Regiment RA [TA];

Harrow [Greater London]; V ACF [*2]
*1 Northolt Road, drill hall, demolished, part of site occupied by Cadet Centre; described as Church Lads' Bde. HQ in 1894; later TAC then redeveloped for super-market; was 2-storey front block with hall behind; marked on 1970s A-Z;
*2 Elmgrove Road, Harrow, TAC demolished c1999 for redevelopment; new Cadet Centre on site;
*3 High Street, Harrow, **Harrow School**, armoury;
¶ In 1903, HQ 27 Middlesex, [Harrow School] 9 Vol. Bn. KRRC
¶ In 1914, F Coy. 9 Bn. Middlesex Regt.

Hartford [Cheshire]; V
no record of a drill hall; probably used **Leftwich/Northwich**;
¶ In 1914, base for D & H Coys. 5 Bn. Cheshire Regt;

[West] **Hartlepool [County Durham];** PV TAC
*1 Easington Road, c1930s, **Drill Hall,** The New Armoury

in use by signals & RLC units; 2-storey front block with halls behind; early reference to The Armoury, a possible predecessor; 1958 Review records 3 premises in West H'pool in 1933; it is likely the RGA units were based in Heugh and Lighthouse Batteries;

¶ In 1914, base for No.5 Coy. Durham RGA-Defended Ports [Hartlepool]; drill station for B Sqdn. Northumberland Hussars; base for 3 Durham Bty. 3 Northumbrian Bde. RFA [Armoury]; HQ+2-4 Coys.Durham RGA-Defended Ports [Armoury]; base for G Coy. 5 Bn. DLI; base for C Coy. Northern Cyclist Bn [all West Hartlepool];

Hartshill [Stoke-on-Trent]; PV

*1 Wilfrid Place, **Drill Hall**, pre-WWl; 2-storey house/orderly-room, attached to large hall alongside; behind the hall, a 2-storey brick-built office/store; behind that, a long range of gun-stores, stables, garages; in use by N Staffordshire Hospital Transport; re-development imminent [2003];

¶ In 1914, HQ+Bty. + Ammunition Column, N Midland RGA [Heavy]

¶ In 1939, 51 Medium Regt. RA [TA];

Harwich [Essex]; PV ACF [p324]

*1 Main Road, Dovercourt, **Drill Hall**, pre-WWl; E-plan building with 2-storey wing at one end, & single-storey at other; small hall in centre, & annexes behind; HQ of Essex & Suffolk RGA, inscription over doorway with stone canopy & mouldings; alongside, large corrugated-iron-clad hall; now Park Pavilion community centre;new ACF brick hut on site;

¶ In 1914, drill station for A Sqdn. Essex Yeomanry; & HQ + 1 Coy. Essex & Suffolk RGA- Defended Ports;

¶ In 1937, Suffolk Heavy Bde. RA [TA];

Haslemere [Surrey]; PV ACF

*1 Shottermill, Stevenson House, **Drill Hall**, built between 1908 & 1924, most likely, pre-1914; large hall with gabled end to road, buttresses along sides, stuccoed & white-washed; attached staff house; all in Arts-and-Crafts style;

¶ In 1914, drill station for F Coy. 5 Bn. Royal West Surrey Regt.

Haslingden [Lancashire]; PV ACF

*1 Bury Rd/Rifle St, **Drill Hall**, pre-1914; still in TA use in 1983; modernisation has shortened hall to create fore-court;

HAMSTEELS, the drill hall, given up by 1933, now Quebec village hall

wide, red-brick hall, only 5 bays deep;

¶ In 1914, base for G Coy. 5 Bn. East Lancashire Regt;

Hastings [Sussex]; V

*1 Middle Street, drill hall, by 1909; demolished for shops after 1958;

¶ In 1914, drill station for 5 Sussex Bty. 2 Home Counties Bde. RFA; HQ+ A Coy. 5 Bn. Royal Sussex Regt.

Havant [Hampshire]; V

*1 West Street, drill hall, demolished 1960s; now site occupied by shops;

*2 12 East Street, a Recruiting Office in 1915; later building now occupies site;

¶ In 1914, base for F Coy. 6 Bn. Hampshire Regt;

Haverhill [Suffolk]; PV

*1 Burton End, Camps Road, **Drill Hall**, pre-1897; central, lateral hall with porch to road & accommodation blocks at each end; now seven dwellings;

¶ In 1914, base for G Coy. 5 Bn. Suffolk Regt.

Hawkhurst [Kent]; PV ACF

*1 **Cricketers' Arms** PH [now The Kent Cricketer], in use 1908;

*2 High Street, ex-**Drill Hall**, in former Infants' School built 1869; in use by TA until 1960s & by ACF to 2002;

*3 Iron Hall recorded as infantry drill hall in 1910 & 1933; no local knowledge;

¶ In 1908 & 1914, drill station C Sqdn. West Kent Yeo; base B Coy. 5 Bn. The Buffs;

Haworth [West Yorkshire]; PV [p21]

*1 Drill St, **Drill Hall**, pre-1900; single-storey hall with dentillated pediment; two concrete-section huts behind; on gable, monogram [unclear] within belt with legend: "Defence not Defiance"; Maltese cross below buckle; 42 Corps West Riding Rifle Volunteers formed here, 9 April 1866; 1881 Census records presence of a drill sergeant, & a "capacious drill shed" is recorded in1880, soon replaced by the current building paid for by public subscription;

¶ In 1914, base for G Coy. 6 Bn. DoW West Riding Regt.

Haydon Bridge [Northumberland]; PV

*1 2 & 2a Church Street, **Drill Hall**, pre-WWl; L-shaped, 2-storey front block; now converted to private dwellings;

¶ In 1914, base for C Coy. 4 Bn. Northumberland Fusiliers;

Hayle [Cornwall]; PV ACF/ATC [p161]

*1 Commercial Road, **Drill Hall**, 1911; granite single-storey front block with hall behind; small-arms range across yard; datestone 1911 over door; in use in WWll;

¶ In 1914, base for F Coy. 4 Bn. DCLI;

Haywards Heath [Sussex]; PV TAC [*2]

*1 Market Place, drill hall, demolished for supermarket development;

*2 Eastern Road, **TAC**, single-storey brick huts & garages;

¶ In 1914, drill station for A & B Sqdns. Sussex Yeomanry;

Headcorn **[Kent];** V

*1 drill hall behind manor-house, demolished;

¶ In 1908 & 1914, drill station for D Sqdn. Royal East Kent Yeomanry; drill station for C Coy. 5 Bn. The Buffs;

Heaton [Tyne & Wear]; PV TAC

*1 Debdon Gdns, **Drill Hall**, c1930s; long, parallel 2-storey blocks of 20+ bays, with large integral hall in between; yards with garages & workshops; in use RE & Signals;

Hebburn-on-Tyne [Tyne & Wear]; PV TAC

*1 Victoria Road West, **TAC**, 1990s, in use by SAS & Parachute unit; Artillery Drill Hall in use 1914; refurbished 1938;

¶ In 1914, base for 5 Durham [H] Bty. 4 Northumbrian [Howitzer] Bde. RFA;

Heckmondwike [West Yorkshire]; PV ACF

*1 Flush Lane, beside Flush Mills, **Drill Hall**, by 1910; what looks like the garage block of a 1930s TAC has been re-fronted & turned into a Salvation Army hostel; beside, are huts; the whole is contained within a compound set back from the road up Barrack Lane, with military-style gateposts & battlemented wall; on the main road are buildings possibly associated with the drill hall;

¶ In 1914, base for 6 West Riding Bty. 2 West Riding Bde. RFA;

Hednesford [Staffordshire]; PV ACF

*1 Victoria Street, **Drill Hall**, 1894; large hall parallel to street with wide timber porch; in pediment, inscription: "Drill Hall Erected 1894" & badge of 2 Volunteer Bn. South Staffordshire Regt; at one end, later, smaller hall now ACF; at other end, two smaller halls; behind, hall built out on stilts with garages under; behind, detached range; now

Bingo/Social Club;

¶ In 1914, base for F Coy. 5 Bn. South Staffordshire Regt.

Helston [Cornwall]; PV

*1 off Church Street, **Drill Hall**, built 1838 as chapel, adopted as drill hall 1906; now part of Museum; long T-shaped granite hall with bell-cote;

¶ In 1914, drill station for D Sqdn. 1 Devon Yeomanry; base for D Coy. 4 Bn.DCLI;

¶ In 1935-9, 165 AA Bty. 56HAA Regt;

Hemel Hempstead [Hertfordshire]; PV ACF

*1 Bury Road, drill hall, pre-1914, destroyed;

*2 Lower Adeyfield Road, [formerly St Albans Road] **TAC**, 1955; 2-storey front block with hall & garages behind; staff houses; site awaiting redevelopment [2002]; ACF hut to rear.

¶ In 1914, drill station for C Sqdn. Hertfordshire Yeomanry; base for F Coy. 1 Bn. Hertfordshire Regt.; drill station for Hertfordshire Bty. 4 East Anglian Bde. RFA.

Hendon [Greater London]; PV

*1 Algernon Road, Hendon; **Drill Hall**, now Barnet Multi-cultural Centre; pre-WWl building; large two-storey block in front with long hall behind;

¶ In 1914, base H Coy. 9 Bn. Middlesex Regt.; & drill station C Sqdn. Herts Yeo;

¶ In 1947, 880 Forward Observation Bty. [Airborne] RA [TA];

*2 Bittacy Hill, **Mill Hill Barracks;** depot of Middlesex Regt, c1880;few buildings from 19C remain eg a barrack block; also bungalow, guardhouses and equipment sheds of REME Command Depot, now council depot;

Henley-on-Thames [Oxfordshire]; PV TAC [*2]

*1 Market Place, Town Hall, built by Henry Hare, 1900, in Queen Anne style; used by Ox & Bucks LI volunteers;

*2 Queens Rd, **Drill Hall**, in use 1890s; known as Queens Hall; 2-storey, 7-bay, brick front block with hall behind; possible later frontage; beyond that, yard with garages, outbuildings etc; used by cadets & RMR detachment;

*3 Bell St, **Bull Hotel**, 15-17C, had a Morris-tube range;

¶ In 1914, base for C Sqdn. QOOH; base for D Coy. 4 Bn. Ox & Bucks LI;

Hereford [Herefordshire]; PV TAC

*1 Park Street, **Militia Barracks**,1856; 2-storey, red-brick block with porch & arched doorway; now County Record Office;

*2 Harold Street, [adjacent to Park Street] **TAC**; in use by infantry unit; 1958 Review records only one location in 1933;

¶ In 1914, drill station C Sqdn. Shropshire Yeomanry; HQ+A&H Coys.1 Bn. Herefds. Regt.; HQ Welsh Divisional Transport & Supply Column, ASC; HQ+A&B Sections, South Wales Mounted Bde. Field Ambulance RAMC; all at The Barracks

Herne Bay [Kent]; PV ACF [*p39*]

*1 Hanover Square, **Drill Hall**, pre-1908; hall with small entrance porch to one side, covered in green corrugated iron; gothic windows;

¶ In 1908 & 1914, drill station for B Sqdn. Royal East Kent Yeomanry; and base for F Coy. 4 Bn. The Buffs;

Hersham [Surrey]; PV

*1 174 Molesey Road, **Drill Hall**, in use 1913; now clinic & youth centre; large, gabled hall to street, with side annexes, & garage at rear;

¶ In 1913, base [with Esher] for A Coy. 6 Bn. Royal West Surrey Regt;

¶ In 1914, drill station for A Coy. 6 Bn. RWS Regt. [base Esher]; ref Kelly's 1913;

Hertford [Hertfordshire]; PV

*1 28 St Andrews Street, **Yeomanry House**, grand 4-storey house of 1726, with later additions, acquired for military use in 1860; painted sign on side: 'Artillery Barracks'; hall, stabling, workshops etc to rear.

*2 Port Hill, drill hall, built 1897 for 1 Volunteer Bn. Bedfordshire Regt. [foundation stone]; 2/3-storey front block with quadrangle of buildings including hall with stepped gables, & accommodation; currently [2002] awaiting redevelopment; stones to be reset when demolished;

¶ In 1914, HQ & B Sqdn. Herts Yeo; HQ & Ammunition Column, 4 East Anglian Bde. RFA [St Andrews]; HQ & A Coy. 1 Bn. Hertfordshire Regt

¶ In 1923, HQ+342Bty. 86 Field Regt. RA [TA];

Heston [Greater London]; PV TAC

*1 Vicarage Farm Road, **Drill Hall**, c1930s; 2-storey block around hall; main doors in stone with RA & Middlesex crests;

¶ In 1938, 72 [Middlesex] Searchlight Regiment formed as new unit;

¶ In1955-61, HQ 82 AA Bde;

Heswell/Heswall [Wirral]; V

no location identified;

¶ In 1901, one Coy. of 1 Volunteer Bn. Cheshire Regt. based in Heswall;

¶ In 1914, base for H Coy. 4 Bn. Cheshire Regt;

Hexham [Northumberland]; PV TAC   [*p178*]

*1 Hencotes, **Drill Hall**, pre-WWl; massive 3-storey front block with stone doorcase; the top floor timbered; hall behind, then house & stables; modern yard with garages; in use by RLC units;

*2 Westcroft [info' from RFCA]; no record;

¶ In 1914, base for D Sqdn. Northumberland Hussars; HQ+A Coy. 4 Bn. Northumberland Fusiliers;

Heywood [Bury]; V

*1 Longford Street, drill hall, demolished 29.07.1976; large hall, part of complex of five municipal buildings; also used as Trades Hall;

¶ In 1914, base for C & D Coys. 5 Bn. Lancashire Fusiliers;

Higham Ferrers [Northamptonshire]; V

no evidence of drill hall here; probably used Drill Hall at nearby **Rushden**;

¶ In 1914, base for H Coy. 4 Bn. Northamptonshire Regt;

High Wycombe [Buckinghamshire]; PV ACF

*1 Barracks Street, site of Cardwell regimental depot, 1880, near hospital; length of wall, part of barrack-block, converted MT section now ACF Centre; unusually, barracks was TF base;

¶ In 1914, base C Sqdn. Bucks Yeomanry; base B & H Coys. Ox & Bucks LI;

Hinckley [Leicestershire]; PV ACF

*1 Brunel Road, **Drill Hall**, 1923, 2-storey front block with hall behind; similar in style to Shepshed & Melton, but later;

¶ In 1914, drill station D Sqdn. Leics Yeo, & base D Coy. 5 Bn. Leicestershire Regt;

Hindley [Wigan]; PVA

*1 Ladies Lane, drill hall, pre-1908; built onto end of Chapel dated 1700; small, gabled hall to street with adjacent house; demolished for carpark of adjacent supermarket, leaving a back wall, possibly of the house as part of the playgroup accommodation, beyond;

¶ In 1914, base for G Coy. 5 Bn. Loyal North Lancashire Regt;

Hitchin [Hertfordshire]; PV TAC [*1]
*1 Bedford Road [A600/505], **Drill Hall**, Bearton Camp; c1927; 2-storey T-shaped range of buildings includes hall;
*2 91 Bancroft, requisitioned 1939 as HQ of duplicate unit-135 Field Regt;
¶ In 1914, drill station D Sqdn. Herts Yeo; & base G Coy.1 Bn. Hertfordshire Regt.
¶ In 1923, base for 344 Bty [Howitzer], 86 Field Regt. RA [TA] [Bearton Camp];

Holbeach [Lincolnshire]; V
*1 Park Rd, Public Hall was drill hall, cinema, youth centre; demolished for shops;
¶ In 1935, base for B Coy. 6 Bn. Lincolnshire Regt;

Holmfirth [West Yorkshire]; PV ACF[*2]
*1 Huddersfield Road [next to Civic Hall], **Drill Hall**, 1891 [foundation-stone] built for E Coy. 2 Vol. Bn. Duke of Wellington's West Riding Regt [inscription]; stone-built hall with door at each end, & central gable, with frontage to street;
*2 Huddersfield Road, Thongsbridge, 1930s **Drill Hall**, with 2-storey front block, lateral hall behind, & large parade-ground to front; now commercial premises;
¶ In 1914, base for F Coy. 5 Bn. DoW West Riding Regt.

Holsworthy [Devon]; PV
*1 14 Victoria Rd [now Street], in use 1910; 2-storey Edwardian terraced house
*2 North Road, **Drill Hall**, pre-WWl, in use 1935; the hall has been demolished for housing; the drill instructor's house stands, now used as a Social Services centre; 2-storey, stuccoed, with ornate porch & gablet;
¶ In 1914, base A Sqdn. N Devon Hussars; drill station D Coy. 6 Bn. Devonshire R.

Honiton [Devon]; PV ACF [*3]
*1 High Street, armoury/drill hall, in use by 1897 to at least 1910; demolished for extension to Police Station;
*2 Dowell Street, **Drill Hall**, in use from before 1897; now used by Scouts; 2-storey, four-bay, rectangular stone block, with large front doorway;
*3 King Street, drill hall by 1935; burnt down & replaced by

ACF huts;
¶ In 1914, drill station for F Coy. 4 Bn. Devonshire Regt;

Horden [County Durham]; V ACF
*1 Sunderland Road, drill hall, 1938; demolished 2000; ACF hut on site;

Horncastle [Lincolnshire]; PV [p179]
*1 The Wong/48 South St, **Drill Hall** built as British School, 1813, but taken over by Rifle Volunteers as drill hall in 1867; oblong, chapel-like building with gallery at one end; subsequently coach-builders etc, now antiques centre; deemed inadequate in 1901, a new drill hall was built at a cost of £2500;
*2 The Wong, **Drill Hall**,1901, large hall with small-arms range along one side, and staff house at the front on the other; in use by 4/6 Lincolns until at least 1961; since 1970,Town Hall;
¶ In 1914, drill station B Sqdn. Lincolnshire Yeo, & base G Coy. 4 Bn. Lincs Regt;

Horndean [Hampshire]; PV
*1 19 Five Heads Road, **Drill Hall**, used as Rifle Club, 1900-03; hall with double arched entrance to street frontage; orderly room to side; further hall & indoor range behind; to rear, garage compound, now coach garage; hall in use as Masonic Hall; staff house adjoining; in use as school in 1962;
¶ In 1914, base for E Coy. 9[Cyclist] Bn. Hampshire Regt;

Hornsea [East Yorkshire];
*1 Back Southgate, **Drill Hall**, pre-1891; 2-storey front block with small, lateral hall behind; ex-Servicemen's Club since after WWl; attached staff house; other associated dwellings demolished; concert-hall & other extensions to side & rear;
¶ In 1914, drill station for B Sqdn. East Riding Yeomanry; base for H Coy. 5 [Cyclist] Bn. East Riding Regt;

Horsham [Sussex]; PV [p52]
*1 Park Street, drill hall, 1860s; once a furniture store, now demolished for car-park;
*2 Denne Rd, **Drill Hall**,1922; splendid 2-storey front block with Royal Sussex Regt. crest over pillared porch; hall behind; to side a square, 2-storey block, offices & 'Recruit Reception'; large yard with pre-WWll garages on one side, 1970s garages & workshops on another, 1922 MT office &

HEXHAM, the drill hall of the Northumberland Hussars and of the Fusiliers

stores on the last; explosives/inflammables stores [3]; behind is the 1950s ROC regional HQ, used until 1991, due for demolition 2001; next to it, a 1970s range of office/accommodation; also assorted huts for cadets etc; whole site, vacated by TA in 1999, now HDC.

¶ In 1914, drill station A Sqdn. Sussex Yeo; HQ+E Coy. 4 Bn. Royal Sussex Regt.

Horsmonden [Kent]; V

no evidence of dedicated premises; timber shed used by Home Guard in WWll;

¶ In 1908 & 1914, base for D Coy. 5 Bn. The Buffs;

Horton Kirby [Kent]; PV

*1 Devon Road, "**Drill Shed**"; pre-1908; small hall with brick front, but corrugated iron clad sides, & two ventilators in roof-ridge; now used by Royal British Legion;

¶ In 1908, base for H Coy. 5 Bn. Royal West Kent Regt. [drill station Swanley]; by 1914 main location listed as Swanley.

Horwich [Lancashire]; PVA [*p181*]

*1 Beaumont Road, **Drill Hall**, pre-WWl; single-storey orderly-room etc. fronting hall; behind, harness/equipment store approached up ramp; to one side a 25 yard indoor range; across the back, a 2-storey house for PSI; now Resource & Heritage Centre;

¶ In 1914, base for F Coy. 4 Bn. Loyal North Lancashire Regt;

Houghton-le-Spring [Tyne & Wear]; PV

*1 Henry St, **Drill Hall**, pre-WWl; now converted to dwellings- Drill Hall Cottage & Kingfisher House; 2-storey front block with hall behind; 2-storey accommodation & office block down side, with garages to rear; on other side, possibly later, extension;

¶ In 1914, base for G Coy. 8 Bn. Durham LI;

Hove [Sussex]; PV ACF [*p81*]

*1 Marmion St, **Drill Hall**, by 1911; hall with frontage to road; stucco & red-brick facade;

*2 Waterloo St. **Riding School** from 1912; on 1909 map; now Old Market performance space; built 1825 & renovated 1998; *3 Eaton Road, Skating Rink, on 1909 OS map, referred to as Drill Hall in 1958 Review; located on south side of County Cricket Ground; site now occupied by flats;

¶ In 1914, base for 3 Sussex Bty. 1 Home Counties Bde. RFA.

Howden [East Yorkshire]; PV ACF [*2] [*p79*]

*1 Hailgate, **Drill Hall**, pre-WWl; now community centre; 2-storey, L-shaped front block of 5 bays with bow windows, & two doors; canopy probably dates from time as picture-house; hall behind;

*2 Hailgate, **Cadet Centre**, 1997; small, purpose-built hall with datestone;

¶ In 1914, base for E Coy. 5 [Cyclist] Bn. East Yorkshire Regt.

Hownslow [Greater London]; PV ACF [*p50*]

*1 Beavers Lane, **Hownslow Barracks**; buildings of 1790s by Johnson, as well as Cardwell depot Keep/Armoury, hospital, chapel, guardhouse, & barrack blocks;

*2 202a [now 210, *Treaty Lodge*] Hanworth Road, **Drill Hall**, 1911, closed 2001; 2-storey, 10 bay, front block with elaborate doorway; crest over door: 8 Bn. Middx Regt. South Africa 1900-1902; at each end of building, datestones-TF 1911; hall behind, then 2-storey c1930s block; now hostel & Cadet Centre;

¶ In 1914, HQ+C Coy. 8 Bn. Middlesex Regt.

*3 71 Whitton Road, **Drill Hall**; 2-storey Victorian house apparently reduced from its original size, since it once accommodated sergeants' mess, canteen, reading room & gymnasium; it is quite close to backing onto the drill hall on Hanworth Road, so may have been replaced by this in 1911; the drill shed in 1860 was the Riding School of nearby Whitton Park, house demolished in 1947;

¶ In 1903, HQ 2 Vol. Bn. Middlesex Regt

Hoylake **[Wirral];** PV ACF/ATC

*1 New Hall Lane, **Cadet Centre**; marked on 2000 street atlas as TAC; now only two huts + underground range remain;

¶ In 1914, drill station for H Coy. 4 Bn. Cheshire Regt; [also **Parkgate**];

¶ In 1939, 149 Field Regiment RA [TA] formed here as duplicate unit;

Huddersfield [West Yorkshire]; PV TAC[*2] [*pp70,312*]

*1 Ramsden St, **Armoury** or **Riding School,** 1847; built for 2 West Yorkshire Yeomanry; later HQ of 2 Volunteer Bn. Duke of Wellington's Regt; classical facade with large central arch; reliefs of horses each side; most probably used until 1904 opening of St Pauls St; subsequently a cinema & a

HORNCASTLE, the converted British School which served as drill hall till 1901

HORNCASTLE, the "new" drill hall with house, hall, and range, now Town Hall

public house;

*2 St Pauls St, **Drill Hall**; castellated front block with turrets & gatehouse; foundation stone by Lord Roberts of Kandahar, 1899; fine crest of 2 Volunteer Bn. West Riding Regt; large hall behind & very extensive yard with garages etc. to side;

¶ In 1914, base D Sqdn. Yorks Dragoons; HQ+A-E Coys. 5 Bn. DoW West Riding R;

Hull [East Yorkshire]; PV TACs [*1 *3 & *4] [pp27,181]

*1 Anlaby Road, **Wenlock Barracks**, pre-WWl; castellated facade to hall behind; adjoining L-shaped, 2-storey office/mess block; [p181]

*2 Walton St, **Riding School/ Drill Hall**, 1905, of East Riding Yeomanry; large hall with adjoining garages; now leisure centre;

*3 Endike Road, **Halifax Barracks**, 1980s on site of earlier buildings in use up to 1956 by East Riding Yeomanry + regulars;

*4 Park St/Londesborough St, **Londesborough Barracks**, 1864; 2-storey front block with large hall behind, and further 2-storey cross-wing; yard with garages to side; over the entrance arch, the white rose crest of the East Yorks Regt;

*5 Eagleton House, Park St. was HQ 5 [Cyclist] Bn. E Yorks. Regt. newly-formed in 1908; Colonial St/ Park St, drill hall, c1910; demolished;

*6 Holderness Rd, E Hull, **TAC**, 1980s buildings, on site of...

*7 [Sutton-on-Hull], Mona House TAC, in use by RE [TA] in 1963;

¶ In 1914, A Sqdn. E Riding Yeomanry, [Walton Street];HQ+A-F Coys. 4 Bn. East Yorks Regt. [Londesborough Barracks], G&H Coys. [East Hull]; HQ+A-D Coys. 5 [Cyclist] Bn. East Yorks Regt. [Park Street]; HQ 2 Northumbrian Bde. RFA [Wenlock Barracks], 1&2 E Riding Btys. & Ammunition Column, 2 Northumbrian Bde. RFA [Park St]; HQ+1-4 Coys.Defended Ports, E Riding, RGA [Park St]; HQ+ No.1 Works Coy. & No. 2 Electric Lights Coy. E Riding RE Fortress [Colonial St]; York & Durham Bde. Coy. Northumbrian Divnl. Transport & Supply Column, ASC [Walton Street];

Hulme [Manchester]; PV TACs [p35]

*1 Barrack Street, **Hulme Barracks**, 1890; all that remains is a terrace of War Office model housing for NCOs;

¶In 1914, HQ+HQ Coy.+ 2 Bde. Coys. E Lancs Divnl. Transport & Supply Col ASC;

*2 Burlington Street, **Drill Hall**, built 1885, by Hillkirk, for Rifle Volunteers; converted, by Beaumont, 1939 to Macdougal [University] Sports Centre; enormous hall fronted by 2-storey front block with 4-storey tower, apparently re-modelled in 1930s; entrance passage flanked by guard-rooms etc, with second hall in original styling; at rear, a gateway & remnants of perimeter wall;

¶ In 1885, base for 16 Lancashire [3 Manchester] Corps of Rifle Volunteers, in 1888, became the 4 Vol Bn. Manchester Regt; subsequently to be re-numbered 7 Bn.

¶ In 1914, HQ+A-H Coys. 7 Bn. Manchester Regt;

*3 Chester Road, **Militia Barracks**, c1850; 10-bay symmetrical front with two 3-bay pediments forms L-shaped block with outbuildings; subsequently Canal Offices;

*4 4 Higher Cambridge Street; drill hall, in use by MUs OTC; appears to have been subsumed by....

*5 Boundary Lane, **University Barracks**, c1990s; large 3-storey block with pitched roof; large yard with garages etc; in use by OTC;

*6 3 Stretford Road, in use from 1914; apparently demolished;

*7 Leamington Place, Old Garratt Street; no such place now; HQ 1 Lancashire Light Horse Volunteers 1872;

¶ In 1947, base for 465th HAA Regiment [Stretford Road];

Huntingdon [Cambridgeshire];

*1 Cowper Road, **Militia Barracks**, pre-1872; 2-storey main block with central tower & gabled bays; yellow brick with rusticated detail around doorways; care home;

*2 St Mary's Street, **Drill Hall**, in use c1900-1945; hall, offices & former indoor small-arms range; now sale rooms.

*3 3 Cromwell Walk, modern ACF building + indoor range; possible residue of former drill hall complex;

¶ In 1860, 1 Corps Hunts Rifle Volunteers formed, attached to 1 Hunts Light Horse Volunteers for administration purposes; 1872 transferred to 1 Cambs. Admin. Bn; HQ moved to St Neots 1876; 1880 became J Coy. 1 Cambs. Rifle Volunteer Corps;

¶ In 1914, base for H Coy. [one of 4 Coys. recruited in

Hunts.] 5 Bn. Beds. Regt; HQ Hunts. Cyclist Bn. [St Mary's Street];

Hurst [Tameside]; PV
 *1 Mossley Road, **Ladysmith Barracks,**1841-3; formerly, long range to street through gateway; three other ranges around parade-ground with pedimented officers' mess in centre of far range opposite entrance; all this demolished since 1969; only gate & loopholed & bastioned wall remain; all interior given over to houses; barracks was Depot of Manchester Regt. from 1845-1958;

Hurstpierpoint; PV ACF
 *1 91 High Street, **Drill Hall**; two cottages dated 1768 with large hall built on behind;
 ¶ In 1914, base for B Coy. 4 Bn. Royal Sussex Regt;

Huyton [Knowsley]; PV TAC
 *1 Liverpool Road, Alamein Barracks, **TAC**, c1930s; long, low, 2-storey front block with hall behind; inscription for 33rd. Signal Regt. [Volunteers];
 *2 Bluebell Lane, No2 Camp, TAC in 1947; no trace;

Hyde [Tameside]; PV
 *1 Mottram Road, **Armoury**, pre-WWl; large gabled hall parallel to road; extension to rear down Halton Street; now religious centre;
 ¶ In 1914, base for C Coy. 6 Bn. Cheshire Regt;

Hythe [Kent]; V
 *1 building in Great Conduit Street used as drill hall by 1866; may subsequently have become PO sorting office; now rebuilt;
 *2 Military Road, School of Infantry and Musketry, built at town's east end 1807-8; possible venue;
 ¶ In 1908 & 1914, drill station for D Coy 4 Bn. The Buffs; & H Coy. Kent Cyclist Bn;

I

Ilford [Greater London]; PV TAC [*1] ACF [*2]
 *1 Gordon Road, former drill ground covered whole block, **TAC**: 'Gordon Fields', c1980s; signals & transport units;
 *2 Horns Road, Newbury Park, drill hall, demolished; new **Cadet Centre** on site; *Artillery Close,* opposite;
 ¶ In 1950, 32 & 33 AA Workshop Coys. REME, [Essex] TA;

Ilfracombe [Devon]; V ACF

HORWICH, a low hall with two-storey cross-wing behind

HULL's Wenlock Barracks still in use as a TAC

*1 Avenue Road, armoury/drill hall, in use 1910; demolished for car-park;

*2 Winsham Terrace, ACF Centre;

¶ In 1914, base for No.1 Heavy Bty. Devonshire RGA-Defended Ports;

Ilkeston [Derbyshire]; PV ACF

*1 Stanton Rd/Havelock St, **Drill Hall**, 1909; extended for new indoor range 1912; part of orderly room block survives as offices; rest re-developed as housing;

*2 Albert St, **Drill Hall**, 1929 in records but 1930 datestone, 2-storey front block & hall behind; sign over door: '5 Bn. Sherwood Foresters' & datestone; cadet hut & garage added 1950; [p184]

¶ In 1914, drill station D Sqdn. Derbys Yeo, & base G Coy. 5 Bn. Sherwood F'sters;

Ilkley [West Yorkshire]; PV [p28]

*1 Leeds Road, **Drill Hall**, pre-1900; lateral hall linking two, 2-storey wings, fronts main road; behind, various annexes & garages/gun-stores; now the nucleus of an industrial estate- "*Drill-Hall Motors* " etc;

¶ In 1914, drill station for A Sqdn. Yorkshire Hussars; base for 11West Riding Howitzer Bty. 4 West Riding [Howitzer] Bde.

Ilminster [Somerset];

no recorded drill hall; Butts Farm, HQ of 11[Somerset] Bn. Home Guard in WWll;

¶ In 1914, drill station for D Sqdn. W Somerset Yeo; drill station H Coy. 5 Bn. SLI;

Ingatestone [Essex]; PV

*1 Fryerning Lane, **Drill Hall**, pre-WWll; 2-storey front block, with hall behind; porch added; later engineering workshop, now play-group;

¶ In 1914, drill station for No 2 Section Essex Bty. RHA

¶ In 1937, HQ No.4 Essex Group AA Searchlights;

¶ In 1950, 3 Coy. 10 Para Bn. TA; & detachment R Bty. 563 LAA/SL Regt;

Ipswich [Suffolk]; PVA TAC [*4] [p52]

*1 Great Gipping St, drill hall/armoury of Suffolk Militia, c1850s, demolished, for...

*2 Portman Road, drill hall, demolished;

*3 Woodbridge Rd, **Drill Hall**, 1909-10; 2-storey front block in brick, with royal coat-of-arms over entrance arch; large hall behind, with further stores   etc.   to   rear; community centre;

*4 Yarmouth Road, **TAC** 1978; replaced WWll hutted camp; 2-storey, prefabricated construction; TA crest.

¶ In 1914, base for C Sqdn. Suffolk Yeomanry; HQ + 2 Suffolk [H] Bty. 3 E Anglian [Howitzer] Bde. RFA, [Great Gipping Street]; base for 4 Coy. Essex & Suffolk RGA, Defended Ports; HQ+A-D Coys. 4 Bn. Suffolk Regt. [Portman Road]; HQ+A-B Coys. 6 [Cyclist] Bn. Suffolk Regt; HQ+A-C Sections, 1 East Anglian Divisional Field Ambulance, RAMC, [Woodbridge Road]; East Anglian Clearing Hospital, RAMC.

Ironbridge [Telford & the Wrekin]; PVA

*1 St Luke's Road, **Armoury**, early-19C building; in use 1906-1926; stone house & workshop; grand 19C house in South View, adjoins at one end;

*2 Waterloo St. drill hall, pre-WWl until 1947, factory & garage; demolished for housing c1990s;

¶ In 1863, HQ of 6 Corps Shropshire Rifle Volunteers moved here from Much Wenlock; 1880 became D Coy.1 Corps. & 1887 D Coy.1 Vol. Bn. KOSLI;

¶ In 1914, base for D Coy. 4 Bn. KOSLI.

Islington [Greater London]; PV TAC [*7]

*1 1-2 **Barnsbury Park**, had become Offord Rd. [*2] by 1933; now a house;

¶ In 1903, 1 London REs;

¶ In 1914, Islington listed as drill station for C & D Sqdns. Hertfordshire Yeomanry;

*2 Offord Road, Islington, drill hall, demolished, War Memorial now installed in St Mary Magdalene Church, Holloway Road; in use 1933;

¶ In 1914, HQ, Bty. & Ammunition Column for both 1 & 2 London RGA [Heavy];

*3 17 Penton Street, drill hall, demolished; replaced by Public Carriage Office

¶ In 1903, 21 Middlesex, [Finsbury Rifles] 7 Vol. Bn. KRRC

¶ In 1914, 11 Bn. London Regt. [Finsbury Rifles]

*4 112 Shaftesbury Street, backs onto Wenlock Street;

¶ In 1903, 4 Volunteer Bn. Royal Fusiliers [late1Tower Hamlets]

¶ In 1914, HQ+A-H Coys. 4 Bn. London Regt. [Royal Fusiliers]

*5 Wenlock Street, ex-**Drill Hall**, backing on to Shaftesbury Street; long, 2-storey block to street; City crest beside door; Printing-works;

*6 Nailour Street, Holloway;

¶ In 1903, East London [Tower Hamlets] RE; only 'temporary' use still in 1910;

*7 65 Parkhurst Road, **Drill Hall**, 217 Field Sqdn. RE, TA; 3-storey 1930s-style main block with garaging to rear; [*p184*]

J

Jarrow-on-Tyne [Tyne & Wear]; V

*1 Western Road, in use 1914; demolished for factories;

*2 Beech Street [info' from RFCA], demolished for housing;

¶ In 1914, HQ+1 & 2 Works Coys. Durham REs-Fortress [Western Road];

Jersey [Channel Islands]; St Helier;

*1 Beau Sejour, Rouge Bouillon, Militia HQ in 1911;

*2 St Helier Arsenal, Light Infantry HQ in 1911; the network of arsenal buildings erected around 1806 to provide support for the Militia largely survives, converted into dwellings, an example being that at St Marys consisting of three linked, cube-shaped pavilions; that at St Helier was similar but larger;

Jesmond [Tyne & Wear]; PV TAC [*2]

*1 Hutton Terrace, Sandyford Road, **Drill Hall**, pre-WWl; long 2-storey, range of buildings with two cross-wings making an inverted F-shape; the two cross-wings form a courtyard, accessed through an archway; the angle on to the street contains the main doorway with stone mouldings; another similar doorway onto Sandyford Road; at the rear, a yard, & 2-storey, double-fronted staff house; around the corner, in Hutton Terrace, new 3-storey apartment blocks may represent a rebuilding of the original; beyond these, a 2-storey brick house; behind the site, more buildings which were possibly integral;

*2 **St Georges TAC**, c1980s; in use infantry & RMP units; low, square 2-storey block in dark grey brick, enclosing a lateral hall; yards;

¶ In 1914, HQ+E & H Coys. Northern Cyclist Bn; HQ+A-C Sections 1 Northumbrian Div'nl Field Ambulances RAMC; 1 Northern General Hospital RAMC;

K

Kearsley [Bolton]; V

*1 Manchester Rd, Militia Barracks, then, "Man & Scythe" PH, listed but demolished;

Keighley [West Yorkshire]; PV TAC

*1 Lawkholme Lane, **Drill Hall**, pre-WWl; stone-built complex with two halls, two blocks of offices/messes/staff quarters;

¶ In 1914, base for D & E Coys. 6 Bn. DoW West Riding Regt.

Kendal [Cumbria]; PV ACF

*1 Queen Katherine Street, **Drill Hall**, pre-1900; 2-storey orderly-room block, gate-tower with pyramid roof, hall with two arched entrances & two dormers, line south side of street; indoor range along back of hall; small yard; [*p186*]

*2 Aynham Road [corner of Q Katherine St] TAC, post-WWll, demolished & replaced by block of flats;

¶ In 1914, base for A Sqdn. Cumberland & Westmorland Yeomanry; base for F & G Coys. 4 Bn. Border Regt; base for B Section 3 West Lancashire Divnl. Field Ambulances RAMC; West Lancashire Clearing Hospital RAMC;

Kensal Green [Greater London];

*1 Pember Road, church hall used in 1915 by Cadet Bn; status unknown;

Kensington & Chelsea [Greater London]; PV TAC [*3] [*p73*]

*1 206 Brompton Road, **Drill Hall**; operated as Piccadilly Line tube station from 1909-32; adapted as AA Operations Room during WWll; referred to by General Pile as 'the Signals drill hall'; used by TA after the War; ops room in underground lift-shafts; drill hall above ground; early-Victorian frontage with brick-arched extension behind; concrete towers atop the shafts; now offices;

*2 304 Kings Road, Chelsea, drill hall; building of right vintage standing but does not look appropriate; now Osborne & Little interior designers who know nothing of such former use; possible confusion with Clapham or *3; may have been only HQ;

¶ In 1903, HQ 4 County of London Yeomanry, [Kings Colonials]

*3 Kings Road, **Duke of York's HQ**; built 1803 as a school for the children of soldiers; from 1912 used, & still functions as a drill hall; partly redeveloped;

¶ In 1914, HQ+A-D Sqdns. 1 County of London Yeomanry,

ILKESTON, the replacement drill hall of the Sherwood Foresters

ISLINGTON's Parkhurst Road drill hall still in use

[Duke of Cambridge's Hussars]; HQ, 3&4 Field Coys. 2 London Divnl REs; HQ+1-4 Sections, 2 London RE Divisional Signal Coy; HQ+A-H Coys. 18 Bn. London Regt. [London Irish Rifles]; HQ+4·6 London Bde. Coys. ASC Divnl. Transport & Supply Columns; HQ+A-C Sections 2 & 3 London Divnl. Field Ambulances RAMC; 1 & 2 London, General & Clearing Hospitals, RAMC; 1 & 2 London Sanitary Coys. RAMC;

¶ In 1967, FANY HQ until 2003; in Mercury Ho.from 1993 until its demolition in 2000;

*4 Rutland Yard, Knightsbridge, no such address now; in use 1910;

¶ In 1903, HQ Middlesex Yeomanry, [Duke of Cambridge's Hussars]

*5 Kings Road, Chelsea, St Marks College; no longer in existence;

¶ In 1914, B Coy. 10 Bn. Middlesex Regt.

*6 Iverna Gardens, **Drill Hall**, pre-WWl; ornate gate onto Adam & Eve Mews, large hall behind;

¶ In 1903, 3 Volunteer Bn. KRRC

¶ In 1914, HQ + A-H Coys. 13 Bn. London Regt. [Kensington];

¶ In 1955, base for 499 HAA Regiment [Iverna Gardens];

*7 Grove House, Hollywood Rd. drill hall in use 1910; not found;

*8 83 Lexham Gdns, South Kensington; HQ FANY, 1911-14;

*9 Earls Court Road; HQ FANY, 1914-20;

*10 27 Beauchamp Place; HQ FANY, 1920-30;

*11 55-6 Sloane Street; FANY Corps Regimental Club & HQ, 1946-67;

Keresley [Coventry]; V

*1 Greens Road, ex-TAC closed in mid-1990s; function taken over by Canley; site occupied by housing: *Regiment Close & Battalion Close* ;

Keswick [Cumbria]; PV

*1 Penrith Rd, Denton House, **Drill Hall**, c1914; 2-storey house with porch & bow window, attached to low hall with further building beyond; outdoor centre/hostel;

¶ In 1914, drill station for B Sqdn. Westmorland & Cumberland Yeomanry; base for C Coy. 4 Bn. Border Regt;

Kettering [Northamptonshire]: PV ACF

*1 Station Rd, drill hall, c1930s and earlier; " tank store", & smaller building reported, prior to their demolition for new housing; a steel-clad garage, & temporary-brick office remain on adjoining yard of ARTEX company;

¶ in 1914, base C Sqdn. Northants Yeomanry, & for F Coy. 4 Bn. Northants Regt.

¶ In 1939, base for A Coy. 4Bn. Northants Regt. & 403 Coy. 585 SL Regt. RA [TA]

¶ In 1947, base for part of 585 SL Regt.

Keynsham [Somerset]; PV TAC [*2]

*1 Bath Hill, **Drill Hall**, in use 1914; large, stone-built, chapel-type hall, of 5 bays with large windows, 'chancel' extension beyond, & porch in front; now Health & Fitness club; reputed to have seated 500;

*2 Ashmead Rd **Drill Hall**; 1930s front block & hall, formerly fronting main road; 1980s block & extended garaging to rear;

¶ In 1914, drill station for D Sqdn. N Somerset Yeomanry; base C Coy. 4 Bn. SLI;

Kidderminster [Worcestershire]; PV TAC [*1]

*1 Birmingham Road, The Shrubbery, **Drill Hall**; early 19C house with portico, adapted for military use with drill shed added to rear; disposed of mid 1990s, now a care home; on the porch the divisional sign of 23 Independent Armd. Bde; TA still on site;

*2 George St, **Drill Hall**, pre-WWl; now snooker hall; asbestos-roofed brick shed; if used by 1 Volunteer Bn. Worcestershire Regt. then pre-1908;

*3 Sutton Park Road, rifle range

¶ In 1914, base for A Sqdn. Worcestershire Yeomanry; 2 Worcestershire Bty. 2 South Midland Bde. RFA [George Street]; HQ+A Coy. 7 Bn. Worcestershire Regt.

Kimberley [Nottinghamshire]; PV

no dedicated building; probable venue at Station Hotel [c1880] with indoor range at Brewery; used both by Rifle Club c1907, and by Home Guard WWll; Volunteers arrived by train to drill at Swingate Colliery [site now Kimberley Primary School];

¶ In 1912, base for F Coy. 8 Bn. Sherwood Foresters;

Kimbolton [Cambridgeshire]; V

*1Castle venue for Earl of Manchester's Hunts. Mounted Rifles formed 1861, & joined with Cambridgeshire Mounted Rifles in 1863;

¶ In 1914, drill station for D Sqdn. Bedfordshire Yeomanry; D Coy. Hunts Cyclist Bn. drawn from St Neots & Kimbolton;

Kingsbury [Greater London]; PV TAC [p57]

*1 Honeypot Lane, Kingsbury, **Drill Hall**, c1930s; in use RE Commando Sqdn. TA; 2/3-storey block around lateral hall; two front doors, one with Middlesex county crest, & one with Middlesex Regt. crest;

¶ In 1947, base for 595 LAA Regiment RA [Middlesex] formed 1938 at Willesden;

Kings Heath [Birmingham]; PV TAC [*2]

*1 33 Mossfield Road, ex-**Drill Hall**; pre-WWl; 2-storey front block with pediment; now converted as 'Yeomanry Court' into 8 flats, datestone MM; [p186] crest inscribed 'Comitatis Wigoriensis [County of Worcs]; vacated in 1990s, for.....

*2 Dawberry Fields Road, Roger Nutbeem House **TAC**; in use by RAMC & Intelligence units; L-shaped block with garages etc around large yard;

¶ In 1914, drill station for B Sqdn. Worcestershire Yeomanry

Kings Lynn [Norfolk]; PVA ACF [pp96,256]

*1 Purfleet Quay, **Drill Hall**, Warehouse, formerly Peatling & Caldron wine-shippers, now labelled P CORTLAND, DRY STORAGE [by 1992] on front, but used as offices by Norfolk Probation Service, bears legend on side: HEADQUARTERS ARMY SERVICE CORPS NORFOLK & SUFFOLK BRIGADE

*2 Providence St, Volunteer Stores, sharing site with PH, marked on 1886 OS Map; area re-developed for housing;

*3 Broad St, drill hall of Norfolk Regt. until 1936; now under Bus Station;

*4 Wellesley St, **Drill Hall**, opened 1936 to replace Broad St; hall, 70' x 45' nearly twice size of Broad St, porch, armoury, indoor range, band room, and club; staff quarters at rear; space for 50 cycles; designed as gas & shrapnel-proof ARP station; converted c1970 to Regis Rooms; now King Centre church;

*5 Providence St, **Drill Hall**, 1930s; 2-storey front block with single-storey offices to side, & large hall behind; staff house on one side at front; to rear a large 1960s 2-storey hall on stilts over garaging; these now in-filled for conversion to flats; front block now youth centre;

¶ In 1914, base for D Sqdn. Norfolk Yeomanry; base for A

KENDAL, the original drill hall; a replacement TAC has already come and gone

KINGS HEATH, this Mossfield Road drill hall of the Yeomanry is now flats

Coy. 5 Bn. Norfolk Regt.; base for C Coy. 6 [Cyclist] Bn. Norfolk Regt. & base for Norfolk & Suffolk Coy. East Anglian Divisional Transport & Supply Column, ASC;
¶ In 1938 Norfolk Yeomanry converted to AT regiment;

Kingston-upon-Thames [Greater London]; PV TAC [*3] [p57]
*1 Kings Road, **Barracks**, 1875, Cardwell depot of East Surrey Regt. by Maj. Seddon; castellated armoury block with two square towers & gate-tower; other 19C buildings remain but most of site cleared for MoD housing;
*2 Orchard Road, drill hall, pre-WWl; demolished; a Royal Mail office may have incorporated remnants;
*3 Portsmouth Rd/Surbiton Rd, **Drill Hall**, 1939; a three-storey front block with hall behind, & further 3-storey garage block; in one corner,19C house as cadet centre; imposing neo-Georgian style, brick with stone dressings;
*4 24 Claremont Road, Surbiton, pre-WWl; ex RAMC HQ; still stands; early-Victorian 3-storey terrace houses, with elaborate terra-cotta decoration, now with ground-floor shops;
*5 62 Claremont Road, Surbiton; ex-**TAC** & Army Careers Office with inflammables store & garaging, etc behind; large semi-detached early-Victorian villa, in large plot;
¶ In 1903, 3 Volunteer Bn. East Surrey Regt;
¶ In 1913 & 14, HQ+D E & F Coys. 6 Bn. East Surrey Regt. [Orchard Road];
¶ In 1913, HQ+A-C Sections 3 Home Counties Bde. Field Ambulances [62* Claremont Road, Surbiton];
¶ In 1914, HQ+A-C Sections 3 Home Counties Divnl. Field Ambulances [24 [sic] Claremont Road, Surbiton]; Home Counties Clearing Hospital [no address];
¶ In 1939, HQ 30 [Surrey] Searchlight Bn. RE [TA];

Kington [Herefordshire]; PVA
*1 5 [or 21] Headbrook, **Drill Hall**, converted from Victorian school: Broughton Ho. c1908; in use by ACF to 1990s; now private house; large, 2-storey, L-shaped block with porch; to rear, a free-standing indoor range, garages & outbuildings;
¶ In 1914, drill station C Sqdn. Shropshire Yeomanry; base D Coy.1Bn. Heref. Regt

Kirkburton [West Yorkshire]; PV
*1 Huddersfield Rd, **Drill Hall**, c1911; superseded Mill [now demolished]; now health centre; hall fronting road with

186

RA in 1914;

Loddon [Norfolk]; PV ACF
*1Upper Bungay Road, **Drill Hall**, c1939; small hall with porch; behind are pair of Home Guard explosives & inflammables stores;
¶ In 1914, drill station for A Sqdn. Norfolk Yeo; & for H Coy. 4 Bn. Norfolk Regt.

Loftus [North Yorkshire]; PV ACF
*1West Road, **Drill Hall**, by 1910; 2-storey front block with two long, low halls, end-on behind; still in TA use in 1933; converted to housing;
¶ In 1914, drill station for G Coy. 4 Bn.Princess of Wales' Own Yorkshire Regt;

London, the City; PV TACs [*2, *5 & *13]; [p19,20]
*1130 Bunhill Row, 1857, base for London Militia permanent staff; then drill hall; demolished for re-development;
¶ In 1903, 1 London, [City of London Rifle Volunteer Bde.]
¶ In 1914, HQ+A-H Coys. 5 Bn. London Regt. [London Rifle Bde.]
¶ In 1914, HQ+A-H Coys. 8 Bn. London Regt. [Post Office Rifles]
*2 City Road, Finsbury, **Armoury House**, 1857; HQ of Honourable Artillery Coy; barracks by Jennings; stone-built in the Tudor style with round & square towers, arrow-slits, crenellations; 19C house+hall behind, crowned by odd green cupola;
¶ In 1903 & 1914, HQ of HAC; 2 horse artillery batteries & 4 companies of infantry;
*3 57a Farringdon Road, **Drill Hall;** arch to street with 'Drill Hall' sign & date 1887; door to hall with badge, [City Arms, Maltese cross & crown] & date 1888; glass-roofed hall parallel to street; further access in Saffron Hill [OTC] see *5;
¶ In 1903, 2 London, [2 City of London Rifles] 11 Vol. Bn. KRRC;
¶ In 1914, HQ + A-H Coys. 6 Bn. London Regt. [Rifles];
*4 39 Finsbury Square, under City Gate House, c1920s office block;
¶ In 1914, HQ+A-D Sqdns. City of London Yeomanry, [Roughriders]
*5 110-115 **Saffron Hill**, London University OTC's garages;
*6 24 Sun Street, drill hall, demolished for Finsbury Avenue

development;
¶ In 1903, 3 London, [3 City of London Rifles] 12 Vol. Bn. KRCC;
¶ In 1914, HQ+ A B C F G & H Coys. 7 Bn. London Regt;
*7 42 & 44 Sun Street, demolished for Finsbury Avenue development;
¶ In 1903, 1 Cadet Bn. KRRC;
*8 Barbican, Staines House, re-developed;
¶ In 1903, 1 City of London, RGA
*9 51 Clifton Street, drill hall; Royal Green Jackets, 4 Vol. Bn.; demolished and replaced by office development-Holderness House;
*10 Guildhall
¶ In 1903, HQ City of London Yeomanry [Roughriders]
*11 Leonard Street, Artillery Barracks; demolished; resident units moved to Offord Road, Islington in 1920;
¶ In 1903, 2 Middlesex, RGA
¶ In 1914, HQ+7 8 & 9 Btys. 3 London [Howitzer] Bde. RGA
¶ In 1914, HQ+7 8 & 9 Btys. & Ammunition Column, 3 London Bde. RFA
*12 2 Throgmorton Avenue, RHQ, now Carpenters' Hall
¶ In 1903, 24 Middlesex, 8 Vol. Bn. Rifle Bde.
*13 79-85 Worship Street, **Drill Hall;** in use Royal Green Jackets; c1930s three-storey facade, with hall behind; extensively renovated 2001;
*14 Lower Thames Street, **Custom House;** 1813-17, river front rebuilt by Smirke 1825; nearly 500' long in Portland stone & brick;
¶ In 1903, 15 Middlesex, [Customs & Docks], 3 Vol. Bn. Rifle Bde.
*15 Artillery Lane, 1682, used for gunnery practice by HAC & Tower Ordnance;
*16 Vineyard Walk, Clerkenwell; in use 1910;
*17 118-122 Holborn, HQ FANY, 1907;

Long Ashton [Somerset];
no recorded drill hall; Research Station HQ of 7[Somerset] Bn. Home Guard; their admin. HQ at Wraxall Manor in WWll;
¶ In 1914, drill station for 1 Field Coy. Wessex Divnl. REs;

Longbenton [Tyne & Wear]; PV
*1 Fusilier Armoury former **TAC**; factory-type buildings no

longer in military use;

Longridge [Lancashire]; PVA

*1 Little Lane, drill hall,1914; demolished for housing; formerly three sections in parallel behind a façade; the middle section was the hall with a turreted front; the datestone and royal coat-of-arms are preserved by the War Memorial in Berry Lane;

¶ In 1914, base for B Coy. 4 Bn. Loyal North Lancashire Regt;

Long Stratton [Norfolk]; V

no record of a drill hall here ever;

¶ In 1908, base for Sgt. Potter's [stretcher] Bearer Coy. of 4 [Vol] Bn. Norfolk Regt.

¶ In 1914, drill station for A Sqdn. Norfolk Yeo; & base for C Coy. 4 Bn. Norfolk Regt.

Long Sutton [Lincolnshire]; PV ACF [Park Lane, 1957]

Longton [Stoke-on-Trent]; PV TAC

*1 Uttoxeter Road, Meir, drill hall, demolished for road-widening; resited to....

*2 Anchor Road, Baskeyfield House, **TAC**, 1980s; main block & extensive garages/ workshops; in use by REME & RE units;

¶ In 1914, A Coy. 5 Bn. North Staffordshire Regt.

Looe, West [Cornwall]; PV

*1 The Downs, Westdowns Court apartments are conversion of pre-WWl drill hall; impossible to discern original structure but may still be present;

*2 North Road, **Drill Hall**, cWWll; timber-clad hut with substantial hipped, tiled, mansard roof;

¶ In 1914, base for No.3 Coy. Cornwall RGA-Defended Ports;

Lostwithiel [Cornwall]; PV

*1 The Parade, **Drill Hall**, pre-WWl; single-storey, corrugated-iron-clad hall, gabled & roughly L-shaped; under threat of demolition [2003];

¶ In 1914, drill station for E Coy. 5 Bn. DCLI;

Loughborough [Leicestershire]; PV TAC

*1 Granby St, drill hall, demolished c1990 for car-park; traces of boundary walls remain; mentioned in connection with Home Guard WWll;

*2 Leicester Rd, **Drill Hall**, 1937, in use, [Transport]; main block with hall to rear, & staff house;

¶ In 1914, base C Sqdn. Leics Yeomanry, & HQ & H Coy. 5 Bn. Leicestershire Regt.

Loughton [Greater London];

*1 no specific location identified;

¶ In 1914, base for E Coy. 4 Bn. Essex Regt.

Louth [Lincolnshire]; PV

*1 Town Hall, 1853, depot of Lincolnshire rifle volunteers;

*2 Charles St [Eve St], drill hall for volunteer artillery built c1870, in use 1892; demolished;

*3 Northgate, 19C **Drill Hall** with pedimented facade; possible admin block across rear; high garage built to face rear; large parade-ground type space to side, now car-park; hall now RBL; in use 1933;

*4 Victoria Rd, **Drill Hall**, built 1930s, single-storey front with hall behind & garages to rear; large royal coat-of-arms over main door; in use until at least 1961; now converted as theatre & recently, further refurbished;

¶ In 1892, base D Coy. 1 Vol. Bn. Lincs Regt; base 4 Bty. Vol. Artillery [Eve Street];

¶ In 1914, base for B Sqdn. Lincolnshire Yeomanry; 3 Lincolnshire Bty. RFA, 1North Midland Bde; & base for D Coy. 5 Bn. Lincolnshire Regt;

¶ In 1933, base for unit of 5 Bn. Lincolnshire Regt. [***3**];

¶ In 1961, D Troop, Q Bty. 440 LAA Regt RA TA [***4**];

Lowestoft [Suffolk]; PV ACF

*1 Arnold St, **Drill Hall**, 1871; for 1 Suffolk Artillery Volunteers; pediment over entrance arch with cannons & crowns; back demolished for ring-road; now garage;

*2 St Peters St, **Drill Hall**, pre1914; staff house stands, & garage remains as martial arts centre; adjacent another hall, in WWll HQ of D Coy. Lowestoft Bn.Home Guard, now HG Club;

*3 St Peters St, **Drill Hall**, c1930s; single- & double-storey offices etc round two sides of a large hall; staff house;

¶ In 1914, drill station D Sqdn. Suffolk Yeo; base 1 Suffolk [H] Bty. 3 East Anglian [Howitzer] Bde. RFA, [Beccles Road, now St Peters St.], + Ammunition Column, [Arnold St.]; base E Coy. 4 Bn. Suffolk Regt & E Coy. 6 [Cyclist] Bn.Suffolk Regt.

Ludlow [Shropshire]; V

*1Portcullis Lane, drill hall; sold in 1970s; auction house,

*1Fakenham Rd, **Drill Hall** adjoining Railway Institute built after 1880; drill hall in existence by 1914; this may explain absence of one at **Cromer**, designated base for F Coy 5 Bn. Norfolk Regt; the hall is timber & was originally twice present size, half having been demolished to create access for new industrial estate; it is likely that the social facilities of the Institute were utilised by the territorials;

¶ In 1914, drill station for F Coy. 5 Bn. Norfolk Regt;

Melton Mowbray [Leicestershire]; PV TAC [*p47*]

*1 Asfordby Rd, **Drill Hall**, 1914 datestone over main door; imposing front block with hall behind & garages to sides; still in use; similar building style to Shepshed;

¶ In 1914, baseA Sqdn. Leicestershire Yeo, & C Coy. 5 Bn. Leicestershire Regt.

Middlesbrough [North Yorkshire]; PV TACs [***2**, ***4** & ***5**] [*pp77,201*]

*1 Bright St, **Drill Hall**, in use 1914; walled compound with WD marker stone at one corner [No 2] & gate-post; hall with 2-storey orderly-room block alongside & garage; on the other side, a later, single-storey building [*p201*]; now used by NACRO & Age Concern;

*2 Stockton Rd, **TAC**, c1950s, in use by infantry unit; square, two-storey block containing hall; yard with garages & caretaker's house;

*3 Lytton St drill hall; demolished for Care Home;

*4 Brambles Farm, **TAC**, c1980-90s; in use by signals units; 2-storey front block & hall behind; to rear, separate 2-storey block & garages+ yard with further garaging;

*5 Ridgeway, Coulby Newham, **Hollis VC Armoury TAC**, c1990s; in use by infantry unit; double quadrangle of two-storey office accommodation, garaging, workshops etc;

¶ In 1914, base for D Sqdn. Yorkshire Hussars; HQ+Bty.+ Ammunition Column Northumbrian RGA-Heavy; HQ+No.1 Electric Lights Coy. N Riding REs-Fortress [Bright Street]; base for A & B Coys. 4 Bn. Princess of Wales Own Yorkshire Regt;

Middleton [Rochdale]; V

*1 Manchester New Road, drill hall in use 1914; demolished for shopping precinct;

¶ In 1914, base for A & E Coys. 6 Bn. Lancashire Fusiliers;

Midhurst [Sussex]; PV

*1 Market Place, **Church Rooms**, originally Town Hall dating from C16 with C18 front; listed in 1958 Review, as in use 1909; also used 1930s instead of **Petworth**;

¶ In 1914, drill station for D Coy. 4 Bn. Sussex Regt;

Midsomer Norton [Somerset]; PV ACF

*1 High Street, **Drill Hall**, pre-WWl; the front block is a 2-storey Georgian House, now Riverside Bar; behind is a hall with indoor range;

¶ In 1914,base for G Coy. 4 Bn. Somerset LI;

Milborne Port [Somerset]; PV

*1 Old **Town Hall**, in use 1914; 2-storey, 18C L-shaped hall, pediment & bellcote;

¶ In 1914, drill station for G Coy. 4 Bn. Dorsetshire Regt;

Millom [Cumbria]; PV ACF [*p201*]

*1 Moor Rd, **Drill Hall**, pre-WWl; large, gabled hall with lion badge on peak of facade; single-storey front block with GR monogram over brick doorway; another brick archway into side of hall;

¶ In 1914, base for H Coy. 4 Bn. Royal Lancaster Regt;

Milnsbridge [Golcar to WO] **[West Yorkshire];** PV [*p205*]

*1 Scar Lane, **Drill Hall**, c1910; red-brick hall & 2-storey orderly-room block on corner site; to one side a small, battlemented tower with another block beyond; at the back 2-storey house for drill instructor, linked to hall; behind that a garage; in style, similar to Mossley & Springhead; not on 1912 OS map or in Kelly's, but in use as recruiting office by Autumn 1914, and claimed as in use1910 in 1958 return;

¶ In 1914, HQ+ A & B Coys. 7 Bn. DoW West Riding Regt.

Milton Keynes [Buckinghamshire]; PV TAC

*1 Blakelands, **TAC**, 1980s; large 2-storey office/accommodation block; large yard with garages; in use, Royal Greenjackets;

Minchinhampton [Glos]; PV

*1 High Street, **Drill Hall**; 19C building used by RBL, TA & ACF; hall now gym, range now skittle alley, all now the Cotswold Club;

¶ In 1947, detachment 523 LAA Regt. RA TA;

Minehead [Somerset]; PV ACF [***2**] [*p75*]

*1 Quay Lane, **Armoury** of SLI in 1914; small brick-built gabled hall, with half-moon window, & two small annexes; marked on 1920s map;

*2 Alcombe Road, **Drill Hall**, 1953; single-storey front block of 5 bays & L-shaped wings; garages etc to rear; now used

by Social Services, Ambulance Service, Red Cross etc;
¶ In 1914, drill station A Sqdn. W Somerset Yeomanry; drill station B Coy. 5 Bn. SLI;

Mirfield [West Yorkshire]; PV ACF
*1 Crowther Rd, **Drill Hall**, 1934; quadrangular, 2-storey mess & office block, with central hall; yard behind with garages; Day Centre; foundation stone in front wall;
¶ In 1914, base for H Coy. 5 Bn. DoW West Riding Regt.

Mitcham **[Greater London];** V
no location yet identified; possible drill hall at Rosehill roundabout in angle of Reigate Avenue, A217, & Green Lane, B278, ngr TQ260665; large double-fronted house with bay windows & enclosed staircase; 'temporary brick' hall alongside;
¶ In 1913 & 14, base for D Coy. 5 Bn. East Surrey Regt;

Monkseaton **[Northumberland];** V
*1 Deneholm, info from RFCA; possible staff housing still, but no trace otherwise;

Morecambe [Lancashire]; PV ACF [*2]
*1 Morecambe St West, **Drill Hall**, built c1870 as Lyric Theatre; in 1891 was a Music Hall; used as drill hall pre-WWl, as a shell-filling factory during WWl, as a St John Ambulance HQ in 1921, as a drill hall again up to WWll, & as an ex-Service-men's Club from 1939 to the present;
*2 Charles St, TAC, in use in 1983; now only cadet huts remain;
*3 Pedder St, built as a chapel, 1855; Sea Cadets since 1950s as TS Duke of Lancaster;
*4 Anderton St listed in Kellys 1914; no such road now;
¶ In 1914, base for E Coy. Royal Lancaster Regt;

Moreton Hampstead [Devon]; PV
*1 Station Rd, **Drill Hall**, in use 1910; now Masonic Hall; 2-storey hall with out-buildings; adjacent barn with garage doors may be connected;
¶ In 1914, drill station C Sqdn. 1 Devon Yeo; base G Coy. 5 Bn.Devonshire Regt;

Moreton-in-Marsh **[Glos];** V
*1 Jameson Court, off Fosse Way, drill hall demolished c1960s; site occupied by c1980s housing; HAA unit in WWll;
¶ In 1914, drill station for H Coy. 5 Bn. Gloucestershire Regt;

¶ In 1947, detachment 523 LAA Regt;
Morley; PV
*1 Ackroyd St, **Drill Hall**, 1912; 2-storey front block with pediment over entrance arch; hall behind, then cross-wing; closed 1962, now pet supplies shop;
¶ In 1914, base for H Coy. 4 Bn. KOYLI;

Morpeth **[Northumberland];** V
*1 Copper Chare, drill hall, from 1910; demolished for housing;
¶ In 1914, base for C Sqdn. Northumberland Hussars; base for A Coy. 7 Bn. Northumberland Fusiliers;

Mossley [Tameside]; PV
*1 Manchester Road, **Drill Hall**, c1914; single-storey front block with hall behind alongside road & railway; at one end, small, castellated tower, porch & garage block; at other, 2-storey house for drill instructor; all in red brick; garden machinery dealer; style very similar to Springhead/Lees & Milnsbridge, both nearby;
¶ In 1914, base for F & H Coys. 7 Bn. Duke of Wellington's Regt;

Mountsorrel [Leicestershire]; PV
*1 **Drill Hall** in Main Street built 1901 [plaque] by Mountsorrel Granite Co. as offices; three-storey block, now house, & social club; hall, now workshop; built of granite with upper parts in brick; now haulage company yard;
¶ In 1914, drill station C Sqdn. Leics Yeo, and base F Coy. 5 Bn. Leics Regt.

N
Nailsworth [Glos]; PV
*1 21-5 Fountain St, **Drill Hall** in use WWll [by HG] & then by TA; linked two-storey warehouse-type buildings behind Victorian terraced frontage; one now Scouts, other 'The Studio'; front block is ironmongers shop; ex-ACF hut on nearby playing-fields;
¶ In 1947, detachment 523 LAA Regt. RA TA;

Nantwich **[Cheshire];** V
*1 Church Lane, contact address for Cheshire Regt. in 1914;
*2 Dog Lane, drill hall location; site re-developed;
¶ In 1914, drill station for C Sqdn. Cheshire Yeo; base F Coy. 7 Bn. Cheshire Regt;

Newark-upon-Trent [Nottinghamshire]; PV ACF [*p52*]

*1 60 Carter Gate, Beaumont Cross, **Drill Hall**, pre-1900; hall to street, arched entrance, hipped roof, 7 bays deep; now carpet shop, previously SA Hall; in use up to 1912; referred to as 'Hall' in 1914;

*2 Albert St, Militia Stores, built c1855; later depot of Notts. section of 4 Bn. Sherwood Foresters [Special Reserve] in 1912; extensive additional buildings on OS Map 1914; still in use 1949; demolished;

*3 24 Castle Gate, HQ 8 Bn.Sherwood Foresters TF; now Architectural practice offices; 19C building with blocked coach-arch; in use 1912;

*4 34 Castlegate, drill hall in 1912;

*5 Sherwood House, Sherwood Avenue, **Drill Hall**, 1914 for 8 Bn. Sherwood Foresters; neo-Georgian 2-storey block with elaborate detailing in stone; to rear, garages & additions of 1938 & 1956; in use until 1996; now architectural & engineering consultancy;

*6 Bowbridge Rd. Bowbridge Camp, TAC in 1949; huts remain as part of Junior School;

*7 REME Depot, WWll-1970s, alongside A1, mainly rebuilt, now motorcaravan dealer-ship;

¶ In 1892, HQ + B & C Coys. 4 Notts. Vol. Bn. S'wood Foresters [Cartergate];

¶ In 1912, HQ 8 Bn. Sherwood Foresters [24 Castlegate]; base for B Coy. 8 Bn. Sherwood Foresters [34 Castlegate];

¶ In 1914, base A Sqdn. Sherwood Rangers, & B Coy. 8 Bn. Sherwood Foresters;

¶ In 1949, HQ + one Sqdn. The Nottinghamshire [Sherwood Rangers Yeomanry] RAC, TA [Barracks, Albert Street]; HQ [Sherwood House], + base for one Coy. 8 [Motor] Bn. The Sherwood Foresters, TA [Bowbridge Camp]; base for one Coy. 307 [Northern Command] Bn. WRAC, TA [Bowbridge Camp];

Newburn-upon-Tyne [Northumberland]; PV [p54]

*1 Townfield Gardens, **Drill Hall**, 1924, for 4 Bn. Northumberland Fusiliers; lately Motor Museum; 3-storey Tudor front block with oriel over entrance, projecting tower, double doors at side; hall behind; small yard to side, behind, 2-storey staff house with bow windows to front & to side; date-stone over door- 'mcmxxiv', & '4th NF' carved in doorcase;

¶ In 1914, base for G Coy. 4 Bn. Northumberland Fusiliers;

MIDDLESBROUGH, the Bright Street drill hall showing WD-marked gate-post

MILLOM, drill hall with Kings Own Royal Lancaster Regt. lion & GR cipher

Newbury [Berkshire]; PV TAC

*1 St Michaels Rd, **Drill Hall**, pre-WWl; 2-storey front block, with hall alongside at right-angles; yard behind with single-storey buildings & garages etc;

¶ In 1914, base C Sqdn. Berks Yeomanry; base E Coy. 4 Bn. R Berkshire Regt; **Newcastle [Tyne & Wear];** PVA TACs [*2 & *4]

see also Gosforth, Heaton, Jesmond, Walker & Wallsend

*1 Northumberland Rd, **Riding School**, 1849; computer centre for University; possibly designed by Dobson; another drill hall demolished and re-developed;

¶ In 1914, HQ+A Sqdn. Northumberland Hussars; HQ+A-H Coys. 6 Bn. N Fusiliers;

*2 **St Cuthberts Keep**, Holland Dr, c1990s; centre Northumbrian Universities OTC; square, low, steel & glass block, in yard;

*3 Barrack Rd, **Fenham Barracks**, early-19C artillery barracks; gate-lodges & guardrooms of 1806 in commercial use, two 2-storey barrack-blocks converted to flats and student accommodation; some lengths of wall with musketry loops & corner bastions remain;

*4 Fenham Barracks **TAC**, c1950s; in use by Yeomanry & RAMC units; 2-storey front block set in yard with garages etc;

*5 Barras Bridge, Assembly Rooms, in use 1914; re-developed;

*6 St Mary's Place, St George's [Drill Hall], mentioned 1914, in use 1947; no trace

¶ In 1914, HQ+Northumberland Bde. Coy. Northumbrian Divnl. Transport & Supply Column ASC [St Georges Hall]; HQ+1-4 Sections Northumbrian Divnl. Signal Coys REs [Barras Bridge]; HQ+1 & 2 Field Coys. Northumbrian Divnl. REs; HQ+1-3 Northumberland Btys. & Ammunition Column 1 Northumbrian Bde. RFA [Fenham];

Newcastle-under-Lyme [Staffordshire]; PV TAC [*2]

*1 Town Centre, **Militia Barracks**, pre-1850; quadrangular with pitch-roofed tower at each corner, & machicolated clock-tower over entrance arch; 2-storey buildings around four sides of courtyard; now workshops; used by North Staffs Rifles until c1880; vacated by TA 1939;

*2 Liverpool Road, Crossheath **Drill Hall**, c1939; symmetrical 15-bay, 2-storey front block with lateral hall behind; staff house to side;

¶ In 1914, drill station B Sqdn. Staffordshire Yeo; base G Coy. 5 Bn. N Staffs. Regt.

Newhaven [Sussex]; PVA ACF

*1 Fort Rise, drill hall, now demolished for flats; W side of road, used by Volunteer RGA & REs;

*2 Bridge Street, drill hall, used by RN; demolished for housing;

¶ In 1914, drill station for No.1 Works Coy. Fortress REs;

Newmarket [Suffolk]; PV ACF [p107]

*1 Rayes Lane, 'Victoria Drill Hall', 1938; hall & large garage front main road; now garden machinery supplier; office, indoor-range & mess to rear;

¶ In 1914, base for H Coy. 5 Bn. Suffolk Regt.

New Mills [Derbyshire]; PV

no definite location; possibly Institute at Batemill Road, Thornsett;

¶ In 1914, drill station for H Coy. 6 Bn. Sherwood Foresters;

Newport [Isle of Wight]; PV TAC [*1] [p46]

*1 Drill Hall Rd [W side], **Drill Hall**, 1860; built for Princess Beatrice's Isle of Wight Rifles; L-shaped, single-storey front block with gabled porch; badge of IoW Rifles + date over door; large hall behind with clerestory; later, single-storey block with garages, on one end; earlier work in grey brick, later in red;

*2 Drill Hall Rd [E side], **Drill Hall**, 1910; large, red-brick, gabled hall to road, with 3-bay, 2-storey facade, arched windows & door, pediment over central bay, & console & urn decoration; date in tympanum; 2-storey block behind hall, with garage entrances, range etc; built for RFA; backing onto the drill hall was a skating-rink of 1910, used as an extension during WWll, but demolished soon after; adjoining staff houses;

¶ In 1914, drill station for A Sqdn. Hampshire Carabiniers; drill station for 5 Hants [H] Bty. 2 Wessex Howitzer Bde. RFA; HQ+C,D & G Coys.8 Bn. Hampshire Regt;

Newport Pagnell [Buckinghamshire]; V

no location identified as in use in 1895;

¶ In 1914, drill station for A Sqdn. Buckinghamshire Yeomanry;

Newquay [Cornwall]; PV

*1 Crantock St, **Drill Hall**, 1900; large, single-storey, gabled hall, entered by low steps at one end, & crow-stepped at other end; date in keystone over window: 1900, with VR, & A° 60; small-arms range built on later;

¶ In 1914, drill station for G Coy. 5 Bn. DCLI;

Newton Abbot [Devon]; PV ACF [*2]

*1 60 East St, HQ of volunteers in 1897, still in use 1910; site next to hospital now developed for housing;

*2 The Avenue/Wharf Rd, drill hall, in use 1935; building, looking to be pre-WWl in date, used as an indoor range, survives as car-repair workshops; two Romney huts remain, & later ones accommodating the ACF Centre; a large hall-like structure, now in commercial occupation, could represent the original c1914 drill hall; only the huts were in ACF use by early 1980s;

¶ In 1914, drill station for C Sqdn. 1 Devon Yeomanry; drill station for No. 1 Works Coy. Devonshire REs-Fortress; base for E Coy. 5 Bn. Devonshire Regt;

Newton Aycliffe [County Durham]; PV TACs [*1 & *2]

*1 Greenwell Road, **Barnard Armoury**, c1930s, in use by medical unit; two-storey block with glazed oriel at one corner [cf Neasham Rd, Darlington]; yard with garages etc. at rear; [p205]

*2 Northfield Way, **Aycliffe Armoury**, c1990s, in use REME units; two-storey blocks opposite each other linked by garages & workshops;

Newton-le-Willows [St Helens]; PV Sea Cadets [*2]

*1 Park Rd, drill hall in use 1914; demolished for redevelopment;

*2 Cross Lane, **Drill Hall**, built 19C as chapel; in use 1940; TS Warspite; large 2-storey chapel with added front block; outbuildings & garage to side; NB adjacent chapel not connected;

¶ In 1914, base C Sqdn. Lancashire Hussars; base E & G Coys. 4Bn.S Lancs Regt;

Normanton [West Yorkshire]; PV ACF

*1 28 Granville Street, Carlton House, **Drill Hall**, pre-WWl; 2-storey front block with arched doorway, & decorative features; now housing; hall has been demolished; ACF hut adjacent; in between, c1950s staff house;

¶ In 1914, base for C Coy. 4 Bn. KOYLI

Norris Green [Liverpool]; PV

*1 Townsend Avenue, **Drill Hall**, 1936; in use 5/8 Kings; 2-storey, V-shaped front block with main door in angle;

datestone, 1936, & badge of Kings Liverpool Regt. over; hall, accommodation blocks & garages adjoining;

¶ In 1947, 5 Bn. The King's Regt;

Northallerton [North Yorkshire]; PV TAC [*1]

*1 16-18 Thirsk Road, **Drill Hall**, pre-WWl; house, two-storey orderly-room block, and hall, all in line to street; inscription "4 Bn. Green Howards", over door to hall;

*2 Alverton Factory, TAC; not traced, [information from RFCA];

¶ In 1914, HQ & H Coy. 4 Bn. Princess of Wales Own Yorkshire Regt.

Northampton [Northamptonshire]; PV TAC [*4] [p255]

*1 Barrack Road, **Gibraltar Barracks**, 18-19C depot of Northants Regt.; most of site sold to Royal Mail 1980; one 19C barrack-block still remains, now housing;

*2 Wootton, **Quebec Barracks**, completed 1941 as new depot for Northants Regt.; subsequently, as Simpson Barracks, depot of Royal Pioneer Corps; demolished 1990s;

*3 Racecourse, **Talavera Barracks**, hutted camp in both World Wars; demolished 1948;

*4 Clare St, **Drill Hall/Armoury**; built 1859 as militia armoury, at a cost of £7000, & used as a drill hall from 1880; in brick with stone dressings as a mock mediaeval castle with gatehouse, corner towers, arrow-slits etc.; still in TA use [REME]; extra land acquired 1937;

¶ In 1914, HQ & A Sqdn. Northamptonshire Yeomanry [Clare St.], HQ, & A-D Coys. 4 Bn. Northamptonshire Regt. [Clare St.]; ASC Divisional Transport & Supply Coy. East Midland Bde Coy;

¶ In 1938, base for 401 & 402 Coys. 585 SL Regt;

¶ In 1939, HQ of 4 Bn. Northamptonshire Regt. in isolation hospital at old [Gibraltar] barracks, moved to a house in Langham Place;

¶ In 1948, base for part of 585 SL Regt;

Northfleet [Kent]; V

*1 Lawn Road, in use 1914; demolished for school;

*2 Grove House in use 1933;

¶ In 1914, base for 5 Coy. Kent RGA;

¶ In 1914, drill station for 2 Coy. Kent RGA- Defended Ports;

¶ In 1933, Kent [Fortress] RE;

North Shields [Tyne & Wear]; PV ACF [*1]

*1 Military Road, drill hall, in use 1914; demolished c1990s, care home on site; enclave for cadet huts;

*2 Union Rd, **Old Cliffords Fort**, built c1672 as part of Tyne defences; in use from 1882 as base for Tyne Division RE [Vol] Submarine Miners; within original loopholed enceinte, six of the Miners' buildings stand, some, much-altered by the addition of lofts for fish-drying; also HQ building;

¶ In 1914, drill stn. for C Sqdn. North'd Hussars; HQ+1 & 2 Coys.Tynemouth RGA-Defended Ports [Military Road];HQ+ four Coys. Tyne REs-Electrical Engineers;

North Walsham [Norfolk]; V

*1 Corn Hall, built 1848, demolished for car-park, used by TF/TA units;

*2 Kings Arms St, cadets' premises, now demolished, moved to school;

*3 Manor Rd Board School [still in operation] provided venue for 1914 mobilisation [4.08.14] of 6 [Cyclist] Bn. Norfolk Regt. The officers' quarters were in The Grange, & officers' & sergeants' messes in Kings Arms Hotel;

*4 Grammar School Rd provided HQ for RNAS Mobile AA Bde. in WWl;

¶ In 1914, base for A Sqdn. Norfolk Yeo; & drill station for F Coy. 5 Bn. Norfolk Regt.

Northwich [Cheshire]; PV   TAC

*1 Darwin St, **Drill Hall**, 1911; single-storey hall with annexes to side; inscription over door: 'GR Cheshire Territorial Force Association MCMXl';

¶ In 1914, base for C Sqdn. Cheshire Yeomanry;

Norwich [Norfolk]; PVATAC [***11**]

*1 Britannia Barracks, this Cardwell depot of 1886-7 has an armoury rather than a Keep, a 2/3-storey arcaded block which was probably the officers' mess, turrets, & loop-holed walls; now part of Gaol;

*2 Chapelfields, drill hall, 1866; built for the Rifle Volunteers around a tower of the mediaeval city walls & consequently crenellated; demolished 1963 for inner ring-road; referred to as Theatre Street as well;

*3 52 All Saints' Green, **Ivory House**; grand 4-storey Georgian house of 1771-2, became the Militia Barracks in 1860; Victorian drill shed to rear & other outbuildings; also known as Surrey St artillery barracks;

*4 23 Cattlemarket Rd, **Drill Hall**, built c1800 as house; in

TF use from 1911-31; 3-storey, grand, brick & stone, 5-bay house, with rear extension; architectural practice, no. 23a The Old Drill Hall; ghost of crest on pediment;

*5 44 Bethel St, **Drill Hall**, built c1870s & requisitioned by TF 1908; long timbered range to street with coach-arch through to yard; fascia once with legend: "Headquarters 2nd East Anglian Field Ambulance"; behind, large hall, built 1876 as skating rink [with 73 St Giles Street address], 1882-92 SA, then Tacey & Lincoln, builders' merchants, now Country & Eastern interior design;

*6 22 Tombland, **Erpingham House**, built c1800; in use by Yeomanry by 1901-14; HQ Norfolk TF Association 1912-31; 3-storey, 3-bay, grand Regency house, rubble & rusticated stone dressings; restaurant;

*7 18a Prince of Wales Rd, built c1900; 3-storey, 3-bay terraced house; in use 1914, as **HQ** Norfolk & Suffolk Infantry Bde;

*8 41 Silver Rd, built c1890; in use 1900, as **HQ** 4 Vol. Bn. Norfolk Regt; simple terraced cottage;

*9 21 Northcote Rd/ Magdalen Rd, built c1890; in use 1901 **HQ** Norfolk Yeomanry; end-of-terrace house;

*10 137 Rosary Road, York House, destroyed by bombing 1940; in use by volunteers & TF 1904 & 1908;

*11 325 Aylsham Road, **Drill Hall**, 1930s, neo-Georgian buildings for a TA artillery unit; two-storey front block with semi-circular projections, hall, gun-sheds, garaging to rear; artillery crest over doorway;

¶ In 1868, HQ 1 West Norfolk Militia [All Saints Green];

¶ In 1883, HQ 1 Corps, Norfolk Rifle Volunteers [Chapelfields];

¶ In 1895, 1 Cadet Bn. Norfolk Regt. [Theatre Street Drill Hall];

¶ In 1900, HQ 1 Norfolk Artillery [Eastern Div] RGA [Surrey Street Barracks]; HQ 4 Vol. Bn. Norfolk Regt [Silver Road];

¶ In 1901, HQ Norfolk Yeomanry [21 Northcote Road];

¶ In 1904, HQ 1 Norfolk RGA Volunteers [Surrey Street Barracks]; HQ Norfolk Imperial Yeomanry [Erpingham House]; HQ 4 Vol Bn. Norfolk Regt [York Ho];

¶ In 1908, HQ Norfolk Yeomanry & Eastern Mounted Bde [Erpingham House]

HQ 4 Bn. Norfolk Regt. [Chapelfields]; HQ 6 [Cyclist] Bn.

Norfolk Regt. [York House]; base for 1 & 2 Norfolk Btys. + 1 East Anglian Ammunition Column, 2 East Anglian Bde. RFA [Surrey Street Barracks];

¶ In 1914, HQ & A Sqdn. Norfolk Yeomanry, [Cattle Market St]; HQ, 2 & 3 Norfolk Btys. & Ammunition Column,1 East Anglian Bde. RFA [The Barracks, Surrey St]; HQ, A & B Coys. 4 Bn. Norfolk Regt. [St Giles]; HQ, A & H Coys. 6 [Cyclist] Bn. Norfolk Regt. [Cattle Market St]; HQ, A B & C Sections, 2 East Anglian Divisional Field Ambulance, RAMC, [Bethel St]; HQ Norfolk & Suffolk Inf. Bde. [18a PoW Rd];

¶ In 1922, HQ 2 Bn. East Anglian Div. RE [Cattlemarket St]; 4 Coy. East Anglian Divnl. Train RASC [Cattlemarket St]; 84 E Anglian Bde. RFA [Surrey St. Barracks];

¶ In 1931, HQ + 4 Bn. Norfolk Regt. [Chapelfields]; HQ + B Coy. 161 East Anglian Field Ambulance RAMC [Ivory House]; HQ 163 East Anglian Infantry Bde. including 4 & 5 Bns. Norfolks, 4 Bn. Suffolks, & 1 Bn. Cambridgeshires [Erpingham House]; 429 [Norfolk Yeomanry] Field Bty. RA; 2/50 Field Coy. 54 East Anglian Divnl. RE; 3 Light Bde. RA [all Cattlemarket St];

Nottingham [Nottinghamshire]; PVA   TACs [***3** & ***9**] [*p33,51,74*]

*1 Castle Road, drill hall, converted in 1872 for Robin Hood Volunteer Rifles, from a riding-school which was built 1798 for the Yeomanry cavalry; in its final state this was a large stone-built hall with castellated round tower attached, & a clock set to Horse Guards' time; demolished 1926; a riding school was still in TA use in 1933;

*2 168 & 174 Derby Road, **Drill Hall**, c1910; large 4-storey brick-built block with stone dressings & neo-Baroque detail; most of the ancillary buildings & the hall itself have disappeared; at the rear is a brick building with pitched roof & two vents on the ridge, maybe stabling;

*3 5-6 Clinton Terrace, Derby Rd, 5-storey regency house, now **HQ** of **RFCA**, E Midlands;

*4 Orderly Room of RHR, Nottingham Castle, in use from after 1859 until 1893; used as gardener's store; single storey, stone-built, with pitched roof;

*5 Racecourse Grandstand used as Orderly Room & Armoury from 1893; demolished;

*6 26 Park Row, in 1912 HQ of Notts & Derby Mounted

MILNSBRIDGE, one of several drill halls in the area with a battlemented tower

NEWTON AYCLIFFE's Greenwell Road, similar to Darlington's Neasham Road

Bde; third of terrace of four 4-storey Regency houses; no outbuildings;

*7 116 Raleigh St, in use 1912 by RHA; large detached Victorian villa, with substantial outbuildings to rear; flats;

*8 Forest Rd/Balmoral Rd, **Upnah House**, TAC in use 1949; stone-built double-fronted Victorian house; halls added to rear post-1914; described in 1949 as having canteens, messes, lecture rooms, indoor games facilities & space for dances & socials; now Girls' School;

*9 Triumph Road **TAC**, 1953, 2-storey block+garages; in use; anti-bomb screen added 1990s;

*10 Coppice New Road, [now Ransom Rd] Mapperley, rifle range; lodge, originally with RHR monogram etc over porch; not found;

*11 Trent rifle range; lodge with ammunition store etc; built 1895, by Major Brewill, adjutant of 2 Bn. & a local architect; still inhabited & called **Trent Rifle Lodge**; another lodge to south of Range by lock, formerly lock-keeper's cottage; Yacht Club-house;

*12 University Park, OTC, 1949;

¶ In 1912, HQ Notts & Derbys Mounted Bde. [26 Park Row];

¶ In 1914, HQ & C Sqdn. South Notts Hussars; HQ & A-H Coys. 7 Bn. Sherwood Foresters; HQ Notts RHA+Ammunition Column [116 Raleigh St]; ASC Divisional Transport & Supply Column, Notts & Derby Mounted Bde; RAMC Notts & Derby Mounted Bde. Field Ambulance; all at Derby Road save RHA;

¶ In 1949, HQ + one Bty. 307 [S Notts Hussars Yeomanry] Field Regt. RA, TA; HQ 577 LAA/SL Regt. [the Robin Hoods, Foresters, RA, TA [Derby Road]; HQ + Sqdn. 350 S Notts Hussars Yeomanry Heavy Regt. RA, TA [Derby Road]; HQ 528 [Notts] LAA [Mobile] Regt. RA, TA [Derby Rd]; HQ + one Troop, 48 Counter-Bombardment Regt. RA, TA [5 Clinton Terrace]; HQ + one Sqdn. 21 [NM] Corps Signal Regt. TA [Derby Road]; base for one Coy. 8 [Motor] Bn. Sherwood Foresters [Derby Rd]; HQ + one Coy. 307 [Northern Command] Bn. WRAC [Derby Rd]; base for 2504 [County of Nottingham] LAA Sqdn. R Aux AF [Upnah House];

Nuneaton [Warwickshire]; PV ACF [***2**]

*1 Mill Walk, drill hall from houses converted by Ebenezer

Brown c1865, & in use as a theatre in later part of 19C; demolished in air raid 1941;

*2 Pool Bank Road, **Drill Hall**, opened by Sir John Ardagh, 28.ix.1903, with lease extended for further twenty years on 3.vii.1931; now martial arts centre; large hall with orderly-room alongside; staff house adjoins; ACF huts on adjacent plot;

¶ In 1914, drill station C Sqdn. Warwicks. Yeo; base H Coy.7 Bn. Warwicks. Regt;

O

Oakham [Rutland]; PV ACF [*pp12,208,332*]

*1 Catmos St, **Drill Hall** & **Riding School** of Rutland Yeomanry Cavalry of 1790s; two-storey stone-built quarters, 'Catmos Cottage', riding school, stables with more accommodation over etc; now Museum;

*2 Penn St, **Drill Hall**, very similar to Melton & Shepshed, so similar in date: 1914; 2-storey front block, hall behind, garages etc;

¶ In 1914, drill station A Sqdn. Leics Yeomanry, & base B Coy. 5 Bn. Leics. Regt;

Okehampton [Devon]; PV ATC [***3**]

*1 Market St, drill hall, in use 1910; demolished for re-development;

*2 Park Row, **Drill Hall**, possibly pre-WWl; 2-storey front block with Wrenaissance-style details & hall behind; 2-storey block with gables built on a curve; linking block with dormers; backs onto river; now Conservative Club;

*3 Tor Road, **Cadet Centre**, huts;

¶ In 1914, base for B Coy. 6 Bn. Devonshire Regt;

Oldham [Oldham]; PV ACF/ATC [***1** & ***3**] [*pp35,250*]

*1 Rifle St, **Drill Hall**,1897; red-brick, castellated 2-storey front block with tower at each end & central gatehouse; hall reputed to hold 1000 men; 2-storey detached ACF block to side; closed 2002, now warehouse; [*p249*]

*2 Bow St, Yeomanry Stores in 1909; not traced;

*3 Park Lane, Royton, ATC **HQ**; post-WWll huts;

¶ In 1914, base for A Sqdn. Duke of Lancasters Own Yeomanry; HQ+A-H Coys. 10 Bn. Manchester Regt;

Old Trafford [Manchester]; V

*1 73 Seymour Grove, in use 1914; demolished for housing; now "Trafford Plaza";

¶ In 1914, HQ+1 & 2 Field Coys. East Lancashire Divnl. REs; HQ+Nos. 1-4 Sections East Lancashire Divnl. Signal Coys. REs [all Seymour Grove];

Ongar [Essex]; V ACF
*1 Marden Ash Hill, drill hall, c1935; demolished early 1980s for Coopers Mews;
¶ In 1914, base for G Coy. 4 Bn. Essex Regt.
¶ In 1950, detachment of Q Bty. 304 Field Regt. Essex Yeomanry.

Ore [Sussex]; PV
*1 Grove Road, **Drill Hall** by 1909 recorded in 1958 Review; large, gabled hall onto pavement, with office to one side, & garage to other; now timber merchants;
¶ In 1914, base for H Coy. 5 Bn. Royal Sussex Regt.

Ormskirk [Lancashire]; PV A ACF [Moorgate]
*1 Wigan Road, drill hall demolished for bus garage; two-storey, gabled front block with timbered details & oriel over porch; hall & house behind;
¶ In 1914, base for F & H Coys. 9 Bn. Kings Liverpool Regt;
¶ In 1947, 22 Corps. Ord. Field Park; & 50 Army Ord. Maintenance Corps. RAOC;

Orpington [Kent]; PV ACF/ATC [*2]
*1 Village Hall, in use 1908;
*2 Anglesea Rd, **Drill Hall**, c1930s; two-storey front block with lateral hall behind; yard with Romney hut garage; staff house; inscription over main door: 'B Coy. 4 Bn. Royal West Kent Regt, & white horse crest;
¶ In 1908 & 1914, base for F Coy. 4 Bn. Royal West Kent Regt [Village Hall];

Ossett [West Yorkshire]; PV ACF [p208]
*1 Station Rd, **Drill Hall**, pre-1900; square, stone-built front block, with hall behind; then crosswing with segmental pediments; range across back of yard, and later ACF building; door into hall with inscription '4 Bn. KOYLI';
¶ In 1914, base for D Coy. 4 Bn. KOYLI.

Oswestry [Shropshire]; VA ACF
*1 Willow Street, drill hall; demolished late-1990s for housing; ACF on site;
¶ In 1914, base for B Sqdn. Shropshire Yeomanry; base for H Coy. 4 Bn.KOSLI.

Otley [West Yorkshire]; PV
*1 Boroughgate, drill shed, roofed in 1907, in Meeting-House Yard, later Masonic building;
*2 Nelson St, former Methodist chapel, built 1772, and bought for RE Volunteer Coy. as drill hall pre-1907; sold to Yorkshire TA Association c1908, when the gun-shed was built; demolished late 20C for re-development;
¶ In 1914, HQ+ 10 West Riding Howitzer Bty. 4 West Riding [Howitzer] Bde.

Ottery-St-Mary [Devon]; PV
*1 Mill St/Tar Lane, **Drill Hall**, pre-WWl; 2-storey front block with hall & out-buildings behind; now supermarket; no location given in 1910;
¶ In 1914, base B Sqdn. 1 Devon Yeo; drill station F Coy. 4 Bn. Devonshire Regt;

Oundle [Northamptonshire]; PV ACF [p332]
*1 Benefield Rd, **Drill Hall**,pre-1914; 19C house attached to 2-storey block all in stone, with brick hall, garage, small-arms range, & two WWll explosives & inflammables stores, all to rear; until recently a museum; now community facility;
¶ In 1914, drill station for B Sqdn. Northamptonshire Yeomanry;
¶ In 1939, base for B Coy. 5 Bn. Northamptonshire Regt. & temporary base for a battalion of the Leicestershire Regt;
¶ In 1948, base for a coy. of 5 Bn. Northamptonshire Regt.

Oxford [Oxfordshire]; PV TACs [*3 & *4] [pp53,210]
*1 James Wolfe Rd, Hollow Way, extending south to Barracks Lane, **Cowley Bks**; 1870s Cardwell depot of Ox. & Bucks LI; in use until 1957; Keep demolished in early 1960s to provide BT parking; two barrack blocks: Moore & Napier still stand in use by BT; officers' mess now residential accommodation for Oxford Brooks University; a bunker lies under new hostels, possibly Cold-War HQ of UKWMO;
*2 **12 Lonsdale Road**, semi-detached late-Victorian house; in 1914 HQ of 2nd South Midland Mounted Bde;
*3 Manor Rd, drill hall, in use pre-1900 -1950s; ecclesiastical-style buildings incorporating converted sports facilities included two drill halls, offices etc; demolished for University buildings, eg St Catherines College [1960];
*4 Tidmarsh Lane [near Paradise St], Yeomanry Riding School, in use pre-1900-1920s; demolished for commercial premises next to Brewery;
*5 Marston Rd, **Harcourt House**, 1957; very long 2-storey frontage, with crests of QOOH, & Ox & Bucks LI; to one

OAKHAM's Penn Street, closely related to Melton Mowbray & Shepshed

OSSETT, drill hall with traditional layout, and 4th Bn. KOYLI badge over door

side a compound, still in TA use, with garaging, workshops etc; currently government offices; opened by Earl Alexander of Tunis, [plaque inside front porch].

*6 Mascall Avenue, Slade Park, Headington, **Drill Hall**, c1938 complex of buildings; L-shaped 2-storey block, backed by hall & stair-tower; to the front, another hall, & garages; refurbished mid-1980s, opened by Douglas Hurd, then Home Secretary; to one side, a 3-storey barrack-block, staff house etc; sheltered housing.

*7 Elsfield Way, **Drill Hall**, c1938; probably built for AA unit; large hall with first-floor range & L-shaped offices, messes etc; garage & two staff houses; used as stop-gap between ***3** & ***5**, and for new City of Oxford AA Bty; converted to offices by addition of mezzanine floor; [p210]

*8 Oxpens Rd, **TAC**; 1990s 4-storey building houses Oxford Universities OTC;

¶ In 1860/1, Rifle Volunteer Corps formed in University & Town

¶ In 1914, base for HQ + A Sqdn. QOOH; base for HQ, A B & H Coys. 4 Bn. Ox & Bucks LI; HQ S Midland Mounted Bde; 3 Southern General Hospital RAMC; HQ South Midland Infantry Bde;

¶ In 1951, HQ Coy.+ a rifle company 4 Bn. Ox & Bucks LI; Q Bty. HQ+ one troop 299 Field Regt; TA Association offices; OTC & Air Sqdn. [all Manor Road];

¶ In 1957, 299 Field Regt. [QOOH] & 4 Bn. Ox & Bucks LI, at Harcourt House;

Oxton [Wirral]; PV TAC

*1 Wexford Rd, **Drill Hall**, apparently 1930s, still in use by RLC unit; long 2-storey front block, brick with stone dressings, hall etc behind; plaque with RA badge over main door; extensive staff housing;

P

Paddington [Greater London]; VA

*1 207-9 Harrow Rd/Porteous Rd, Paddington, drill hall, demolished for elevated Westway; in use 1910 & 1933;

¶ In 1903, HQ 18 Middlesex, 5 Vol. Bn. Rifle Bde.

¶ In 1914, 14 Bty. 5 London Bde. RFA; drill station for 3 Bn. London Regt;

Padiham [Lancashire]; PV

*1 [21] Mill Street, in use 1914; a possible identification is a

2-storey, stone, 6-bay building, formerly used by RBL, now undergoing renovation;

*2 Thompson Street, **Drill Hall**, 1914 & 1952; 2-storey, 3-bay, front block, in millstone-grit, with hall & house behind; to side, 2-storey, L-shaped, 5-bay, stone-fronted extension, built by Turnbull builders in 1952; now used by motor-sport company, with added garaging;

¶ In 1914, base for E Coy. 5 Bn. East Lancashire Regt;

Padstow [Cornwall]; V

*1 New Street, drill hall; in use 1935; demolished for housing;

¶ In 1914, base for No.1 Heavy Bty. Cornwall RGA-Defended Ports;

¶ In 1935, 56 [Cornwall] AA Bde. & 201 Howitzer Bde;

Paignton [Devon]; PV TAC [*p68*]

*1 Palace Avenue, **Drill Hall**, c1870; now Palace Theatre; the drill hall recorded in 1910 as being in the Public Hall; behind the main hall is another red-brick hall, now badminton courts; a single-storey strong structure with thick concrete roof, now town morgue, may have been the armoury;

*2 York Rd, **TAC**, c1970s + later; three-storey centre block with two-storey wings containing garages;

¶ In 1914, base for 2 Devonshire Bty. 4 Wessex Bde. RFA;

Parkstone [Dorset]; PV

*1 Alder Rd , **Drill Hall**, c1930s; two-storey front block, large hall behind; garage block adjoins further, smaller hall; now used by Royal Mail; WWll Home Guard use;

¶ In 1914, drill station No.2 Coy. Dorset RGA-Defended Ports; D Coy. 4 Bn. Dorsets;

¶ In 1939-45, base for 12/54 Heavy Regt. RA [TA];

Patricroft [Salford]; PV [*p210*]

*1 Cromwell Road, **Drill Hall**, pre-1900; tall, gabled hall with pediment & finials; doorways in side of hall to Pembroke Avenue, 2-storey house to side of frontage; legend: "Defence Not Defiance" on facade;

¶ In 1914; base for F Coy. 5 Bn. Manchester Regt;

Patshull House;

*1 18C house by Gibbs; 5th Earl of Dartmouth [d1891] raised a company of rifle volunteers in 1860; range in park;

¶ In 1900, base for G Coy.1 Vol. Bn. South Staffordshire Regt; [gone by 1913]

Peckham [Greater London]; V

*1 53 Copeland Rd, drill hall; area totally redeveloped for housing;

¶ In 1903, 2 Cadet Bn. The Queen's [Royal West Surrey Regt.]

*2 Messrs Tilling's Riding School; not traced;

¶ In 1903 used weekly by 2 Coy. of London Yeomanry, Westminster Dragoons;

*3 1-7 Linden Grove; in use 1933; end of street re-developed;

Penge [Greater London]; PV ACF [*1 & *2]

*1 64 High Street, **Drill Hall**; large double-fronted Victorian house, with out-buildings & cadet hut to rear; marked in 1970 street atlas;

¶ In 1914, base for C Coy. 4 Bn. Royal West Surrey Regt. at **Crystal Palace**;

*2 101a Parish Lane, Kent House, **Drill Hall**; long 10-bay, 2-storey block to street with arch to hall behind; now community use; ACF hut on adjacent site; [*p212*]

¶ In 1933, 4 Bn. Royal West Kent Regt;

Penistone [South Yorkshire]; PV

*1 Thurlstone Rd, **Drill Hall**, 1938 [date formerly on rainwater-heads]; now Leisure Centre; large hall with single-storey entrance foyer & side annexes; behind, large doors, now blocked, & two attached garages; to side, staff house, much rebuilt; a tank was once driven in through the rear doors but went through the floor;

Penrith [Cumbria]; V

*1 Portland Place, drill hall, by 1910; demolished for offices; in the 1880s volunteers drilled in the Market Hall in winter, & in the field next to the White Ox Inn in summer; drill hall not on 1900 OS map;

¶ In 1914, HQ+B Sqdn. Westmorland & Cumberland Yeomanry; base for D Coy. 4 Bn. Border Regt;

Penryn [Cornwall]; PV ACF [New St. Station Road]

*1 Upper Market St, **Town Hall** [1839] used by volunteers; museum;

*2 88 Lower Market St, drill hall formerly to rear of existing house; then used by SA; demolished;

¶ In 1914, base for No.3 Works Coy. REs-Fortress;

¶ In 1935, drill hall in use by RE unit;

Penzance [Cornwall]; PV ACF, ATC & HM Coastguard

*1 Chyandor Cliff, Chyandor Barracks, **Drill Hall**, 1912;

OXFORD's Elsfield Way drill hall built for an AA unit, now cleverly converted

PATRICROFT, a drill hall proudly displaying the Rifle Volunteers' motto

hall, converted to house; gun-store, drill instructor's house, all of 1912 or later, no military presence earlier;

¶ In 1914, drill station for D Sqdn. 1 Devon Yeomanry; base for No.2 Heavy Bty. Cornwall RGA-Defended Ports; base for A Coy. 4 Bn. DCLI;

¶ In 1935, 56 [Cornwall] AA Bde. & DCLI;

Pershore [Worcestershire]; PV

*1 Defford Rd, **Drill Hall**, pre-WWl; now Fire Station; 2-storey L-shaped front block & hall alongside; other buildings, domestic & offices; in red brick with decoration;

¶ In 1914, drill station D Sqdn. Worcestershire Yeo; base C Coy. 8 Bn. Worcs. Regt.

Peterborough [Cambridgeshire]; PV TAC [*6] [p52]

*1 Queen St, drill hall, built 1868 for 6 Corps Northants. Rifle Volunteers [formed 1860]; in use until 1927 by 336 [Northants] Bty. RFA; demolished c1975 for shop development;

*2 St Leonard's St, drill hall, built 1867 by Northants RE Volunteers; included orderly room, stores, & modelling shed; unit disbanded 1908; drill hall taken over by B Sqdn. Northants. Yeomanry; demolished 1911 for building of Crescent Bridge;

*3 London Rd, Fletton, 'Coffee Palace' built by London Brick Co. 1898, for use of employees; taken over by G Coy. 5 Bn. Bedfordshire Regt. prior to 1914; also base for F & G Coys. Hunts Cyclist Bn; demolished;

*4 London Rd, Fletton, drill hall/ 'TA hut', built 1921, for D Coy. 5 [Hunts] Bn. [T] Northants.Regt; demolished c1930;

*5 Lincoln Road, Millfield, **Drill Hall**, built 1927 for HQ+A,B &C Coys. 5 Bn Northamptonshire Regt. & 336 [Northants] Bty. RFA; a 2-storey front block with halls behind; also staff houses, garages, explosives/inflammables store; indoor range demolished 1999; now City Youth Centre; in 1939 mobilisation centre for TA units; adjacent **PSA Hall** used as canteen, & neighbouring **Unity Hall** in Northfields Road as classroom;

*6 'Shortacres', London Road, Fletton, **Drill Hall** built as house acquired by TA 1938; opened as HQ 402 Bty. 585 SL Regt. RA [TA] successor to 4 Bn. Northamptonshire Regt; double-fronted Edwardian house & hall behind, extensive garaging etc; post-WWll became TAC for unit of R Anglian Regt;

¶ In 1914, base for B Sqdn. Northants. Yeomanry; base for

yard behind; now Register Office; lodge on road;

*3 Tilehurst Rd, artillery drill hall completely re-built as housing 'Artillery Mews' in 1999; porch with RA crests;

*4 19-20 St Marys Butts, Army Information Office, leased in 1959; in large, 3-storey block with coach-arch; at rear, 19C buildings set in yard;

¶ In 1914, HQ + B Sqdn. Berkshire Yeomanry [Castle Hill]; HQ+ Baty. & Ammunition Column, Berkshire RHA; HQ+A&B Coys. 4 Bn. Royal Berks Regt. [St Marys Butts]; 2 South Midland Mounted Bde. Supply & Transport Column ASC; [Castle Hill].

Redcar [North Yorkshire]; V

no location identified; there were barracks in Warrenby after 1919, until 1990s; site now council depot; also provision for accommodating troops on South Gare, around batteries or in fortified depot of Submarine Miners;

¶ In 1914, base for F Coy. 4 Bn. Princess of Wales Yorkshire Regt;

Redditch [Worcestershire]; PV TAC [*3}

*1 Church Road, drill hall, pre-WWl; destroyed; Worcs Regt. badge survives in replacement building;

*2 Easemore Rd, **Drill Hall**, late 19C; used by Yeomanry & artillery; 2-storey, L-shaped front block backed by hall; crest over doorway; now 'Community House', dance studio;

*3 Winyates Way, North Moons Moat, Kohima House **TAC**, post-WWll; RHQ + HQ Sqdn. 37 Signal Regt. [Volunteers];

¶ In 1914, drill station for B Sqdn. Worcestershire Yeomanry; 3 Worcestershire Bty, 2 South Midland Bde. RFA [Easemore Road]; H Coy.8 Bn. Worcestershire Regt.

¶ during WWll recruiting to 267 [Worcester] Bty. RA [Easemore Road]

Redhill [Surrey]; PV TAC

*1 Batts Hill, Linkfield House, **Drill Hall**; early-19C house & lodge; yard with 1960s garages & other buildings;

Redruth [Cornwall]; PV ACF

*1 Foundry Row [E side], **Drill Hall**, 1912; complex of single-storey buildings including hall; small-arms range demolished; detached MT shed; datestone;

*2 Foundry Row [W side], **Drill Hall**, c1938; large barrel-shaped structure, similar in profile to Falmouth, & employing reinforced concrete;

*3 Chapel St, Oak House, drill hall, not traced;

*4 ACF Centre, Drump Rd;

*5 Foundry Row [West side], old **Drill Hall**, Armed Forces Careers Centre; 19C house with outbuildings;

*6 East End, armoury of 1 Vol. Bn. DCLI in 1897; not traced;

¶ In 1914, base for G Coy. 4 Bn. DCLI;

¶ In 1935-9, 165 AA Bty. 56 HAA Regt;

Reigate [Surrey]; PV [p216]

*1 Chart Lane, **Drill Hall**, pre-WWl; in use by bomb disposal unit & Surrey Yeomanry; detached Victorian house beside large hall with stable-type buildings to rear; garage & indoor range behind house;

¶ In 1914, base for A Coy.5 Bn. Royal West Surrey Regt.

Retford [Nottinghamshire]; PV [p105]

*1 Ashley Place, London Rd, in use 1892

*2 34 Albert Rd, **Drill Hall**, pre-1912; small mission-like T-shaped hall, now used for storage; Yeomanry Store in 1912;

*3 Storcroft Rd, drill hall, in use 1912; no trace, possible site occupied by 1970s bungalows; possibly same site as ***1**;

*4 Hallcroft Rd, ex-**TAC**, 1956; front-block & yard with garages etc. & staff house to side;

¶ In 1892, base for A Coy. 4 Vol. Bn. Sherwood Foresters [Ashley Place];

¶ In 1908, Kelly's lists 34 Victoria Road as HQ TF including HQ Notts & Derby Mounted Bde; & 8 Bn. Notts & Derby Regt. [Sherwood Foresters];

¶ In 1912, HQ Sherwood Rangers [34 Albert Road]; base for A Coy. 8 Bn. Sherwood Foresters [Storcroft Road];

¶ In 1914, base D Sqdn. Sherwood Rangers, & A Coy. 8 Bn. Sherwood Foresters;

¶ In 1936, base for C Sqdn. Sherwood Rangers [London Road];

¶ In 1949, base for one Sqdn. The Nottinghamshire [Sherwood Rangers Yeomanry] RAC, TA [London Road TAC]; base for one Coy. 8 [Motor] Bn. The Sherwood Foresters [London Road TAC];

Richmond [Greater London]; PV ACF

*1 Park Lane, **Drill Hall**, pre-WWl; complex of imposing buildings with badge of 6 Bn East Surrey Regt; now Royal Mail sorting office; Cadet Centre in garages;

¶ In 1913 & 14, base for B & C Coys. 6 Bn. East Surrey

PLYMPTON's drill hall is now an auction house

REIGATE's free-standing C19 hall still accommodates a TA bomb-disposal unit

Regt. [Park Lane];

Richmond [North Yorkshire]; PV
*1 Alma Barracks, 1874-7; Cardwell depot of Princess of Wales Own Yorkshire Regt. [Green Howards]; officers' mess stands as old people's home, & barrack blocks converted to residential, 1990s-present, with supplementary building in same style on parade-ground; also drill-shed [1913, now a dance studio]; armoury, gymnasium/drill-hall [1938, now a Leisure Centre]; guardroom, CO's house, HQ building, stabling, etc; the whole surrounded by a high, stone, loopholed wall, with castellated turrets at the entrance; very similar style, arrangement, layout & design of buildings to Wellesley Park in Halifax;
*2 Temple Square, Cravengate, **Militia Barracks** of N Yorks Militia; three two-storey ranges around a quadrangle, in local stone; probably built c1850, now residential;
*3 The Castle, contained barracks in 1914, now demolished;
*4 23 Newbiggin & corner of Bargate, **Drill Hall**, 3-storey, stone early-19C house with mullions etc, converted to Job Centre, 1966; now CAB;
¶ In 1914, base for E Coy. 4 Bn. Princess of Wales Own Yorkshire Regt; HQ Northumbrian Division, TF;

Ringwood [Hampshire]; PV
*1 Market Place, **Corn Exchange**, 1866; in use as a drill hall by 1894 until after WWl; then leased as a cinema, converted as a modern cinema in 1937, now shopping centre; Italianate, 3 bays, big arched window;
¶ In 1914, base for C Coy. 7 Bn. Hampshire Regt;

Ripley **[Derbyshire]**; V
*1 Argyll Road, drill hall, demolished for old peoples' housing;
¶ In 1914, drill station A Sqdn. Derbys Yeo, & base E Coy. 5 Bn. Sherwood F'sters;

Ripon [North Yorkshire]; PV ACF [***3**] [*p82*]
*1 Park St, **Drill Hall**; built at end of 17C as theatre; used as drill hall by 1896 until 1912; in use 1914 as Spa Hotel Garage, then garrison cinema; then used for storage of buses; refurbished 2004;
*2 Somerset Row, **Drill Hall**, 1912; now Hugh Ripley Hall, used by TA up to 1960s; now used by community groups; mix of two-storey & single-storey components of range to street; hall behind; all in red brick;

*3 Clotherholme Road, **Drill Hall**, 1989; compact T-shaped block [cf Howden] used by ACF/ATC; near to Claro Barracks;

¶ In 1914, drill station for C Sqdn. Yorkshire Hussars; base for H Coy. 5 Bn. Prince of Wales Own West Yorkshire Regt.

Robertsbridge [Sussex];

*1 Drill Shed from 1911; out-of-use by 1933; no local knowledge;

Rochdale [Rochdale];

*1 Moss Lane, Yeomanry Stores in 1909; area re-developed;

*2 27 Baron Street, **Drill Hall**, after 1883 & before 1908; very large T-shaped hall, with, on one side, 2- & 3-storey orderly-room block and, on the other, single-storey, bow-fronted quarters for drill instructor; on gable of hall, crest of 2 Volunteer Bn. Lancashire Fusiliers, formed from 24 Corps Lancs. Rifle Volunteers in 1883, subsequently 6 Bn. Lancs Fusiliers in 1908; still in use by TA in 1983; now garage;

¶ In 1914, drill station A Sqdn. Duke of Lancasters Yeomanry; HQ+B C D & F Coys. 6 Bn. Lancashire Fusiliers;

Rochester [Kent]; PV TAC [***2**]

*1 Corn Exchange in use 1910;

*2 St Margarets Road, **Drill Hall**, pre-WWI; large sheds; in use by RE unit;

*3 Fort Clarence, manned by TF/TA in 1910 & 1933;

¶ In 1908, drill station for B Sqdn. West Kent Yeomanry;

¶ In 1914, drill station for B Sqdn. West Kent Yeomanry; base for No. 1 Coy. Kent RGA Defended Ports [Fort Clarence];

¶ In 1933, 166 Bty. 55 [K] AA Bde. RA [TA], [Fort Clarence];

Romford [Greater London]; PV TAC [***1**]

*1 312-14 London Road, **Drill Hall**, 1930s; 2-storey admin block, staff housing, halls, garages & workshops;

¶ In 1950, Q Bty. 563[M] LAA/SL Regt. [28 Essex] TA

*2 South Street, drill hall, demolished; ACF HQ in new office-block on site;

¶ In 1950, Q Bty. 285 Airborne Light Regt. RA [Essex] TA

*3 Upminster, no specific location;

¶ In 1950, detachment R Bty. 563 [M] LAA/SL Regt. [28 Essex]; 23 [S] Corps. Troops Column. RASC, TA; & 1564 Supply Coy. RASC, TA;

*4 17 **Victoria Rd**, semi-detached Edwardian house in commercial use; next door but one, a detached house more likely to fit the bill; possible re-numbering;

¶ In 1914, 2 Essex Bty. 2 East Anglian Bde. RFA.

¶ In 1914, base for H Coy. 4 Bn. Essex Regt. at Hornchurch;

¶ In 1914, drill station for H Coy. 4 Bn. Essex Regt. at Rainham;

¶ In 1914, drill station for H Coy. 4 Bn. Essex Regt. at Harold Wood;

Romsey [Hampshire]; PV

*1 Cornmarket, **Corn Exchange**, 1864; in use as a drill hall until after WWI; floor inserted & converted to offices in 1924; now Barclays Bank; classical, 3-bay front with Corinthian pilasters;

¶ In 1914, drill station for C Sqdn. Hampshire Carabiniers; base C Coy. 9 [Cyclist] Bn. Hampshire Regt;

Ross-upon-Wye [Herefordshire]; PV ACF [*p220*]

*1 Alton Road, **Drill Hall**, 1930s; sold mid-1990s; now snooker hall + light industrial; ACF on site; 2-storey front block, large hall block behind, incorporating indoor range, inflammables store etc; to rear, large yard with two, single storey, gabled buildings, block of five garages, and a large, high, detached garage/gun-store;

¶ In 1914, drill station C Sqdn.Shropshire Yeomanry; base B Coy.1 Bn. Heref. Regt.

Rothbury [Northumberland]; PV

*1 Main St, **Jubilee Institute**, 1887; stone-built hall & offices; used for drill by TF; Rothbury was social centre for C Sqdn. Northumberland Hussars, many of whose officers were provided by the Armstrongs of nearby Cragside;

¶ In 1914, drill station for C Sqdn. Northumberland Hussars, & for F Coy.7 Bn. NF;

Rotherham [South Yorkshire]; PV TAC [***2**]

*1 Wharncliffe Street, drill hall, 1873; 2-storey front block, with castellated tower, containing armoury, orderly-room, living accommodation etc; large hall behind with shed [?indoor range] along one side; in use until 1936, when unit converted to AA, & there was a need for specialist gun-stores etc; moved to ***2**; used as dance-hall & night-club [Clifton Hall] until demolished in 1991, after an unsuccessful preservation campaign;

*2 Fitzwilliam Road, **Drill Hall**, 1936; 2-storey front block with lateral hall behind; yard with garages & later accommodation block; in use; art-deco motifs over doorways;

*3 Deepdale Road, Kimberworth, ACF Centre; apparently demolished c1998, cadets moved to *2;

*4 Wentworth Woodhouse, grand 18C house of Fitzwilliams, with stabling etc;

¶ In 1914, drill station for A Sqdn. Yorkshire Dragoons; HQ+ Bty. & Ammunition Column, West Riding RHA [Wentworth Woodhouse]; HQ+ A B & F Coys. 5 Bn. York & Lancaster Regt;

Royston [Hertfordshire]; V

*1 Melbourn Street, The Armoury, pre-1914, demolished, maybe for police station;

¶ In 1914, base for E Coy. 1 Bn. Hertfordshire Regt.

Ruardean [Gloucestershire]; V

never a drill hall here; locals trained at **Ross-on-Wye** or **Cinderford**;

¶ In 1914, base for E Coy. 1 Bn. Herefordshire Regt.

Rubery [Worcestershire]; V ACF

*1 Callow Bridge Rd; ex-TAC, sold 1970/80s for housing; ACF hut+house on site;

¶ In 1914, drill station for F Coy. 8 Bn. Worcestershire Regt.

Rugby [Warwickshire]; PV TAC [*3]

*1 Park Rd/Lancaster Rd, **Drill Hall** pre-WWl; hall with bays to side; 2-storey block of later date behind; staff house to side; now community use;

*2 Edward Street, **Drill Hall**, pre-WWl; Dutch-barn profile with later dormer windows, & single storey additions behind;

*3 Edward Street, Seabroke House, **TAC**, 1980s;

¶ In 1914, drill station C Sqdn. Warwickshire Yeo; base 5 Warwickshire [Howitzer] Bty. & drill station 4 Bty. 4 S Midland [H] Bde. RFA; base E Coy. 7 Bn. Warwicks;

Rugeley [Staffordshire]; PV

*1 Anson St; **Drill Hall**, pre-WWl; 'Victory Church Centre'; 2-storey front block with arched doorway & adjoining office accommodation; behind, a large hall with huts to rear; small-arms range down side of hall; scars where crests have been removed;

¶ In 1914, base for D Coy. 6 Bn. North Staffordshire Regt.

Runcorn [Halton]; PV   TAC [*2] [pp27,220]

*1 Greenway Road, **Drill Hall**, 1869; 2-storey, 4-bay front

block with polychrome brickwork & sandstone dressings; hexagonal, castellated tower at one end; tall, pointed gable over entrance; large hall behind; over door, badge of Cheshire Rifle Volunteers & 1869 datestone; also motto: "Defence not Defiance" above door; now fitness centre; [p220]

*2 Crown Gate Barracks; **TAC** in use Cheshire Yeomanry [Signals]; square, brick 1970s main building + garage block;

¶ In 1859, 7th Corps Cheshire Rifle Volunteers;

¶ In 1880, base for F & G Coys. 2 [Earl of Chesters] Vol. Bn. Cheshire Regt;

¶ In 1914, base for G Coy. 5 Bn. Cheshire Regt;

Rushden [Northamptonshire]; PV ACF

*1 Victoria Road, **Drill Hall**, c1927; 2-storey front block with gable & stone detailing, hall, garages etc. to rear; staff house attached; may well have accommodated units nominally based at nearby **Higham Ferrers**;

¶ In 1914, drill station C Sqdn. Northants Yeomanry, & H Coy. 4 Bn. Northants Regt.

¶ In 1936, company transferred from 4 Bn. to 5 Bn. Northamptonshire Regt.

¶ In 1948, base for company of 5 Bn. Northamptonshire Regt;

Rusholme [Manchester]; PV TAC

*1 Norman Road, **Drill Hall**, c1930s; 2-storey front block with projecting semi-circular porch; hall behind, & garages etc in yard to rear; in use by signals unit;

Ryde [Isle of Wight]; PV

*1 St James St in use 1911; probably part of Town Hall/Market Hall, 1830, enlarged 1864; now Ryde Theatre;

*2 St Johns Wood Rd, **Drill Hall**, 1910; 2-storey, red-brick T-shaped front block with inscription on gable: '1910 Territorial Forces'; behind, long, low hall, clad in green corrugated-iron; behind that, out-buildings; also WWll concrete shelter/store;

¶ In 1914, drill station for A Sqdn. Hampshire Carabiniers; HQ+drill station for 4 Hampshire [H] Bty. & Ammunition Column 2 Wessex [Howitzer] Bde. RFA; base for A Coy. 8 Bn. Hampshire Regt;

Rye [Sussex]; PV

*1 Ferry Road, drill hall was recruiting office in 1914; demolished;

*2 Winchelsea Road, drill shed moved from Winchelsea Beach,1915; made of corrugated-iron sheets, numbered for re-erection, over timber frame; now boatyard; other military-type structures adjacent- timber hut, Handcraft hut etc;

¶ In 1914, drill station D Sqdn. Sussex Yeo; base E Coy. 5 Bn. Royal Sussex Regt.

S

Saffron Walden [Essex]; V

*1Station St, drill hall, demolished c1990 following use for educational purposes;

¶ In 1914, base for D Coy. 8 [Cyclist] Bn. Essex Regt.

¶ In 1950, Q Bty. 646 LAA Regt.

St Albans [Hertfordshire]; PV

*1 Artillery Buildings, Harpenden Road; pre-1914; a pair of staff houses remains, & another apparently contemporary house [21 Harpenden Road] may have been the orderly room; 25" map c1930 shows 'Riding School'; now housing development 'Edmund Beaufort Close', nos. 6 & 7 look early 20C;

*2 Holywell Hill, site acquired prior to September 1939 for planned expansion/re-organisation of Herts.Yeomanry field regiments; still in use 1947;

*3 99 Camp Road, **TAC** in converted bakery opened 1987; single-storey buildings & garages; closed in 2000;

¶ In 1914, base for C Sqdn. Herts Yeo; 1 Herts Bty. 4 East Anglian Bde. RFA, [Artillery Buildings]; & base for B Coy. 1 Bn. Hertfordshire Regt.

¶ In 1923, base for 341 Bty. 86 Field Regt. RA [TA] [Riding School];

St Austell [Cornwall]; PV ACF [***2**]

*1 Mount Charles off Clifden Road, **Drill Hall**, c1930s next to social club, large, featureless shed, built prior to WWll, for AA unit; derelict;

*2 Cadet Centre, South Street; hut with water-tower behind concrete wall with pillars; could be WWll; later huts to rear;

*3 3 Victoria Place, **Drill Hall**, listed in Kelly's as in TA use 1935; large, stone building with balustrade at roof level with Cornwall coat-of-arms [motto *One And All*] is remembered as TA meeting-place; charity shop & Fish-&-Chip shop at ground level;

*4 East Hill, **Drill Hall**, 1911; complex of buildings with large gabled hall & parallel two-storey admin. block to street, with 1911 datestone; behind, cross-wing, triple gabled sheds, and three-storey house etc; listed in Kelly's as in use in 1935, by DCLI; now Band Club + commercial use;

¶ In 1914, base for D Coy. 5 Bn. DCLI;

St Blazey [Cornwall]; PV ACF

*1 Station Road, 1997/8; single-storey modern **Cadet Centre**, in concrete with buttresses, has replaced earlier building, which may have been another geodetic barrel; Battery House, adjoining, described by occupant as ex-Army house, may be the front-block of an earlier drill hall, as it has a distinctive double-pitched roof; a second building, now also a dwelling, resembles a gun-shed; also a hut on site;

¶ In 1914, drill station for No.1Heavy Bty. Cornwall RGA-Defended Ports [**Par**]

St Columb Major [Cornwall]; PV

*1 Fore Street, **Armoury/ Drill Hall**, by 1897; newsagents shop & store; two-storey front block with large hall behind;

¶ In 1914, base for G Coy. 5 Bn. DCLI;

St Helens [Isle of Wight]; PV

*1 Upper Green Rd, **Drill Hall**, pre-WWl; stone-built, of 4-bays, dormer windows; subsequently Post Office, & bicycle repairers; now residential, "The Old Cottage";

¶ In 1914, base for B Coy. 8 Bn. Hampshire Regt;

St Helens [St Helens]; PV A [***1** & ***2**] TAC[***3**]

*1 Croppers Hill, Engineer Hall, 1869; name survives as 'Croppers Hill Court' housing development near ***3** but two buildings to rear may remain from original barracks ;

*2 Mill Street, **Drill Hall**, 1861; long, 15-bay hall side-on to street; at one end a 2-storey block of 3 bays; then three more bays under a pediment with 1861 datestone; then a pedimented doorway with square columns & capitals; then seven, full height bays with another pediment over the middle bay, bearing motto: "Defence not Defiance"; now TS Scimitar; on corner of Mill St & Volunteer St, [*p222*] a further **Drill Hall** in use in 1930s;

*3 Prescot Road, Jubilee Barracks, c1980s,**TAC** in use by RA & RE units; square, 2-storey block with extensive yard & garages, within stone perimeter wall of former barracks; see ***1**;

¶ In 1914, base for B Sqdn. Lancashire Hussars; HQ+1-2

ROSS-on-WYE, a 1930s drill hall now a snooker centre

RUNCORN's drill hall retains its original 1869 roof

Field Coys. W Lancs Divnl. REs & HQ+No.1 Coy. W Lancs Divnl. Signals Coys.REs [both Engineer Hall]; HQ+A, C-E & G Coys. 5 Bn. South Lancashire Regt; HQ+A & C Sections 3 West Lancashire Divnl. Field Ambulances RAMC [Engineer Hall];

¶ In 1947, 107 Field Regt. RE [Croppers Hill]; 596 LAA Regt. [Mill Street];

St Ives [Cambridgeshire]; V [p57]

*1 corner of Free Church Passage/Bull Lane, drill hall, known to exist in 1914 as venue for mobilisation of Hunts Cyclist Bn; demolished; is remembered as a long, low, timber building;

¶ In 1914, drill station for H Coy. 5 Bn. Bedfordshire Regt. & base for C Coy. Hunts Cyclist Bn. drawn from St Ives & Somersham;

St Ives [Cornwall]; PV

*1 Chapel Street, **Drill Hall**, pre-1900; granite building 3 bays wide with porch;

*2 Alexandra Road, **Drill Hall**, c1938; large barrel-shaped hall; also detached probable gun-store, & garages etc. attached to hall; now in use as a distribution depot; used throughout WWll & after;

¶ In 1914, base for No.5 Coy. Cornwall RGA-Defended Ports;

St Just in Penwith [Cornwall]; PV

*1 Chapel Street, **Drill Hall**, pre-1900; granite, 2-storey rectangular building with pitched roof; large arched doorway now window; cannons and crown crest like at Marazion; now Town Hall;

*2 Penzance Road, **Drill Hall**, 1911; single-storey hall parallel to road; datestone/crest over porch; now Recreation Centre ;

*3 Penzance Road, **Drill Hall**, 1938; directly behind *2, large barrel-shaped hall; concrete block facades with curved asbestos roof between; a Cornwall TA Assocn. crest, dated 1938; now in use as builders' merchants & bowling club; possibly used by AA unit;

¶In 1914, drill station for No.2 Heavy Bty. Cornwall RGA-Defended Ports; base for H Coy. 4 Bn. DCLI;

St Leonards-on-Sea [Sussex]; PV

*1 Bulver Hythe, **TAC**; 2-storey square block c1970s in use; yard with garages etc; adjacent earlier drill hall in process of disposal, 2000;

*2 Hatherly Rd, **Drill Hall**, in use in 1909; 2-storey admin. block alongside large hall; cartouche on decorative gable appears blank;

*3 Tower Road West, **Drill Hall** in use 1914; nos. 10-14 consist of a double-fronted Victorian/Edwardian house with archway through to hall behind; now builders premises;

¶ In 1914, drill station for D Sqdn. Sussex Yeomanry; base 5 Sussex Bty. 2 Home Counties Bde. RFA [Hatherly Road]; base for 2 Field Coy. Home Counties Divnl. RE [Tower Road West]

St Neots [Cambridgeshire]; V

*1 Ware Road, drill hall, in use 1914, rebuilt 1922, demolished c1990s;

*2 Priory Hill House, base for Northants Battery, RFA on mobilisation in 1914.

¶ In 1914, drill station for D Sqdn. Bedfordshire Yeomanry, formed here in 1902; drill station for D Coy. 5 Bn. Bedfordshire Regt; & base for D Coy. Hunts Cyclist Bn. drawn from St Neots & Kimbolton.

Sale [Trafford]; V

*1 Tatton Place, drill hall, in use 1914; subsequently a Fire Station; demolished for Town Hall extension, 2002;

¶ In 1914, drill station for A Sqdn. Cheshire Yeo; base C Coy. 5 Bn.Cheshire Regt;

Salford [Salford] see also Clifton & Patricroft; PVA   TAC

*1 Cross Lane, drill hall, pre-1908; demolished, area completely re-developed; polychrome brick, castellated, tower, gables etc;

*2 Haldane Road, Haldane Barracks, **TAC**, c1990s; large block with pitched roofs etc; cf University Barracks, Manchester; in use by RLC unit;

¶ In 1914, HQs A-H Coys. 7 & 8 Bns. Lancashire Fusiliers;

Salisbury [Wiltshire]; PVTAC

*1 28a Butcher Row, in use 1914; redeveloped 1970s;

*2 Market House [1859], Orderly Room, in use 1911, by ASC & Wiltshires; demolished for railway extension;

*3 Wilton Road, **Drill Hall**, by 1939; [p222] L-shaped Voysey-ish front block with tile-hanging, dormers, pedimented gable & hall within the L-shape; to rear, garages;

*4 Portway, Old Sarum House **TAC**, in HQ building of former RAF station, c1935; in use by B Sqdn. Royal Wessex Yeomanry + ACF;

¶ In 1914, drill station for A Sqdn. Wiltshire Yeomanry; base for A Coy. 4 Bn. Wiltshire Regt; drill station for 1 South-Western Mounted Bde. Transport & Supply Column ASC; HQ 1 SW Mounted Bde. [Butcher Row];

Saltash [Cornwall]; PV   ACF [p95]

*1Elwell Rd, **Drill Hall**, pre-1900; 2-storey front block with gabled gate-tower; hall behind & 2-storey cross-wing; not in use in 1939; now fitness club;

¶ In 1914, base for B Coy. 5 Bn. DCLI;

Saltley [Birmingham]; V ACF [*2]

*1 Common Lane, Metropolitan [Railway] Works, in use by 1912; buildings still stand;

*2 Washford Heath Road, drill hall, demolished; ACF on site;

¶ In 1914, base for B Coy. 8 Bn. Warwickshire Regt; HQ+Birmingham Bty. South Midland [Warwickshire] RGA [Heavy];

Sandbach [Cheshire]; PV ACF[*3]

*1 Scotch Commons, Armoury in 1892; site re-developed;

*2 Crewe Road, Armoury in 1914; no apparent trace, unless in school;

*3 Middlewich Road, **Drill Hall**, by 1939; conversion of school/Sunday school building behind chapel; long hall with porch; 2-storey orderly-room block at one end; indoor range along the back with underground magazine;

¶ In 1914, base for G Coy. 7 Bn. Cheshire Regt;

Sandgate [Kent]; PV

*1 Castle Road, **Drill Hall**, in use 1908; saw stand-down parade 75 AA Regt. in 1955; later used by Sea Cadets; 8-bay, two-storey front block, with stone door-case; lateral hall & outbuildings behind; derelict;

¶ In 1908 & 1914, base for H Coy. Kent Cyclist Bn;

Sandown [Isle of Wight]; PV ATC

*1 Broadway, HQ in **Artillery Barracks** in 1911, drill hall in 1937; centre block + part of one wing of Artillery Barracks, c1880, still stand, built in red & white chequered brickwork; site now Council offices & Leisure Centre; ATC hut at one end may suggest that this was where the drill hall stood, if it was, in fact, a separate building, rather than part of the U-shaped barracks;

¶ In 1914, base for E Coy. 8 Bn. Hampshire Regt;

Sandringham [Norfolk]; V

ST HELENS, on the corner of Mill Road & Volunteer Street
[photo: NW RFCA]

SALISBURY, this drill hall displays an eclectic mix of styles

no location identified; may have used **Dersingham** ;
¶ In 1914, base for E Coy. 5 Bn. Norfolk Regt;

Sandwich [Kent]; PV
*1 The Quay, **Drill Hall**, 1869; built for 2CPAV [Cinque Ports Artillery Volunteers]; inscription on gable; large hall fronting quay adjoining Fisher Gate; entrance arch;
¶ In 1908, base for 3 Home Counties [CP] Bde. RFA Ammunition Column;
¶ In 1914, base for small-arms section of 3 Home Counties Bde. RFA;

Scarborough [North Yorkshire]; PV TAC[*5]
*1 Burniston Road, **Burniston Barracks,**1861; artillery barracks, expanded 1870s as part of Cardwell reforms; redeveloped for housing; the barrack-square survives surrounded by brick huts including the guardroom; the rest demolished for housing:
*2 North Street, HQ 2 North Riding Yorkshire Rifle Volunteers, 1880-1893; base for 5 Bn. Princess of Wales Own Yorkshire Regt. TF from 1908-34; site redeveloped;
*3 Temperance Hall, HQ 2 Volunteer Bn. Princess of Wales Own Yorks Regt. from 1892-?1907; demolished ;
*4 St Johns Road, **Drill Hall**, in use 1934-58; now factory premises; 6-bay, single-storey hall with small cross-wing & indoor-range alongside; large, low, flat-roofed, single-storey space to one side; formerly yard with huts to other; land-locked between two residential streets;
*5 Coldyhill Lane, **TAC**,1958; two-storey front block with lateral hall, and garages to rear in yard;
¶ In 1914, drill station D Sqdn. Yorks Dragoons; North Riding Bty. 2 Northumbrian Bde. RFA; E & F Coys. 5 Bn. Princess of Wales Own Yorkshire Regt; drill station for Yorkshire Mounted Bde. Transport & Supply Column ASC;

Scilly Isles ; PV ACF
although there had been land & sea fencibles previously, there were no volunteer troops on Scilly during the time of the TF & TA; RN gunners drilled on the Garrison, and the area outside the gate is still known as the Parade; no dedicated early drill hall, but a **Cadet Centre** in a hut on the Garrison;

Scunthorpe [North Lincolnshire]; PV TAC[*2]
*1 Cole Street, **Drill Hall**, 1913, replacing earlier building;

neo-Georgian two-storey front-block and pediment, in brick with stone dressings around door & widows; hall behind; in use until 1938, when site could not accommodate necessary expansion of garages, workshops etc; now Blind Society centre;

*2 Cottage Beck Road, [actually in Frodingham] **Drill Hall**, 1938; two-storey front & side block, with hall in L-shape; garages, staff houses etc to rear; stone front doorway with 'Egypt' & 'X' crest over; 1991 TAVR Cadet Centre with Yorkshire rose crest;

¶ In 1914, Scunthorpe, drill station for D Sqdn. Lincolnshire Yeo; & Frodingham, base for G Coy. 5 Bn. Lincolnshire Regt;

¶ In 1933, base for D Coy. 5 Bn. Lincolnshire Regt. [*1];

¶ In 1938, base for 384 AA Coy. RE [TA] part of 46 [Lincolnshire Regt] AA Bn;

Seaburn [Tyne & Wear]; PV TAC
*1 Dykelands Road, **Drill Hall**, c1930s; RAMC & RE units; 2-storey, 20-bay front block with 10-bay return, in red brick & stone dressings; two entrances with stone doorcases; in the angle, a large hall, 2 smaller ones, & a 2-storey 14-bay block along the back; large yard with 5 double garages, indoor range & other outbuildings;

Seacombe [Wirral]; PV
*1 Riverview Road, **Drill Hall**, in use 1914; 2-storey, L-shaped front block with hall behind; now sports hall;

¶ In 1908, Lancashire Fortress REs based in HMS Annettin in Clarence Dock, Wallasey; camps were held at The Warren, New Brighton;

¶ In 1914, base for Nos.5 & 6 Coys. Lancs & Cheshire RGA-Defended Ports; unit responsible for manning Liscard Bty. in New Brighton;

Seaford [Sussex]; PV
*1 Broad Street, **Drill Hall**, by 1909; 2-storey 5-bay front block with arched doorway, and gable; hall behind; later garage behind that;

¶ In 1914, HQ+ No. 1 Works Coy. Fortress RE;

Seaforth [Sefton]; V
*1 Barracks/TAC in use 1947; demolished for Container Port;

¶ In 1947, 306 HAA Regt; 13 Parachute Bn; 6 Para Field Ambulance [West Lancs] RAMC; 6 Airborne Workshop

REME TA;

Seaham Harbour [County Durham]; PV
*1 Tempest Street, drill hall in use 1914; garage blocks remain but rest demolished for office building of factory;

¶ In 1914, HQ+1 Durham Bty. + Ammunition Column 3 Northumbrian [County of Durham] Bde. RFA;

Seaton Delaval [Northumberland]; PV
*1 Prospect Avenue, **Drill Hall**, pre-WWl; now timber yard; gabled hall with lancet window over doors; 2-storey office/accommodation along one side; indoor-range & armoury/gunshed alongside; all rendered; when unit converted to medium artillery in 1930s, comment made that accommodation was inadequate;

¶ In 1914, base for No.3 Coy. Tynemouth RGA-Defended Ports;

Selby [North Yorkshire]; PV ACF
*1 Armoury Road, **Drill Hall**, c1875; inscription over door: "Selby Rifles"; the 38 Corps of West Riding Rifle Volunteers formed here 1 January 1861, and was incorporated into 1 Corps as L Coy. in 1880; in 1908 became 5 Bn. West Yorkshire Regt; E-shaped hall with forward facing wings, one containing doorway; decorated brickwork etc. similar to Colliergate, York [built 1872]; formerly a staff house attached on railway end; two later staff houses behind; in commercial use;

¶ In 1914, base for D Coy. 5 Bn. Prince of Wales Own West Yorkshire Regt.

Settle [North Yorkshire]; PV
*1 Castleberg Road, **Drill Hall**, 1864; now Scout hut; stone-built, barn-type hall, with end door at raised level, and door into semi-basement;

¶ In 1914, base for F Coy. 6 Bn. DoW West Riding Regt.

Sevenoaks [Kent]; PV ACF/ATC [*1]
*1 Argyle Road, **Drill Hall**, pre-1908; large hall & 2-storey orderly-room block with entrance archway, occupying corner site; over road, a later, c1930s, garage block, now converted to 2-storey cadet centre;

*2 Cramptons Rd. **Drill Hall** in use 1933; recorded as transferred by 1958 to Air Ministry; possibly now the Community Centre;

¶ In 1908 & 1914, drill station for B Sqdn. West Kent Yeomanry; base for G Coy. 4 Bn. Royal West Kent Regt;

Shaftesbury [Dorset]; PVACF

*1 35 Bell Street, **Armoury**, in use 1911; large detached Victorian villa, now a nursery school;

*2 Victoria Street, **Drill Hall**, pre-WWl; 3-storey front block to street, with archway through to hall, with cross-wing behind as garages; range of 19C stabling adjacent; staff house cf Wareham; still in use 1939;

¶ In 1914, drill station D Sqdn. Dorset Yeo; drill station E Coy. 4 Bn. Dorset Regt.

Shanklin [Isle of Wight]; V

*1 Landguard Road, drill hall, by 1911; destroyed by enemy bombs during WWll; site now occupied by publisher's warehouse;

¶ In 1914, drill station for E Coy. 8 Bn. Hampshire Regt;

¶ In 1937, detachment of Hants. Regt. IoW Rifles Heavy Bde. RA [TA];

Sheerness [Kent]; V

*1 235 High Street, artillery drill hall, in use 1908; demolished for health centre;

*2 Sheerness Lines and artillery barracks, bastioned lines of 18C and 1860s with gun emplacements & accommodation; in use 1908 & 1933;

¶ In 1908, drill station for B Sqdn. Royal East Kent Yeomanry; base for 2 & 3 Coys. [235 High Street] + drill station for 1-5 Coys. Kent RGA [Sheerness Lines]; drill station for E Coy. 4 Bn. The Buffs;

¶ In 1914, drill station for B Sqdn. Royal East Kent Mounted Rifles; HQ+ drill station for No.1 Coy.Kent RGA- Defended Ports; drill station for E Coy. 4 Bn.E Kent Regt;

¶ In 1933, 169 Bty. Kent Heavy Bde. RA [TA];

Sheffield [South Yorkshire]; PV TACs [*2, *5,*6,*7 & *8] [*pp39,46,71,72*]

*1 Langsett Road, **Hillsborough Barracks**,1848-54; converted sympathetically to a supermarket; boundary walls with castellated towers looped for musketry; ranges of accommodation with gatehouses front & back; institute, stabling, barrack blocks, drill-shed, all virtually complete; stonebuilt;

*2 Glossop Road, **Somme Barracks**, 1907; built for 1 WYREs; L-shaped with tower in angle; used by RE unit + OTC;

*3 Middlewood Road, ex-TAC; hutting for cadets & pair of staff houses;

*4 Crabtree Road; in list of old leases, nothing evident now;

*5 Hurlfield Road, Manor Top, **TAC**; buildings of c1970s + one older shed & a brick building maybe older still;

*6 Endcliffe Vale Road, **Endcliffe Hall**, TAC; large Italianate house of 1860 for Sir John Brown, steel magnate; in the grounds large stables with tower, contemporary with house; also drill hall, guardroom & indoor range, probably a little later; modern garages across yard; badges of Duke of Wellington's Regt. & of York & Lancaster Regt; HQ of Y&L Regt. in guardroom by gate;

*7 Barnsley Road, **Norbury Hall**, 19C house with additions; Cadet Centre;

*8 Greenhill Parkway, **Bailey Barracks**, c1980s; two large 2-storey blocks forming an L-shape; entrance into large yard with garages; in use by engineer units;

*10 **Brook House**, 2 Gell Street [1914]; square 2-storey early-Victorian house with portico;

*11 Edmund Rd, **Drill Hall**, also known as Norfolk Barracks, 1878-80 by ME Hadfield & Son; tower with crest of Duke of Norfolk; with small-arms range in cellar, first-floor stabling; built for artillery unit; now warehouse;

¶ In 1914, base A Sqdn. Yorks Dragoons; HQ+7-9 West Riding Btys.+ Ammunition Column, 3 West Riding Bde. RFA [Norfolk Barracks]; HQ+1&2 Field Coys.West Riding Divnl. RE [Glossop Road]; HQ+ No. 1 Section + Nos. 2-4 West Riding Sections, West Riding Divnl. Signals Coys. RE; HQ+A-H Coys. 4 Bn. York & Lancaster Regt; HQ+A-C Sections, 3 West Riding Divnl. Field Ambulances RAMC [Brook House]; 3 Northern General Hospital RAMC; HQ 3 West Riding Infantry Bde;

Sheldon [Birmingham]; PV TAC

*1 Barrows Lane **TAC**, 1930s ; in use W Midlands Regt. & RE; 2-storey front block with wings; lateral hall behind; yard to rear with garages; fusilier badge carved on gable over door; Warwickshire Regt. badge in stone on grass in front of entrance;

Shelton [Stoke-on-Trent]; PV [*p250*]

*1 Victoria Square/Park, probably 1897; imposing facade with tall arts & crafts-style towers & pedimented front in between with arch; large hall behind; adjoining one side a staff house, & the other later garages; inscription over arch:

"Headquarters Hanley Companies 1st Vol Bat N S Reg1857-1897";

¶ In 1914, HQ+1&2 Staffordshire Btys. & Ammunition Column, 2 N Midland Bde.RFA HQ+ No.1 Section North Midland Divnl. Signals Coys. RE;

Shepherds Bush [Greater London]; PV TAC [2]
*1 South Africa Road, White City, **Drill Halls**, c1930s; very large, mainly 2-storey admin blocks & halls, with garages etc. to side; in use 4 Para + signals units;
*2 Wood Lane, Shepherds Bush, **Drill Hall**, large red brick hall of 1898, with house & offices behind in Bulwer St; the facade richly decorated in terracotta with crossed cannon, & medallions; a plaque records its use by 1 City of London Volunteer Artillery; architect was Shearburn of Dorking; now Village[sic] Hall; [p250]
¶ In 1914, HQ 19 Bty. 7 London Bde. RFA;
¶ In 1939, 88 HAA Regiment RA [TA] formed at White City;

Shepshed [Leicestershire]; PV [p227]
*1 Kings Road, **Drill Hall** similar in style to Melton, dated 1914 over main door; two two-storey blocks and garage alongside, front onto the street; now in industrial use;
¶ In 1914, base for G Coy. Leicestershire Regt.

Shepton Mallet [Somerset]; PV ACF[*2]
*1 Commercial Road, Armoury of Yeomanry in 1910; not identified;
*2 Drill Hall Lane, Charlton Road, **Drill Hall**, pre-WWl; stonebuilt gabled hall & adjoining house; outbuildings & annexes behind; across the yard, what is now the indoor range in an L-shaped block of former stables & cart-sheds;
¶ In 1914, base for C Sqdn. N Somerset Yeomanry;drill station for F Coy. 4 Bn. Somerset LI; drill station for Ammunition Column Somerset RHA;

Sherborne[Dorset]; PV ACF [*6]
*1 Acreman Street, drill hall, in use 1911; demolished but stone with Dorset Regt. crest survives next to CCF School Armoury;
*2 Coldharbour, drill hall, in use 1911 by Yeomanry; demolished;
*3 Priestlands Crescent, HQ of Yeomanry, in 1911; possibly Priestlands House;
*4 Greenhill, Yeomanry Stores, in 1911; no building

identified;
*5 Lenthay Rd, **Drill Hall**, possibly pre-WWl; in use 1947 by Yeomanry; single-storey hall with house alongside; another hall/garage to road, & other sheds, garages etc; in commercial & residential use [Honeycombe Court];
*6 Blackberry Lane, ACF Centre;
*7 Sherborne School, Armoury; two small halls & outbuildings, buttressed & rendered; also several WWll-vintage huts; see *1;
¶ In 1914, base for B Sqdn. Dorset Yeomanry; base for G Coy. 4 Bn. Dorset Regt;

Sherwood Lodge [Nottinghamshire]; PV ACF
*1 large, brick-built 18C house with pedimented front; used as location for Robin Hood Rifles' camps, 1886, 1867 & 1890; seat of Col. Seely, CO 1875-91; house demolished 1974 for Police HQ; lodges of 1893 & 1903 remain;

Shifnal [Shropshire]; V
*1 Cheapside, drill hall, pre-WWl; demolished for shops c1970s; HG use WWll;
¶ In 1914, base for E Coy. 4 Bn. KOSLI.

Shirley [Solihull]; PV
*1 Haslucks Green Rd, ex-**Drill Hall**, 1930s; sold 2001 for retail/leisure; two-storey front block with lateral hall behind; yard with garages etc;

Shoeburyness [Essex];
*1 **Horseshoe Barracks**, most built 1856; artillery development & ranges; recently restored and converted to private housing.
¶ In 1950, WRAC units [TA]

Shoreham-by-Sea [Sussex]; PV
*1 The Harbour, **Sea Scouts' HQ**, SSS Chieftain; late-C19 single-storey brick hall with tiled, hipped roof, & gabled porch; may have been drill hall;
¶ In 1914, drill station for 3 Sussex Bty. 1 Home Counties Bde. RFA;
¶ In 1939, 113 Field Regiment RA [TA] formed as duplicate;

Shrewsbury [Shropshire]; PVA
*1 Coleham, **Drill Hall**, c1865; sold 1994/5 by TA; Barnabas Centre; large hall with attached sheds etc behind, & later extensions to side; at rear, officers' mess, c1970s but in Victorian style, now a house-builder's offices;
*2 near to *1 the Yeomanry's riding school, demolished

2001 for housing;

*3 3 Belmont, 3-storey Georgian house, formerly **HQ** Welsh Divn. & 4 Bn. KOSLI, now Solicitors' offices; to rear a hall and attached house dated 1904 reached by *Barracks Passage*; church hall;

*4 High St, HQ Welsh Border Mounted Bde. + Infantry Bde; an address below High St on the corner of Wyle Cop & Dogpole was, until c1990, in Army use; this is 19C 3-storey office/shop premises; Yeomanry HQ listed as 55 High Street in 1914 Kelly's Directory; NB Armed Forces recruitment offices re-located round the corner in Market Square, in a building which replaced council offices in High St;

*5 Copthorne Road, **Copthorne Barracks**; 1870s Cardwell depot of Shropshire Light Infantry; guardroom, Keep, two barrack-blocks, officers' mess from original buildings; also later ones; now HQ 5 Div.+143 Bde; 1990s **TA** compound in use by units formerly located at Coleham;

*6 The Mount, at the junction with *Barracks Lane*, **Corunna House**, 1889; built as home of CO of Volunteer Bn. KOSLI now home of Barracks CO; large, red-brick, detached, late-Victorian mansion;

*7 Sundorne Road, **TAC**, 1930s; in use by signals units; long 2-storey front block with large yard for garages etc to rear;

*8 *Armoury Way* off London Road;

¶ In 1891, base for Shropshire & Staffordshire Volunteer Artillery;

¶ In 1914, HQ+ A Sqdn. Shropshire Yeomanry; HQ+BTY. Shropshire RHA; HQ+A Coy. 4 Bn. KOSLI; HQ Welsh Divn; HQ Welsh Borders Mounted Bde; HQ Welsh Borders Infantry Bde;

Sidcup [Kent]; PV

*1 St Marks School used 1908;

*2 1958 Review records infantry drill hall in 1910; no trace of St Marks on maps; possible location of drill hall on Hatherley Road, where **Public Hall** built 1881 still stands, used by car dealer;

*3 **Lamorbey House** built C18, now Rose Bruford College, was TA HQ in 1939;

¶ In 1908 & 1914, base for E Coy. 5 Bn. Royal West Kent Regt;

Sidmouth [Devon]; PV   ACF

*1 Esplanade, **Drill Hall**, by 1897; site given in perpetuity by

Militia officer; large gabled hall + outbuildings;

¶ In 1914, drill station B Sqdn. 1 Devon Yeo; base F Coy. 4 Bn. Devonshire Regt;

Sittingbourne [Kent]; PV

*1 East Street, **Drill Hall**, pre-1908 [foundation stone illegible, perhaps1907]; tall hall fronted by single-storey, ornate, foyers/entrances, one with painted-over inscription on gable: "4 Bn. The Buffs"; now used as a Pentecostal church; appears to have begun life as Foresters Hall;

¶ In 1908 & 1914, drill station for B Sqdn. Royal East Kent Yeomanry; base for E Coy. 4 Bn. The Buffs;

¶ In 1939, HQ 89 HAA Regt; RA [TA];

Skegness [Lincolnshire]; PV ACF

*1 Grantham Drive, **Cadet Centre**; 1980, not on established site; 'drill field' on 1905 map, maybe for Robin Hoods' summer camps, or for local use, or both;

¶ In 1914, drill station for B Sqdn. Lincolnshire Yeomanry, [Louth]; & for C Coy. 5 Bn. Lincolnshire Regt. [Spilsby]

Skelton [North Yorkshire]; PV

*1 High St/Marlborough Rd, **Drill Hall**, pre-WWl; for a time Working Men's Club, now flats; two-storey, 5-bay front block, hall behind, crosswing & further extension;

¶ In 1914, base for G Coy. 4 Bn. Princess of Wales Own Yorkshire Regt;

Skipton-in-Craven [North Yorkshire]; PV *[p227]*

*1 Otley Street, **Drill Hall**, 1892; stone-built complex of hall, office/mess/range etc around small courtyard; now offices; date above porch, &, above that, in gable, inscription:" Volunteer Drill Hall";

¶ In 1914, HQ+A & B Coys. 6 Bn. DoW W Riding Regt; HQ 2 W Riding Infantry Bde;

Slaithwaite **[West Yorkshire]; V**

*1 Manchester Road, drill hall, demolished for housing;

¶ In 1914, base for C Coy. 7 Bn. DoW West Riding Regt.

Sleaford [Lincolnshire]; PV ACF

*1 West Banks, Orderly-room & Armoury in use 1892;

*2 Carre Street, drill hall, demolished 1980s;

*3 Church Lane, **Drill Hall**, now SKDC Community Council office;

*4 The Drove, **Drill Hall**, built c1950s; hall + single-storey offices, garage & outbuildings;

¶ In 1892, base for E Coy. 2 Vol. Bn. Lincolnshire Regt;

Company, 2nd. Vol. Batt. Suffolk Regt.' over main door; large hall behind;

¶ In 1860, 11th Corps of Suffolk Rifle Volunteers formed at Sudbury;

¶ In 1880, the new 6th Corps formed with HQ & D Coy. at Sudbury;

¶ In 1887, the 6th Corps was redesignated 2 Volunteer Bn. Suffolk Regt;

¶ In 1914, drill station for B Sqdn. Suffolk Yeo; & base for D Coy. 5 Bn. Suffolk Regt;

Sunderland [Tyne & Wear];

*1 Livingstone Road, drill hall, in use 1890, 3 Volunteer Bn. DLI; demolished for redevelopment of whole area, post-1967;

*2 Bishopwearmouth, S of church, c1890, drill hall of Sunderland artillery volunteers; demolished for redevelopment;

¶ In 1914, drill station for B Sqdn. Northumberland Hussars; HQ+A-F Coys. 7 Bn. Durham LI; base for No.1 Heavy Bty. Durham RGA-Defended Ports; base for Durham LI Bde. Coy. Northumbrian Divnl. Transport & Supply Column ASC; base for A & B Coys. Northern Cyclist Bn;

Sutton [Greater London]; PV TAC

*1 Lenham Road, drill hall, in use 1913; no trace; area redeveloped as a car-park;

*2 Stonecot Hill, Farringdon House, drill hall, c1930s; long 27-bay, three-storey front block with hall behind; yard with garages etc; stone dressings around door; demolished since 2005; new TAC to be built on site;

¶ In 1914, base for C Coy. 5 Bn. East Surrey Regt;

Sutton Coldfield [Birmingham]; V ACF

*1 Rectory Road, St Georges Barracks, post-WWll, mostly demolished for housing development, some 1960s blocks remain, but further housing planned;

*2 former **TAC** currently in use by MoD as Aquatrine House; 2-storey L-shaped 1960s block with extensive garaging to rear; due for disposal & redevelopment in 2002;

*3 St Bernards Road, ACF Centre, hutted; in use, on site of demolished drill hall now redeveloped for housing; [p234]

Sutton-in-Ashfield [Nottinghamshire]; PVA [p106]

*1 Alfreton Rd, **Drill hall**,1938; two-storey block and curved roof hall, with garages and other additions including

SPARKBROOK's Dennis Road drill hall retains only traces of its past inside

SUDBURY's drill hall was base for a company of the Suffolk Regiment

SUTTON COLDFIELD's St Bernards Road once a drill hall, then given a nuclear bunker beneath it, now only a humble Cadet Hut remains on this site

TAPLOW's drill hall retains its Army Service Corps badge from pre-Royal days

staff flat, of 1953, behind;

¶ In 1914, C Coy. 8 Bn. Sherwood Foresters; more recently South Notts Hussars;

¶ In 1949, base for one Coy. 8 [Motor] Bn. Sherwood Foresters;

Swadlincote [Derbyshire]; PV [p141]

the drill hall for Swadlincote is at **Church Gresley**; confirmed in 1958 Review;

¶ In 1914, base for H Coy. 5 Bn. Sherwood Foresters;

Swaffham [Norfolk]; PV TAC

*1 Sporle Road, **Drill Hall**, 1936; 2-storey offices etc wrapped around lateral hall, with garages etc to rear;

¶ In 1914, drill station for C Sqdn. Norfolk Yeomanry; for D Coy. 5 Bn. & for G Coy. 6 [Cyclist] Bn. Norfolk Regt.

Swanage [Dorset]; PV

*1 Kings Road East, later fronting onto High Street, drill hall; now demolished, but the indoor range survives beneath the adjacent RBL building;

¶ In 1914, base for No. 1 Coy. Dorset RGA-Defended Ports;

Swanley [Kent]; PV ACF

*1 Swanley Lane, **Drill Hall**, pre-1908; small T-shaped, single-storey hall, stuccoed & painted white; in use 1933;

¶ In 1908, drill station for H Coy. 5 Bn. Royal West Kent Regt;

¶ In 1914, base for H Coy. 5 Bn. Royal West Kent Regt;

Swindon [Wiltshire]; PV TAC

*1 Prospect Place, **The Armoury**, datestone 1932, on possibly earlier building; double-pile, 2-storey block with cross-wing, now care home; attached behind, single-storey structure with gable containing datestone, & inscription: "HQ [Wilts] Royal Artillery [RA]";

*2 Church Road/Place; **TAC**; 2-storey U-shaped block with garages across the fourth side; TA crest; probably post-WWll re-building on old site;

¶ In 1914, base for D Sqdn. Wiltshire Yeomanry; HQ+Wiltshire Bty. 3 Wessex Bde. RFA [Prospect Place]; HQ+No. 1 Works Coy.Wiltshire REs-Fortress [Church Road]; base for H Coy. 4 Bn. Wiltshire Regt; HQ+A & B Sections 1 SW Mounted Bde. Field Ambulances RAMC [Church Place *sic*];

T

234

SHELTON's Victoria Sq. drill hall, HQ of the Hanley coys. of the N Staffs Regt.

FORT AUGUSTUS, the drill hall of 1913 became a War Memorial Hall

ULLAPOOL, the drill hall with bowstring roof, and adjoining staff house/office

NEWPORT, the pre-1900 drill hall in Dock Street, now a fitness club

PEMBROKE, below the castle, the drill hall with PoW feathers over the archway

MACCLESFIELD, the French chateau-style armoury of the Militia Barracks

NORTHAMPTON's Militia Barracks in toy fort style, still a TAC

WHITBY, a relatively recent TAC has already been released for commercial use

READING Brock Barracks, the Keep of this Cardwell depot, now a TAC

KINGS LYNN's ASC drill hall on the quayside occupies a former warehouse; it is said that the inscription was in shot during the filming of "Revolution" set in 1776

¶ In 1914, drill station for F Coy. 5 Bn. West Yorkshire Regt.

Weymouth [Dorset]; PV

*1 Lower St Albans Street; in use 1911; demolished for re-development;

*2 North Quay, Sidney Groves Memorial Hall; in use 1911; demolished;

¶ In 1914, drill station for A Sqdn. Dorset Yeomanry; HQ+drill station for No. 3 Coy. Dorset RGA-Defended Ports [Sidney Hall]; HQ+ No.1 Electric Lights Coy. + drill station for No. 3 Coy. Dorsetshire REs Fortress;

Whaley Bridge [Derbyshire]; PV

*1 New Horwich Rd, **Drill Hall**, pre-WWl; large, stone-built hall on three levels built into side of hill; symmetrical front facing downhill with high gable with clock over doorway, entered up steps; at rear, facing onto road, a garage door; offices;

¶ From 1860 a detachment of the 7 Corps of Derbyshire Rifle Volunteers was based here, but in 1866 the 18 Corps was formed here;

¶ In 1914, base for H Coy. 6 Bn. Sherwood Foresters;

Whalley Range [Manchester]; PV TAC [*2] [*p58*]

*1 215 Upper Chorlton Road, Lancaster House, drill hall, in use1914; demolished, and site occupied by new housing: "Yeomanry Court' at back of Whalley Road;

¶ In 1914, HQ+C Sqdn. Duke of Lancasters Yeomanry;

*2 Kings Road, **Drill Hall**, 1903; built for RAMC Vols.-legend over doorway; corner site with twin octagonal towers flanking doorway in three-storey gate-tower with coats-of-arms & inscription; along Darnley Street, 5-bay,Tudor, red-brick, two-storey, castellated block with gabled dormers; along Kings Road, a similar block, 2 storeys & 5 bays; then a long & wide hall with castellated doorway in the side; still in use by RAMC units & others;

¶ In 1914, HQ+A & B Sections 1 2 & 3 E Lancashire Divnl. Field Ambulances

*3 Norton St, **Drill Hall**, pre-WWl; now Royal Mail South West Delivery Office; two-storey, 5-bay front block with Baroque detail, & large hall behind;

*4 Milner St. **Drill Hall**, c1930s; two-storey, 5-bay front block, the three central bays projecting, tower, with lateral hall behind; currently empty;

¶ In 1914 unspecified locations: 2 Western General Hospital

WESTMINSTER, the Regency Street volunteer Electrical Engineers' drill hall

WIDNES, Rifle Volunteers' drill hall

257

RAMC; East Lancs Clearing Hospital RAMC; ***2-*4** occupy same island site but are 3 distinct elements;

Whitburn [Tyne & Wear]; PV
*1 Mill Lane, **Camp & Range**, 1912; 2-storey, L-shaped house, & administration building remain from original build; hutted accommodation now of modern brick;

Whitby [North Yorkshire]; PV *[p255]*
*1 Spring Hill, **Drill Hall**; red brick hall added to 18C three-bay ashlar house with elaborate doorcase; now Bagdale Hall Hotel;
*2 Fairfield, Whitby Industrial Estate, former **TAC** c1990; now joinery factory; striking brick & glass hall with sloping steel sheeting roof; yard with garages etc behind; only in use for a few years;
¶ In 1914, drill station for N Riding Bty. 2 Northumbrian Bde. RFA;

Whitchurch [Hampshire]; V
probably no dedicated building; London Street, Parish Hall, built 1908, used for most village activities;
¶ In 1914, base for H Coy. 9[Cyclist] Bn. Hampshire Regt;

Whitchurch [Shropshire]; V ACF
*1 Mill Street, TAC demolished; new ACF Centre built on site, in 1990s;
¶ In 1914, drill station B Sqdn. Shropshire Yeomanry; base for B Coy.4 Bn. KOSLI;

Whitehaven [Cumbria]; PV ACF [***3**]
*1 Catherine St, drill hall, pre-WWl; in use by Home Guard in 1940; demolished for supermarket;
*2 Catherine St, **Militia Barracks**, from 1857, built 1809 - 1829 as linen mill; then Dobson & Musgrave factory; 1992 converted to apartments; long, 4-storey building with three-bay pediment;
*3 Howgill Street, **TAC**, in use 1983; hutted, now used by ACF;
¶ In 1914, base for C Sqdn. Westmorland & Cumberland Yeomanry; drill station for Ammunition Column 4 E Lancs [Howitzer] Bde. RFA; base A Coy. 5 Bn. Border R;

Whitley Bay [Northumberland]; V
no trace of dedicated drill hall ever;
¶ In 1914, base for G Coy. Northern Cyclist Bn;
¶ In 1947, base for 464 HAA Regiment RA [TA]

Whitstable [Kent]; V ACF [***1**]
*1 Cromwell Road, drill hall; in use up to WWll; demolished; ACF hut adjacent;
*2 Waverley Hall, in use 1908; not known locally;
¶ In 1908, drill station for F Coy. 4 Bn. The Buffs; base for Section C 2 Home Counties Field Ambulance RAMC [Waverley Hall];
¶ In 1914, drill station for F Coy. 4 Bn. East Kent Regt; drill station for F Coy. Kent Cyclist Bn; base C Section 2 Home Counties Divnl. Field Ambulance RAMC;

Whittlesea [Cambs]; V
*1 Station Road, drill hall, demolished 1960s.
¶ In 1860, 4 Corps Cambridgeshire Volunteer Rifles formed, in 1880 became F Coy. Cambridgeshire Rifle Volunteers.
¶ In 1914, base for F Coy. 1 Bn. Cambridgeshire Regt.

Whitwell [Hertfordshire]; V
*1 Village hall was drill hall; now re-developed as 'Oldhall House', apartments;
¶ In 1914, drill station for G Coy. 1 Bn. Hertfordshire Regt;

Widnes [Halton]; PVA TAC [***2**]
*1 Victoria Road, **Drill Hall**; badge of 49th Corps, Lancashire Rifle Volunteers on keystone over door; 2-storey, symmetrical, 5-bay front block, in polychrome brick, dentillated cornice, turrets & arrow-slits; large hall behind; once billiard hall, now piano show-room; *[p257]*
*2 Peel House Lane, Ubique Barracks, **TAC** in use by REME; square, brick, main building c1970s, & large factory-type garage/ workshop block; may be replacement for drill hall in use 1930s with 7-bay, pedimented front block & hall behind, and garages to one side;
¶ In 1860 the 49th Corps Lancashire Rifle Volunteers formed at Newton-le-Willows &, in 1862 was attached to the 9th Corps at Warrington, eventually becoming G Coy. 1 Vol. Bn. S Lancs. Regt. there in 1886; in 1860, the 77th Corps was formed at Widnes, but had disappeared by 1863;
¶ In 1914, base 14 Lancashire Bty.3 West Lancashire Bde. RFA; drill station West Lancashire Divnl. REs; base for H Coy. 5 Bn. South Lancashire Regt;
¶ In 1947, No.51 AA Workshops, REME;

Wigan [Wigan]; PV TAC [***4**]
*1 Commercial Buildings, Rifle Volunteers' Store in 1869; no trace;

*2 Bank St. in use 1914; street now redeveloped on new line;
*3 Powell Street, drill hall, pre-1908; long, lateral hall to street frontage, [cf Mill Street, St Helens]; pediment with inscription: Wigan Volunteer Drill Hall, coat-of-arms, & two roundels with crown & bugle; all demolished in August 1986 for road-widening; carvings & inscriptions preserved at....
*4 Canal Street, Kearsley House **TAC**, in use by RAC-Yeomanry; two-storey, L-shaped hall/admin block, with single-storey annexe in re-entrant angle; yard with garages etc; stonework from Powell Street [***3**] in forecourt;
¶ In 1914, drill station for A Sqdn. Lancashire Hussars; HQ+A-E Coys. 5 Bn. Manchester Regt. [Bank Street];

Wigton [Cumbria]; PV
*1 George St, **Armoury**, c1860s; for 11 Corps Cumberland Rifle Volunteers, & then N Coy. 1 Volunteer Bn. Border Regt; two-storey, 8-bay front block with pediment over centre two bays; now Armoury Cottages 1992;
*2 West St, **Drill Hall**, 1938; single-storey front block with hall behind; and indoor range to rear; Border Regiment badge over door with 1938 datestone;
¶ In 1914, drill station for D Sqdn. Westmorland & Cumberland Yeomanry; base for F Coy. 5 Bn. Border Regt.
¶ In 1938, base for D Coy. 5 Bn. Border Regt;

Willenhall [Woverhampton]; PV ACF [***2**]
*1 Market Place, drill hall in use 1912, re-developed;
*2 Leve Lane, **Drill Hall**, opened 1924; single-storey front block with lateral hall behind; further building added on behind that; ACF hut + miniature range in Romney hut; now pie factory; opposite is WWll decontamination centre and further garaging, possibly for Civil Defence;
¶ In 1914, base for D Coy. 6 Bn. South Staffordshire Regt.

Willesden [Greater London]; PV [p51]
*1 Pound Lane, **Drill Hall**; pre-WWl; now hostel; 3-storey main block in Flemish Renaissance style, with single-storey pedimented pavilions at each end of the facade; complex trophy sculpture in gable with 'TF' in centre; crests in pediment over main door with Middlesex & Duke of Cambridge's coats of arms incorporated; in brick with elaborate stone dressings.
¶ In 1914, HQ+A-E Coys. 9 Bn. Middlesex Regt.

Williton [Somerset]; PV ATC [Priest Street]

*1 former **Drill Hall**, now Chapel Cottage behind Post Office, built as Girls' Friendly Society Hall; single-storey, sandstone hall with porthole window in gable-end wall;
¶ In 1902 & 1906, base for D Coy. 2 Vol. Bn. SLI; drill instructor recorded;
¶ In 1914, drill station for A Sqdn. W Somerset Yeomanry; base for B Coy. 5 Bn. SLI *Wilmslow* **[Cheshire];** V
*1 Church Street, drill hall, by 1914; after WWl there was a Public Hall, which stood until whole street was re-developed in 1970s;
¶ In 1914, base for H Coy. 7 Bn. Cheshire Regt.

Wilton [Wiltshire]; PV
*1 Russell St, **Drill Hall**, in use from 1870; built as school room on first floor of rectangular stone building next to church; by 1939 in use as TA Social Club;
¶ In 1914, base for B Coy. 4 Bn. Wiltshire Regt;

Wimbledon [Greater London]; PV ATC[***2**]
*1 105 Merton Road, Coombe Villa, in use 1913; W side, numbers stop for probable road re-alignment;
*2 Merton Road, E side, **Drill Hall**, c1950s; two-storey front block, hall behind; in use by ATC & community;
*3 17 St George's Road, drill hall, in use 1913; demolished for car-park;
¶ In 1903, HQ 2 Volunteer Bn. East Surrey Regt. [St George's Road];
¶ In 1913 &14, base for D Sqdn. Surrey Yeomanry [Coombe Villa];
¶ In 1913 &14, HQ+E F & G Coys. 5 Bn. East Surrey Regt. [St George's Road];

Wimborne [Dorset]; PV ACF [***2**]
*1 20 West Borough, **Armoury**, in use 1911; two-storey brick house;
*2 Blind Lane, drill hall, pre-WWl; demolished for housing; ACF hut on site;
¶ In 1914, drill station for C Sqdn. Dorset Yeo; base for F Coy.Dorset Regt;

Winchester [Hampshire]; PVA TAC [***6**]
*1 Hyde Close, **Drill Hall** in use as Yeomanry HQ in 1914; built 1795 by Sir John Soane as a school-room; carpet warehouse; plain, brick block of 5 bays across, & 6 bays deep; front half original with arched windows in recessed blank arcading; the back half served as a munitions factory

during WWll, then a TAC, was next rebuilt as offices, and, most recently [2005] converted to residential use;

*2 Castle Hill, new HQ for 1 Volunteer Bn. Hampshire Regt. opened by Duke of Connaught, 11 August 1892; demolished for new County Council Offices,1930s;

*3 Romsey Road, Peninsular Barracks, begun 1683 as a royal palace designed by Wren; only completed in 1758 & altered after use as a prison to become Cardwell depot of Rifle Bde. 1881; destroyed by fire 1894 but rebuilt in its original style; three long 4-storey blocks in brick with stone pediments converted to apartments or in use as museums; also weapons training shed & guardhouse;

*4 Southgate Street, Lower Barracks, c1880; Cardwell depot of Hampshire Regt; guardroom, barrack-blocks & chapel /school;

*6 Newburgh St. **Drill Hall**; large building marked on 1909 OS map; 1932 map shows large extension to rear labelled 'Drill Hall'; now new road through extension site, and c1960s **TAC** on original site;

¶ In 1914, HQ+B Sqdn. Hampshire Carabiniers [Hyde Close]; HQ+A&B Coys. 4 Bn. Hampshire Regt; drill station HQ Coy. Wessex Divnl. Transport & Supply Column ASC; drill station for B Section 3 Wessex Divnl. Field Ambulances RAMC;

Windermere [Cumbria]; PV ACF

*1 Park Road, **Drill Hall**, pre-WWl; 2-storey front block now very domestic looking; hall behind, with indoor range alongside; outdoor pursuits centre; all stone-built;

¶ In 1914, drill station for A Sqdn. Westmorland & Cumberland Yeomanry; base for H Coy. 4 Bn. Border Regt;

Windsor [Berkshire]; PV TAC

*1 96 Bolton Road, **TAC**, 1963; in use by Yeomanry signals unit; front block with hall behind; yard with garages etc;

¶ In 1914, base A Sqdn. Berks Yeomanry; base D Coy. 4 Bn. Royal Berkshire Reg;

Wingham **[Kent];** V

*1 The Green, Canterbury Road, drill hall, built as Wesleyan chapel, which may have dated from 1839; in use by 1899, and in 1907, when used by 1 Volunteer Bn. The Buffs, under Rev. Sargent, OC & acting Chaplain; demolished;

*2 High Street [corner with N Court Road] drill hall, known as Red Hut; also demolished;

¶ In 1899, base for I Coy. East Kent Volunteers;

¶ In 1908, base for C Coy. 4 Bn. The Buffs;

¶ In 1914, drill station for C Coy. 4 Bn. East Kent Regt;

Wirksworth **[Derbyshire];** V

*1 Canterbury Rd, drill hall, remembered as Nissen hut; demolished for housing;

¶ In 1914, drill station C Sqdn. Derbys Yeo; & base E Coy. 6 Bn. Sherwood F'sters;

Winsford [Cheshire]; PV [p318]

*1 Dingle Lane, **Drill Hall**, 1900; large hall to road with black & white gabled facade; tall, castellated, red-brick tower with datestone & inscription; adjoining two-storey house/orderly-room; now Top Ten Bingo;

¶ In 1914, drill station C Sqdn. Cheshire Yeo; base E Coy. 7 Bn. Cheshire Regt;

Wisbech [Cambridgeshire]; PVA ACF

*1 North Brink, **Corn Exchange**, orderly room from 1860 to post-1893 of 2 Corps Cambridgeshire Volunteer Rifles; in 1880, E Coy. Cambridgeshire Rifle Volunteers;

*2 4 North Terrace, drill hall until 1902, when later rebuilt as..

*3 Sandylands, TAC closed c2000, awaiting redevelopment; new premises to be built for ACF further along road to incorporate regimental crest of Cambridgeshires;

¶ In 1914, drill station D Sqdn. Norfolk Yeo; & base E Coy. 1 Bn. Cambs. Regt;

Witham **[Essex];** VA

*1 Guithavon Road, drill hall, demolished 1974;

¶ In 1914, drill station for G Coy. 5 Bn. Essex Regt.

¶ In 1950, detachment P Bty. 646 LAA Regt.

Witney [Oxfordshire]; PV [pp44,55]

*1 Langdale Hall, **Drill Hall**, opened 1927; 3-storey, 9 bay, front block with porch; behind, large hall; behind that cross-wing; now in community use; plaque refers to Volunteer Bn. Ox. & Bucks. LI;

*2 Marlborough Lane, **Drill Hall**, in use from c1860 in ex-Friends' Meeting House,1712; barn-like structure with side windows, and window over front door;

*3 High Street, **Corn Exchange,** built 1863; used as drill hall at different times up to WWll use by Home Guard;

¶ In 1914, drill station for B Sqdn.QOOH; base for F Coy. 4 Bn. Ox & Bucks LI;

Woking [Surrey]; PV   ACF

*1 259 Walton Road, late-Victorian terrace house remains; in use 1913 & 14;

*2 Walton Road, **Drill Hall**, pre-WWl; two-storey front block with arched door at each end; hall behind, with two-storey cross-wing behind that; in use as Woking Youth Centre, church, & ACF Centre; similar in style to Chertsey, dated 1902;

¶ In 1914, drill station B Sqdn. Surrey Yeomanry; base for H Coy. 5 Bn. Royal West Surrey Regt. with a drill station at Knaphill near [or in] Inkerman Barracks; Surrey Bde. Coy. Home Counties Divnl.Transport & Supply Column, ASC [259 Walton Rd

Wokingham [Berkshire]; PVA [p31]

*1 Denmark St, **Drill Hall**; built 1881 by Captain Walter, for L Coy. 1 Volunteer Bn. Berkshire Regt; surviving front block of two storeys comprising 4 cottages & central archway; the original datestone now re-set on the back of the arch; the hall, which measured 70' by 33', had a front porch, and a store and armoury at the rear entered by a separate entrance; demolished in the mid-1970s for shopping precinct;

¶ In 1914, drill station A Sqdn. Berks Yeomanry; base H Coy. 4 Bn. R Berks Regt;

Wolverhampton [Wolverhampton]; PV TAC [*2]

*1 Park Road East/Devon Road, **Drill Hall**, 1911; high, symmetrical, two-storey block with castellated bow windows & doorway projection, flanked by single-storey wings; lateral hall now demolished; front block converted to housing and rest of site built on; inscription over doorway: 'Staffs Territorial Force Association'; stylistically similar to Booth Street, Stoke [1913] also referred to as West Park, & New Hampton Road East;

*2 Wolseley House, Fallings Park, **TAC**, post-WWll; extensive site entered between two staff houses, and inner gates; large two-storey modern block with three-storey centre, incorporates halls; yard with garages;

*3 Stafford Street, The Deanery; base for RAMC; although 17C, by Wren, now demolished and rebuilt as University buildings on Wulfruna Street, drill hall in use until 1958;

*4 Albert Road TAC in 1958;

¶ In 1914, base D Sqdn. Staffordshire Yeo; HQ, 4 Staffordshire Bty. & Ammunition Column, 3 N Midland

Bde. RFA [West Park]; HQ+A & B Coys. 6 Bn. S Staffs. Regt; HQ+A-C Sections, 3 North Midland Divnl. Field Ambulance RAMC [The Deanery];

¶ In 2001, HQ W Midlands Regt; 210 Bty. 104 Regt. RA [TA]; HQ 23 SAS Regt;

Wolverton [Buckinghamshire]; PV ACF [p327]

*1 Mill Mead House by railway station, **Drill Hall**, 1914; two-storey front block with Swan badge, 1914 date-stone, & Buckinghamshire Volunteer Bn. legend; behind, hall with vents on ridge; now sports hall; staff house adjacent; hutted Cadet Centre;

¶ In 1914, base for F & G Coys. Oxon. & Bucks. Light Infantry;

Wooburn [Buckinghamshire]; PV

*1 **Drill Hall**, c1930; single-storey front block with hall behind; later additions behind that; garages across yard used by ACF until c1975; now used by construction firm; Buckinghamshire Swan over entrance;

¶ In 1940, HQ C Coy. 4 Bn. Bucks. Home Guard

Woodbridge [Suffolk]; PV ACF

*1 Quayside, **Drill Hall**, pre-1914; hall with cupola; 1/2-storey extensions at each end; staff house;

¶ In 1914, drill station for C Sqdn. Suffolk Yeomanry; drill station for G Coy. 4 Bn. Suffolk Regt; & drill station for 1 East Anglian Divisional Field Ambulance, RAMC;

Woodford [Greater London]; PV

*1 Chingford Mount Road, ex-TAC; demolished 1990s after continued use by FE College; but pair of staff houses remain;

¶ In 1950, HQ+P & Q Btys. 599 [Essex] HAA Regt. RA, TA;

*2 Prospect Road, Woodford Green, **Drill Hall**, single-storey L-shaped block containing hall, with garages behind; c1930s; now a church;

¶ In 1950, HQ+315 Sqdn. 134 [Essex] Construction Regt. RE, TA;

***Woodlesford* [West Yorkshire];** V ACF

*1 Oulton Lane, drill hall demolished for housing c2000; ACF hut on site;

Woodstock [Oxfordshire]; PV [p262]

*1 New Rd, **Drill Hall**, pre-WWl; two-storey front block, hall behind, parallel to road; drill-instructor's house in line; hall in use as Community Centre, house occupied [2002] by son of WWll RSM of O&B LI;

WOODSTOCK, drill hall of the Oxfordshire &
Buckinghamshire Light Infantry

WOOLER's drill hall may have been an alternative to Belford which,
though the HQ of a company of the Northumberland Fusiliers,
appears to have no drill hall

¶ In 1914, base for B Sqdn. QOOH; drill station for F Coy. 4 Bn. Ox & Bucks LI;

Wooler [Northumberland]; PV *[p262]*
  *1 A697 southern by-pass route, **Drill Hall**, pre-WWl; a cinema in the 1950s, carpet warehouse; two-storey, 7-bay front block, projecting, gabled porch with moulding over doorway; hall behind, with two-storey block to side for offices/ accommodation; outbuildings to rear;
  ¶ In 1914, drill station for C Coy. 7 Bn. Northumberland Fusiliers;

Woolwich [Greater London]; PV TAC [***5**]
  *1 10 Beresford Street, Woolwich; no trace;
  ¶ In 1903, HQ 3Vol. Bn. The Queen's Own [Royal West Kent Regt.]
  *2 Bloomfield Road, Plumstead; no trace;
  ¶ In 1903, 2 Kent RGA
  *3 Brookhill Road, Woolwich, no trace
  ¶ In 1903, School of Ambulance
  ¶ In 1914, HQ+A-C Sections, 4 London Divisional Field Ambulances RAMC
  *4 Charles Street, Plumstead, no such address now,
  ¶ In 1914, HQ+1-3 London Bde. Coys. Divisional Transport & Supply Columns ASC
  *5 Green Hill, Congreve Lines **Drill Hall**; 19C sheds, gun-stores etc; in use as **TAC**;
  ¶ In 1914, HQ, 4 & 5 Btys, & Ammunition Column, 2 London Bde. RFA
  *6 Crescent Road, Plumstead;
  ¶ In 1903, social club for 2 Kent RGA; in use 1910 & 1933;
  *7 St Margarets Rd [Grove?], Woolwich, Oaklands; no such address; in use 1933;
  ¶ In 1914, HQ+21 & 22 Btys. & Ammunition Column, 8 London [H] Bde. RFA;
  *8 52 Wellington St; in use 1910; ***9** 159 Greenwich [High] Road; in use 1910;

Worcester [Worcestershire]; VA TAC
  *1 Crookbarrow Lane, **Norton Barracks**,1877; Cardwell depot of Worcestershire Regt; now housing estate but Keep + ranges to both sides, converted to flats, and a pair of late 19C houses on the Brockhill Lane side of the sports field, still stand;

*2 Lansdown Road, drill hall, cWWll; complex of temporary buildings to provide depot for 267 Field Regt.; re-activated 1948; demolished for housing;

*3 16 Silver Street, Barracks, late 19C, certainly pre-WWl; replaced by new **TAC** c1980 at Dancox House; old photo shows typical late Victorian drill hall frontage with bay windows, balcony with flagstaff over doorway, red-brick with stone dressings etc;

*4 24 Southfields Street, drill hall, late 19C; only a wall with tethering rings remains of the Yeomanry barracks, & later TAC;

*5 Sabrina Avenue, Barbourne, riding school opened November 1910; demolished 1980s;

*6 Pound Walk, timber, gabled Yeomanry stables in use at Perdiswell Racecourse;

*7 Gheluvelt Park, Barbourne, contains a former circular riding track used by the Yeomanry;

¶ In 1914, HQ+D Sqdn. Worcestershire Yeo; HQ+1 Worcestershire Bty. 2 S Midland Bde. RFA [24 Southfields Street]; HQ+A&B Coys. 8 Bn. Worcs. Regt. [Silver Street];

Wordsley [Dudley]; PV

*1 Wordsley Green, **Drill Hall**, 1884; built by subscription when D Coy. 1 Vol. Bn. S Staffordshire Regt. moved from Kingswinford; in 1907 presented to community by Wm Richardson in memory of his late wife; unit moved to Bloxwich, perhaps by 1908; large red-brick hall with gable-end to street flanked by turrets; at rear end, 2-storey orderly-room block; one stone commemorates the foundation, & another the presentation to the village; now called "Richardson Hall" as community centre;

¶ In 1884, base for D Coy. 1 Volunteer Bn. South Staffordshire Regt;

Workington [Cumbria]; PVA TAC [***3**]

*1 Portland Street, Covered Market used by volunteers 1803 to end of 19C;

*2 Edkin Street, drill hall, pre-1900, castellated, in use 1941 as HQ 8 Bn.Border Regt; demolished for re-development;

*3 Annie Pit Lane, **TAC**, 1965; two-storey Z-plan main block in yard with garages etc;

¶ In 1914, drill station for C Sqdn. Westmorland & Cumberland Yeomanry; HQ+2 Cumberland Howitzer Bty.+ Ammunition Column, 4 E Lancs [Howitzer] Bde. The Cumberland Artillery, RFA; HQ+B & C Coys. 5 Bn.Border

Regt.

Worksop [Nottinghamshire]; PV TAC [***6**]

*1 Bridge Place, Cattle Market Hotel, used by Yeomanry; demolished;

*2 Bridge Street, Officers' Mess of Rifle Volunteers, drills held in disused malt-kiln; not traced;

*3 Potter Street, in use 1892; not traced;

*4 Newgate Street, in use 1912; not traced;

*5 Shaw Street, **Drill Hall**, early 20C; in use 1912; now community use;

*6 Park Street, Scofton House, **TAC**, by 1949, rebuilt & re-opened 29 June 1974 by Princess Anne;

¶ In 1885, G Coy. [late 7 Corps] 2 Nottinghamshire Rifle Volunteer Corps;

¶ In 1892, HQ 4 Notts Vol Bn. Sherwood Foresters [Potter Street];

¶ In 1912, base for G Coy. 8 Bn. Sherwood Foresters [Shaw Street];

¶ In 1914, base C Sqdn. Sherwood Rangers, & G Coy. 8 Bn. Sherwood Foresters;

¶ In 1949, base for one Bty. 528 [Notts] LAA [Mobile] Regt. RA, TA [Park Street]; base for one Coy. 8 [Motor] Bn. Sherwood Foresters [Shaw Street]; base for one Coy. 307 [Northern Command] Bn. WRAC, TA [Park Street];

Worthing [Sussex]; PV ACF [***3**]

*1 12 Bath Place, 1886-1931, **Drill Hall**; [H Coy. 2 Reserve Bn. R Sussex Regt.]; subsequently a billiard hall; still stands & accommodates Woolworths;

*2 Ivy Arch Road, **Drill Hall**, 1921-49; [228 Bty.RFA; & ACF]; used by Parcel Force for some time, now light industrial; two-storey front block, 5-bay, with pediment over door; hall behind largely consisting of gun-store;

*3 Little High Street, **Drill Hall**, pre-WWl; two-storey, 5-bay front block with decorative brickwork; hall behind; former garage/ gunstore to side, Cadet Centre;

*4 Upper Brighton Road/Forest Road, post-WWll; purpose-built **TAC**; now Masonic Hall & function suite;

¶ In 1914, drill station for A Sqdn. Sussex Yeomanry; base for Ammunition Column 1 Home Counties Bde. RFA; base for H Coy. 4 Bn. Royal Sussex Regt.

Wotton-under-Edge **[Glos];** V

*1 Ludgate Hill, Church Mill used as drill hall; site cleared & occupied by Library;

¶ In 1947, detachment 5 Bn. Gloucestershire Regt;

Wycombe Abbey [Buckinghamshire]; VA
used by Buckinghamshire Yeomanry as base during 1850s; the Orangery, Cloisters & stable-yard were used for orderly room, officers' mess etc;

Wymondham [Norfolk]; PV [p73]
*1 Pople St, **Drill Hall**, 1930s, rebuilt 1980s; arched doorway in single-storey gabled entrance block; hall behind & tall garage/gun-store to side.

¶ In 1914, drill station for C Sqdn. Norfolk Yeo; & base for F Coy. 4 Bn. Norfolk Regt.

Y

Yateley **[Hampshire];** V
*1 Reading Road, drill hall, built between 1896-1910; reference to Drill Room in 1888, possibly in big house; yellow, corrugated-iron building; built by John Packman Stilwell for F Coy. 4 Bn. Hampshire Regt; accounts show still run by Hampshire Regt. on income from hirings until 1939, when leased to RBL for 1/- pa; ex-Servicemen's club set up 1946; burnt down 1957, shopping parade built on site early-1960s; also 900 yard rifle-range on Common;

¶ In 1914, base for F Coy. 4 Bn. Hampshire Regt;

Yatton [Somerset]; ACF [High Street]

Yaxley **[Cambridgeshire];** V
*1 Chapel St, drill hall in hut with indoor rifle-range; burned down around 1963; Girls' School was venue for mobilisation of Hunts Cyclist Bn. in 1914;

¶ In 1914, drill station for G Coy. 5 Bn. Bedfordshire Regt; & base for H Coy. Hunts Cyclist Bn. drawn from Yaxley & Farcet.

¶ In 1931, base for D Coy. 5 [Hunts] Bn. Northamptonshire Regt.

Yeovil [Somerset]; PV TAC[*1]
*1 Southville Road, **Drill Hall**, pre-WWl; 2-storey front block with gate-tower; hall behind, & then 2-storey cross-wing; garages & indoor range;
*2 1 The Park, *The Armoury*, pre-1900; formerly **Volunteer Armoury**, now public house; L-shaped block with much Victorian decorative detail; 16 Corps, Somerset Rifle Volunteers formed at Yeovil in 1860;

*3 Houndstone Farm, 1963; tithe barn converted as officers' mess of Q Own Dorset & W Somerset Yeomanry;

¶ In 1914, base for D Sqdn. West Somerset Yeomanry; drill station for B Sqdn. Dorset Yeomanry; base for E Coy. 5 Bn. Somerset LI;

York [North Yorkshire]; PV TACs [*4-*7 & *9]
*1 9 St Leonards Place, 1844-5; three-storeys, stucco, balconies etc; no. 9 is the end of the crescent with a portico; **TF Divisional HQ**, 1914;
*2 Colliergate, **Drill Hall**, 1872; large hall with highly-decorated brick- and tile-work around doorway and windows; built for 1 Corps, York Rifle Volunteers formed in 1859, they became the 1 Volunteer Bn. of West Yorkshire Regt. in 1887, with A-E Coys. in York; currently used for retail;
*3 Fulford Road, **Imphal Barracks**, 1877-80; Cardwell depot of the Prince of Wales Own West Yorkshire Regt; Keep, guardhouse, messes, barrack-blocks etc. all remain;
*4 20 St Georges Place, 1892; large detached 'Sweetness & Light' house; stone doorway with crest, & coat-of arms [1911] from a former drill hall; now **HQ RFCA**;
*5 Burtonstone Lane, **Lumley Barracks**, 1911; designed by Walter Brierley; long, lateral hall, with projecting wings at each end, and central, arched doorway; large yard with garages etc. to rear;
*6 Fulford Road, **Yeomanry Barracks**, 20C; in use by QO Yeomanry;
*7 Fulford Road, **Worsley Barracks**, 20C; in use by West Riding Regt;
*8 Hungate, ex-**Drill Hall**, 1930s; two-storey block at right-angles to street, with row of garages parallel; now storage; *9 Burton Stone Lane, **Duncombe Barracks**, 1970s; in use by West Yorkshire Regt. & MI Coy;
*10 St Leonards Place, **de Grey Rooms**, 1841-2; built by GT Andrews as Officers' Mess of Yorkshire Hussars, on annual visit to York;

¶ In 1914, HQ+B Sqdn. Yorkshire Hussars; HQ+Bty. + Ammunition Column, West Riding RGA - Heavy; HQ+A-C Coys. 5 Bn. West Yorkshire Regt; Yorkshire Mounted Bde. Transport & Supply Column ASC [Lumley Barracks]; HQ Coy. West Riding Divnl. Transport & Supply Column ASC [Lumley Bks]; HQ West Riding Div; HQ 1West Riding Infantry Bde.& HQ Yorkshire Mounted Bde. [9 St Leonards];

GAZETTEER OF DRILL HALLS & TA CENTRES:
SCOTLAND

Notes

Entries show surviving buildings in **BOLD** and destroyed or non-existent buildings in ***BOLD ITALIC.*** The region is given in brackets, shown as follows:

[A&B]   ARGYLL & BUTE including Dunbartonshire
[B]   BORDERS Berwick, Peebles, Roxburgh & Selkirk
[C]   CENTRAL including Stirling & Falkirk
[D&G]   DUMFRIES & GALLOWAY including Ayrshire
[E&L]   EDINBURGH & LOTHIAN
[F]   FIFE including Clackmannan
[G&L]   GLASGOW including Lanarkshire, Renfrewshire, Paisley
[G]   GRAMPIAN including Angus & Moray
[H&I]   HIGHLANDS & ISLANDS
[P]   PERTHSHIRE including Dundee

Where the site has been visited by the author, a V is shown;
Where a site has been photographed by the author, a P is shown;
Where the author has an archive photo' of a [demolished] building, an A is shown;
Where a site still functions as a TA Centre, TAC is shown;
Where a site is used by cadets, ACF and/or ATC are shown;
Regiments are sometimes shown as follows:
A&SH = Argyll & Sutherland Highlanders
CH = Cameron Highlanders
BW = Black Watch
GH = Gordon Highlanders
HLI = Highland Light Infantry
KOSB = Kings Own Scottish Borderers
RS = Royal Scots
RSF = Royal Scots Fusiliers
SH = Seaforth Highlanders

Aberdeen [G]; P [*1-*3, *8]; V[*1-*9]; TAC/ACF [*1-*3 & *5];
*1 Bridge of Don, Gordon Barracks, built c1850s for regular troops; now **TAC** on a reduced site, part of which is occupied by FE; imposing granite Scots Baronial HQ block with crow-steps, bartizans etc; barrack blocks and guardhouse around drill-square;
*2 125 Don Street, **TAC**, c1980s, in use by OTC; 2-storey, brick & glass buildings;
*3 Viewfield Road, St Luke, **RHQ** Gordon Highlanders; early-20C arts-&-crafts house, formerly a private residence, latterly RHQ & museum;
*4 North Silver Street, 1899, drill hall, used by Artillery Volunteers; occupied a trapezoidal site in the angle of Ruby Place & Ruby Lane; demolished for office-block: Ruby Ho;
*5 Fonthill Road, barracks in use 1914, demolished for housing; cadet centre in small enclave on site, c1980s pavilion;
*6 80 Hardgate, drill hall, opened 1898, demolished for housing;
*7 Woolmanhill, drill hall, in use 1914, demolished for offices;
*8 28 Guild Street, HQ 4 Bn. Gordon Highlanders in 1908, grand 5-storey Customs House with classical detail, in official & commercial use;
*9 Albert Hall, 14 Union Wynd, HQ Aberdeen Coys. RAMC, in 1908; entire street re-developed for offices, no trace;
*10 Great Southern Rd [angle of Bloomfield Rd] hutted camp bought 1939, disposed of 1967 for vehicle testing station & housing;
¶In 1914, HQ+G Sqdn. 2 Scottish Horse; HQ+1-3 Btys. & Ammunition Column 1 Highland Bde. RFA [*4]; No.1 Coy.

North Scottish RGA-Defended Ports [*5]; HQ+2 Field Coy. Divnl. REs. [*6]; HQ+1-4 Sections RE Divnl. Signals Coys. [*6]; HQ+No.1 Works Coy. City of Aberdeen REs-Fortress [*6]; HQ+A-H Coys. 4 Bn. Gordon Highlanders [*7 in 1920]; base for 3 Coy. Highland Divisional Transport & Supply Column ASC [*5]; HQ+A-C Sections 1 & 2 Highland Divnl. Field Ambulances RAMC [*5];1 Scottish General, & Highland Clearing Hospitals RAMC;

Aberfeldy [G]; V
*1 Wades Place, drill hall, demolished for housing;
¶ In 1914, drill station B Sqdn. 1 Scottish Horse; base H Coy. 6 Bn. Black Watch;

Aberlour [Charlestown of] [G]; PV
*1 Victoria Terrace, **Drill Hall**, apparently built as school, between church & station; T-shaped building with bell-cote; to be renovated as art gallery;
¶ In 1914, drill station for B Coy. 6 Bn. Gordon Highlanders;

Aboyne[G]; PV
*1 Golf Road, **Drill Hall**, possibly WWl era; single storey, double hut-type building, but remembered on site over several generations;
¶ In 1914, drill station for G Sqdn. 2 Scottish Horse; base forF Coy. 7 Bn. GH;

Achiltibuie [H&I];
*1 **Drill Hall**; timber hut & indoor range; now Pipe School;
¶ In 1914, drill station for E Sqdn. Lovat Scouts;

Alexandria [A&B]; PV
*1 158-60 Middleton Street & 1-5 Overton Street, **Drill Hall**, by 1889 ;2-storey front block, now two dwellings; behind, & formerly joined, single storey hall, now house; described in 1912 as "commodious hall & drill instructor's house" harled & washed;
¶ In 1914, base for F Coy. 9 Bn. A & S Highlanders;

Alford [G]; V
*1 Kingsford Road, drill hall in 1908; demolished for housing;
¶ In 1914, drill station for F Sqdn. 2 Scottish Horse; base for F Coy. 6 Bn. GH;

Airdrie [Lanark];
*1 Craig Street, drill hall, given up 1910; site re-developed as housing;
¶ In 1914, drill station for Lowland Divisional REs;

Alloa [F]; PV
*1 Bank Street, drill-room & armoury of Volunteers, 1860;
*2 Union Street, drill hall in 1864 & 1866; at this time, the Corn Exchange in Union Street was used; the house next door accommodated the drill instructor; the Armoury was also housed in the Old Court House;
*3 The Whins, Armoury in 1871;
*4 Marshill, Ochil House, built as Tontine Inn, 1806; later converted to prison; acquired for **Drill Hall**, 1882; a large hall, offices, armoury etc. added; 2-storey, 3-bay villa; arch on one side has inscription: "1st C & KRV Drill Hall 1882"- Clackmannan & Kinross Rifle Volunteers; two companies raised in Alloa in 1859, & by 1883, had become the 1st Corps of 8 companies; drill hall demolished for housing, but Ochil House + archway remain;
¶ In 1914, drill stn. B Sqdn. Fife & Forfar Yeomanry; base E & H Coys.7 Bn. A&SH;

Alness [H&I]; PV
*1 Birkdale, 38 Perrins Road, **Drill Hall** from pre-WWl to 1938, then Scout Hut, now private residence; hut with timber cladding & render, with pitched slate roof; projecting annexe on one side;
*2 Invergordon Road, **Perrins Hall**, 1903; built as recreational/educational centre for Perrins Sauce workforce; bought by TA in 1938; now reverted to community centre; stone-built, free-Scots Renaissance with mass of detail; conical roof on reading-room, crow-stepped gables, finials etc;
¶ In 1914 base for G Sqdn. 2 Lovat's Scouts; base for G Coy. 4 Bn. SH;

Alva [F]; PV ACF [p269]
*1 77 Park Street, **Drill Hall**, by 1899; two-storey, 3-bay front block with Dutch Gable over door, & semi-dormers; harled & white-washed with brick dressings; hall behind & indoor range etc;
¶ In 1914, base for F Coy. 7 Bn. A & S Highlanders;

Alyth [P]; PV
*1 St Ninians Road, [The Old] **Armoury**, by 1910; double-banked Victorian house with later extension doubling its size; now a private dwelling; still in use 1933;
¶ In 1914, drill station for C Sqdn. 1 Scottish Horse; drill station for E Coy. 6 Bn. BW;

corners; large hall behind & further single-storey extensions to side; now residential;

¶ In 1914, base for H Coy. 5 Bn. Seaforth Highlanders;

Cathcart [G&L]; PV

*1 Earls Park Avenue, drill hall; hall & garages appear incorporated in 1970s industrial building: "Systems House";

*2 Woodgreen Avenue, Carmunnock Road **TAC**,1959; square, single-storey 'pavilion' type building, in yard with garages & huts;

¶ In 1914, base for Ammunition Columns, 3 Highland [Howitzer] Bde. RFA;

¶ In 1959, base for 445 LAA Regimental Workshops, REME [TA];

Catrine [D&G]; V

*1 Bridge Lane, drill hall, pre-1910; out-of-use by 1933 and demolished;

¶ In 1914, base for B Coy. 5 Bn. Royal Scots Fusiliers;

Chirnside [B]; PV

*1 High Street, **Drill Hall**, 1871; stone-built, gabled hall to street frontage; house & other buildings behind; inscription to 7th Berwickshire Rifle Volunteers, formed here 1863; currently a social club;

¶ In 1914, drill station for E Coy. 4 Bn. KOSB;

Clackmannan [F]; V

*1 Pennyschool Place, drill hall; demolished for old people's housing c1970s;

¶ In 1883, H Coy. 1 Clackmannan & Kinross Rifle Volunteers formed here;

¶ In 1914, drill station for H Coy. 7 Bn. A & S Highlanders;

Clydebank [A&B]; V

*1 Douglas Street, Public Hall, built 1884; multi-use building served as drill hall; demolished for school, 1970s;

¶ In 1914, base for G & H Coys. 9 Bn. A & S Highlanders;

Coatbridge [Lanark]; PV [*2]

*1 Water St, drill hall, given up 1910, no trace;

*2 Quarry Street, Drill Hall, by 1910; large hall encased by single-storey offices etc. around three sides; entrance in half-hexagonal tower; yard with garages; derelict, demolished c2004;

¶ In 1914, base C Sqdn. Lanarkshire Yeomanry & 1 Field Coy. Lowland Divnl. REs;

Coldstream [B]; PV

*1 High street, behind & attached to Church, ex - **TAC**, marked on OS map c1950; now British Legion hall; offices and large square hall;

¶ In 1914, drill station for A Sqdn. Lothian & Border Horse; base E Coy. 4 Bn. KOSB

Connell [A&B]; V

*1 Main Street, drill hall in former blanket mill, with hall above & tack-room below; replaced by present village hall on site in 1994;

¶ In 1914, base for H Sqdn. 2 Scottish Horse;

Coupar Angus [P]; PV

*1 Athole Street, **Drill Hall**, pre-WWl; long, narrow block with house at one end, & 3-bay hall at other, with end door; now Red Cross;

¶ In 1914, base for C Sqdn. 1 Scottish Horse; drill station for E Coy. 6 Bn. BW;

Cowdenbeath [C]; V

*1 Stenhouse Street, chapel converted to drill hall; 1930s demolished for housing;

¶ In 1914, base for D Coy. 7 Bn. Black Watch;

Cowie [C]; PV

*1 Station Road, **Drill Hall**, pre-WWl; hall attached to large [Drill Hall] House; another, later hall beyond;

¶ In 1914, base for B Coy. Highland Cyclist Bn;

Crieff [P]; PV ACF [*p251*]

*1 Meadow Lane, **Drill Hall**, pre-WWl; oddly asymmetric building with dormers, clerestory, timber & sandstone details, & butressed side-walls; to rear, two possibly later buildings incorporating an indoor range;

¶ In 1914, drill station for D Sqdn. 1 Scottish Horse; base for D Coy. 6 Bn. BW;

Cromarty [H&I]; PV

*1 High Street, **Drill Hall**, 1887; single-storey hall by Maitland; a wheel window with clock in the gable & datestone; now Victoria Hall; built for Artillery Volunteers;

¶ In 1914, base for No.2 Coy. North Scottish RGA-Defended Ports;

Cumbernauld [G&L]; PV TAC

*1 Glencryan Rd, **TAC**, c1980s 2-storey, red-brick blocks, one L-shaped+garages;

¶ In 1914, drill station for B Coy. 9 Bn. A & S Highlanders;

Cumnock [D&G]; PV

*1 Townhead, **Drill Hall**, pre-WWl; now changing-rooms for local football team; front block, 3 bays in the front, 7 in the back; sold by 1933, & hall demolished;

¶ In 1914, base for B Sqdn. Ayrshire Yeomanry; base for E Coy. 5 Bn. RSF;

Cupar [F]; PV   TAC

*1 Castlebank Road, **Militia Barracks**, built 1842 as a prison; bleak central block in Tudor style received balconies on the S side, on conversion in c1890; **TAC** in use by Scottish Yeomanry;

¶ In 1914, base for A Sqdn. Fife & Forfar Yeomanry; base for E Coy. 7 Bn. BW;

Dalbeattie[D&G]; PV

*1 Burn Street, **Drill Hall**, pre-WWl; 3-bay, gabled, 2-storey front block with Gothick windows, & chimneys set diagonally at four corners; small hall behind; now "Hallburn", converted to flats;

¶ In 1914, base for F Coy. 5 Bn. KOSB;

Dalkeith **[E&L];** V

*1 Eskbank Road, drill hall, demolished for Post Office building;

¶ In 1914, drill station B Sqdn. Lothians & Border Horse; base E Coy. 8 Bn. RS;

Dalmellington **[D&G];** V   ACF

*1 Broom Knowe, drill hall, demolished; ACF hut on site;

¶ In 1914, base for H Coy. Royal Scots Fusiliers;

Dalry [D&G]; PV   ACF[off-site]

*1 20 James Street, **Drill Hall**, pre-WWl; 2-storey, 3-bay front block in brick with sandstone doorcase; hall & indoor range behind; now MRC Fitness Studio;

¶ In 1914, base for F Coy. 4 Bn. Royal Scots Fusiliers;

Darvel **[D&G];** the men from Darvel used the drill hall in *Newmilns* ;

¶ In 1914, base for G Coy. Royal Scots Fusiliers;

Denny [C]; PV   ACF

*1 Herbertshire St, **Drill Hall**, c1930s, & extended 1959; 2-storey front block with hall behind; yard & garages; extensions at both ends of front block, Masonic Lodge; garages in commercial use; *2 Duke St, Cadet Centre, c1970s, long, low building;

Dingwall [H&I]; PV

*1 off High Street, drill hall, pre-WWl; hut & range destroyed by fire c1980s;

*2 Ferry Road, **TAC**, known locally as Seaforths' Barracks; probably built between 1900 & WWl; hall with verandah, 2-storey orderly-room block, & [later?] 2-storey block form an open quadrangle; within the larger yard, huts, garages etc; two cadet huts opposite, across road, & rifle-range with original fittings in butts, next door;

*3 High Street, Militia Barracks on 1903 map; demolished for Council offices 1965;

¶ In 1914, base for C sub-Section, Ammunition Column, 4 Highland [Mtn] Bde. RGA-Mountain; HQ+ B Coy. 4 Bn. Seaforth Highlanders;

Dornoch [H&I]; PV   ACF [*p42*]

*1 The Square, **Drill Hall**, 1882; the Jail, built 1842-5, was closed & sold to the Sutherland Highland Rifle Volunteers for £220; they inserted the grand staircase, & added the free-standing hall in the yard behind, with access via a new entrance to the right of the jail, with inscription over the doorway, in 1896-7; also indoor range, cadet hut & garage to rear; much of the building is now shops & gallery;

¶ In 1880, base for B Coy. 1 Sutherland [Sutherland Highland] Rifle Volunteer Corps, becoming, in 1881 a Vol. Bn. of the Seaforth Highlanders;

¶ In 1914, base for F Coy. 2 Lovat's Scouts; base for B Coy. 5 Bn. SH;

Douglas **[G&L];** V

*1 site of drill hall 100 yards inside Douglas & Angus Estate gates past Polish memorial; demolished; only concrete base remains visible; *2 1958 Review notes armoury, PSI's house & stores in Addison Drive; houses stand on one side of street;

¶ In 1914, base for A Sqdn. Lanarks Yeomanry; drill station B Coy. 8 Bn. HLI;

Dufftown [G]; PV

*1 Church Street, **Drill Hall** in use 1908; single-storey, L-shaped stone, school-like building, with indoor range projecting behind; in use by community education;

¶ In 1914, drill station for E Sqdn. 2 Scottish Horse; base for B Coy. 6 Bn. GH;

Dumbarton [A&B]; PV   TAC

*1 Bonhill Road, Hartfield House **TAC**, A&SH Bn.HQ; built

1853, 2-storey, stone mansion with porch & classical detail;

*2 Latta Street, **Drill Hall**, 1912; original hall at one end of drill square, with later, single-storey offices built along front face; formerly stabling behind hall; large double garages along one side of square; huts along another;

¶ In 1914, base No. 3 Coy. Clyde RGA-Defended Ports; HQ+C Coy. 9 Bn. A&SH;

Dumfries [D&G]; PV TAC[***3**] [*p39*]

*1 Newall Terrace, **Drill Hall**, 1890, by Crombie; red sandstone front block, with oriel topped by octagonal spire & crown over entrance; crow-stepped gables with pyramid-roofed square bartizans on outer corners; behind, long, low, dry-dashed hall; hall roof has cast-iron rib construction;

*2 English Street, **County Police Barracks**, 1876, by Barbour; Scots baronial style, in red sandstone; it would seem to incorporate barracks of Scottish Borderers Militia, built 1854; the accommodation provided in 1877, for the Militia included magazine, drill-shed, guardroom, 4-stall stable, pay office, tailor's shop, living-quarters for 11 staff-sergeants, & stores for 800 men;

*3 Edinburgh Road, **TAC**, in use; 19C red sandstone villa with French & Renaissance details; also pair of later staff houses;

¶ In 1914, base for D Sqdn. Lanarkshire Yeomanry; HQ+A Coy. 5 Bn. KOSB;

Dunbar [E&L]; PV

*1 Lauderdale House, 1790-2, by the Adams; converted to military use 1859; in early 20C, a regular cavalry depot & base for Yeomanry; in WWll, an officer training school; adjacent two-storey barrack-block of 1911, built for TF & demolished for Leisure Centre 1980s; elaborate, single-storey building, possibly, magazine, or HQ for barracks, once used by ACF, still stands; main house now run by a housing association;

*2 High St, **Drill Hall**, pre-1900; built for Haddingtonshire Artillery Volunteers; hall with outbuildings & indoor range; now Royal British Legion;

¶ In 1914, base A Sqdn. Lothians & Border Horse; drill station D Coy. 8 Bn. RS ;

Dunblane [P]; PV

*1 124-6 High Street, former Free Church opposite St Blanes; built 1843, served as school, library, **Drill Hall** etc;

3-bays, windows through two storeys, segmental arch over entrance, rubble masonry;

¶ In 1914, base for D Sqdn.1 Scottish Horse; base for C Coy. 6 Bn. Black Watch;

Dundee [P]; P[1,3-6]; V[1-10]; TACs[3-6];

*1 Brown Street/Douglas Street, **Dudhope Drill Hall**, 1909; long, gabled, admin block with cross-wing fronting Brown Street; hall behind with door onto Douglas St; three doors to Brown Street, one labelled "Officers"; plaque on admin block gable reads "City of Dundee Territorial Force 1909"; ER monogram on arch into hall [now blocked]; in use as night-club;

*2 52 Taylor's Lane; not found;

*3 Dalkeith Road, Oliver Barracks, **TAC**, RAMC + Black Watch, 1980s-type factory units & 2-storey admin block;

*4 Strathmore Ave, **TAC**; house, single-storey, later 2-storey blocks with hall behind; earlier buildings could be 1930s;

*5 Park Wynd, **Drill Hall,** in use by OTC; 1970s-style 2- & 3-storey stone & glass block incorporating garages;

*6 Mid Craigie Road, **TAC** in use by signals unit; 1970s-style, large yard with long block of garage/workshop-type buildings;

*7 Bell Street, Albany Quarters, in use by Volunteer Artillery, 1908; street re-developed as University of Tayside;

*8 107 Victoria Road, HQ Black Watch Bde. bearer coys. in 1908; site developed for housing;

*9 Queens College, OTC HQ & Mess opened c1956;

*10 Barrack Road, Barracks, apparently demolished;

¶ In 1914, base for C Sqdn. Fife & Forfar Yeomanry; HQ+City of Dundee Bty.+ Ammunition Column 2 Highland Bde. RFA [Dudhope]; HQ+No.1Works Coy. REs-Fortress [Taylors Lane]; HQ+A-H Coys. 4 Bn. Black Watch; G-H Coys. 5 Bn. Black Watch; 4 Coy. Highland Divnl. Transport & Supply Column ASC; HQ+A-C Sections 3 Highland Divnl. Field Ambulances RAMC [Dudhope];

Dunfermline [F]; PV TACs [1-2];

*1 Bruce House, 53 Elgin Street, **Drill Hall**, 1911-12; Wrenaissance building by Gillespie & Scott; front block with an added, upper floor & adjoining staff house with segmental, pedimented gable; hall behind; in use by RLC unit;

*2 Bothwell House, Elgin Street, **Drill Hall**, pre-WWl; two-

273

storey, 5-bay front block with small pediment over centre bay; hall behind, & yard with garages;

¶ In 1914, base B Sqdn. Fife & Forfar Yeomanry; HQ+Bty. & Ammunition Column, Highland RGA-Heavy; base A Coy. 7 Bn. BW; base E Coy. Highland Cyclist Bn;

Dunkeld [P]; PV TAC

*1 Cathedral St/High St, **Drill Hall**, 1900 & earlier; 2-storey 3-bay early-Victorian house with small hall behind may represent earliest build; mouldings on doors & windows; badge removed from over door; adjacent large E-shaped, 2-storey, 7-bay symmetrical block with sandstone dressings, & coloured badge of Scottish Horse, dated 1900, over door; another hall contained within its wings; large court to rear with garages, gunsheds, indoor range etc;

¶ In 1914, HQ+B Sqdn. 1 Scottish Horse;

¶ In 1940, base for 79 & 80 Medium Regiments formed from Scottish Horse;

Dunoon [A&B]; PV TAC

*1 Corner of Argyll St & Queen St, drill hall in use 1914; replaced c1960, by USN Commissary; in turn replaced by Co-op supermarket;

*2 Hafton Estate, Ardnadam, [Sandbank Business Park],**TAC**, c1980s, Highland Regt; square with pyramid roof;

¶ In 1914, HQ+D Coy. 8 Bn. A & S Highlanders;

Duns [B]; PV [p92]

*1 Tiendhill Green, Militia Stores, 1857; demolished, new house built 1895;

*2 South St, **Drill Hall** [Volunteer Hall], 1895; 2-storey front block, with decorated gable & finials; crest of 2 Volunteer Bn. KOSB over door; large hall behind, + indoor range & outbuildings;

¶ In 1914, drill station A Sqdn. Lothian & Border Horse; base D Coy. 4 Bn. KOSB;

Earlston [B]; V

*1 near Westfield Road, TA Centre marked on OS map c1950; demolished;

¶ In 1914, drill stations A Sqdn. Lothians & Border Horse, and D Coy. 4 Bn. KOSB;

Easdale [A&B]; PV

*1 on the island near the Harbour, former **Drill Hall**, c1870; square, slate rubble structure with high pyramid roof, whose

central mast was recovered from a ship-wreck; completely refurbished 2004;

*2 on the edge of Ellanabeich village on the mainland, **Easdale Hall**, datestone 1870, built as drill hall; simple rectangular, gabled hall, with low extension, probably added later, at one end;

¶ In 1914,drill station for H Sqdn. 2 Scottish Horse; base for H Coy. 8 Bn. A&SH;

East Kilbride [Lanark]; PV TAC

*1 Whitemoss East, **TAC**, c1980s; HQ Scottish Yeomanry; large one- & two-storey block, extensive yard with garages etc;

East Linton [E&L]; PV

*1 Main Street, **Drill Hall**, pre-WWl; refurbished as Community Centre; gabled facade of hall to street with arched doorway;

¶ In 1914, drill station for A Sqdn. Lothians & Border Horse, & for D Coy. 8 Bn RS;

East Wemyss [F]; PV [p275]

*1 9-11 The Haugh, **Drill Hall**, pre-WWl; 2-storey, 3-bay front block, with single-storey wing on one side, & 2-storey house on other; the gable of the front block is the same height as the ridge of the hall; hall ends in blind, buttressed wall; now "Auld Drill Hall" residence;

¶ In 1914, drill station Fifeshire Bty. 2 Highland Bde. RFA; base G Coy. Highland Cyclist Bn;

Edinburgh [E&L]; P[1-3, 5-8, 11-17]; V[1-17]; TACs [3 8 12 14 15 & 17]

*1 18 Dundonald Street,19C; narrow, 4-storey terrace house;

¶ In 1914, HQ+B & D Sqdns. Lothians & Border Horse;

*2 30 Grindlay Street, **Drill Hall**, 1888; through archway into Grindlay Court; hall with roof-lights, fronted by post-WWll offices; in commercial & residential use;

¶ In 1914, HQ+1 & 2 Btys. & Ammunition Column, 1 Lowland Bde. RFA;

*3 124 McDonald Street, **Drill Hall**, 1912, by Rhind; built for RA, in Renaissance style; 3-storey, 3-bay house with pediment & canopy over door; later hall behind; **TAC**, in use by Intelligence Corps;

¶ In 1914, HQ+Bty. & Ammunition Column, Lowland RGA-Heavy;

*4 Easter Road Barracks, in use 1914; apparently no trace remains;
¶ In 1914, HQ+Nos.1-4 Coys. Forth RGA-Defended Ports; HQ+A-C Sections, 3 Lowland Divisional Field Ambulances RAMC;
*5 28 York Place, **Drill Hall**, pre-WWl; 3-storey, 3-bay terrace house, behind, hall with curved roof, outbuildings & garages etc. access from alley;
¶ In 1914,HQ+No.1 Works Coy. & No.2 Electric Lights Coy.City of Edinburgh REs [F]
*6 Forrest Hill, **Drill Hall**, 1872, by Menzies; a single-span girder roof of 29m; cast-iron balcony at N end; to the right, later hall, 1902-4, by Cooper & Taylor; bare Scots Renaissance style; in front of the entrances, a wide semi-elliptical arch with rope hoodmould, & an aedicule on the parapet; a variety of inscriptions detailing the raising of The Royal Scots in 1859, & the re-building of its HQ here, in 1905;
¶ In 1914, HQ+A-H Coys. 4 & 5 Bns. Royal Scots;
*7 33 Gilmore Place, **Drill Hall**,1911; 2-storey, 11-bay front block with three stone doorways; hall behind demolished 2000; now converted into flats; some details of old building incorporated in new build: datestone, Royal Scots badge, gunloops;
¶ In 1914, HQ+A-H Coys. 6 Bn. Royal Scots;
*8 89 East Claremont Street, **Drill Hall**,1912, by Rhind; free Renaissance, with pedimented centrepiece, & semi-dormers on upper floor; large hall & outbuildings behind; **TAC** in use by 52 Lowland Regt; [*p275*]
¶ In 1914, HQ+A-H Coys. 9 Bn. Royal Scots;
*9 Brandon Terrace, in use 1914; no obvious building remains;
¶ In 1914, Lowland Mounted Bde. Transport & Supply Column, ASC; 2 Lowland Divisional Transport & Supply Column, ASC;
*10 2 Lindsay Place, in use 1914; street completely redeveloped;
¶ In 1914, 2 Scottish General Hospital, RAMC;
*11 **10 Dublin Street**, early-19C five-storey terrace house;
¶ In 1914, HQ Lowland Mounted Bde.
*12 Granton Square, **TAC**, built 1838 as Granton Inn; subsequently RNR HQ , HMS Claverhouse; 7 bays & porch

EAST WEMYSS, the "Auld Drill Hall" is now a family home

EDINBURGH's East Claremont Street drill hall, built in 1912 & still a TAC

275

FALKIRK's drill hall in Cow Wynd, is now a school of dancing

with Doric columns; on N face, balcony overlooking the sea; stables & coach-yard to E; now 205 Field Hospital RAMC [TA];

*13 Chesser Crescent, ex-**TAC**, c1935 + 1960s additions; large hall, a second L-shaped hall, garages etc; later 3-storey offices; now [2002] empty;

*14 Colinton Road, Duke of Edinburgh House, Edinburgh Universities' OTC; modern **TAC**, next to grey stone mansion, with small hall to side, now School of Military Piping & Drumming; possibly earlier home of OTC;

*15 Alnwickhill Road, **Drill Hall**, pre-1900; large, stone, 2-storey mansion serves as front block; behind, low hall, outbuildings, & 2-storey cottages; beside, is a modern **TAC** in use by REME unit; two-storey, flat roofed blocks, set in large yard;

*16 71 Gilmore Place, small, late-19C terrace house;

¶ In 1908, HQ 1 Lothian Bde. Bearer Coys;

*17 Lanark Road, **TAC**, c1970s; in use by parachute unit; large, low, brick block with flat roof; yard with garages etc;

*18 West Pilton Camp in use 1947;

¶ In 1947, base for 519 LAA Regiment RA [TA];

¶ In 1914, HQ Lothian Infantry Bde. unspecified location;

Elgin [G]; PV TAC [***2**] [*p71*]

*1 Cowper [now Cooper] Park, **Drill Hall** in use 1908; large hall with crow-stepped gables & transepts, one of which is extended & has bartizan at corner; behind, 2-storey block with dormers; tall tower in angle of hall & transept; support services for adjoining public library; badge of 3 Volunteer Bn. Seaforth Highlanders on gable;

*2 Edgar Road, **TAC**, in use 51 Highland Regt; c1990s-style with pyramid-roof;

¶ In 1914, base E Sqdn. 2 Scottish Horse; HQ+B-C Coys. 6 Bn. SH;

Ellon [G]; PV

*1 Station Road, **Victoria Hall**, 1901; built by public subscription which absorbed funds of Rifle Volunteers; 2 Volunteer Bn. Gordon Highlanders given exclusive use of one room, 24' by 16' as Armoury, & shared use of the building; large block with gables & turret; halls, outhouses, possible indoor range etc; now community centre;

¶ In 1914, drill station for F Sqdn. 2 Scottish Horse; base for E Coy. 5 Bn. GH;

Evie [Orkney] [H&I]; no location identified;

¶ In 1914, base for No.5 Coy. Orkney RGA-Defended Ports;

Falkirk [C]; PV

*1 Cow Wynd/St Crispins Place, **Drill Hall**, 1898-9 [*p276*]; by A & W Black for Volunteers; 2-storey, 6-bay, front block with pediment; in tympanum, crest of 4 Vol Bn. A & SH; asymmetrically-placed front door under cornice; large, utilitarian hall behind; now School of Dance/Gymnastics;

*2 Bog Rd, ex-**TAC**, c1960s; flat-roofed block, water-tank, & steel-clad sheds; next door earlier, c1940s, garage block;

¶ In 1914, base for C Coy. 7 Bn. A & S Highlanders;

Fauldhouse [E&L]; PVA

*1 Bridge Street, **Drill Hall**, probably 1908; 3-storey front-block with large hall behind; long, single-storey indoor range alongside; on other side, Baillie Miners' Institute & Welfare, date-stone 1908; whole complex now social club, except indoor range which is Chinese take-away & tanning studio;

¶ In 1914, base for F Coy. 10 [Cyclist] Bn. Royal Scots;

Fochabers [G]; PV

*1 Westmorland Street, drill hall; demolished, for housing, only indoor range survives on Market Green;

¶ In 1914, base for E Coy. 6 Bn. Seaforth Highlanders;

Forfar [P]; PV TAC [**2**]; ACF [**1**];

*1 Brechin Road/Lochside Road, **Drill Hall**, pre-WWl; large, 2-storey block with arched windows in lower storey; projection on rear for staircase; small hall, now garage to rear; cadet huts to side;

*2 146/8 Castle Street, **TAC**, 51 Highland Regt; typical Crown building with GR monogram & 1937 date over Wrenaissance doorway [possibly built as Labour Exchange or Post Office], now serves as single-storey front block for TAC with yard & sheds to rear;

¶ In 1914, base for D Sqdn. Fife & Forfar Yeomanry; base for B Coy. 5 Bn. Black Watch; base for D Coy. Highland Cyclist Bn;

Forres [G]; PV ACF [*p166*]

*1 High Street, **Drill Hall**, c1914; high, gabled 2-storey front block, hall behind; indoor range down one side; badge & inscription: '6 Battn. Seaforth Highlanders', makes it later than 1908, when designated 3rd Volunteer Bn;

¶ In 1914, drill station for E Sqdn. 2 Scottish Horse; base for A Coy. 6 Bn. SH;

Fort Augustus [H&I]; PV [*p251*]

*1 **War Memorial Hall**, 1913; designed by Ross as a drill hall; round-arched windows & battlemented porch; now Mill shop;

¶ In 1914, drill station for A Sqdn. 1 Lovat's Scouts; drill station for E Coy. 4 Bn. CH;

Fort George [H&I]; PV

*1 depot of Royal Highland Fusiliers [formerly that of Seaforth Highlanders] in mid-C18 barracks within extensive bastioned fort rebuilt 1746 onwards;

Forth [G&L];

*1 Main Street, Armoury Buildings in 1914, behind Old School; demolished in 1950s for new school;

¶ In 1914, base for E Coy. 8 Bn. HLI;

Fortrose [H&I]; PV

*1 Cathedral Square, Mackerchar Hall, **Drill Hall**, 1881, by Robertson; sandstone hall with romanesque detail in doors & windows; the staff house appears to be integral; now RC church;

¶ In 1914, drill station for C Coy. 4 Bn. Seaforth Highlanders;

Fort William [H&I]; PV ACF

*1 Mary Street, **Drill Hall**, pre-WWl; reconstructed & converted to housing but appears to retain some original features & form; staff house may be represented by Surveyors' offices on site; locals talk of demolition but the renewed structures appear to be authentic stylistically;

*2 Glen Nevis Place, Cadet Centre, c1980s; simple hall with annexe;

¶ In 1914, drill station for A Sqdn. 1 Lovat's Scouts; base for E Coy. 4 Bn. CH;

Fraserburgh [G]; PV

*1 29 Grattan Place, **Drill Hall**, pre-!901; 2-storey stone front block with crow-stepped gables & tourelles; slightly projecting door arch flanked by hand-gun-loops; hall behind, traces of a further extension; tablet with "VR" on gable; now a church;

¶ In 1914, drill station for F Sqdn. 2 Scottish Horse; base for G & H Coys. 5 Bn. GH;

Gairloch [H&I]; PV

*1 opposite Low Road, **Drill Hall**, pre-WWl; corrugated-iron-clad hut;

¶ In 1914, base for D Coy. 4 Bn. Seaforth Highlanders;

Galashiels [B]; PV TAC

*1 St John Street, **Volunteer Hall**, built 1874-5 for 1 Selkirkshire Rifle Volunteers or Gala Forest Rifles; two-storey, five-bay front block with crow-stepped gable, and hall behind, all in yellow sandstone; now council offices;

*2 Paton Street, **Drill Hall**, built 19C as offices of Mid Mill; taken over by TF, 1908; gymnasium & indoor range added; 2-storey, 7-bay, L-shaped block, in stone; on side, a small, harled, drill instructor's house; to other side of entrance, 2-storey orderly room block with half-hexagonal front & stone doorcase; behind, hall & garages etc;

¶ In 1914, drill station C Sqdn. Lothian & Border Horse; HQ+F & G Coys. 4 Bn. KOSB

Galston [D&G]; PV

*1 Barr Castle, 15/16C tower-house served as drill hall post-WWl;

¶ In 1914, drill station for G Coy. 4 Bn. Royal Scots Fusiliers;

Garmouth [G]; PV

*1 in village centre, **Drill Hall**, pre-WWl, probably in use 1908; 2-storey house with hall behind with three projecting annexes to side; bought from TA in 1970s for under £1000 as community centre;

¶ In 1914, base for G Coy. 6 Bn. Seaforth Highlanders;

Glasgow [G&L]; P [***1-*3, *5-*8, *10-*12**]; V [***1-*13**]; TACs [***7-*8**]; [*pp31,77,89,90,164,252*]

See also Cathcart, Coatbridge, Govan, Govanhill, Johnstone, Maryhill, Partick, Pollockshaws, Rutherglen and Springburn

*1 Yorkhill Parade/Gilbert Street/172 Yorkhill Street, **Drill Halls**; built 1900-01 for 6 Bn. HLI, by McNab; castellated Tudorbethan orderly room block of hard red brick, with red sandstone dressings; big circular office & staircase projection, striped in yellow brick, fronting the hall, with inscription: "6th Bn. HLI"; striped brickwork repeated in large new extension converting the whole complex to residential use; drill hall marked around the corner in Yorkhill Parade, demolished for housing;

¶ In 1914, HQ+A B & D Sqdns. Glasgow Yeomanry; base for 4 Coy. Lowland Divnl. Transport & Supply Column ASC; HQ+A-H Coys. 6 Bn. HLI; HQ+A-B Sections Lowland Mounted Bde. Field Ambulances ; HQ+A-C Sections 1 & 2

Lowland Divnl. Field Ambulances ; 3 & 4 General Hospitals, RAMC;

¶ In 1947, base for 474 HAA Regiment RA [TA];

*2 8 Newton Terrace, Charing Cross, built 1864-5; 4-storey terraced house with classical detail, former **HQ** of 3 Lowland Bde. RFA & $ Lowland [Howitzer] Bde. RFA; now Gold's, solicitors; backs on to

*3 c135 Berkeley Street, Charing Cross, **Drill Hall**, in use 1914; military facade to street with castellated tower, stair-turret, arched doorway etc; now Sikh Temple;

¶ In 1914, base for 1 City of Glasgow Bty. 3 Lowland Bde. RFA;

*4 81 Greendyke Street, Glasgow Green, drill halls; demolished for offices;

¶ In 1914, HQ+A-H Coys. 9 Bn. HLI;

*5 261 West Princes Street, **Drill Hall**, 1895-7, by Bell, with red sandstone facade; pedimented porch with columns, carved crests in panels this building superseded a drill hall in Great Western Road, built in 1866-7 for £1250, and cost £16000; hall behind now Robin Anderson Theatre, Scottish National Ballet;

¶ In 1914, HQ+A-H Coys. 5 Bn. Cameronians;

[***6** 518 Sauchiehall Street, built 1903, for photographer by CR Mackintosh; only recently HQ Royal Highland Fusiliers; 3-storey, 3-bay house in the Dutch style;]

*7 University Avenue, **Drill Hall**, 1900, by Barclay, HQ of GUs OTC; 2-storey front block with gable over doorway, & turrets; rebuilt hall behind; possible hall to side; University OTC crest over door;

*8 63 Houldsworth Street, **TAC**, c1980s; in use by parachute unit; industrial type building clad in steel sheets;

*9 149 Cathedral Street, drill hall in use by 1908; area re-developed;

¶ In 1914, HQ+A-H Coys. 8 Bn. Cameronians;

*10 24 Hill Street, Garnethill, **Drill Hall**, 1895; [*p252*] massive, square hall with 4-way rooflight at apex; square tower at corner, & gate with loops above & inscription, no longer legible; this took over from drill hall which was blown down in a storm; now Haldane Building, Glasgow School of Art;

¶ In 1914, HQ+A-H Coys. 5 Bn. HLI;

*11 69 Main Street, Bridgetown, drill hall opened 1902 at a cost of £12000; now 4-storey terraced tenement building, possibly associated with

*12 James Street, **Drill Hall** where a black & cream tiled front is part of the 1938 transformation into the Kings Cinema; now furniture store;

¶ In 1914, HQ+A-H Coys. 7 Bn. HLI;

*13 7 West George Street, now offices & shops;

¶ In 1914, HQ Lowland Division;

*14 4 Francis St, Shettleston, drill hall, HQ & PSI's house, given up 1910 & 1911;

¶ In 1910, Lowland Divisional Telegraph Coy. RE & 2 Lowland Field Coy. RE;

¶ In 1914, locations unspecified: drill station for C Sqdn. Lanarkshire Yeomanry; Lowland Clearing Hospital; HQ HLI Bde; HQ Scottish Rifle Bde; 4 City of Glasgow [H] Bty. & Ammunition Column, 4 Lowland [Howitzer] Bde. RFA;

Glenrothes [F]; PV TAC

*1 Baltimore Road, **TAC**; in use by RLC unit; 1980s-style, square, 2-storey block clad in forest green steel sheeting; garages in yard;

Golspie [H&I]; PV [p165]

*1 Old Bank Road, **Drill Hall**, 1892; large shed with wooden walls, & corrugated- iron roof with dormers, by Bisset for the Duke of Sutherland; central tower with pagoda roof; hall, armoury, 2-storey, stone, caretaker's house [c1910] & miniature range; pair of Drill Hall Cottages, 1896;

¶ In 1914, HQ+A Coy. 5 Bn. Seaforth Highlanders;

Gourock [G&L] PV ACF

*1 Shore St. Gamble Institute, 1876, likely base for volunteers;

*2 Binnie Lane, **Drill Hall**, c1930s; corrugated-iron-clad structure on brick base, possible range in basement, though outdoor range at Drumshantie; now church; **Cadet Hut** adjacent;

¶ In 1914, base for H Coy. 6 Bn. A & S Highlanders;

Govan [G&L]; PV TAC[*2] [p92]

*1 Elder Street, in use 1914; area re-developed;

*2 130 Whitefield Road, **Drill Hall**, built 1905-6, by Burnet et al, for RNR; 2- & 3-storey orderly-room block, with angle bartizans; the adjoining hall with sturdy north tower; all in red brick, rendered & pink-washed; 205 Field

Hospital, Graham House, RAMC; yard with garages;

¶ In 1914, ***1**base for 5 City of Glasgow [H] Bty.4 Lowland [Howitzer] Bde.RFA;

¶ In WWll, base for DEMS training;

Govanhill [G&L]; PV

*1 Victoria Road, [35 Coplaw St], **Drill Hall**, 1884-5, by Wilson, for 3 Lanarkshire Rifle Volunteers; domestic Gothic style, with battlemented square tower & circular corner turret with pepperpot; converted to residential use; over door, badge of 7 Bn. Cameronians; subsequently used as health & fitness studio;

*2 Butterbiggins Rd, **Drill Hall**, pre-1914; long low single-storey frontage with hall behind; archway in centre with inscription, partially-obscured by modern sign: "......Volunteer Artillery";

¶ In 1914, ***1**HQ+A-H Coys. 7 Bn. Cameronians; ***2** base for 4 City of Glasgow [H] Bty. & Ammunition Column, 4 Lowland [Howitzer] Bde. RFA;

Grangemouth [C]; PV TAC [*3]

*1 Old Town Hall, used as drill hall from 1860; demolished;

*2 Talbot Street, drill hall, 1887, was Dockers' Welfare until demolished 1967;

*3 Central Avenue, **TAC**, post WWll; 2-storey, flat-roofed admin. blocks forming L-shape; large hall; yard with extensive garaging;

¶ In 1914, drill station for 3 [Gordon Bde.] Coy. Highland Divisional Transport & Supply Column ASC;

Grantown-on-Spey [G]; PV

*1 High Street, Community Centre, 1897; possible earlier venue; high gabled hall with large window, archway access, & circular turret;

*2 Forest Road, **Drill Hall**, pre-WWl; stone, 2-storey front block with three dormers & ashlar dressings; hall behind; now RAF outdoor pursuits centre;

¶ In 1914, base for F Coy. 6 Bn. Seaforth Highlanders;

Greenock [G&L];

*1 Eldon St, **Fort Matilda**, coast defence battery, 19C; part survives under Royal Marine Reserve/RN/Coastguard establishment, built 1940s;

*2 8 South St, **Drill Hall**, pre-WWl; 3-storey, 3-bay, stone house to South Street; massive hall behind, with outbuildings & garages to street; also smaller hall with 2-

storey front block attached, between main hall [leisure centre] & house;

*3 Finnart St, in use 1914; small hall cWWl, Scout Hut;

*4 37 Newton St, HQ 1st Vol Bn. A&SH in 1907;

¶ In 1914, ***2** HQ+1 & 2 Renfrewshire [H] Btys.3 Highland [Howitzer] Bde. RFA; drill station C Sqdn. Glasgow Yeomanry; ***1**HQ+No.2 Electric Lights Coy. Renfrewshire REs-Fortress; ***3** HQ+A-D, F & G Coys. 5 Bn. A&SH;

Haddington **[E&L];** V

apparently no dedicated drill hall ever; in 1859 The White Swan in Brown Street changed its name to The Rifle Arms with the motto: "Defence not Defiance";

¶ In 1908, HQ 7 Volunteer Bn. Royal Scots;

¶ In 1914, drill station A Sqdn. Lothians & Border Horse; HQ+A Coy. 8 Bn. RS;

Halkirk [H&I]; PV ACF

*1Church Street, **Drill Hall**, built as Millkirk chapel in 1854; converted as drill hall c1910; single-storey hall with gabled porches now residential; indoor range to rear; all in stone;

*2 Crescent Street, cadet hut, c1950s; brick with slate roof;

¶ In 1914, base for G Coy. 5 Bn. Seaforth Highlanders;

Hamilton [Lanark]; PV ACF

*1 Bothwell Road, Hatton House, **Drill Hall**, pre-WWl; small, sandstone hall surrounded by post-WWll buildings; in use as cadet centre;

*2 Muirhall, Muir St, in use 1910; still a TAC in 1947; this had HQ, drill hall, messes, indoor range, armoury & PSI's house; also TF Association offices; near Depot of regulars; area re-developed;

*3 *Barrack Street* may be reference to former Militia Barracks c1857;

¶ In 1914, HQ+A & B Coys. 6 Bn. Cameronians;

Hawick **[B];** PVA ATC

*1 Dovecot Street, drill hall, demolished for housing & supermarket; one hut remains on site; formerly very extensive halls etc;

*2 Union Street, ATC meet in mill attached to 19C Masonic Hall;

¶ In 1914, base for C Sqdn. Lothian & Border Horse; base B & C Coys.4 Bn. KOSB;

Helensburgh [A&B]; PV [p252]

*1 East Princes Street, **Rifle Volunteers' Hall**, 1885 by Dixon; corrugated-iron hall with semi-circular window to gable, full-length lantern, & ridge-cresting to roof;

¶ In 1914, base No. 2 Coy. Clyde RGA-Defended Ports; base A Coy. 9 Bn. A&SH;

Helmsdale [H&I];

*1 Harbour Street, **Drill Hall**, C18 building once barracks, converted to drill hall in 1891; 2-storey gabled house at one end, with flat-roofed 2-storey hall at other; rendered, & on two floors with outside stair; now shop;

*2 Dunrobin Street, **Drill Hall**, pre-WWl; inscription: "Artillery Hall" over door; 2-storey front-block, house to one side, orderly-room etc. to other with door through to hall behind; residential;

¶ In 1914, drill station for F Sqdn. 2 Lovats Scouts; drill station for D Coy. 5 Bn. SH;

Holm **[Orkney] [H&I];** no location identified;

¶ In 1914, base for No.6 Coy. Orkney RGA-Defended Ports;

Huntly [G]; PV [p36]

*1Deveron Street, **Drill Hall**, c1908; large, stone, gabled hall with 2-storey front block & 3-storey castellated tower; indoor range along one side; inscription on gable: " A Coy. 4th VBGH"- ie the situation in 1908;

¶ In 1914, drill station for F Sqdn. 2 Scottish Horse; base for H Coy. 6 Bn. GH;

Innerleithen [B]; PV

*1Main Street, **Drill Hall**, 1877; gabled hall to road; on one side, orderly room in same stone; extended building behind; now Cleikum Mill; restored as dwelling[s];

¶ In 1914, drill stn. C Sqdn.Lothian & Border Horse; base H Coy. 8 Bn. Royal Scots;

Inveraray **[A&B];** PV

*1 Barn Braes, site of drill hall, 1913; converted to picture-house by Margaret, Duchess of Argyll c1960s; demolished, vacant plot;

¶ In 1914, base for A Coy. 8 Bn. A & S Highlanders;

Invergordon **[H&I];** V

*1Joss Street, drill hall, demolished;

¶ In 1914, base for F Coy. 4 Bn.Seaforth Highlanders;

Invergowrie **[P];** PV TAC

*1Main Street, **TAC**; in use by 23 SAS Regt; single- & 2-storey buildings around hall, set in yard with garages; some structures may date from pre-WWl;

¶ In 1914, drill station for C Sqdn. 1 Scottish Horse;

Inverness [H&I]; P [**2,5-7**]; V[**1-7**]; TAC [**7**];

*1 Cameron Barracks, off Perth Road, 1880-6, by RE office, Edinburgh; three, stone-built, 2-storey ranges around the parade-ground, with gablets & crow-steps; at one angle, a large square gate-tower; at another, paired, machicolated drum-towers; completely hidden from public view;

*2 Telford Road, **Militia Depot**, c1850; on OS map 1904; demolished for housing; only square castellated gate-towers stand;

*3 Academy St, in use 1914; not on 1904 map;

*4 Margaret St, drill hall in use by 1904; demolished for offices;

*5 Rose Street, **Drill Hall**, by 1904; [*p283*] 3-storey front block with central arch; large hall behind with prominent crow-stepped gable as rear wall; top storey of front block now tile-hung & whole building adapted as "The 45" bar & hotel; shops in rear of hall fronting bus-station;

*6 **10 Bank St**, HQ Seaforth & Cameron Bdes. Bearer Coys. in 1908; one of a pair of semi-detached stone-built houses c1870; now gallery;

*7 Gordonville Road, **TAC**, post-WWl, in use by 51 Highland Regt; 2-storey hall with shallow frontage; alongside, two-storey, 9-bay admin block; yard with garages etc;

¶ In 1914, base for H Sqdn. 2 Lovat's Scouts; HQ+Bty. Inverness RHA [Margaret St]; HQ+A & C Coys. 4 Bn. Cameron Highlanders; base for Highland Mounted Bde. Transport & Supply Col ASC [Academy St]; HQ+A-B Sections Highland Mounted Bde. Field Ambulances RAMC [Rose St]; HQ Highland Mounted Bde. [Academy St];

Inverurie [G]; PV

*1 Jackson Street, **Wyness Hall**, c1870; purpose-built drill hall, but presenting as chapel; gabled hall to road, with porch; alongside, flat-roofed hall with offices, probably representing extensions by the TA over the years; stone indoor range across the back; now community centre, court, community education office etc;

¶ In 1914, drill station for F Sqdn. 2 Scottish Horse; base for E Coy. 6 Bn. GH; drill station for 2 Highland Divnl. Field Ambulances RAMC;

Irvine [D&G]; PV TAC

*1 Corsehill Mount, **TAC**, c1970s; large, dark, brick, brutalist block, yard & garages;

¶ In 1914, HQ+1 Ayrshire Bty. 2 Lowland Bde. RFA; base for B Coy. 4 Bn. RSF;

Jamestown **[A&B];** V

*1 Milton Loan, beside sawmill; demolished 1970s, vacant plot;

¶ In 1914, base for E Coy. 9 Bn. A & S Highlanders;

Jedburgh [Borders]; PV [*p25*]

*1 Abbey Place, **Drill Hall** in public Hall built 1900-01 to replace Corn Exchange; French Renaissance style in red sandstone; earlier vaulted malt barn under hall served as armoury;

*2 High Street, **Drill Hall**, in church built 1757, & rebuilt 1818; 5-bay stone block with hipped roof & adjoining two-storey house; now RBL;

¶ In 1880, base for A Coy. 1 Roxburgh & Selkirk [The Border] Rifle Volunteer Corps;

¶ In 1914, drill station for C Sqdn. Lothian & Border Horse; & for A Coy. 4 Bn. KOSB;

Johnstone [G&L]; PV ACF

*1 Dimity Street, **Drill Hall**, pre-1900; 2-storey, 3-bay front block, crow-stepped gable over big arched doorway, & dormer each side; single-storey room to one side with similar features; all in sandstone; hall now demolished; crest in gable above door; ACF & ATC huts adjacent;

¶ In 1914, base for E Coy. 6 Bn. A & S Highlanders;

Keith [G]; PV TAC

*1 Union Street, **Drill Hall**, pre-1908; in use by 51 Highland Regt; complicated group of stone, institutional buildings; hall [with bellcote] has an extension to one side, & adjoins a 2-storey, gabled admin block on the other; the space between the extension & a further, square, 2-storey block, is filled, along the side of the hall, by a more recent single-storey structure; high up on the hall projection inside a stone moulding, is the badge of the Gordon Highlanders;

¶ In 1914, drill station for E Sqdn. 2 Scottish Horse; HQ+C Coy. 6 Bn. GH;

Kelso [B]; PV

*1 Bowmont Street, **Drill Hall**, pre-WWl; small gabled hall backs onto street; behind, a 2-storey block & a garage, opening onto the street behind;

¶ In 1914, drill station C Sqdn. Lothian & Border Horse; base A Coy.4 Bn. KOSB;

Kemnay [G]; PV

*1 off Station Road, **Drill Hall**, pre-WWll; corrugated-iron-covered shed; bought from TA by Scouts in 1958 for £100; now Scout hut;

¶ In 1914, base for G Coy. 7 Bn. Gordon Highlanders;

Kilmarnock [D&G]; PV

*1 Agricultural Hall,1862-3, adjoining Corn Exchange, used as volunteer drill hall; demolished;

*2 John Finnie Street, **Drill Hall**, Carleton House, small business advisory service; square, 2-storey early-19C classical house with balustrade, fronting John Finnie Street, & occupying a corner site; hall behind entered through a pedimented archway in Grange Place;

*3 Titchfield St, **Drill Hall & Recruiting Office**; 3-storey front block with bow windows, battlements, crow-steps, tower, & big arched windows at ground level; behind, PSI's house, now Samaritans; there was once an indoor range; hall, if there ever was one, now disappeared; local name for path to recruiting office: "Hellfire Alley";

¶ In 1914, base for C Sqdn. Ayrshire Yeomanry; base for 2 Ayrshire Bty. 2 Lowland Bde. RFA; HQ+A & H Coys. 4 Bn. Royal Scots Fusiliers;

¶ In 1939, base for 79 Lowland Field Regt. & duplicate unit 78 Regt;

¶ In 1950, base for 279 Field Regt. RA [TA]; [Carleton House];

Kilsyth [C]; PV A[*2];

*1 Drill hall at Burntgreen in 1911, no local information;

*2 Shuttle St/Townhead, drill hall in 1914; demolished for roundabout on relief road;

¶ In 1914, drill station for D Coy. 7 Bn. A & S Highlanders;

Kingussie [H&I]; PV

*1 High Street, **Drill Hall**, 1911; single-storey, 6-bay front block with lots of classical detail: pediments, finials, gablet etc; date & badge of Queens Own Cameron Highlanders over doorway; large hall behind;

¶ In 1914, base for F Coy. 4 Bn. Cameron Highlanders;

Kinross [F]; PV ACF

*1 Swansacre, **Drill Hall**, pre-WWl; square front block with

pointed arch over doorway; stone & brick, harled & white-washed; hall & sheds behind; to one side, 2-storey block, probably staff house, but possibly earlier Armoury;

¶ In 1914, drill station for B Sqdn. Fife & Forfar Yeomanry; base G Coy.7 Bn. A&SH;

Kintore [G]; PV

*1 High Street, Village Hall, 1894; may have served as drill hall; 2-storey front block, hall, & vestibule; no local knowledge of alternative venue;

¶ In 1914, base for F Sqdn. 2 Scottish Horse;

Kirkcaldy [F]; PV TAC [*p325*]

*1 Hunter St/Hill St, **Drill Hall**, 1913; in use by RA unit; HQ Offices of Fife County TF Association; 4-bay, 2-storey block with arts & crafts decorative touches; hall behind backing on to Hill St. 1980 shopping centre; next door L-shaped block of c1930s; 2- & 3-storey block fronting quadrangle of garages, gun-sheds etc;

¶ In 1914, HQ+ drill station A Sqdn. Fife & Forfar Yeomanry; base No.5 Coy. Forth RGA-Defended Ports; base C Coy. 7 Bn. BW; HQ+A Coy. Highland Cyclist Bn;

Kirkconnel [D&G]; PV ACF

*1Main Street, **Drill Hall**, pre-WWl; gabled hall with porch, & lower blocks each side, one, probably an indoor range;

¶ In 1914, drill station for D Coy. 5 Bn. KOSB;

Kirkcudbright [D&G]; PV

*1 High Street, drill hall next to Maclellans Castle, demolished;

*2 Dee Walk, **Drill Hall**, pre-WWl; L-shaped with hall in one arm, stabling & offices in the other, & tower in the angle; now fish-processors;

¶ In 1914, base 3 [Kirk't] Bty. 2 Lowland Bde. RFA; drill station G Coy. 5 Bn. KOSB;

Kirkintilloch [A&B]; VA

*1 Kerr Street School, from 1874, provided early base 10 Corps Dunbartonshire Rifle Volunteers, formed 5 March, 1860;

*2 St Andrews UF Church, Cowgate, also known as Meeting House & the Marshall Church; simple block with porch, acquired 1897, & converted as drill hall; shown on OS map 1958; demolished;

¶ In 1914, base for B Coy. 9 Bn. A & S Highlanders;

¶ In 1914, drill station B Sqdn. Lothians & Border Horse; base H Coy. 7 Bn. RS;

Nairn [H&I]; PV [*p286*]
*1King Street, **Drill Hall**, built 1843 as Free Church, in use as drill hall by 1914; large hall, 4 bays long, with 2-storey block behind; attached on one side, a 2-storey flat-roofed block, probably added by TA; & two low, gabled huts; community centre;
¶ In 1914, drill station for H Sqdn. 2 Lovat's Scouts; base for Ammunition Column Inverness RHA [King Street]; base for B Coy. 4 Bn. Cameron Highlanders;

Newmains **[G&L];** V
*1School Road, ACF hut burned down; may have occupied original site;
¶ In 1914, base for G Coy. 8 Bn. HLI;

Newmilns **[D&G];** V
*1Greenside, drill hall, pre-WW1; demolished soon after WW1;
¶ In 1914, drill station for G Coy. 4 Bn. Royal Scots Fusiliers;

New Scone [P]; PV
*1 Queens Road, **Armoury**, in use by 1910; built as church c1870; plain nave with some later additions behind; now Parish Hall;
¶ In 1914, base for F Coy. Highland Cyclist Bn;

Newton Stewart **[D&G];** V
*1 Victoria Road, drill hall formerly adjacent to Crown PH, where Volunteers' social functions took place; demolished for pub car-park;
¶ In 1914, base for H Coy. 5 Bn. KOSB;

North Berwick **[E&L];** V ACF
*1 High Street, Foresters Hall, may have been drill hall; converted to Playhouse Cinema in 1928; demolished for shops & housing; no evidence for dedicated drill hall;
*2 Dunbar Road, **Cadet Centre**; substantial hut; NB adjacent RBL building;
¶ In 1914, drill station A Sqdn. Lothians & Border Horse; base D Coy. 8 Bn. RS;

Oban [A&B]; PV
*1 Breadalbane Street, **Argyllshire Gathering Hall** late 19C has look of a drill hall;
*2 Drimvargie Ridge, drill hall, 1911; demolished for 1990s housing;
¶ In 1914, drill station for Argyllshire Bty. 4 Highland [Mountain] Bde. RGA; drill station for H Coy. 8 Bn. A & S Highlanders;

Old Meldrum [G];
*1 4 King Street, **Drill Hall**, built c1873, acquired by TA 1913; house fronting King Street, hall formerly joined on, not now part of property; a single-storey rectangular admin block, has a two-part hall to rear; now in process of being converted to house & store for vintage vehicles;
¶ In 1914, base for F Coy. 5 Bn. Gordon Highlanders;

Paisley [G&L]; PV TAC [*2]
*1 31 Whitehaugh Avenue, **Drill Hall**, pre-1900; [*p289*] front block, in stone, like L-plan tower-house, with hall alongside; large, blocked archway into hall; door into front block has crest with grenade, & RA motto; yard with garages; may be former Militia Barracks;
*2 63 Hawkhead Road, **TAC**, c1980s; in use by RE unit; square pavilion-type main block; yard with garages;
*3 66 High Street, **Drill Hall**, mid-19C, imposing classical building, former Town Hall[?] now Museum, fronts double-banked halls, previously drill hall from 1901; *1 & *3 both in use 1910 & 1933;
¶ In 1914, base for C Sqdn. Glasgow Yeomanry; base for No. 1 Works Coy. Renfrewshire REs-Fortress; HQ+A-C Coys. 6 Bn. A & S Highlanders [High St];
¶ In 1941, base for 91 AT Regiment from converted 5 Bn. A & S Highlanders;

Partick [G&L]; PV TAC [*1];
*1 Crow Road, **TAC**, c1980s; industrial-type buildings;
*2 Jordanvale Avenue, Whiteinch, ex-**TAC**, c1970s; steel-clad sheds, already redundant;

Peebles [B]; PV
*1Walkershaugh, **Drill Hall**, pre-1900; large hall with single-storey extensions at each end, & 2-storey PSI's house along part of the back; in rubble masonry with sandstone dressings; now leisure centre;
¶ In 1908, HQ 6 Volunteer Bn. Royal Scots;
¶ In 1914, drill station B Sqdn. Lanarkshire Yeomanry & C Sqdn. Lothian & Border Horse; base G Coy. 8 Bn. Royal Scots;

Penicuick/Glencorse [E&L]; PV TAC/ACF [*p75*]

*1 Glencorse Barracks, beside the A701; the nucleus with octagonal tower is Greenlaw House of 1803; also Cardwell-type keep, & other stone buildings of 1870s; use as training barracks for Scottish infantry units;

*2 Eastfield Farm Road, **TAC**, 1957; in use as Cadet Centre; large E-plan front block with central pediment, & date over porch; hall encased; yard with garages etc; accommodation includes three staff houses; all buildings in cream-coloured render;

¶ In 1914, drill station B Sqdn. Lothians & Border Horse & F Coy. 8 Bn. Royal Scots

Perth [P]; P[*2-*4, *6-7]; V[*1-*7]; TAC[*2];

*1 Barrack Road, Barracks, demolished for Police Station; part of perimeter wall remains;

*2 Dunkeld Rd, **Queens Barracks**; two pairs of former staff houses, one now Army recruiting office, front road, with large, new, 1980s-style hall in yard with garages etc; building continuing [2003];

*3 3 St Leonards Bank, **Highland House**, former HQ 51 Highland Bde; Georgian house with Gothic features in walled courtyard; vacated by TA;

*4 7 St Leonards Bank, square, classical house with porch & roof-top balustrade, again, in walled court; also vacated by TA in 2002;

*5 Tay Street, drill hall, pre-1914; demolished for fake Scottish Baronial office-block in 1996; 6/7 Black Watch moved to old Gymnasium, Queens Barracks, prior to a projected move to a new drill hall at Muirton Toll, Dunkeld Road, in c1956; plans were not to materialise until 1990s, so a return was made to Tay Street in 1959;

*6 2 Charlotte Street, in use 1914; 4-storey Victorian house, now offices;

*7 16 Victoria Street HQ of Army Service Corps in 1911; 2-storey house, with coach-arch through to rear;

¶ In 1914, drill station for B Sqdn. 1 Scottish Horse; HQ+A-B Coys. 6 Bn. Black Watch [Tay Street]; HQ+1 Coy. Highland Divnl. Transport & Supply Column ASC [Tay Street]; HQ Highland Div. [Charlotte Street];

Peterculter [G]; PV ACF

*1 Malcolm Road, **Drill Hall**; site now in use as Council Roads Dept. depot; ACF hut on site; present buildings may represent conversion of original ones although occupants think not;

¶ In 1914, base for H Coy. 7 Bn. Gordon Highlanders;

Peterhead [G]; PV TAC

*1 Kirk Street, drill hall, demolished for re-development;

*2 Catto Drive, **TAC**, c1920s; in use by 51 Highland Regt; imposing neo-Baroque front block with hall behind; yard with garages etc. to rear;

¶ In 1914, drill station for F Sqdn. 2 Scottish Horse; HQ+B-C Coys. 5 Bn. GH;

Pitlochry [G]; PV

*1near Station, **Armoury**, by 1910; front block, hall & rear block with two large arches, suggesting gun-sheds or stables; now "The Old Armoury Restaurant";

¶ In 1914, drill station for A Sqdn. 1 Scottish Horse; drill station for G Coy. 6 Bn. BW;

Pittenweem [F]; PV

*1 the **Town Hall**, 1871, at Church Wynd, Anstruther East possible drill hall; heavy military aspect: castellatation, corner bartizans etc; anchor & date over front door;

¶ In 1914, drill station for G Coy. 7 Bn. Black Watch [Anstruther];

Pollockshaws [G&L]; PV ACF [*p164*]

*1 230 Auldhouse Road, **Drill Hall**, c1900; free-style, white-washed, with twin saucer-domed towers, & dormers; symmetrical front with gable-topped gate-tower; pillars & railings to match; served **Thornliebank** as well;

¶ In 1914, base for H Coy. 6 Bn. A & S Highlanders;

Port Glasgow [G&L]; PV ACF [*2];

*1 2 King Street, 4-storey 19C house on corner site with turret; large arch now blocked, led to possible hall behind; now in commercial use;

*2 16 Highholm Street, **Drill Hall**, 1932; 2-storey, 7-bay, front block with gable over centre bay & balcony at window; at each side a lower bay under a sloping roof; behind, a large hall parallel to front block; staff house to rear; date on gable; hut & garage to side;

¶ In 1914, HQ+No.1 Coy. Clyde RGA-Defended Ports [King Street]; base for E Coy. 5 Bn. A & S Highlanders;

Portlethen [G]; PV

*1 Crookston Road, **Jubilee Hall**, 1887; plain rubble box with datestone; probably used as drill hall, there being no other obvious venue;

¶ In 1914, base for B Coy. 7 Bn. Gordon Highlanders;

Portpatrick [D&G]; V

*1 Colonel Street, terrace of officers' houses & part of the loop-holed perimeter wall of transit barracks on military route to Ireland;

¶ In 1914, drill station for D Coy. 5 Bn. Royal Scots Fusiliers;

Portree [Skye] [H&I]; PV ACF

*1 Park Road, **Drill Hall**, pre-WWl; 3-storey 6-bay front-block remains with re-modelled hall as council offices;

*2 nearby **Cadet Centre**, c1970s; rectangular gabled hall with two annexes;

¶ In 1914, drill station for C Sqdn. 1 Lovat's Scouts; base for H Coy. 4 Bn. CH;

Prestonpans [E&L]; V ACF

*1 High Street, **Cadet Centre** with Nissen hut indoor range behind Town Hall may have provided venue for drill; no other location;

¶ In 1914, base for C Coy. 8 Bn. Royal Scots;

Renfrew **[G&L];** V

*1 Campbell Street, drill hall; demolished for housing;

¶ In 1914, base for D Coy. 6 Bn. A & S Highlanders;

Rothes [F]; PV

*1 High Street/New Street, **Grant Hall**, built 1898 as Town Hall; it subsequently became Drill Hall, & has now reverted to community centre; elaborate facade with masses of architectural detail; high hall behind, plus garages, indoor range etc. from TA occupation; foundation stone;

¶ In 1914, base for D Coy. 6 Bn. Seaforth Highlanders;

Rothesay [A&B]; PVA

*1 Russell Street, drill hall in use 1914, no trace;

*2 High Street, **Drill Hall** in use from 1920s until at least 1958; then used by undertakers, now [2004] vacant;

¶ In 1914, HQ+Buteshire [Mtn] Bty. 4 Highland [Mtn] Bde. RGA-Mountain;

Roy Bridge [H&I]; PV [*p28*]

*1 **Drill Hall**, 1869; built for the Mackintosh & his newly-raised 10 Corps Inverness-shire Rifle Volunteers; designed by Rhind incorporating a post office, which occupied the rectangular projection; in 1903 the Lovat's Scouts took over with stables, a riding-school & practice ground nearby; the interior was then adapted;

¶ In 1880, base for K Coy. Inverness-shire Rifle Volunteers;

¶ In 1914, base for A Sqdn. 1 Lovat's Scouts;

PAISLEY's Whitehaugh Barracks carries a Royal Artillery badge over the door

SANQUAR's drill hall, based on a simple design, is now a community centre

Rutherglen [Lanark]; PV TAC [*3]; [p77]

*1 192 Main St, drill hall, given up 1910, site re-developed as shops;

*2 Queen St, drill hall, armoury, mess, PSI's house, indoor range etc. from 1910, marked on 1909 OS map; site now industrial estate but two, harled huts still stand;

*3 9 Polmadie Avenue, **TAC**, c1990s; in use by RLC unit; long, brick & glass block, with full-length roof-light; yard with garages etc;

*4 Camp Rd, Shawfield, ex-**TAC**, c1970s; 3-storey, flat-roofed, L-shaped block, yard & garages, derelict;

¶ In 1914, HQ+2 Field Coy. Lowland Divnl. REs; HQ+1-4 Sections, Lowland Divnl. Signals Coys.REs; drill stn.3 Coy. Lowland Divnl. Transport & Supply Column ASC

¶ In 1933, HQ+242 Field Coy. RE [TA];

St Andrews [F]; P [*3]; V[*1-3]; TAC/ACF[*3];

*1 South Street, Madras College, built 1834; used by Volunteers,1860;

*2 off North Street, Templars' Hall served as drill hall in 1890; demolished 1966 for new University Library;

*3 Wyvern, City Road, **TAC** in use by OTC; large, imposing, stone, Victorian mansion with plenty of detail; cadet hut, garage etc. at lower level;

¶ In 1914, drill station for A Sqdn. Fife & Forfar Yeomanry; base G Coy. 7 Bn. BW;

St Boswells [B]; PV

*1 Main Street, **Public Hall**, 1896, neo-Tudor in sandstone, served as drill hall;

¶ In 1914, drill station for C Sqdn. Lothians & Border Horse, & H Coy. 4 Bn. KOSB;

Saltcoats **[D&G]**; V

*1 local information is that there was never a dedicated drill hall here; shared use of Castle Hill, **Ardrossan**, barely a mile down the road;

¶ In 1914, base E Coy. 5 Bn. Royal Scots Fusiliers;

Sanday **[Orkney] [H&I]**; drill hall in use 1908; no location identified;

¶ In 1914, base for No.2 Coy. Orkney RGA-Defended Ports;

Sanquar [D&G]; PV [p289]

*1 Station Road, **Drill Hall**, pre-WWl; 2-storey front block in red brick with harled panels; 3-bay with central arched entrance; hall behind & indoor range down one side; now in community use;

¶ In 1914, drill station D Sqdn. Lanarkshire Yeomanry; base D Coy. 5 Bn. KOSB;

Selkirk [B]; PV [p68]

*1 Back Row, **Drill Hall**, 1867; classical facade to street, a contrast to adjoining Masonic Hall of 1887, in Scots Baronial; inscription in panel over door: "Volunteer Hall AD 1867"; large hall behind;

¶ In 1914, drill station C Sqdn. Lothian & Border Horse; base H Coy. 4 Bn. KOSB;

Shapansay **[Orkney] [H&I]**;

drill hall in use 1908; no location identified;

¶ In 1914, base for No.3 Coy. Orkney RGA-Defended Ports;

Shettleston **[G & L]**; V

*1 4 Francis Street, drill hall etc given up by 1910; no such address now;

¶ In 1914, drill station for 2 Field Coy. Lowland Divisional REs;

Shotts **[Lanark]**;

*1 Windsor Street, drill hall, sub-let to Ministry of Labour, 1930; demolished for house 1990s; inscribed stone said to be preserved somewhere;

*2 School Street, chapel/church hall used by Home Guard in WWll, and may have had earlier use;

¶ In 1914, base for C Coy. 8 Bn. HLI;

Skeabost [Skye] [H&I]; PV [p39]

*1 towered manor-house of 1870 by Ross, used as **Drill Hall**; now hotel; there are stables in the outbuildings; only building in area;

¶ In 1914, base for C Sqdn. 1 Lovat's Scouts;

Southend [A&B]; PV [p50]

*1 Main Street, **Dunaverty Hall**, built as drill hall, 1913; long, corrugated-iron-clad, single-storey hall, with possible indoor-range along side;

¶ In 1882, base for G Coy. 2 Argyll Rifle Volunteers becoming 5 Vol. Bn. A&SH 1887

¶ In 1914, base for C Coy. 8 Bn. A & S Highlanders;

Springburn **[G&L]**; V

*1 46 Keppochhill Road, Public Halls, 1902-3; vast & church-like with turrets & lots of doors & windows; possible venue for Volunteers; all in red sandstone; ruinous;

¶ In 1914, base for 3 City of Glasgow Bty. 3 Lowland Bde. RFA;

GAZETTEER OF DRILL HALLS & TA CENTRES:
WALES

Notes

Entries show surviving buildings in **BOLD** and destroyed or non-existent buildings in ***BOLD ITALIC.*** The region is given in brackets, shown as follows:

[C]   CLWYD Denbighshire and Flintshire
[D]   DAFYD Ceredigion, Pembrokeshire, Carmarthenshire
[GL]   GLAMORGAN South, West, Mid, Cardiff, Swansea, Neath etc.
[GWE]   GWENT Monmouthshire, Newport, Blaenau Gwent etc.
[GWY]   GWYNEDD Caernarvonshire, Anglesey, Conway etc.
[P]   POWYS Brecknockshire, Montgomeryshire, Radnorshire etc.

Where the site has been visited by the author, a V is shown;
Where a site has been photographed by the author, a P is shown;
Where a site still functions as a TA Centre, TAC is shown;
Where a site is used by cadets, ACF and/or ATC are shown.
WR= Welch Regiment   RWF= Royal Welch Fusiliers   SWB= South Wales Borderers

Aberaeron [D]; PV ACF [***2**]
*1 A482, **Memorial Hall**, used as drill hall; large 2-storey front block, three bays wide by five deep with stone detailing & pediment; wider hall behind; the facade has dates of both World Wars apparently added contemporaneously; this suggests it became a memorial hall subsequent to other use;
*2 Oxford St, **Cadet Centre**; small hall built for Royal British Legion;

Aberbargoed [GL]; PV   ACF
*1 Commercial Rd, **Drill Hall**, 1911; stone & brick hall with house attached behind; stone surround to front door, inscribed "2ND BATT. MON. REGT. "; ACF hut alongside; hall now adult education centre;

¶ In 1914, base for F Coy. 1 Bn. Monmouthshire Regt;

Abercarn [GWE]; V
no dedicated location known ; see **Cwmcarn**;

Aberdare [GL]; V ACF
*1 Cwmbach Road, drill hall, by 1910; used as offices & shops, then demolished for housing being built 2004;
*2 ACF hut at Pit Place, Cwmbach;
¶ In 1914, drill stn. for D Sqdn. Glamorgan Yeomanry; base E Coy. 5 Bn. Welch R.

Abergavenny [GWE]; PV ACF [***2**]
*1 Lewis's Lane, **Drill Hall**, 1895; [*p294*] 2-storey, 7-bay front block, with double doors at each side; behind, large hall & cross-wing; in side of hall, large, arched entrance; all in stone & red brick; memorial stone 27.xii.1895; now soft-furnishings store;
*2 Pant Lane, cadet centre in huts;
¶ In 1914, drill station for C Sqdn. Gloucestershire Hussars;HQ+A Coy. 3 Bn. Monmouthshire Regt;

Aberystwyth [D]; PV   TAC [***3**]
*1 Cardiganshire Militia Barracks, Borth Road, 1869, demolished 1979; Armoury in Shire Hall 1814-55 when demolished; then in Goggerdan Estate town house in Bridge St: armoury, + accommodation for permanent staff;new barracks built 1869;
*2 Glyndwyr Street, **Drill Hall**,1903; 7-bay, gabled hall across end of street; ten bays deep with garage at rear; foundation stone dated 14.iv.1903;
*3 Park Avenue, **TAC**, c1980s; office/hotel-type building with garages & range in yard;
*4 Smithfield Road, HQ of RFA in 1914;
¶ In 1914, drill station for D Sqdn. Pembroke Yeomanry; base for Cardiganshire Bty. 2 Welsh Bde. RFA;

Abertillery [GWE]; PV TAC [*p294*]
*1 Cwm Cottage Road, **Drill Hall**, 1910; 2-storey front block with hall behind, house attached on one side, and

ABERGAVENNY's drill hall, opened in 1895, is now a soft furnishings shop

ABERTILLERY's drill hall carries the Monmouths'. Boer War battle honour

modern additions in yard; South Africa battle honour on gable; inscription over main door: 3RD BATT. MON. REGT;

¶ In 1914, base for E & F Coys. 3 Bn. Monmouthshire Regt;

Acrefair [C] see Ruabon [*p94*]

Ammanford [D]; PV ACF

*1 Margaret Street, **Drill Hall**, by 1910; 2-storey front block, possibly rebuilt, hall, & another two-storey block; behind that a further2-storey block now ACF Centre; also house at one end; now community use;

¶ In 1914, base for H Coy. 4 Bn. Welch Regt;

Bala [P]; PV

*1 Main Street, **Drill Hall**, 1891; large, stone-built, gabled hall with 3-storey, stuccoed entrance block which may have been added later, which, along with blocked side windows, gives it the appearance of a cinema; the foundation stone records date as commemoration of 1889 royal visit; now called "Neuadd Boddug";

¶ In 1914, base for H Coy. 7 Bn. Royal Welch Fusiliers;

Bangor [GWY]; PV   ACF

*1 Glynne Road, **Drill Hall**, 1913; in use as Services Careers Centre + ACF; gun-sheds & stables etc recently demolished for Health Centre;

¶ In 1914, base for C Sqdn. Denbighshire Hussars; HQ+Bty. Welsh RGA-Heavy;

Barmouth **[GWY];** V   ACF

*1 High Street, Assembly Rooms [latterly above Woolworths] used by TA; demolished for re-development;

*2 ACF hut, Park Road;

¶ In 1914, drill station for E Coy. 7 Bn. Royal Welch Fusiliers;

Barry [GL]; PV ACF

*1 Broad Street, **Drill Hall**,1913; [*p295*] 2-storey front-block in neo-Baroque style with halls behind, and indoor range forming quadrangle; 1913 date over main door; now funeral parlour; separate 8-bay, 2-storey, T-shaped house to side, now "Drill Hall Cottages";

*2 Gladstone Road [behind Broad Street], cadet huts;

¶ In 1914, base No. 5 Coy. Glamorgan RGA-Defended Ports; No. 2 Works Coy. Glamorgan REs-Fortress [Gladstone Road]; base C Coy. 7 [Cyclist] Bn. Welch Regt;

*2 King Street, militia barracks by TM Penson, 1857-8, converted into County Offices, 1897-8, by Grierson & Bellis, demolished c1968;

*3 High Street, **Cadet Centre**, 1991; on site of mid-19C market hall, itself replaced by drill hall which stood until 1989; single-storey, L-shaped building with datestone incorporating ACF & ATC arms; behind, original two-storey, red-brick staff house with porch projection; also detached indoor range;

*4 King Street, Cadet HQ marked on street plan; large detached Swiss cottage-style house with balconies & corner turrets dated 1910;

¶ In 1914, drill station for A Sqdn. Denbighshire Hussars; base A Coy. 5 Bn. RWF

Monmouth [GWE]; PV [p16]

*1 Castle House, 17C and later; HQ of premier territorial unit, taken over by TA in 1927;

*2 85 Monnow Street in use in 1914;

¶ In 1914, drill station for C Sqdn. Gloucestershire Hussars; base [with **Usk**] for G Coy. 2 Bn. Monmouthshire Regt;

Montgomery [P]; PV

*1 Kerry Street, **Armoury**, in early-19C house; now 3-storey house & shop, in terrace with 2-storey, 3-bay house with Gibbs door-surround; unevenly-stuccoed; whole terrace has dentillated cornice and may originally have been the Armoury- hall & house together;

¶ In 1914, drill station for C Sqdn. Montgomeryshire Yeomanry; drill station for A Coy. 7 Bn. Royal Welch Fusiliers;

Morriston [GL]; PV

*1 Banwell St. Barracks/**Drill Hall**, in use by 1910; large hall with small 2-storey block at one end; original roof-structure, but whole now clad in steel-sheet; in use as gymnasium & sun-bed centre;

¶ In 1914, base for Ammunition Column, 1 Welsh [Howitzer] Bde. RFA; drill station for E Coy. 6 Bn. Welch Regt;

Mostyn [C]; V ACF [***2**]

*1 Dock Road, drill hall, pre-WWl; later John Owen's Sawmill timber-store; demolished;

*2 ACF hut at Glan-y-Don;

¶ In 1914, drill station for D Coy. 5 Bn. Royal Welch Fusiliers;

Mountain Ash [GL]; PV

*1 21 Dyffryn Road, **Drill Hall**, in use by 1910; large hall with three gabled projections to road; pair of semi-detached houses [now Drill Hall House & Library House] to side, one for PSI & one orderly room; once Public Library, now CAB etc;

¶ In 1914, drill station D Sqdn. Glamorgan Yeomanry; base C & D Coys. 5 Bn. WR;

Neath [GL]; PV TAC

*1 Rugby Avenue/Eastlands Road, **Drill Hall**, in use 1910; large hall with a lean-to on the end & 2-storey 9-bay block with arched entrance, form two sides of quadrangle; at one corner, a house, and, by the gate, another single-storey garage/gun-shed; original entrance on Rugby Avenue;

¶ In 1914, drill station for A Sqdn. Glamorgan Yeomanry; drill station 2 Glamorgan [H] Bty. 1 Welsh [Howitzer] Bde. RFA; base for F Coy. 6 Bn. Welch Regt; base for G Coy. 7 [Cyclist] Bn. Welch Regt;

Newport [GWE]; PV TAC [p253]

*1 Barrack Hill, **Raglan Barracks TAC**, 1843-5, two long ranges of barrack blocks, loop-holed perimeter walls, guardhouse etc;

*2 Dock Street, **Drill Hall**, pre-1900; [p253] now [2001] fitness studio; stone-built, castellated; 3-storey front block with turrets, arrow-slits & oriel; hall behind; *****

3 Lime Street, in use 1914; demolished, street untraceable;

*4 Stow Hill, drill hall, demolished; shown on 1884 map as Royal Albert Hall, lease purchased by Vol Bn. 1892 for Drill Hall; there is a commemorative plaque on Stow Hill;

*5 103 Caerleon Road, Yeomanry HQ in 1914;

*6 Stockton Road, ex-TAC; only ever huts, no trace;

*7 Blaen-y-Pant, ex-TAC; site purchased 1938, built 1947; demolished for health centre;

*8 Temple Street, ex-TAC; former Seamen's Mission, purchased 1948;

¶ In 1914, base for C Sqdn. Gloucestershire Hussars; HQ+1 Monmouthshire Bty. & Ammunition Column 4 Welsh Bde. RFA [Lime Street]; HQ+A-D Coys. 1 Bn. Monmouthshire Regt; drill station for 1 Welsh Divnl. Field Ambulances;

Newtown [P]; PV

*1 Back Lane, **Drill Hall**, 3-storey brick block, three bays

MAESTEG's Ewenny Road drill hall now used by light industry

PONTYPOOL, this derelict drill hall of 1901 looks to be vulnerable [2004]

wide, & six bays deep, with eaves cornice; painted legend on side next to court: "THE HEADQUARTERS 5TH VOL BATTALION South Wales Borderers" the word "FUSILIERS" seems to have been partly erased; set for re-development 2003;

¶ In 1914, base for C Sqdn. Montgomeryshire Yeomanry; HQ+B Coy. 7 Bn. RWF;

¶ In 1914, the depot of the newly-raised Welsh Horse was moved here from Cardiff;

Pembroke [D]; PV [*p254*]

*1 Westgate Hill/Castle Terrace [Main Street in 1914], **Drill Hall**,1913, by HJP Thomas; two stone-built, symmetrical, 2-storey, 2-bay houses linked by an archway leading to hall or [now] yard; over arch, PoW feathers + legend: 'Pembrokeshire Territorial Force Drill Hall';

*2 **Defensible Barracks** in use until at least 1956;

¶ In 1914, drill station for A Sqdn. Pembroke Yeomanry; base for B Coy. 4 Bn. WR;

¶ In 1953, base for 408 Coast Regiment RA [TA] [Defensible Barracks]

Pembroke Dock [D]; PV ACF

*1 Pembroke Street, Victoria House, HQ of RGA in 1914; built c1835 as Victoria Hotel, altered c1905 [?1908 for RGA/TF?];

*2 Cadet Centre at Pier Road;

*3 Pennar Barracks, built 1875 for Submarine Miners; some remains;

¶ In 1914, drill station for No. 3 Coy. Pembroke RGA-Defended Ports;

Penarth [GL]; PV ACF [*1 & *2]

*1 Woodlands Place, ex-TAC; drill hall in use 1914; site re-developed for housing, only one brick building remains;

*2 Dingle St more ACF & ATC huts by the station;

¶ In 1914, base for No. 4 Coy. Glamorgan RGA-Defended Ports;

Penmaenmawr [GWY]; PV ACF

*1 Bangor Road, **Drill Hall**, by 1910; long, low hall with porch, all in patterned brick, a reconstruction of original building; behind, a semi-sunken indoor-range;

¶ In 1914, base for F Coy. 6 Bn. Royal Welch Fusiliers;

Pentre [Ystrad] [GL]; PV ACF

*1 Treharne Street, **Drill Hall**, pre-1914; long [25+ bays] 2-

storey block, pierced by arch through, forming access over railway level-crossing; 8-bay block west of arch, with slightly lower roofline, may be later addition; in use by ACF; known locally as "The Barracks"; confirmed as **Ystrad** venue in 1958 Review;

¶ In 1914, base for Welsh Border Brigade Company Divisional Transport & Supply Column ASC listed as based at adjoining *Ystrad* [Rhondda];

Penygroes [GWY]; PV ACF

*1 Victoria Road, **Drill Hall**, by 1913; large, gabled & aisled hall timber-framed & stuccoed; now Health Centre; adjacent, small gabled hall in use by cadets;

¶ In 1914, base for C Coy. 6 Bn. Royal Welch Fusiliers;

Pontypool [GWE]; PV

*1 Rock Hill, Pont-y-Moel, Armoury, in use until 1901, demolished; site occupied by garage; marked on OS map c1900;

*2 Osborne Rd, **Drill Hall**, 1901; [War Office approval in 1912]; large hall sandwiched between & behind 2-storey blocks of offices, orderly rooms etc; detached house at one end; [*p304*]

¶ In 1901, HQ A Coy. 3 Vol. Bn. South Wales Borderers;

¶ In 1914, HQ+A-C Coy. 2 Bn. Monmouthshire Regt;

Pontypridd [GL]; PV TAC

*1 Tram Road, **Drill Hall**, in use 1914, recorded on 1919 OS map but not on 1900; rebuilt c1950 as TAC located on re-named road, now Broadway; 2-storey block & garages, one possibly original shed, & house;

¶ In 1914, base for D Sqdn. Glamorgan Yeomanry; HQ+A & B Coys. 5 Bn.Welch R.

Port Talbot [GL]; V ACF

*1 Ynys Street, drill hall & riding school, in use 1914; later DHSS offices; demolished 1992 for housing- Island Mews;

*2 ACF off Forge Street;

¶ In 1914, drill station for A Sqdn. Glamorgan Yeomanry; HQ, Bty. & Ammunition Column Glamorgan RHA; base for H Coy. 7 [Cyclist] Bn. Welch Regt. [Aberavon];

Porthcawl [GL]; V ACF [off South Road]

no dedicated premises known, but 1958 Review records: 'ceased 1928';

¶ In 1914, drill station for B Sqdn. Glamorgan Yeomanry;

Porthmadoc [GWY]; PV ACF

*1 Snowdon Street, **Drill Hall**, pre-WWl; large, gabled hall built in rubble masonry with rendered facade; later extension on one side & garages on other; detached stone building & cadet hut to rear; now RBL;

¶ In 1914, base for B Coy. 6 Bn. Royal Welch Fusiliers;

Prestatyn [C]; PV TAC [*2] [*p74*]

*1 drill hall in old town used until 1929; demolished for garage;

*2 Marine Road, **TAC**; built pre-WWll as bus-garage & taken over in 1953 by TAVR artillery unit; now occupied by TA REME unit; large L-shaped, 2-storey front block with canopy on corner where the petrol pumps stood; above this, a square tower with pyramid roof; two roundels on the tower, presumably once clock-faces, are now occupied by RA & REME painted logos; behind, large hall; to side, yard, garages & workshops;

¶ In 1914, drill station for B Sqdn. Denbighshire Hussars;

Presteigne [P]; PV ACF

*1 Hereford Street, **Drill Hall**, pre-WWl; single-storey, gable-ended hall to road; offices at front, hall with side door behind;

¶ In 1914, drill station for D Coy. 1 Bn. Herefordshire Regt;

Pwllheli [GWY]; PV ACF [*p306*]

*1 North Quay, The Harbour, **Drill Hall**, by 1913; 7-bay, 2-storey hall with central doorway, parallel to quayside; along the back, an indoor-range; at one end, an L-shaped, 2-storey orderly-room/house; hall appears to have future heritage use;

¶ In 1914, base for G Coy. 6 Bn. Royal Welch Fusiliers;

Queensferry [C]; PV TAC

*1 Station Road, Harry Weale VC **TAC**; c1980s; 2-storey, red-brick & pitched roofs;

Rhayader [P]; PV

*1 West Street, **Drill Hall**; long, 12-bay stone building, in use as a Leather Works in 1903; subsequently a drill hall, in use by 1910, out-of-use by 1933; supermarket;

¶ In 1914, drill station for D Sqdn. Montgomeryshire Yeomanry; base for G Coy. 1 Bn. Herefordshire Regt;

Rhosllanerchrugog [C]; PV ACF

*1 Osborne Road, **Drill Hall**, 1938; single-storey hall with castellated porch, linked to orderly-room block; over porch

PWLLHELI, house, orderly-room and hall are ranged laterally along the street

RHYL's John Street drill hall still functions as a TAC

door: "DRILL HALL 4TH. BATT. R.W.FUS. 1938"; to rear of yard, post-WWll ACF hut &, possibly earlier, indoor range;

¶ In 1914, base for G Coy. 4 Bn. Royal Welch Fusiliers;

Rhyl [C]; PV ACF [p306]

*1 John Street, **Drill Hall**, 1914; 2-storey, L-shaped front block with pediment containing Royal arms above stone Baroque doorway; on side, two gables & fire-escape, suggesting use as accommodation; behind, hall & indoor range; inscribed panel over door: "Territorial Drill Hall, 1914";

¶ In 1914, drill station for B Sqdn. Denbighshire Hussars; base C Coy. 5 Bn. RWF;

Rhymney GWE]; PV

*1 Old Brewery Lane, **Drill Hall**, 1910; hall flanked by two 2-storey blocks with gabled roofs; to one side, later garages & sheds; sold 1956; now the Brewery Social Club, and commercial garage;

¶ In 1914, base for G Coy. 1 Bn. Monmouthshire Regt;

***Risca* [GWE];** V ATC [Thistle Way]

*1 no dedicated building, confirmed 1958 Review, see ***Crosskeys*** ;

¶ In 1914, base for 2 Monmouthshire Bty. 4 Welsh Bde. RFA;

Ruabon [C]; PV [p94]

*1 grounds of Wynnstay Hall used for drilling, pre-WWl;

*2 Acrefair, opposite Air Systems works, **Drill Hall**, pre-WWl; 2-storey, 7-bay, tall front block with pediment over centre bay; to side, single-storey stores block with 5 dormers; behind, 2-storey staff house & terrace of cottages; behind front block, hall & indoor range; all in decorative mix of red/blue brick; in use as youth & community centre;

¶ In 1914, drill station for A Sqdn. Denbighshire Hussars; base C Coy. 4Bn. RWF;

Ruthin [C]; PV

*1 Denbigh Road, **Drill Hall**, pre-WWl; small, single-storey, 6-bay, stone-built hall with porch, lengthways to road, behind wall; blocked arched window in one gable-end; modern additions at each end; currently in community use;

¶ In 1914, drill station B Sqdn. Denbighshire Hussars; drill station B Coy. 4 Bn. RWF base North Wales Bde. Coy. Welsh Divisional Transport & Supply Column ASC;

St Asaph [C]; PV
*1 no evidence locally for existence of dedicated drill hall; Dean's Library, 1894, castellated rectangular block with oriel over porch, suggested as possibility; Kinmel Camp may have been venue for local units; no reference in 1958 Review;
¶ In 1914, drill station for C Coy. 5 Bn. Royal Welch Fusiliers; drill station for North Wales Bde. Coy. Welsh Divisional Transport & Supply Column ASC;

Saundersfoot [D]; PV
*1 Francis Street, **Drill Hall**, in use 1914; 2-storey block at one end of long low hall; now converted to dwellings-"Admiral's Mews";
¶ In 1914, base for No. 2 Coy. Pembroke RGA-Defended Ports;

Sirhowy **[GWE];** no premises, see **Tredegar**; confirmed 1958 Review;
¶ In 1914, base for D Coy. 3 Bn. Monmouthshire Regt;

Swansea [GL]; PV TACs [*1 *3 & *6];
*1 Glamorgan Street, **John Chard VC House TAC**, c1970s; yellow-brick blocks with pyramid roofs in L-shapes around courtyard;
*2 Richardson St, Central Drill Hall, in use 1910; site backs on to *1 & building next to the TAC entrance may be part of original drill hall;
*3 Alamein Rd, Morfa Industrial Estate, **TAC**, 1986, in use; red-brick hall, chalet-style offices, courtyard & garage block;
*4 17 Castle St, TAC; now Services Careers Centre, may have previously been offices, 1930s-style city-centre terrace;
*5 42 Castle St, in use as RA HQ in 1914;
*6 The Grange, Blackpill, **TAC**, in use; large 2-storey brick block & garages etc; adjacent AA Operations Room;
*7 Hafod, in use 1914, out-of-use 1927; drill hall demolished for MOT garage; on 1919 map;
*8 7 Rutland St, in use 1914; livery stables listed in 1910 Kelly's; redeveloped as shopping centre;
*9 Royal Arsenal mentioned 1881 as Volunteers' HQ; marked on 1889 map in angle of Glamorgan & Richardson Streets;
*10 St Helens Road, mentioned in Kelly's 1914 with Richardson Street;

¶ In 1914, base for A Sqdn. Glamorgan Yeomanry; HQ+1 Glamorgan [H] Bty. 1 Welsh [Howitzer] Bde.RFA; HQ+B-D Coys. & E Coy. [Hafod] 6 Bn. Welch Regt; S Wales Mounted Bde. Transport & Supply Column ASC [Rutland Street]; HQ+A-C Sections3 Welsh Divnl. Field Ambulances RAMC;

Talgarth [P]; PV ACF
*1 Hay Road, **Drill Hall**, pre-WWl; hall with stone house attached; out-of-use by 1933; B&B Lodge;
*2 **Town Hall**, from 1877, possible early venue for Volunteers;
*3 Church Lane, Old School, venue for ACF since new school built c1970;
¶ In 1861, base for Vl Corps Brecknockshire Rifle Volunteers;
¶ In 1914, base for F Coy. Brecknockshire Bn. South Wales Borderers;

Tenby [D]; PV ACF [*2]
*1 1 Greenhill Avenue [now The Norton], **Drill Hall**, in use by 1910; converted into apartments [Regency Court];
*2 cadet huts at Station Approach;
¶ In 1914, base for A Sqdn. Pembroke Yeomanry; drill station for No. 2 Coy. Pembroke RGA-Defended Ports;

Towyn [GWY];
*1 Brook Street, Neuadd Pendre, originally **Drill Hall**,1910; large, lateral hall with twin-gabled front porch projection, & flat-roofed extension along the back; AA gun garage/gun-shed on opposite side of road, now in use by double-glazing company;
¶ In 1914, base for F Coy. 7 Bn. Royal Welch Fusiliers;

Tredegar [GWE]; PV
*1 Park Place, **Drill Hall**, 1910; converted to housing, 2004; 2-storey house with large hall attached; later addition on end with garage;
¶ In 1914, base for G Coy. 3 Bn. Monmouthshire Regt;

Tregaron [D]; PV ACF
*1 The Square, **Memorial Hall** served as drill hall; 2-storey, 4-bay, stone-built hall with dressed stone mouldings over doorway & windows; hall behind; ACF use;
¶ In 1914, drill station for D Sqdn. Pembroke Yeomanry;

Treharris **[GL];** V ACF
*1 The Park, drill hall, in use 1910, demolished for housing development; ACF hut behind site at rear of Oaklands

Terrace;

¶ In 1914, base for F Coy. 5 Bn. Welch Regiment;

Trimsaran [D];

*1Bryncaerau Road, **Drill Hall**, c1930s; 3-bay hall, with turreted facade, at right-angles to lower orderly-room block; recently re-furbished for ACF use;

Tumble [D]; PV ACF [*2]

*1 High Street, drill hall, demolished; site now War Memorial gardens;

*2 54 Gwendraeth Road, ACF Centre;

¶ In 1914, drill station for F Coy. 4 Bn. Welch Regt;

Usk [GWE]; PV

*1 3-5 Porth-y-Carne Street, **Drill Hall**, in use in 1914; Georgian house late18C & attached hall; now Presbytery and RC church hall; generally held to have been used by TF but resident priest has no knowledge of it;

¶ In 1914, base [with **Monmouth**] for G Coy. 2 Bn. Monmouthshire Regt;

Welshpool [P]; PV ACF

*1 Brook Street, **The Armoury**, pre-1900; 2-storey, stuccoed block at front of site, post-dates the red-brick, 2-storey block behind; in between is a range clad in corrugated-iron; attached to the front block is a stone, single-storey, lodge-type structure, probably residential, & earlier; to the side is stone & corrugated-iron hall; also other outbuildings; the Militia had gone by 1814, & the Rifle Volunteers soon disappeared, to reform only in 1897; only the Yeomanry enjoyed continuous embodiment from 1831; it seems likely that the stone buildings & the red-brick one, later enlarged, date from c1900; the front building [now ACF] from post-1908; the hall is now a Leisure Centre;

¶ in 1803 HQ of Yeomanry Cavalry at Trehelig Gro;

¶ in 1833 newly-built Armoury of Militia below Bron y Buckley Wood;

¶ In 1914, HQ+B Sqdn. Montgomeryshire Yeomanry; base for C Coy. 7 Bn. RWF;

Whitland [D]; V ACF[*2]

*1 A40 road, TA Centre, demolished for Spring Gardens Industrial Estate;

*2 ACF huts at Fairfield, A40;

¶ In 1914, drill station for C Sqdn. Pembroke Yeomanry;

Wrexham [C]; PV TAC [*3] [*p93*]

*1 Town Hill, Town Hall, 1715, demolished 1940; used by Militia until 1857;

*2 Regent Street, **Militia Barracks**, 1856-7; now Museum & Archive Office; quadranglular with round corner turret at each angle, & gabled ranges & loggia;

*3 Kings Mills Road, **Hightown Barracks**, built originally as Militia Barracks, in 1877 became depot of Royal Welch Fusiliers; red-brick barrack-blocks arranged around parade-ground, with Keep, QM Stores etc. now TAC;

*4 1 Erdigg Road/ corner of Chapel & Poplar Streets, drill hall in use 1912 by Yeomanry; demolished for housing & playing-field;

*5 Poyser Street, **Drill Hall**, 1902; brick facade to street with stepped gables & terracotta detailing; large central doorway, window over, flanked by smaller entrances; castellation & arrow-slits; staff house adjoins to side; inscription: 4TH BN RWF DRILL HALL; moulded dragon with architect's & builders' names; large hall with long roof-light; in good repair, in commercial use;

¶ In 1914, HQ+A Sqdn. Denbighshire Hussars [Erdigg Road]; HQ+A Coy. 4 Bn. Royal Welch Fusiliers [Poyser Street];

Ystrad [Rhondda]; see **Pentre**; V

¶ In 1914, base for Welsh Border Bde. Coy. Divnl. Transport & Supply Column ASC;

Ystradgwnlais [P];

*1Gurnos, boundary with Cwmtwrch-Isaf, **Drill Hall**, c1914; two large corrugated-iron-clad sheds, in 2003, for sale;

¶ In 1914, base for H Coy. Brecknockshire Bn. South Wales Borderers;

APPENDIX 1
Militia/Yeomanry barracks, Yeomanry riding schools,
Submarine Miners Depots, and Cardwell Reform local infantry depots

This Appendix gives details of buildings connected to the volunteer forces of different types, but not, generally, of actual drill halls, although subsequently, some will have become such, either because of changes in a unit's organisation or designation, or as later TACs. A good example of this latter point is Carnarfon, whose Militia Barracks was leased to the County Territorial Association in 1910, roundabout the time that a drill hall was added to the complex fronting onto Victoria Road. Similarly, both Lincoln and Grantham Militia Barracks were taken over by the TF, each having a drill hall added in 1913.

This Appendix includes:

- **Militia & Yeomanry Barracks & Armouries**, many of them, pre-1860
- **Yeomanry Riding Schools**, mostly pre-1860
- **Locations of the Submarine Miners Depots**, both Volunteer & Militia
- The Cardwell period **Barracks & Depots** of the Line Regiments, 1870s-80s

NOTE: **bold print** denotes buildings still in existence at time of compilation

MILITIA & YEOMANRY Barracks & Armouries

Aberystwyth: HQ of Cardiganshire Militia in Shire Hall in 1814, demolished 1855, so moved to Goggerdan Estate town house in Bridge Street accommodating HQ, Armoury & permanent staff; new barracks built 1869, in Borth Rd; converted to council housing 1945, then demolished 1979.

Alnwick: formerly in Bondgate Without; demolished for Playhouse Cinema c1920

Barnard Castle: built 1864, gate & guardhouse remain; now sheltered housing.

Bishops Stortford: Yeomanry barracks at Silver Lees, now a Car Stereo Shop; built in 1865, this was the home of the 1st Hertfordshire Volunteer Light Horse, whose life-size hart emblem now stands over the porch of the former White Hart in North Street, now a bookshop; the regiment was dissolved when the secretary ran off with the funds; the present building has a pillared porch, and the adjacent former stables retain tethering rings.

Bloomsbury, London: Eastman Dental Hospital on Grays Inn Road, built 1842 as barracks for Light Horse Volunteers; [Pevsner, London volume ll, 1952]

Buckingham: large double-banked early nineteenth-century house on West Street described in town trail as Volunteer Barracks; Yeomanry House in Hunter Street, three-storey early-Georgian house with outbuildings, stables, yard with gallery, possible riding-school, hall etc; in 1845 it was HQ of Royal Buckinghamshire Hussars, lately re-formed from existing Yeomanry troops; Beckett refers to Militia Barracks of 1802.

Burnley: Clifton Street built 1854, demolished 1981 for motorway works.

Bury [Lancashire]: Elton Square, demolished for housing development, late 1970s.

Bury St Edmunds: built 1857 in King Street, now housing, Yeomanry Close; it was, more likely, the base of the West Suffolk Militia, rather than Yeomanry.

Carnarfon: built 1855 in stone, classical quadrangular building with balustrade around roof, and projecting front bay; acquired by TAFA 1961 and still used.

Cardiff: Stores in Castle rebuilt by Burges 1862, in romantic mediaeval style.

Carlisle: Stores built 1881 in inner ward of Castle; adjacent Officers' Mess is now the Museum of the Border Regiment.

Carmarthen: Armoury in Spillman Street in 1852; then Carmarthen Barracks, may be present Picton Barracks TAC.

Chelmsford: Stores of West Essex Militia built in Market Road c1855; adapted into drill hall 1902; demolished for APU extension; foundation stone re-set at new Springfields Tyrrells TAC.

Chester: Stores in Castle, the opposite wing to officers' mess, contains Armoury.

Chichester [East Row/East Walls]: depot & parade-ground up to 1879; no trace.

Cirencester: built 1857 on Cecily Hill; Cotswold stone buildings, castellated with oriel over main doorway set in square tower with octagonal stair-turret; at one end, quarters for four sergeants, at

FINSBURY, the HQ of the Honourable Artillery Company

the other, the Armoury/stores with semi-circular projection to the street; cf former Gloucester Armoury. [*p66*]

Colchester: Stores of East Essex Militia built in Stanwell Street 1855; became drill hall in 1887, demolished for re-development 1983.

Cupar: built 1842 as prison, later converted to Militia Barracks; now TAC.

Derby, Rowditch Bks. built 1859 for Derbyshire Militia; guardroom & two barrack-blocks survive on Uttoxeter New Road.

Devizes: built 1856, became police HQ 1879, demolished1964.

Dingwall: west end of High Street, demolished for County Council offices.

Dorchester: the Keep, and also the Little Keep, joined to small, square pavilions, have been described as original elements of the Militia Barracks which was adapted as the Dorsetshire Regiment's depot in the 1870s.

Durham: built 1865, L-shaped block with octagonal tower over main door; other two-storey barrack-blocks & outbuildings around yard; bowling-green on former drill-square; now in community use.

Dumfries: built 1857, in Scottish Baronial style, incorporating the Police Barracks in 1876. In 1877, it carried stores for 800, and accommodation for 11 staff.

Duns[e]: built 1857 on Tiendhill Green; demolished 1895 for a house.

Ely: Orderly-room, armoury, hospital and two rows of staff houses, all survive;parade-ground now a car-park.

Falmouth: the HQ, orderly-room, officers' mess and stores of the Cornwall & Devon Miners' Royal Garrison Artillery [Militia] had been accommodated in the Keep of Pendennis Castle from c1849; in 1902, a pastiche Tudor extension was added to the front of the Keep, and a new barracks for the RGA built in the castle; although the barracks survives, the Keep extension was demolished when the castle went to the Office of Works in 1921.

Finsbury: built 1857 for Honourable Artillery Company; early buildings in Tudor style with turrets & arrow-slits; later neo-Georgian additions; still in use. [*p310*]

Finsbury: Bunhill Row, built 1857 for permanent staff of London Militia.

Gloucester: apparently of similar design to Cirencester; now under Prison.

Grantham: built 1857 as stone quadrangle with gatehouse block and four corner towers; armoury etc along side walls; drill hall added across back wall in 1913; behind is a court of staff houses in brick; now Crown Prosecution Service offices, offices and auction house; identical to Lincoln but in stone. [*p46,66*]

Hamilton: built c1857 and commemorated by *Barrack Street*.

Hereford: built 1856; two-storey block; now County Records Office.

High Wycombe: Wycombe Abbey was HQ of the Royal Bucks. Kings Own Militia with the orderly-room in the stable-yard from 1839.

Huntingdon: mid-1850s two-storey yellow-brick block with tower and projecting bays; now nursing home.

Ipswich: Stores of East Suffolk Light Infantry Militia built in Great Gipping Street, c1855; demolished.

Inverness; largely destroyed but for gate with flanking square loop-holed towers.

Lancaster: built 1854 in South Road; symmetrical Scottish Baronial style with tourelles on corner turrets, and gatehouse [1899] to side with pepper-pot roofs on bartizans; now Storey's Social Club, BBC Studios and offices.

Lichfield: Armoury built 1854 in Victoria Square, Birmingham Road; demolished.

Lincoln: 1857, brick two-storey block with central gatehouse; quadrangle with corner towers, single-storey buildings, stables etc, along two sides; drill hall of 1913 along fourth; adjacent Adjutant's house, and, on Mill Road, two terraces of staff housing, including one cottage labelled 'Drummer's', both painted and carved name; identical to Grantham but in brick.

Macclesfield: built c1875 in Crompton Road; Armoury in French chateau style; all in stone with perimeter walls with corner-towers and gatehouse with turret; also HQ building and ranges of stables etc. [*p254*]

Manchester: built c1850 in Chester Road, Hulme; 10-bay symmetrical front with two 3-bay pediments; subsequently Canal Office, currently [2002] empty.

Manchester [Kearsley Road]: became *Man & Scythe* PH, then demolished.

Milford Haven: in 1885, HQ of Royal Pembrokeshire Artillery Militia was in Fort Hubberstone.

Mold: the barracks of the Flintshire Militia, by Penson junior, was built 1857-8 in Chester Street; converted to Council Offices in 1897, and demolished for the new Shire Hall in 1960.

Montrose: Asylum, built 1799, converted to Militia Barracks; demolished.

Newark: Albert Street, demolished post-WWll.

Newcastle-under-Lyme: built c1850; quadrangle with ornamental gate-tower, corner towers and buildings ranged around the courtyard; now used as craft workshops; NB identical building formerly in Stafford.

Northampton [Clare Street]: 1859 Militia Stores, in toy fort style with round corner-turrets, and central gatehouse with drum-towers, forming the front range of a horse-shoe-shaped block; the land was extended in 1937 in order to provide facilities for newly-raised armoured car company; still in use as TAC. [*p255*]

Norwich [All Saints Green] Ivory House of 1771 became Militia Barracks in 1860; later on it was the artillery drill hall, known as Surrey Street Barracks; Victorian drill shed to rear was recently [2004] demolished.

Paisley [31 Whitehaugh Street]: it is possible that the extant barracks buildings here, represent the original barracks of the129th Renfrew Militia Regiment. [*p289*]

Plymouth: Mutley Barracks was built around 1860 for 25th South Devon Regiment of Militia; in stone in an embattled Tudor style with oriel over gate-tower, a hall, square tower, mullions, chimneys etc; now used by Plymouth College.

Pontefract: built 1871 for West Riding Rifles Militia [?]; used for a time as a school; demolished soon after 1990, for supermarket; only the stone, castellated gatehouse remains; NB there was no Yorkshire Militia unit at Pontefract in 1850, units being recorded at Beverley, Doncaster, Richmond and York, but local tradition says the Pontefract unit was Militia although its title suggests it was Rifle Volunteers [18th Corps of West Riding RV formed at Pontefract 3 March 1860]; the gatehouse, however, *does* suggest Militia.

Preston; rectangular block with turrets, built 1857; demolished for Inland Revenue offices c1980s.

Richmond, Temple Square, Cravengate: open quadrangle of three stone ranges, probably eighteenth century; base for 22nd North York Light Infantry Militia.

Stafford: marked as Police Barracks on 1901 OS map, this was the identical building to that at Newcastle-under-Lyme [qv].

Stockport: built 1862 by Bowman in Greek Street, in the style of a Rhineland burg; tall octagonal tower with copper witch's hat roof; two-storey Armoury with steep pitched roof and dormers, two-storey bay windows flanking main entrance, and slits at ground level; behind that, a long, low hall and further outbuildings; within a boundary wall with loop-holed corner tower; still TAC. [*p265*]

Stowe [Buckinghamshire]: one of the 18C landscape temples in the Park, now owned by The Landmark Trust, is recorded as having served as a Militia Armoury, and subsequently for school cadet force.

Uxbridge: the staff of the 58th Royal West Middlesex Regiment of Militia was based here from 1830; The Shrubbery, 222 High Street, now Pizza Express was the Adjutant's house, and the cadre of NCOs lived in Hillingdon End, opposite the entrance to Hillingdon House, residence of their Captain; in 1853, the Royal Elthorne Light Infantry Militia was formed in Uxbridge, with officers' accommodation in The Greenway, where three such houses remain: numbers 64-68; the middle one is now called

HUDDERSFIELD, the 1847 Riding School of the Yorkshire Dragoons

PAULL POINT Fort, officers' quarters of the Humber Submarine-Miners

Blandford House; the former Dry Canteen is now a public house, called *The Militia Canteen*, as is the former forage barn, now *The Load of Hay*; the barracks, now demolished formerly stood in Enfield Place.

Welshpool: in 1833, [recently-constructed] Armoury of Montgomeryshire Militia was below Bron y Buckley Wood; may be the present Armoury on Brook Street.

Wetherby: Yeomanry barracks converted into farm; demolished c2002 for housing.

Whitehaven: a four-storey linen Mill in Catherine Street, built between 1809 and 1829, was adapted by 1857 to serve as the Militia barracks; then a factory until 1992 when it was converted into apartments.

Wrexham: prior to 1857, the Militia were based in the Town Hall, demolished in 1940; the Barracks, built in Regent Street in 1857, by Penson senior, form an H-shaped block with the cross-piece of guard-room and stores fronted by a loggia; the two wings, with four round towers at the outer angles, contained quarters for permanent staff, & cells for offending militia-men; now museum.

YEOMANRY Riding Schools

Ayr, Wellington Square: built for Ayrshire Yeomanry, a regiment which stayed in existence throughout the nineteenth century; it is at one end of a late-Georgian terrace with the drill hall at the other end; each hall is fronted by a two-storey, double-fronted house; the riding-school has another two-storey structure beyond it; the whole is now a cafe and fish & chip shop.

Bromley, the West Kent Riding School on Bromley Common, probably provided facilities for the West Kent Yeomanry, with HQ, Yeomanry House, nearby.

Buckingham, Hunter Street: the brick building adjoining Yeomanry House may have been a riding-school for the Yeomanry.

Hove, Waterloo Road, Old Market built 1825, converted 1998 to public space; [*p81*]

Huddersfield, Ramsden Street: built 1847, by Wallen, for 2nd West Yorkshire Yeomanry; used until 1904, then became Hippodrome, now public house; grand two-storey block with arched entrance, and carved horses in relief, on panels fronting a large hall. [*p312*]

Hull, Walton Street: built 1905 for East Riding Yeomanry at the back of Wenlock Barracks; large hall with raised roof-light, and attached former stabling with accommodation over; now leisure centre.

Newcastle-upon-Tyne, Northumberland Street: riding-school by Dobson, mid-nineteenth century; two-storey structures front and rear with higher open, full-height space in between; University of

Northumbria computer centre.

Nottingham: outside Castle Gate, built 1798 for Yeomanry, stone with round tower & battlements;1872 adapted as drill hall for Robin Hood Rifles; demolished.

Oakham, Catmose Street: built late eighteenth century for Rutland Fencibles; at one end, Catmose Cottage, two-storey stone house with oriel over doorway, and Georgian detailing; at other, quarters over stabling; in between, the riding-school itself, now used as Museum; other buildings behind. [*p12*]

Oxford, Tidmarsh Lane/Paradise St. in use into 1920s; demolished.

Shrewsbury,Coleham: demolished 2001 for housing development.

Southampton, Carlton Place, from 1820s; Georgian terrace with 10-bay-deep red-brick riding school behind; in use by OTC.

Worcester, Sabrina Avenue, Barbourne, opened 1910, demolished 1980s; timber stables in Pound Walk, still used by **Perdiswell** racecourse; Yeomanry's former circular riding track now incorporated in Gueluvelt Park, Barbourne.

It should be remembered that those County Associations which maintained Royal Horse Artillery batteries such as Hampshire, Shropshire, or Glamorgan, provided riding schools like those of their Regular counterparts at **St John's Wood**. There was once such a riding school, for the Glamorgan RHA, at Port Talbot. Other artillery units also provided such facilities as at Bradford, for the West Riding Artillery, or at Dover. Regular Cavalry riding schools survive at **Aldershot**, **Exeter**, **Dorchester**, and **Colchester**.

Locations of Submarine Miners: Volunteer and Militia

As part of the Coast Defences, most ports of any importance were provided with minefields which were electrically controlled. These were roundly condemned by Sir George Sydenham Clarke writing in 1907, and, on the advice of the Admiralty, they were abolished. They had been introduced after the American Civil War, and there were Militia units from 1878, and volunteer units from 1883, re-organised, in 1886, and again in 1888, into divisions.

The **VOLUNTEER** Submarine Miners were based in the following ports:

TYNE [HQ at North Shields] at **Old Cliffords Fort**, dating from 1882, along with several of the Miners' buildings, now curing-houses, survive. [*p56*]

New Cliffords Fort, built in 1928 as the drill hall of the Tyne Electrical Engineers, still stands in Tynemouth and is still a TAC.

SEVERN [HQ at Burt Road, Cardiff] this area has been re-developed.

CLYDE [HQ at Greenock] they were based at **Fort Matilda**, rebuilt for the Navy in the period leading up to WWll, and now used by Royal Marines Reserves and HM Coastguard.

HUMBER [HQ at Hull] the Miners were based in the fort at **Paull Point**; built inside a former gun-pit, the concrete cell, from which the mines were activated, survives on the rampart; of their depot, to the north of the fort, only High Paull House, the former officers' quarters, now survives as two dwellings; the jetty was destroyed early in the 20th century; in 1891 the duties of this Humber volunteer unit were transferred to the Militia. [*p312*]

TEES [HQ Middlesbrough] the depot on the **South Gare** still stands inside its compound surrounded by a concrete, loop-holed wall with bastions at three of its corners; it is now used by the yacht club.

FORTH [HQ Leith] originally based on HMS Dido, moored off Leith, in 1905 they moved to new premises in North Queensferry, with a pier, stores etc. and their HQ was moved to 14a Queen Street, Edinburgh.

TAY [HQ Dundee] established in the castle at **Broughty Ferry** by 1888.

MERSEY [HQ Liverpool] raised from K Company of the 1st Lancashire Rifle Volunteers; **Fort Perch Rock**, known to have been re-modelled by the REs in 1896 when a generator was added, may have provided the location.

FALMOUTH [HQ Falmouth] the Miners' HQ was at Arwenack House, Bar Road, and the area of workshops and pier etc. was extended eastwards c1898, into a part of the port recently demolished for housing; the volunteers like those in Hull, had relinquished their duties to the Militia in 1891.

The **MILITIA** Submarine Miners Divisions were located as follows:

PORTSMOUTH: HQ was probably either at **Ravelin House**, the CRE's office, or at the **Hampshire Terrace** drill hall of the Hampshire RE Volunteers; the actual mining operations were first centred on **Fort Blockhouse**, where piers and stores etc were erected in 1879; in 1884, the Gosport Submarine Miners [responsible for the whole Spithead/Portsmouth area] moved into **Fort Monckton**, where a training school was established with testing of mines located at the adjacent **Fort Gilkicker**; once the RN took over in 1907, the Mining School at HMS Vernon would have become the HQ; a school of Electric Lights [Searchlights] was at Gilkicker, and Monckton reverted to being a base for REs [Fortress].

NEEDLES: **Fort Victoria**, built in 1855, but made obsolete by improvements in gunnery, was equipped as a Submarine Mining Depot in 1891; an 18 inch gauge tramway was laid for moving armed mines to the pier for laying by boat; specialist stores and offices were built in the courtyard of the fort; much of this survives; an observation post was added to the western end of **Old Needles Battery** in 1885, for the purpose of operating the minefield, but in 1899 was converted to a searchlight position as alternative, less-exposed posts had been built at **Cliff End** and, on the mainland, at **Hurst Castle**.

PLYMOUTH: there were two control points for the minefields which were laid either End of the Breakwater; the generator etc. in a brick-vaulted chamber built into the ditch of **Fort Picklecombe** [now apartments] exists but on the hill above, the observation post has been demolished; above **Fort Bovisand**, the 1896 observation post survives in a quarry; lower down are searchlights, originally dedicated to illuminating the southern minefield.

THAMES & MEDWAY: both estuaries were heavily-defended by forts, batteries and minefields and in 1902 it became necessary to split into two divisions; there was a school of Submarine-Mining at Gillingham, and **Shornemead Fort** was the test-bed for practical training and experimental techniques; there was an enclosure for the miners by Gillingham Pier, into which construction of Brennan Torpedoes was removed from **Brompton Barracks** in 1896.

HARWICH; the Miners' HQ, stores and workshops stand beside **Landguard Fort** on the Felixstowe side of the harbour; a low, pentagonal building, once accessible from the fort, with 1878 date-stone over doorway; now a Museum.

MILFORD HAVEN: the Submarine Mining Depot is at the west end of Pembroke Dock at **Pennar Barracks**, built 1875, of which there are some remains.

CARDWELL Barracks of 1870-1880 period; Depots of the Line Regiments.

These Regimental Depots were the family homes of the Regular Army Regiments of the Line, and, as such, had a significance for their Volunteer Battalions of, first, the Volunteer Force, after 1908 the Territorial Force, and, from 1920, the Territorial Army. Many were newly-constructed for the task, often following a common design, with a Keep, generally a square or rectangular block with two or three corner-towers, serving as the Armoury, an arched gateway alongside, and up to a dozen or so two- or three-storey barrack-blocks. A HQ building, hospital, guardroom, CO's house, officers' mess, sergeants' mess, canteen and ancillary buildings completed the extensive layout, often within a stout perimeter-wall with loop-holed corner towers. Most of the building-types were built from common designs, there being two distinct designs for officers' messes, for instance, one seen at **Bodmin** and **Oxford** being three-storeyed with projecting wings. The other, seen at **Leicester**, **Reading** and **Halifax**, is of two-storeys with a porch, and half-hexagonal projection to one side. The Armouries at **Norwich**, and at **Richmond** [Yorkshire], consist of three-storey blocks without towers, and at **Great Yarmouth**, a similar block, but of only two storeys. That at **Kingston-upon-Thames**, is a rectangular, two-storey block with a central, higher square gate-tower, and a higher square tower at each end. The two-storey Armoury at **Chichester** is Z-plan, with a circular turret, rising at one end, above one of the jambs. As well as the purpose-built barracks of this period, many existing structures were adapted. **Carlisle Castle**, the **Tower of London**, and **Chester Castle**, for instance, are among the oldest in this category, but the large number of existing barracks now to be incorporated into the Scheme, included **Berwick-upon-Tweed**, **Fort George**, and **Hownslow**. The established Militia armouries at **Bodmin** and **Dorchester** were also adapted and enlarged.

In the list of Cardwell-era infantry barracks below, those with significant surviving remains are shown in **bold**. Also shown are the regiments whose depots these were. This list does not include Cavalry or Artillery Barracks unless shared as at **Preston** or **Exeter [Higher]**, for instance. Nor does it include the Royal Artillery Barracks at **Woolwich**, the Royal Engineers Brompton Barracks at **Chatham**, or the Guards' [quadruple] depot at **Caterham**.

The survival of a Keep is shown: [K], and an Armoury: [A]. New Cardwell barracks are shown: §; the rest are adaptations of earlier buildings.

§Aberdeen [Bridge of Don]: barrack-blocks of two-storeys with crow-stepped gables ranged around parade-ground; central block with bartizans; guardroom with verandah; still in military use.
• Gordon Highlanders

Ayr: formerly adjacent to Citadel; demolished.
• Royal Scots Fusiliers

§Bedford[K]: buildings either side of the keep remain, in use by the Freemasons. The keep is very similar to those at **Cardiff** and **Worcester**.
• Bedfordshire & Hertfordshire Regiment

Berwick-upon-Tweed: built 1721 in Ravensdowne, designed by Hawksmoor; three ranges of two-storey barrack-blocks forming an open quadrangle with wall and Gateway on fourth side; open to the public as ancient monument. By 1914, the KOSBs had moved to Dumfries.
• Kings Own Scottish Borderers

APPENDIX 2
Present uses of former drill halls / TACs

Large numbers of drill halls remain in use as perfectly serviceable buildings in a wide range of new applications. Those still extant are recorded in **bold**.

AMBULANCE STATION
The drill hall at **Hailsham** [London Road] accommodates the local service.

AUCTION HOUSE
Kirkby Lonsdale, **Plympton** and **Bournemouth** [Holdenhurst Road] are examples.

BALLROOM
The pre-WWl drill hall at **Eastleigh** is a ball-room & dance school. The solid wood floors of many drill halls ensure that it is often for dancing that the locals remember them. At Woodlesford, now destroyed, locals remember having to dance around the gun mounted in the middle of the floor.

BANK
Chipping Campden, and **Romsey** are two of a very few examples.

BINGO HALL
Winsford may be the only example [p318].

CAR PARK
At the **Thorp Street**, Birmingham, drill hall, whilst the orderly room block with its castellated towered gateways has become a Chinese restaurant, the roof-less shell of the actual hall is now a car-park.

CHARITY SHOPS
Turriff, **Builth Wells** and **Wakefield** [Vicarage Road];

CHURCH or other RELIGIOUS CENTRE
Many drill halls were converted from redundant chapels, but none appears ever to have reverted, but a number of drill halls have subsequently become places of worship. These include **Rugeley**, **Fortrose**, **Sittingbourne**, **Kings Lynn** [Wellesley Street], **Connahs Quay**, **Gourock**, **Stranraer**, **Spennymoor**, and the house at **Batley**; at **Halstead** [Essex] a Kingdom Hall; at **Glasgow** [Berkeley Street], a Sikh temple; and at **Bedford** [Ashburnham Road], a Hindu Centre;

CINEMA
Several, such as **Broadgate**, Lincoln, include cinema facilities, but Inveraray was converted by the Duchess of Argyll into a cinema in the 1960s, her Hollywood contacts enabling her to secure films ahead of cinemas in the cities. **Coleford** currently operates as a cinema.

CLUB [ex-Services]
These include Royal British Legion at **Dunbar**, **Porthmadoc**, **Jedburgh** and **Coldstream**, RN Association at **Leamington**, and others at **Evesham**, **Barrhead**, **Malton** and **Birdwell**.

CLUBS [political]
Okehampton [Park Row] [conservative]

COMMUNITY CENTRE
One of the most common uses; good examples exist at **Elland**, **Halifax** [Arden Road], **Howden**, **Sandwell**, **Cefn Coed**, and **Treeton**.

CORN EXCHANGE
A number of Corn Exchanges doubled as drill halls as at **Blandford**, **Ringwood**, **Romsey**, **Wisbech**, **Alford**, **Boston**, **Biggar**, Grimsby, **Witney**, **Tunbridge Wells** and **Tonbridge**

COUNCIL DEPOT
Examples include **Hartshill**, **Hackney** [Hillman Street], and **Tunstall**.

EXHIBITION CENTRE
The quayside drill hall at **Blyth** [Northumberland] is the centre-piece of a Heritage development, part of a wider re-generation project.

FIRE STATION
Pershore serves as a fire station, as once did Sale.

FITNESS CENTRE
Plenty of examples here: **Burslem** [gymnastics], **Felixstowe** and **Nuneaton** [martial arts], **Prudhoe** and **Guisborough** [fitness], **Morriston** [gym & sunbeds], **Dalry** [tanning & sauna],

FOOTBALL CLUBHOUSE
Cumnock Juniors use the front-block of the old drill hall as changing-rooms.

FUNERAL PARLOUR
One at **Barry**, and, until recently, in **Rothesay** [High Street].

HEALTH CENTRE
Hailsham [Sturton Place], **Beverley**, and **Kirkburton** are all health centres.

HOTEL/PUBLIC HOUSE

Some volunteer units, as at **Formby, Carnforth, Clacton, Stony Stratford, Hawkhurst, Diss, Skeabost, Blaina** and **Staplehurst**, were always based on local hotels or pubs; at **Whitby** [Spring Hill], the drill hall has become a hotel, and at **Huddersfield** [Ramsden Street], and **Bromley** [East Street] former drill halls have become pubs [respectively, the *Rat & Parrot* and *Philatelist & Firkin*-now *O'Neils*], and at **Uddingston** a bar [known to three passers-by, by three different names].

HOUSING [flats]

Many examples including **Guiseley, Tredegar, Kings Heath, Houghton-le-Spring, Fort William** [*p318*]**, Dartmouth, Petersfield** and **Skelton**.

HOUSING [private houses]

Apart from many surviving staff houses which have continued in private hands, there are a number of instances of small, and sometimes not-so-small, drill halls being converted into private houses as at **Ventnor** [Zig-zag Road], **Fishguard, Haverhill, Kington, Dalbeattie, Law,** and **Oldmeldrum**.

INDUSTRIAL PREMISES

A wide range of uses here: **Cardiff** [Norbury Road] film-processing, **Maesteg,** steel fabrication, **Kirkcudbright,** frozen fish, **Great Yarmouth** [Southtown Road], printing, **Llay** instruments & gauges, **Weston-super-Mare** [George St] plumbing & heating, **Briton Ferry** assorted, **Whitby** furniture, and **Arnold** now printing but previously, making false teeth.

INSTITUTE

Egham [Literary], and **Llanfair-Caereinion** Institutes both doubled as drill halls. The drill hall at **Melton Constable** is attached to the Railway Institute, and at **Fauldhouse,** it adjoins the Baillie [Miners'] Institute. The Perrins Centre in **Alness** was acquired by the TA, but has now reverted to its original use.

LEISURE/SPORTS CENTRE

There are plenty of these including **Darlington, Birkenhead, Penistone, Seacombe, Dumfries, Great Yarmouth** [Nelson Road], **Greenock, Darlington** [Larchfield Street]; both **Birdwell** and **Driffield** are Shooting Clubs; **Newport** [Gwent, Dock Road] is a Power Gym & Boxing Club.

MASONIC and other such HALLS

Very occasionally such a hall doubled as a drill hall as at **Knaresbrough** and Poole [Hunger Hill] [both Oddfellows]; a very few drill halls have been taken over such as **Brightlingsea** [Free Foresters], and **Kirriemuir, Thurso** [Olrig Street], **Worthing** [Upper Brighton Road], **Denny, Haltwhistle,** and **Horndean** [all by the Masons].

MOTOR TRADE

Drill halls clearly lend themselves to use as Garages as at **Seaton Delaval, Boness, Brampton** [Cumbria], **Rhymney, Basingstoke** [Goat Lane], **Bungay** [Scales Lane], and **Padiham** [Mill Street], or as Show-rooms as at **Dudley** [Trindle Road], for cars, or **Fakenham** for motor-cycles.

NIGHT-CLUB

Examples include **Walsall** [Whittimere Street], **Inverness** [Rose Street], and **Bilston** [Mount Pleasant]; Stafford's *Zanzibar* club, if a conversion rather than a re-build, is another example.

NURSERY[childrens]

Munlochy, Rugby [Park Road], and **Ingatestone**.

NURSING HOME

Redditch, Kidderminster [The Shrubbery], **Cosham**.

OFFICES

Barnsley [publishers], **Skipton** [solicitors], **Norwich** [All Saints Green] [BBC], and [Cattlemarket Road] [architects], **Exeter** [Butts Road] [British Red Cross].

PIE FACTORY

Willenhall, not to be confused with Harleston, the Pye [Communications] factory.

PIPE-BAND PRACTICE HALL or BAND CLUB

Ballater [Pipe-band], **St Austell** [East Hill] [Band Club], possibly **Burntisland**.

POLICE STATION

Tenbury Wells would appear to be the only example.

PUBLIC HALL

Sometimes, as at **Westerham,** the public hall became the drill hall; sometimes the public hall doubled as the drill hall, as at **Landeilo** and **Formby** [both Jubilee Halls], or at **Paignton, Bloxwich, St Boswells** and **Godalming**; often the drill hall has subsequently become the public hall as at **Llandovery** or **Lochgelly**; and at **Cromarty, Campbeltown, Tisbury** and **Ellon** [all four Victoria Halls]; whilst at **Wordsley,** a dedicated drill hall was built by public subscription, opening in 1884, and, in 1907, was presented to the community as the Richardson Hall. The use of Memorial Halls as military establishments, as **Aberaeron,** and **Tregaron** were, is quite unusual, but at **Freshwater,** the Cameron Hall, named for the son of the local photographer, was the original drill hall from its opening in 1899.

RESTAURANT

Birmingham [Thorp Street], **Norwich** [Bethel Street], **Barnstaple** [Bear Street], **Ayr** [Wellington Square], **Midsomer Norton** & **Ashton-in-Makerfield**.

ROYAL MAIL SORTING OFFICE

This was the destiny of very many drill halls either using the original buildings, as at **Manchester** [Norton Street], **Parkstone** [Alder Road], **Cardigan** [Finch Square], and **Richmond-on-Thames,** or in new buildings on the site, as at Walthamstow, or